Third Edition

DOMESTIC *Violence*

The Criminal Justice Response

■ Eve S. Buzawa
University of Massachusetts, Lowell

■ Carl G. Buzawa

SAGE Publications
International Educational and Professional Publisher
Thousand Oaks ■ London ■ New Delhi

For information:

Sage Publications, Inc.
2455 Teller Road
Thousand Oaks, California 91320
E-mail: order@sagepub.com

Sage Publications Ltd.
6 Bonhill Street
London EC2A 4PU
United Kingdom

Sage Publications India Pvt. Ltd.
M-32 Market
Greater Kailash I
New Delhi 110 048 India

Printed in the United States of America

Library of Congress Cataloging-in-Publication Data

Buzawa, Eva Schlesinger.
Domestic violence: The criminal justice response / by Eve S. Buzawa and
Carl G. Buzawa.—3rd ed.
    p. cm.
  Includes bibliographical references and index.
   ISBN 0-7619-247-7 (cloth)
   ISBN 0.7619-2448-5 (paper)
   1. Wife abuse—United States. I. Buzawa, Carl G. II. Title.
   HV6626.2.B89 2002
   364.15′553′0973—dc21

                             2002011108

This book is printed on acid-free paper.

02 03 04 05 10 9 8 7 6 5 4 3 2 1

Acquisitions Editor:	Jerry Westby
Editorial Assistant:	Vonessa Vondera
Copy Editor:	Elizabeth Budd
Production Editor:	Denise Santoyo
Typesetter:	C&M Digitals (P) Ltd.
Indexer:	Pam Van Huss
Cover Designer:	Janet Foulger

Third Edition

DOMESTIC *Violence*

To the victims of domestic violence and those people who are devoting
countless hours to ameliorate the problem

And

To our wonderful children who share our sentiment and commitment
to helping victims of domestic violence

Not Wanting to Leave, Yet Not Safe to Stay
Laura Buzawa

Shadows
 on her sad, vacant face
Bruises
 Hid by a coat of skin colored denial.
Not wanting to leave
 Where could she go?
Not safe to stay
 Did she do something wrong?
Not wanting to leave
 He's the only one who loves me
Not safe to stay
 Obviously it's her fault.
He's so upset
 Not wanting to leave
It's not like anyone would listen anyways
 Not wanting to leave
Who would believe a small passive voice over the
  charming good boy (the façade hiding the ugly monster
  introduced after our brief euphoria of magic)

Not safe to stay
 This time not just for her, but for the life within her womb
 Not wanting to leave
  But he loves her

What to do?
 She only knows two things:
  She doesn't want to leave,
  But it's not safe to stay

Contents

Acknowledgments

I would like to express my sincere gratitude to the many people who helped us with this book. First and foremost, I would like to thank Gerald Hotaling who unexpectedly passed away as we were completing this book. His ideas, creativity, and most importantly, his support and encouragement have been critical to me over the many years we have worked together. I am deeply saddened by his loss and will miss him deeply.

Carl and I would also like to thank Olga Barnett and David Hirschel for their time in reviewing the manuscript and their invaluable comments and suggestions.

We would also like to thank our editor, Jerry Westby, for his continual assistance and guidance during the writing of this manuscript. His expertise, as well as his genuine interest in our book, is deeply appreciated.

Finally, we would like to thank our copyeditor, Elizabeth Budd, who spent countless hours editing this manuscript. Her editorial expertise greatly improved the quality of this manuscript and we are indebted to her for her efforts.

—Eve Buzawa

In Loving Memory of Gerald T. Hotaling
And to all those who will miss him

CHAPTER 1

Introduction

The Role and Context of the Criminal Justice System

Ten years after the publication of the first edition of this book, fundamental issues that many thought would have long been settled—for example, the proper police response—remain open, and new questions have arisen over preferred intervention methods for the system as a whole.

The second edition, published in 1996, focused on the nature and extent of the rapidly evolving criminal justice system and offered tentative observations about the opportunities and limitations of the various approaches being attempted at the time of its publication. In the time since the second edition, there has been a proliferation of research evaluating the impact of innovative intervention strategies. In addition, the failure to critically focus on implementation strategies appears to have possibly resulted in inadequate and simplistic solutions. Rather than fixing problems, many interventions have created new or at least unanticipated ones.

As a result of the changes in perspectives and approaches, as well as the growing body of research, virtually all chapters have been substantially rewritten from the first and second editions. In accordance with the sweeping changes undertaken by the criminal justice system, we have significantly expanded our emphasis on efforts made by the prosecutors' offices and courts, as well as strategies to protect victims through victim advocacy and other services. There is also a discussion of what we know about the efficacy of interventions on offenders and risk factors predicting both offending and reoffending behaviors.

Meanwhile, research since the publication of the second edition has not clearly shown that the enhanced and innovative efforts made by the criminal justice system adequately address serious domestic violence. As we discuss, increased intervention strategies appear effective for certain types of offenders. Such efforts do not seem to greatly affect other types of offenders—specifically, those who are chronic and severe batterers.

In fact, a startling National Institute of Justice–sponsored study published in 2001, conducted a retrospective analysis of partner homicides in 48 of the 50 largest U.S. cities for the period 1976–1996 (corresponding almost exactly with enhanced criminal justice initiatives for domestic violence). This research found that results were inconclusive as to the impact of state statutes, local police and prosecution policies, legal advocacy programs, or the prevalence of hotlines within the city on reductions of domestic homicide rates. In fact, in only slightly more than half the cases were increases in available resources associated with lower rates of domestic homicide. In the other cases, increased resources were associated with *increased* homicide rates, especially for certain categories of victims. Although societal trends may have contributed to some of these findings, rigorous controls were adopted in this study. In any event, the report did not support the widely held belief that increased resources would automatically result in decreased domestic violence as evidenced by the sheer numbers of domestic homicides (Dugan, Nagin, & Rosenfeld, 2001).

Therefore, the primary goal of this edition is to help readers develop an understanding of the context of the interaction between the historic and current criminal justice system responses. We explore the components of the criminal justice system individually, how these components interact, and how this interaction affects outcomes. From this perspective, we attempt to highlight those features that appear most promising toward achieving a goal of consistent positive interventions.

We place emphasis on the emerging—and long overdue—research on victims, addressing three primary areas. First, we believe it is important to address exactly which types of victims and relationships are included under domestic violence statutes. Although the focus of such statutes typically is on intimate partner violence, there is a far more diverse range of relationships that almost all state statutes encompass. Second, not all victims that the statutes encompass are recognized by the criminal justice system. We consider not only differences among victims of domestic violence recognized by the criminal justice system compared with the general population of such victims, but also the differential

treatment they might experience. Third, there has been little attention paid to victim risk factors, preferences, perspectives, and satisfaction with criminal justice intervention, nor to the impact of intervention on revictimization. Instead, attention has typically focused on reoffending by batterers, which is not the same phenomenon. Because it is clear that the system has not consistently provided victims of domestic violence with assistance, this volume emphasizes the impact of these interventions on victims as well as offenders.

Finally, to allow better integration of new research from a range of disciplines that now examine these topics, the organizational structure of this book has been changed. This introductory chapter briefly highlights the topics that are revisited in the course of this book; addresses the effect of the primacy of the criminal justice system on the overall context of societal reactions to domestic violence; explains the difficulty of integrating the varied goals of the criminal justice system into a coherent, consistent policy; and briefly introduces the issue of why the process of change has been so difficult. After this introduction, the heart of the manuscript is divided into four parts: (1) the context of domestic violence; (2) the evolution of the criminal justice response to domestic violence; (3) the current, widely variant actions being taken by the criminal justice system; and (4) our suggestions to improve integration of the criminal justice system into an overall societal response.

We hope this book will offer readers insight into four issues of relevance to modern criminal justice professionals and researchers: First, have internal conflicts in the goals of the criminal justice system led to a loss in mission and clarity, perhaps resulting in victim disempowerment? Second, has the largely uncoordinated process of change in criminal justice agencies led to different "street-level" practices in different jurisdictions and among different classes of victims and offenders? Third, even if a holistic "ideal" criminal justice response is followed using the full power of prosecution and civil restraining orders, does it have only a marginal effect in deterring reoffending and revictimization by the most severe batterers? Even worse, will it present unanticipated negative consequences? Fourth, could successful efforts to control domestic violence have an impact on overall levels of societal violence?

THE PRIMACY OF
THE CRIMINAL JUSTICE SYSTEM

What is the appropriate response to domestic violence? This complex question, still without clearly defined answers, is the subject of intense controversy and debate. Continuing controversy remains concerning the appropriate response of society in general, and the criminal justice system in particular, to domestic violence. In the United States, at least since the 1970s, the criminal justice system—specifically local law enforcement—has had the most significant role in reacting to domestic violence. Before that time, the statutory structure for handling domestic violence can charitably be described as "benevolent neglect" of "family problems." State assistance, if any, went to traditional social welfare agencies handling a variety of family problems. The problem was not viewed as partially the result of persistent government neglect to perform the "societal" responsibility of controlling family violence. Rather, it was believed that if society intervened in all but the most egregious cases, incalculable harm to the family—the basic building block of society—might be permanently weakened.

As we cover extensively in Part II, an almost unprecedented wave of statutory changes since the 1970s, culminating in legislation in all 50 states, irrevocably altered this position. Although differing greatly in their scope and limitations, the new statutes expressly purported to make profound structural change in the response of government agencies to domestic violence by enhancing the police response, granting new criminal sanctions to prosecutors and the judiciary, increasing the availability and enforcement of civil restraining orders, educating the public to the problem and effects of violence in the family, and providing state and later federal funding through the Violence Against Women Act (VAWA) for police, prosecutors, courts, and victim services.

Although possibly unintended, the current effect of such legislation has been to give primary responsibility—and power—for the suppression of ongoing domestic violence to the criminal justice system. Why is this true? In part, it is the result of recognition that the current structure and funding of other institutions does not allow for an adequate response to cases of domestic assault. Service providers such as social welfare agencies or counseling services are not as widely used or known, and, for financial reasons, they may not even be accessible to the general public. They also typically have significant restrictions in serving the public except during "normal" business hours. We do note, however, that during the past decade, there has been a growing recognition of the problem of domestic violence within the medical profession. There have been major strides in recognizing and supporting physicians' role in identification of victims, provision of services, and interfacing with the criminal justice system, shelters, and other service agencies. There is now considerable research studying domestic violence from an epidemiological perspective as well.

In any event, police departments usually are the initial agency contacted in the midst of a domestic violence assault. These are agencies the general public recognizes as providing a free service, 24 hours a day, 7 days a week. Furthermore, in the midst of a crisis, many victims want police intervention because police are easy to contact, provide a highly visible authority figure, and are capable of providing fast response. All-day access is highly significant because research has long demonstrated that "office hours" between 8 a.m. and 5 p.m. on weekdays generate only a small percentage of family assault calls. Hence, contact with the violent family by other local government agencies has often been dependent on police suggestions, referrals, the independent discovery of child abuse, or even sheer accident.

In addition to structural reasons for criminal justice ascendancy in the area of domestic violence, the United States currently has a propensity to use coercive legal powers to "solve" social problems. Despite the existence of alternative prevention and treatment models, the "war on drugs," "get tough" policies on juvenile crime, and drunk driving are seen primarily in the context of "law enforcement" problems. This issue also needs to be placed in an overall societal context, because it does not occur in isolation from other societal trends. Until recently, official retribution for acts committed in private was unacceptable as a concept, or at least as a public or officially recognized goal. It is now a recurring theme that accompanies a penal approach to legislation and decision making. In fact there has been a sharp reversal of the historical process in which the power to punish was largely delegated to professional experts and administrators (Garland, 2001).

This is seen in a number of areas by a series of measures such as fixed sentencing law reforms, mandatory sentences, national standards, truth in sentencing, early release, and so on that have shifted decision making back first to the courts and later to the legislature. The new political imperative is that victims must be protected and their voices heard, memory honored, anger expressed, fears addressed: "the crime victim now is a much more representative character whose experience is taken to be common and collective rather than individual and atypical" (Garland, 2001, p. 144). We expect that this trend—a growing empathy for victims of crimes and a growing sense of anger toward any perpetrator of violence—will continue to grow during the months and years after the September 11, 2001, terrorist attacks, which made clear the extreme vulnerability of the entire population to violent crime.

Apart from the reasons, what is the impact of having criminal justice primacy in the response to domestic violence? In a real sense, the criminal justice system has not only functioned as the initial respondent to domestic violence but also has helped shape current and future societal perceptions and responses to the problem. Have issues of identifying violent offenders, determining guilt, and using criminal justice sanctions to prevent reoffending clouded overall societal concerns about the control of violence? Are there unanticipated consequences? We believe that three important effects may have emerged because of this focus.

First, along with the direct impact of enforcement actions, criminal justice case-processing requirements may have directly defined the parameters of permissible contact by criminalizing certain violent conduct, while tacitly condoning harassment or other strategies of coercive control, actions that in practice rarely result in arrest or prosecution.

Why is this important? As we explore in Part I, domestic violence, more than any other criminal act, includes a wide range of behaviors and relationships. Unfortunately, criminal codes are typically rather blunt instruments, defining *violence* as *individual acts*, usually a physical assault or threat of physical harm intended to cause physical harm. In reality, most researchers now more accurately conceptualize domestic violence as a range of behaviors, some obviously criminal in nature, others more manipulative, which in total are intended to exercise *coercive control* including physical, sexual, psychological, and verbal behaviors used to dominate another person. This perspective focuses on the *pattern* of violent and abusive behavior within the relationship rather than on individual acts of perpetrators.

As we discuss later in this book, only in recent years have criminal codes evolved to the point at which they have begun to recognize myriad forms of abuse by also forbidding "stalking" or "harassment." Although such statutes are an improvement on past legislation focused solely on physical assault, they are not as widely used and contain major inconsistencies; in addition, as an offense, stalking typically is rather difficult to prove. Little is known about the use of these statutes as an effective component for combating abuse in its totality rather than as the individual acts of physical violence found in typical domestic violence laws.

Second, by treating domestic violence primarily as a criminal justice issue, emphasis has largely been placed on the offenders who commit violence and what can deter future violence. From this perspective, deterrence-based theories of offending and reoffending have predominated policy responses. Not surprisingly, largely tactical issues of certainty of apprehension and deterrence via arrest, aggressive prosecution, forced attendance in batterer treatment programs, and "target hardening" via issuance of restraining orders have become the foci of research. Direct victim assistance and victim-centered approaches to the problem have been relegated to incidental status often not considered important by significant policymakers,

activists, or those agencies funding research on the control of domestic violence.

Third, for the criminal justice system to operate effectively, there is an implicit requirement for the identification of a crime with a defined victim and offender in the context of a recognized applicable criminal statute. Because of the severity of its sanctions, criminal law must rely on purely objective criteria for this determination; however, a person's status may not only be difficult to identify, but also may not be a constant in the numerous incidents that may occur during a couple's relationship. Unfortunately, we now know that there are many violent families in which members are alternately violent and victimized in both public and private settings and at various points in their lives. In a recent examination of 2,000 police reports during a 10-year period for all assaults (not just domestic), we found that 18% to 20% (depending on the year examined) of victims were also seen as offenders (Buzawa & Hotaling, 2001).

This victim–offender dichotomy may limit us from seeing domestic assault as a type of interaction that in some cases may be a maladaptive response to familial conflict (see, for example, Johnson's [1995] typology of domestic violence). Furthermore, victims as well as offenders often feel the impact of such labeling. Victims have found that to receive services, they must accept their publicly "framed" status as victim and the community expectations that accompany this label (Wuest & Merritt-Gray, 1999).

Why is this significant? Obviously, this is of concern to the offender because he or she can be arrested. Also, as part of a systematic response, when there is difficulty in determining which party is the victim, police face the choice of either taking no action because there is no legally recognizable victim or, paradoxically, of arresting both parties.

Not surprisingly, there has been considerable concern over increasing rates of dual arrest in some jurisdictions in which both parties to an incident are arrested instead of the customary practice of the police identifying just one offender and one victim (Martin, 1997; Saunders, 1995). Although these dual arrests may have validity, research has suggested that officers use this option as a reaction toward mandatory or presumptive arrest policies, failing to distinguish self-defense on the part of victims (Ferraro, 1989a; Martin, 1997). Exactly when dual arrest is appropriate cannot be determined easily; however, it has clearly been an unanticipated consequence of mandatory arrest laws or policies in many jurisdictions.

Finally, the very statutes in question—domestic violence criminal codes—also often have inexplicable "gaps" in coverage. The relationships included under these acts vary state to state, sometimes only including married individuals or, alternatively, including some or all of the following: current and past intimate partners, anyone living in the same residence, children, siblings, any other "family members," and any relative.

When examining intervention of incidents of domestic violence, researchers and policymakers have seldom addressed relationships other than intimate partner violence. This is significant because research by Maxwell and Bricker (1999) and Buzawa and Hotaling (2000) found that 35% and 61%, respectively, involved present or past intimate partner relationships. Persons under age 18 are extensively involved in these cases with research indicating that anywhere from 40% to 60% of incidents involved a person under age 18 as a witness, offender, or victim.

This issue has been seriously neglected. For example, only one state does not include the victimization of "children" under domestic violence statutes, but although considerable attention is paid to children witnessing domestic violence, similar attention has not been paid to those children who are victims or offenders under such acts. There is a lack of empirical data on how these subgroups might differ in terms of the nature of the incident, the seriousness of injuries, and the criminal justice response.

In addition, researchers often make the mistake of using all data from acts of domestic violence to generalize about male against female intimate partner violence.

HAVE THE MULTIPLE GOALS OF THE CRIMINAL JUSTICE SYSTEM LED TO A LOSS OF CLARITY?

Three of the most frequently articulated goals of the current criminal justice response to domestic violence cases are as follows: (1) punish offenders who commit violent acts; (2) prevent offenders from committing future acts of violence, either through specific or general deterrence or rehabilitation of offenders; and (3) assist and empower the victims of such violence. Although these goals are loosely related, their actual implementation is often contradictory. This is important because there is an apparent lack of agreement about which of these goals to pursue, the relative importance of each, and whether they can be achieved simultaneously.

Some reforms are implicitly, or even explicitly, designed simply to punish offenders. Others explicitly suppress future recidivism by deterring potential offenders. Still other policies, as advocated by VAWA and the stated police and prosecutors' goals for many jurisdictions, appear ready to holistically assist victims by providing ready access to shelters, counseling, financial aid, and assistance while maintaining their safety by rehabilitating offenders.

Can conflicts in goals affect outcomes? We know that efforts to aggressively "punish" abusers may not positively or even perversely influence future violence in a subset of particular cases. In these cases, criminal justice punishment may actually increase an aggressor's hostility and anger that may in turn be directed toward the victim, children, other family members, or a new target. Conversely, research has shown that many abusers never reoffend regardless of the sanction imposed. In these cases, the stigma attached with jail time, a hallmark of the punishment approach, may have little benefit given the low probability of recidivism. Indeed, they may simply interfere with an offender's efforts at rehabilitation by decreasing his or her legitimate opportunity to maintain employment, increasing the likelihood of social isolation and detachment from family, or both. Similarly, victims and children also may be incidentally "punished" by loss of income, family reputation, fines imposed, or other "costs" often effectively thrust on the family unit. In the case of immigrants, there even is an increased risk of deportation for the offender, as well as for the victim and his or her children.

Determining the efficacy and impact of criminal justice intervention depends on which goal is considered paramount. Currently, the criminal justice system fluctuates between punitive responses to domestic violence—ensure arrest, prosecution, and conviction—and violence suppression strategies to deter aggressive behavior without primary regard to their punitive nature, such as advocating a proarrest policy simply for its alleged deterrent effect.

In some jurisdictions, the effect of this dilemma has been the referral of thousands of arrested offenders into "batterer treatment programs," monitored to a greater or lesser extent by probation departments. In other jurisdictions, batterer "rehabilitation" is often not a primary goal, but rather the focus is on general deterrence—the deterrence of a larger class of "potential" batterers concerned with the stigma of an arrest.

One outcome is prevalent, however. Despite frequent official protestations to the contrary, the criminal justice system is rarely victim oriented. This is partially due to an overall belief by key actors (the police and prosecutors as a generalized group) that their agency's primary mission is to protect society as a whole from crimes against the public order, not necessarily to assist a particular victim. Unfortunately, neither a punishment model nor a deterrent model by itself necessarily operates in a manner that empowers, or even protects, many victims of domestic violence.

Even arrest rates for offenders, the most commonly cited statistics of police involvement in domestic violence, limits the importance of other factors that might be more accurate and direct measurements of effective victim assistance. The adequacy of the police response to domestic assault has frequently been measured only by arrest rates, yet there are a number of other potential services that police might perform for victims: informing them of their right to get a restraining order, taking them and their children to available shelters, or assisting them with accessing a variety of needed services. Although these services are usually encouraged or even mandated by statute or departmental policy, their implementation often is not monitored or actual practices within many departments do not indicate compliance. This represents a missed opportunity; research has found that when carried out, such actions highly influence victim satisfaction with the police and their commitment to the criminal justice process (Buzawa, Hotaling, Klein, & Byrne, 1999; Miller, 1999). It may also miss the subtle change in perception toward victims of violence in general as society grows to understand that any person can become a victim of violence and as our collective level of empathy toward victims and our willingness to allow society to assist victims increases.

We must note that some respected researchers readily argue that a crime fighting approach is preferable given the limitations of the intervening institutions. Fagan (1996) argued that the criminal justice system should focus primarily on the detection, control, and punishment of batterers, with only indirect involvement in the provision of extra services to battered women. He stated that an emphasis on victim rights conflicted with the primary mission of these institutions, inadvertently making it easier simply to marginalize "domestic" cases as unpleasant "social work" rather than "fighting real crime."

Despite the validity of this fear, we believe the criminal justice system should consider the impact of their actions on individual victims. As noted earlier, the criminal justice system explicitly operates on the premise that a crime is an offense against the state, hence the crime victim's interests are not the primary focus. Therefore, not only does such intervention increase the state's control over women, it may work against their best interests or their needs. The reality is that in many "private" crimes such as domestic violence, in contrast to "public" crimes such as bank robberies, the victim disproportionately bears the vast majority of the crime's "costs" compared with victims of other offenses. In fact, in earlier days, this was one of the implicit rationales for nonintervention; it was regarded as a "private matter" for which it was advantageous that participants resolve the conflict "informally." In addition, as we discuss in detail throughout this book, enormous burdens are often placed on victims at each stage of criminal justice processing. We also discuss in which ways the lack of victim focus may most come into play (for example, when a policy determination to process all offenders through mandatory arrest, mandatory prosecution, or both is not a victim's preference or, for a variety of reasons, even in her best interests).

WHY CHANGES OCCURRED

Although virtually all observers acknowledge the importance of the police and prosecutors' roles, by the early 1970s it was widely noted that their practices had been of limited effectiveness. In fact, the criminal justice response to domestic violence was repeatedly criticized for its failure to deter future acts of violence and to respond to urgent requests for assistance by victims (Buzawa & Buzawa, 1985; Finesmith, 1983; Hanmer, Radford, & Stanko, 1989a; Langley & Levy, 1978).

The criminal justice response to domestic violence was clearly not ideal, but this did not mean it would be altered. Whereas researchers and practitioners had long acknowledged its role to be inappropriate and ineffective, traditional responses remained relatively unchanged for decades (Parnas, 1967). In fact, three key problems confronted any advocate committed to changing the system. First, police departments as institutions historically were remarkably resistant to change. This made street-level implementation of any directives problematic at best and, of necessity, focused attention on the methods used to facilitate actual behavioral changes. Second, there was the basic disagreement among practitioners, researchers, and feminists over the central tenet of police policies. There had been a recurrent exercise of police discretion to avoid arresting domestic violence offenders whenever possible, assuming this was allowed and supported by probable cause. Finally, prosecutors shared police biases. They were deeply committed to exercising their discretion to filter out cases lacking sufficient public purpose to prosecute. In effect, prosecutorial discretion has historically been used to eliminate not only evidentially weak cases, but also those considered unimportant.

To the extent that misdemeanor domestic violence was judged to be an insignificant crime, it is not surprising that there was a strong bias toward continued dismissal of these cases. From the late 1970s to 1994, an almost unprecedented wave of statutory change sought to alter official reaction to domestic violence. During this time, all states enacted legislation designed to modify official behavior. Such legislation, often the result of the interplay of pressure from feminist groups and actions of concerned legislators and professionals in the criminal justice system, has markedly changed the underlying legal philosophy.

Although differing greatly in their scope and limitations, the new statutes expressly purported to make profound structural change in the response of government agencies to domestic violence. Such changes have primarily been concentrated in three areas: (1) police response to domestic violence; (2) the handling of cases by prosecutors and, to a lesser extent, the judiciary; and (3) methods of educating the public to the problem of domestic violence and providing state funding for shelters and other direct assistance to its victims.

The thesis explored in the second edition of this book was that the process of obtaining change never received adequate attention from "change agents." As a result, a pattern of mandating changes had been decoupled from the administrative detail sufficient to ensure actual constructive changes took place. In this edition, we direct our attention to the positive impact, the limitations, and to the possible repercussions of the numerous reforms that have been adopted—or that are at least "on the books"—for victims of domestic violence.

I

CONTEXT OF THE PROBLEM

CHAPTER 2

Defining and Measuring Domestic Violence and Its Impact

WHAT IS DOMESTIC VIOLENCE?

Many writers have used different expressions to describe violence between intimates. For some, it is a problem of women in marital relationships being assaulted, and the terms *wife abuse* or *wife battering* are most appropriate. Others note that the real problem is the tacit societal acceptance of violence against women. After all, the act of battering occurs just as frequently among couples who are dating or living together but are not married. From this perspective, the term *violence against women* captures the essence of the problem. Others, including the authors of this book, note that although injuries due to violence occur disproportionately against women and that men commit more serious violent acts, both genders engage in violence. For this reason, proponents of this perspective favor the gender-neutral terms *domestic violence, domestic assault, intimate partner violence,* or *intimate partner assault* because they are intrinsically less limiting.

For purposes of this monograph, *domestic violence* is operationally defined as *violence between intimates living together or who have previously cohabited*. When directly relevant, we also study the closely related

phenomenon of "dating violence," in which serious injuries often occur among intimates in the absence of cohabitation. The terms are broadly defined, and we acknowledge that definitions are largely dependent on descriptions by the police, assailants, and victims. Hence, the definition of family violence is societally based. Our adopted definition is gender neutral in that we see violence as a problem of both genders.[1]

In taking this position, we note a dilemma with our definition: It minimizes the disproportionate injuries attendant to male violence against women—that is, although both men and women initiate violence, in most cases violence initiated by women is far less severe. For example, Straus and Gelles, using the National Family Violence Survey (NFVS), found that the injury rate for women was 6 times higher than that for men (3% and .5%, respectively; Straus & Gelles, 1990; see also Gordon, 2000; Morse, 1995; Straus, 1999).

Another data source, the National Crime Victimization Survey (NCVS), reported that in 1998, 85% of the approximately 1 million reported cases of victimization by intimate partners were against women. In the NCVS, approximately half of female domestic violence victims reported physical injury compared with 32% of male victims. Although the rates of serious injury were similar (4% for men and 5% for women), women are significantly more likely to incur minor injuries (more than 4 in 10 women compared with fewer than 3 in 10 men; Rennison & Welchans, 2000).

Male domination is also a component of many acts of female violence, much of which is in the context of self-defense or in anticipation of a male partner's violence. Finally, by virtually all accounts, women experience much greater fear and injury in situations of domestic violence (Bograd, 1988; Kurz, 1992; Yllö, 1993). Despite these facts, we nonetheless consider it appropriate to emphasize that any domestic violence is inappropriate, regardless of gender. As we explore later in this chapter, recent research has challenged the core concept of the predominance of male violence. (In particular, see the discussion of the recent cohort analysis done by Moffit, Robins, & Caspi, 2001. If replicated, this will seriously erode the existing consensus on the relative prevalence of female vs. male violence.)

Although some authors may consider "stalking" a separate phenomenon, we consider it to be closely related and often a precursor to domestic violence—and hence properly covered in this book. We define *stalking* as *the act of deliberately and repeatedly following or harassing another to create fear in the victim or to coerce him or her to accede to the wishes of the stalker.* Unless experienced, this behavior might be assumed to constitute a nuisance, a mere inconvenience to the recipient. Unfortunately, the reality of stalking, especially in the context of domestic violence, is far different— and considerably more dangerous. In this book, we study stalking only as an adjunct to a domestic relationship because it is the heart of our work and addresses the vast majority of stalking incidents.

HOW DEFINITIONS AFFECT MEASUREMENT

Although perhaps considered an arcane subject, we believe an analysis of how domestic violence is measured is critical to the overall study of the criminal justice response to domestic violence. We note this because various studies show extraordinarily different results as to the frequency of abuse and even in terms of basic data regarding whether domestic violence rates are increasing or decreasing over time as reforms are carried out. Hence, it is difficult to measure the impact of such reforms overall or, even more speculatively, on particular types of relationships or subgroups within the population.

Our analysis begins with the understanding that there are seemingly shocking differences in the rates of domestic violence as reported by the various states, the federal government, and the numerous studies and surveys that seek to determine the scope of the problem. To a large extent, this is because unlike "classic" felonies such as murder, robbery, or, to a lesser extent, rape, as we discussed in the first section of this chapter, a consensus has never been reached as to the definition of domestic violence. We believe that this is largely due to widespread continuing differences in how such problems are defined, categorized, and reported. A brief review of these factors demonstrates the problem. It also illustrates the difficulty we have in interpreting the prevalence of domestic violence and establishing empirically if the problem is increasing in magnitude or is being successfully addressed.

Relationships

Although we use *domestic violence* and *domestic assault* in the context of violence between past or present intimates, most state domestic violence statutes typically have far broader definitions of relationships, often including anyone residing in the house or any type of family relationship. Thus, such statutes not only cover our adopted definition of violence committed between two adult, married or unmarried, partners or ex-partners; by their terms such statutes may cover violence between parent(s) or caretakers(s) and dependent children and violence committed by siblings and in other family relationships. Such intrafamily violence may be severe, but its character, causes, and treatment differ markedly from the type of violence discussed in this book.

Nonetheless, although we fully understand that violence among nonintimate relationships requires study, we believe that for purposes of this book it is important to address how intervention for these other relationships differs from that related to intimate violence. It has been an all-too-common practice for all domestic violence data to be aggregated within a state and conclusions drawn about intimate partner violence on many critical variables such as injury, criminal justice decision making, and revictimization. In addition, comparisons are made between states despite differences in the types of relationships and acts that are compared or differences in the scope of legislation.

As we discuss throughout this book, there is significant variation in how cases are processed, providing differences not only in how responses to male-against-female adult intimate partner violence differ, but how legislation and political pressure may have influenced these responses.

It also should be recognized, however, that not all states define an adult intimate partner in the same way. When examining National Incident Based Reporting System (NIBRS) data from nine states, Greenfeld et al. (1998) found that 53.1% of domestic violence cases involved spouses, 4.9% involved ex-spouses, and 42% involved "other intimates." In this case, other intimates is defined as current or past boyfriend or girlfriend relationships (dating violence), common-law spouses, or homosexual relationships. Of the 42% of intimate partner cases falling under the category of other intimate, there is great room for interpretation. What type of relationship between a man and woman constitutes a boyfriend or girlfriend? When classifying a call, do police routinely ask such couples if they have ever resided together or if they have been sexually intimate?

Age

Although counterintuitive, the definition of victims' ages also seems to affect the incidence and reports of domestic violence. There is some overlap in the studies between domestic violence and "child abuse" typically committed in families. The National Crime Survey (NCS) addresses all women 12 and older, many of whom are not likely to be at risk of violence by an "intimate." In contrast, the Uniform Crime Report (UCR) published by the Department of Justice, addresses adults aged 18 and over, as does the National Family Violence Survey. To further confuse the issue, the National Violence Against Women Survey (NVAWS), sponsored by the National Institute of Justice and the Centers for Disease Control and consisting of a survey of 8,000 women and 8,000 men, addressed violence committed against women ages 16 and over (Tjaden & Thoennes, 1998). Because parental violence against teens in this country is at least as prevalent, many of the studies mentioned may be capturing and reporting this phenomenon as domestic violence. Similarly, the more age-restricted studies largely fail to report violence committed between teen partners, relationships that can be quite violent according to statistics.

Behaviors and Acts

Domestic violence, more than any other criminal act, includes a wide range of behaviors, making it difficult to measure. The lack of consensus on what behaviors fall under the rubric of domestic violence results in vastly different figures of its prevalence in the United States. Most state domestic violence legislation has defined violence as an individual act, usually a physical assault or threat of physical harm intended to cause physical harm. In reality, most researchers now more accurately conceptualize domestic violence as a range of behaviors—some obviously criminal in nature, others more manipulative—which in total are intended to exercise coercive control including physical, sexual, psychological, and verbal behaviors used to control a partner. This perspective focuses on the *pattern* of violent and abusive behavior within the relationship rather than on individual acts of perpetrators. For example, the National Center for Injury Prevention and Control has urged that measures of assault behavior include separate measures of physical violence, sexual violence, threats of physical or sexual violence, and repeated acts of emotional and psychological abuse even in the absence of a direct threat (Saltzman, Fanslow, McMahon, & Shelley, 1999). There are several reasons many researchers only consider physical aggression or sexual assault (defined as forced penetration) when measuring violence. First, there is concern that combining serious physical violence with less tangible measures of verbal aggression or controlling and intimidating behavior might cause people to trivialize violence overall (DeKeseredy, 2000). For example, there is less agreement as to whether controlling behavior, such as pressuring a person into unwanted sex, threatening to terminate employment, making demeaning comments, or other acts of psychological aggression, are

as serious or threatening as physical violence. Certainly much of the publicity oriented to educating teens about dating violence and risks of abuse would define such behaviors as risk factors or warning signs of future abuse rather than as actual abusive behavior.

Second, researchers may find it more difficult to measure empirically behaviors other than actual physical acts (Gordon, 2000). In addition, they may believe that these are different behaviors and that failing to distinguish them would preclude the ability to determine causation (DeKeseredy, 2000). Some researchers have attempted to measure both physical violence and abusive or controlling behavior by providing separate measures of their components (e.g., physical or sexual violence, threats of physical or sexual violence, stalking, and emotional or psychological abuse; Buzawa et al., 1999; Buzawa & Hotaling, 2000; Hotaling & Buzawa, 2001). Even within these components there are definitional issues; for example, what constitutes stalking behavior, threatening behavior, and psychological abuse?

One of the primary difficulties is confusion between violent acts and injuries. Many people incorrectly believe that the sole legal criterion for measuring a violent act is *injury*, but physical contact is *not* required as an element of the crime in most statutes. Although criminal law acknowledges differences in assault severity only by a dichotomy distinguishing between simple assault, aggravated assault, and sexual assault, researchers often use the umbrella term *assault* to measure the wide range of behavior on a continuum ranging from minor threats to serious violent behavior.

The UCR states in its discussion of the tabulation of aggravated assault, that attempts are included because it is not necessary that an injury result (Federal Bureau of Investigation [FBI], 1992). Similarly, in 1998, the U.S. National Crime Victimization Survey

(NCVS) published by the U.S. Justice Department's Bureau of Justice Statistics (for estimation purposes) adopted a quite inclusive definition acknowledging that an "assault" may range from minor threats to incidents that are nearly fatal.

State statutes regularly redefine what constitutes legal criteria for "attempts" as well as "acts." Certainly, most surveys take a much broader view of assault than simply measuring injuries. The Canadian Urban Victimization Survey includes in its definition of assault the presence of a weapon, an attack, or a threat. Assault incidents may therefore range from face-to-face verbal threats to an attack resulting in extensive injuries (Fattah, 1991). Some favor an even wider net in defining assault by arguing for the inclusion of verbal aggression, harassment, or behaviors that are emotionally distressing. This can, of course, be carried to the farcical. For example apparently one Canadian town, Brunswick, Nova Scotia, even considered an ordinance that would make exuding the odor of aftershave lotion or mouthwash in public eating establishments a criminal assault (Buzawa & Hotaling, 2000).

HOW WIDESPREAD IS DOMESTIC VIOLENCE? THE PROBLEM OF CONFLICTING STUDIES

As described above, determining the scope of the problem of domestic violence differs widely based on the definition used to measure incidence and prevalence. Given the different definitions of domestic violence and the different measurements used to quantify it, it is not surprising that estimates of violence vary widely.[2]

The general assumption is that both official reports and self-reports understate the problem for a variety of reasons. For example, even a direct question to past victims or perpetrators of violence may not elicit a positive response. After all, people may not always remember, let alone be willing to acknowledge, illegal or inappropriate behavior. Therefore, inaccurate recall due to conscious or unconscious distortion and interpretation of questions may occur. Unfortunately, there is a lack of empirical data verifying the veracity and impact of such bias.

Prevalence rates for domestic violence are usually determined by asking if an individual has experienced an act of physical (or other types of violence) within the prior year or in his or her lifetime. Typically, this information is presented as a percentage for the past year, lifetime prevalence, or both. Prevalence rates are highly dependent not only on the definition, but on the type of population examined. Many studies are done in health care settings, shelters, mental health units, or at colleges or universities, and these populations would likely report strikingly different prevalence rates.

The context for a study, as well as how it is administered, and the format and wording of questions have an impact on findings regarding assaults. Straus (1999) distinguished between "family conflict" and "crime studies" as a source for discrepancies. Minor acts of aggression are more likely to be reported in family conflict surveys in which there are specific instructions given for a wide range of behaviors. Crime studies require the respondent to perceive the aggression as a "crime"; however, many respondents do not perceive minor aggression as constituting criminal "assault."

Although the crime of assault does not require the intent to harm or actual physical injury, many individuals do not perceive such aggression as a crime and fail to report it to researchers (Gordon, 2000; Straus, 1999). The NCVS data do suggest an increased willingness to report to police, however, with 59% reporting in 1998 compared with 48%

in 1993. This contrasts with the NVAWS, which found that only 25% of all physical assaults against females by intimates were reported to the police.

Therefore, crime studies report much lower rates of assault by both men and women. This is supported by Straus's observation that in only 3% or less of conflict studies is an injury reported, compared with 75% (NCS), 52% (NCVS), and 76% (NVAWS) crime studies (Straus, 1999). Furthermore, the NFVS, the National Youth Survey (NYS), and the Dunedin Multidisciplinary Health and Development Study report equal acts of minor aggression by men and women, whereas the NCVS, as noted previously, reported that 85% of the approximately 1 million reported victimizations by intimate partners in 1998 were against women.

The two major national data sources are the UCR (based on police reports), and the NCVS (both published by the Bureau of Justice Statistics), which rely on self-reports of criminal victimization. These are two very different conceptions of crime, which have resulted in very different reported rates. Among incidents of assaults known to police, there are more victims as shown in the NCVS than reflected by the offense rate reported in the UCR. This is partially because a single assaultive offense known to police often involves two or more victims.[3]

Although at a minimum the UCR requires a police report and a "finding" of a crime to count, victimizations under the NCVS are based solely on victim accounts with no corroborating evidence, which is generally not sufficient for police to establish a criminal offense. These differences create large discrepancies between "official" UCR and NCVS and NFVS data. The UCR bases its data on crimes police report to the FBI; however, in 1985, the NFVS reported that as much as 90% of intimate violence was not reported to the police (Straus & Gelles, 1990). In stating this, we note that in 1998, the Bureau of Justice Statistics and the authors of the UCR implicitly rejected this assertion, finding that 53% of women who were assaulted reported these events (Rennison, 2001).

In addition, police record only varying percentages of what is actually reported (we discuss this further in Chapters 5 and 6). In addition, the UCR uses it own definitions and classifications of offenses and requires reporting agencies to conform to these standards. This is exacerbated by the fact that many departments do not submit any data to the FBI, even when doing so is state mandated. Furthermore, the quality of data that police provide is often questionable, and considerable information may be lacking (Buzawa & Hotaling, 2000; Hotaling & Buzawa, 2001). As a result, statistics on domestic violence may either reflect the department's record keeping or the experience of its service population (Pierce & Deutsch, 1990).

There are several additional problems with the UCR. Its data are offender based with no information provided on victims. Although the UCR now requires assaults to be categorized as domestic or nondomestic, it does not include relationship status. Many police departments do not even record this information on incident reports, resulting in the inability to correctly categorize incidents. Of even greater significance, as described earlier, the term *domestic* has varying differences based on state legislation and thus becomes meaningless in an aggregate because relationships and acts encompassed vary among states.

More recently, new format approaches appear to ease at least some of the problems of using official statistics, leading us to hope that this problem will lessen in magnitude. One key improvement to the FBI's UCR is the National Incident Based Reporting System (NIBRS), which has been implemented in several jurisdictions. The NIBRS collects data on 57 types of crimes and includes detailed information on offender–victim demographics, victim–offender relationship, time and place of occurrence, weapon use, and victim injury.[4]

The UCR has provided information on homicides since 1961 in their Supplemental Homicide Report (SHR) and is estimated to have data for 92% of homicides (Greenfeld et al., 1998). These data are far more complete than those in the UCR and include detailed information similar to the NIBRS. As with all UCR data, the accuracy and reliability of police reports limit this data source. Again, domestic homicides are likely to be undercounted for several reasons. First, incidents reported as assaults may result in the victim's death, yet reports are not appropriately modified. Second, relationships are often not clearly defined or are unknown if an offender is not arrested. Even if an offender is subsequently arrested, if this does not occur during the year of the incident, this new information is rarely reported to the FBI. Finally, as with the UCR, many jurisdictions fail to file the SHR or file only for portions of the year. There have also been cases in which entire states have failed to file a report for a given year (Gelles, 2000; Greenfeld et al., 1998). Pierce, Spaar, and Briggs (1988) noted a second problem with existing data. These researchers observed use of police services by two distinct populations of domestic violence victims. The first group typically contacts police on only one occasion. The second are repeatedly victimized and are frequent users of police resources, the "regulars" in police parlance. For example, Pease and Laycock (1996) reported that 43% of domestic violence incidents involved only 7% of households.

Furthermore, victims of domestic violence may seek help from a variety of service agencies, making each agency's database incomplete and sometimes misleading. For example, many victims of intentionally caused injuries seek medical services without filing formal police reports (Barancik, Chattergee, Greene, Michenzi, & Fife, 1983; Pierce & Deutsch, 1990). In fact, Pierce and Deutsch (1990) suggested that police departments may be the primary service provider for less serious domestic violence injuries, whereas physicians, especially emergency medical personnel, become relatively more important as service providers when the injuries become more serious. Further supporting this finding is a recent study reporting that almost half of all women entering a battered women's shelter, which typically disproportionately handles the more serious cases of domestic violence, had not contacted the police (Coulter, Kuehnle, Byers, & Alfonso, 1999).

The lack of continuity in services or in record keeping also makes official estimates suspect. Despite widespread adoption of laws mandating the reporting of domestic violence incidents, there is no effective mechanism to consistently collect data from all public health, welfare, and law enforcement agencies in most jurisdictions.

Finally, classification of calls by police has also been problematic. Assaults frequently receive ambiguous typologies such as "persons investigated" or "services rendered." Police categorized approximately 50% of the 3.2 million service calls Boston received between 1977 and 1982 in such a manner. Alternately, an aggravated assault report may fail to indicate that the assailant was a spouse (Pierce et al., 1988).

Pierce et al. (1988) also found a decrease in specific classification by officers compared with 911 operators that may be attributed to officer "downgrading" the various problem calls received. This lack of consistent reporting is more likely if an assault or burglary involves a domestic problem or if there have been previous requests for police assistance.

Currently, the most sophisticated attempts to identify patterns of repeat service calls to a particular household, conducted by Pierce et al., may be subject to challenge. Such analysis tends to rely on street addresses rather than individual names. One could argue that, due to neighborhood characteristics, specific areas will always comprise families at high risk and heavy occupant turnover as opposed to recidivism of a particular familial unit. This may partially account for repeat calls.

WHAT IS THE INCIDENCE OF DOMESTIC VIOLENCE?

With all of the preceding caveats as to the accuracy of the data, the following is the most accurate practice on the incidence of domestic violence now available.

The NCVS reported that in 1998, women were victims in about 900,000 violent offenses, a decrease from the 1.1 million reported in 1993. Men were the victims of about 160,000 assaults by a violent partner. Intimate partner violence declined 21% in the 5-year period from 1993 to 1998, or 9.8% per 1,000 to 7.5% per 1,000. At the same time, there was a 34% overall decrease in violent crime, so, in reality, intimate partner violence decreased less than other violent offenses.

The NCVS data also revealed that between 1993 and 1998, intimate partner violence was responsible for 22% of violent crime against women compared with 3% of violence against men. Women annually experienced more than 5 times as many violent incidents by an intimate than did men. On average, each year women were the victims of more than 572,000 violent victimizations committed by an intimate compared with approximately 49,000 incidents committed against men. Approximately half of female victims reported a physical injury, and 40%

obtained medical treatment (Rennison & Welchans, 2000).

As a result of problems with NCVS and UCR data, large-scale independent research projects provide good supplemental estimates of levels of domestic violence in America. The key nongovernmental survey is the NFVS, first administered by Straus and Gelles in 1975. They used the Conflict Tactics Scale (CTS; Straus, Gelles, & Steinmetz, 1980) as a mechanism to measure incidence, prevalence, chronicity, and severity of physical assaults as well as how reasoning and verbal aggression is used to resolve conflicts. They completed three national surveys involving personal interviews of 2,143 respondents in 1976 and telephone interviews with 6,002 respondents in 1985 (Gelles & Straus, 1988) and 1,970 respondents in 1992 (Straus, 1990).[5]

Straus reported that about 16% of all households surveyed and approximately 10% of both women and men reported some victimization in the past year with slightly over 3% in any given year suffering severe abuse, e.g. involving punching with a fist, kicking, biting, beatings, and attacks with knives and guns (Straus & Gelles, 1990). They also reported that 39% of all incidents of violence toward wives involved serious violence (Gelles & Straus, 1988). The rate of minor violence in their 1992 survey was 91 per 1,000 (compared with 80 per 1,000 in 1985 and 100 per 1,000 in 1975). Serious assaults were reported at 38 per 1,000 in 1975 and declined to 19 per 1,000 in 1992.

Women's Use of Violence

One controversial difference in the NFVS from NCVS and official data is the very high rates of violence by women. Currently, more than 100 studies have used the CTS and have found rates of violence by women to be as high as men (Straus, 1999). Straus believes this reflects the critical differences between crime studies and conflict studies. Research by Straus and his colleagues suggests that only about 2% of incidents of domestic assault are reported to police (compared with 53% according to the NCVS, as discussed earlier) and that those reported are likely to be the more serious assaults or those for which there is greatest fear of serious injury—most likely by a male perpetrator (Straus & Gelles, 1986, 1990).

This contrasts with the NCVS survey and the NVAWS, which both report considerably higher rates of female compared with male intimate partner victimization (Bachman & Saltzman, 1995; Tjaden & Thoennes, 2000). The NVAWS, based on survey information with 8,000 representative men and women, reported that nearly 25% of surveyed women and approximately 8% of surveyed men said that they were raped or physically assaulted (or both) by a current or former spouse, a cohabiting partner, or a date at some point in their lifetime. From this, they extrapolated that approximately 4.8 million intimate partner rapes and physical assaults were perpetrated against U.S. women annually, and approximately 2.9 million intimate partner assaults were committed against men annually (Tjaden & Thoennes, 2000).

In addition to controversy over which data source more accurately reflects women's use of violence, many researchers argue that the number of acts alone should not be the basis of judging female violence but that the outcome and the context of the violence are also critical factors. First, as Stets and Straus (1990) emphasized, the rate of injury-inflicted assaults was 3.5 per 1,000 for men against women, compared with 0.6 per 1,000 for women against men—6 times the rate of injury.

The NVAWS found that gender differences became even more pronounced when the severity of the outcome was measured. Of the 4.8 million rapes and physical assaults perpetrated against women annually, approximately 2 million resulted in an injury to the

victim, and more than 550,000 required some type of medical treatment for female victims. In contrast, of the approximately 2.9 million intimate partner physical assaults perpetrated against men annually, approximately 580,000 resulted in injuries and only 125,000 required medical treatment. Therefore, although the overall number of injuries—4.8 million compared with 2.9 million—may not be remarkably dissimilar, the difference between the 550,000 women requiring medical care compared with the 125,000 men reveals considerably higher risk to women. In addition, because the NVAWS study included same-sex violence, where a far higher percentage of men were far more likely to be abused by a male partner, the difference in injuries sustained by each sex at the hands of the other is even greater.

As we noted earlier, it has long been suggested that there are major differences in the use of violence between men and women in relationships. Since the early 1980s, some researchers have suggested that women may initiate violence more often then men as a tactical strategy to avoid an imminent violent act against them (Bowker, 1983; Feld & Straus, 1989). In addition, many women may be acting in self-defense or simply fighting back (Hanmer & Saunders, 1984; Renzetti, 1999; Stark & Flitcraft, 1996). This argument is further substantiated by empirical data from a national study of dating violence in Canada, which reported that the majority of women who used violence were acting in self-defense or fighting back (DeKeseredy, Saunders, Schwartz, & Alvi, 1997). Another recent study by Swan and Snow (2002) studied women who had used physical violence with a male partner. They reported that "almost all of the women committed moderate physical violence, 57% committed severe violence, 54% injured their partner, 28% used sexual coercion, and 86% used some form of coercive control"

(Swan & Snow, 2002, p. 311). Almost all these women also experienced physical violence from their male partners. They found that only 12% of women were aggressors; the remaining women reported that the men committed significantly more acts of violence against them with less than 6% experiencing no physical violence by their partner.

Although women committed significantly more acts of moderate physical violence against male partners than their partners committed against them, their partners committed almost 1.5 times the number of severe physical acts against them (although only moderately significant), committed 2.5 times the rate of sexual coercion, and caused 1.5 times as much injury. Also of interest, is that although there were many relationships in which women were more physically aggressive, their male partner was more controlling (50% of relationships). The researchers suggested that this indicates these women were not necessarily in control of their partner's behavior despite the fact that they used more severe violence (Swan & Snow, 2002).

This conclusion may be questionable. The assumption that if one partner uses verbal coercion and the other uses physical violence, the former is really the person in control of the relationship is not really all that clear; the line between physical and psychological abuse may at the least blur. Furthermore, the terms *emotional abuse* and *coercion* were intermingled and include behaviors such as insulting or swearing at a partner. This does not appear to be a commonly accepted measure of coercion.

Moffit et al. (2001) examined a representative sample of 360 couples. These couples were interviewed as young adults, when the incidence of partner violence is greatest. In addition, partners corroborated each others' reports of abuse, and all reports were examined for reliability. Moffit et al.'s research did not support a male aggressor model of violence.

Instead, these researchers found that the range and distribution of abusive acts did not significantly differ by gender. In addition, their findings did not support the belief that women's use of violence is usually motivated by self-defense. The researchers reported that a substantial number of women committed one-sided violent acts during the study period that exceeded the number of male acts. Furthermore, 18% of women initiated assaults despite the fact that both parties agreed that the male partner had committed no acts of abuse, a fact true for only 6% of the male respondents. Finally, the researchers reported that women in the study who were abusive toward their partners were 4 times more likely to have been violent toward someone other than an intimate partner in the same year.

What is interesting is that longitudinal studies have suggested that there are relationships in which women are the initially aggressive partner, but that at a later point in time, men become physically abusive—"men do abuse women who abuse them" (Moffit et al., 2001, p. 23).

The preceding recent studies collectively suggest that female-on-male violence is a widely underreported phenomenon, perhaps because the impact in the form of actual injuries and death is demonstrably less than the converse. It also simply does not fit into the image that many authors, activists, and politicians have of a crime that is almost exclusively within the province of men.

Intimate Violence in Specific Population Subsets

National-level aggregate data often tend to mask major differences among specific groups within the population. For example, data on same-sex relationships suggest that rates of abuse in that subset of the population may actually be higher than in heterosexual relationships. Until recently, we lacked empirical data on the extent of partner violence in same-sex relationships. Initial domestic violence legislation focused on heterosexual partner violence, and service providers including hotlines and shelters typically excluded women victimized by same-sex intimate partners. Therefore, police reports and other sources of official data did not provide data on the extent of these incidents reaching police attention (Hart, 1986). To the extent that many states still do not include same-sex relationships under domestic violence statutes, these victims are unlikely to receive the same access to the criminal justice system that is provided to other domestic violence victims.

Early research was limited to small, unrepresentative samples of same-sex-partner violence. Not only did this make it difficult to generalize from their findings, but the estimates of prevalence varied tremendously, ranging from 17% (Loulan, 1987) to 74% (Lie, Schilit, Bush, Montagne, & Reyes, 1991) depending on the measures used and the time period measured.

The NVAWS was the first study to include same-sex violence as part of a large-scale national survey. It reported that approximately 11% of women in a lesbian relationship reported being raped, physically assaulted, or stalked by their partner. Although a significant percentage, this number was less than the 30% of women who reported such violence when living with a man in a heterosexual relationship. In contrast, in male same-sex couples, the rate of violence was approximately 15% against a partner, whereas men in heterosexual relationships were physically abused by women at a rate slightly less than 8%. Hence, although same-sex violence is clearly an under-addressed issue, this research suggests that men perpetrate more violence in both same-sex or heterosexual relationships, but the highest rates of male violence are in a heterosexual relationship (Tjaden & Thoennes, 2000).

In addition, there were differences reported on the basis of ethnicity. Although the NVAWS reported little difference in intimate partner physical violence and stalking between Hispanic and non-Hispanic women, they found significant differences in rape reported by a current or former partner in these populations. The researchers highlighted the significance of this finding because Hispanic women are less likely than other women to be sexually assaulted by a nonintimate or former nonintimate partner (Tjaden & Thoenees, 2000).

Significant differences have also been reported among different racial groups. The NVAWS found that American Indian/Alaska Native women report significantly higher rates of intimate partner violence than did women of other racial backgrounds, and Asian/Pacific Islander women and men report significantly lower rates. The authors noted that American Indian/Alaska Native women may be more willing to report victimization to interviewers than are other victims (Tjaden & Thoennes, 2000).

Data on intimate partner violence among African Americans vary considerably. Straus and Gelles (1986) reported that African Americans had 4 times the rate of partner violence compared with Whites; however, NCVS data suggest that rates of domestic violence between Black and White women appear to be similar for every age group except between the ages of 20 and 24, when the rates were 29 per 1,000 for Black women compared with 20 per 1,000 for White women (Rennison, 2001). The NVAWS reported higher rates of victimization rates for Black women but found that when other sociodemographic and relationship variables were controlled, these differences disappeared. We discuss these factors in greater detail in Chapter 3.

Finally, overall rates of intimate partner violence among immigrant groups as a defined population subset are extremely difficult to determine. A national survey of criminal justice officials and leaders of six ethnic communities suggest that many recent immigrants fail to report crimes (R. C. Davis & Erez, 1998). In fact, 67% of the officials in the national survey believed that they were less likely to report crimes compared with other victims, and only 12% thought they were as or more likely to report offenses to the police. In addition, domestic violence victims were less likely to report their victimizations, making an overall appraisal of the rates of domestic violence in this group especially problematic.

Data on homicides are the most complete, likely attributable to the severity of the crime and the resulting importance of a thorough police report. Clearly, domestic violence plays a major role in homicide, although in recent years there has been a substantial decrease in the proportion of homicides committed by intimate partners. In 1998, women comprised nearly 53% of homicides; 1,830 female homicides occurred in a relationship known to involve intimate partners. This is a decrease from the 1976 figure of 3,000 intimate partner homicides, which represented 75% of all homicides against female intimate partners (Rennison & Welchans, 2000). It is important to note that White women are the one category of victims for which intimate partner homicide has not shown a substantial decline since 1976 (Rennison & Walchans, 2000). In contrast, there was a 45% decrease in homicides against Black women.

Stalking is also quite prevalent. The most detailed data are from the NVAWS, which estimates that women are approximately 4 times more likely as men to be stalked during their lifetime (8.1% vs. 2.2%). In addition, women are more likely than men to be stalked by current or former intimates. Stalking by a current or former intimate occurs before and during the relationship for 36% of female victims and after termination of the relationship for 43% of female victims (Tjaden & Thoennes, 1998). Victims stalked by a current or former intimate partner are more likely to be threatened (Meloy & Gothard, 1995) and injured (U.S. Department of Justice, 1998; Wright et al., 1996). The NVAWS reported that 82% were physically assaulted, and 31% were raped (Tjaden & Thoennes, 1998).

THE IMPACT OF DOMESTIC VIOLENCE

Injuries and Deaths

It has been estimated that women were injured in approximately half of the domestic assaults committed in 1998 (Rennison & Welchans, 2000). In addition, during the period from 1992 to 1998, domestic assaults were found to be 37% more likely to result in injuries for women than were other types of assault (Simon & Perkins, 2001). Incidents of domestic violence are not merely a problem of one particular social class. Although most criminal justice involvement has been with the lower socioeconomic groups, numerous researchers have noted that although the stress of being indigent, the relative lack of adaptive nonviolence skills, and increased rates of substance abuse may result in higher levels of domestic violence in lower socioeconomic groups, acts of familial violence are by no means restricted to this group (Bassett, 1980; Coates & Leong, 1980; Ferraro, 1989a; U.S. Attorney General's Task Force on Family Violence, 1984). In fact, even the American Medical Association (1992), in a special report published in the *Journal of the American Medical Association*, noted that doctors simply did not recognize widespread signs of abuse in middle-class patients. The article noted that because many of the doctors were White, middle- or upper-class men, they were particularly subject to denying abuse from men with whom they could identify ("Doctors Falter," 1992).

Psychological and Quality-of-Life Effects on Victims

The impact of domestic violence is far higher than the individual acts. Severe physical abuse is more likely to result in greater psychological impact (Follingstad, Brenan, Hause, Polek, & Rutledge, 1991). The degree of psychological impact may not be totally a result of measures of violence such as the amount of force used or injuries sustained but rather based in part on individual subjective factors (Weaver & Clum, 1995).

Victims become emotionally traumatized. The battering syndrome has been found to result in high rates of medical complaints (Stark & Flitcraft, 1988); depression and low self-esteem (Campbell, Kub, Belknap, & Templin, 1997; Campbell & Soeken, 1999; Zlotnick, Kohn, Peterson, & Pearlstein, 1998); psychosocial problems, and later disproportionate risks of rape, miscarriage, abortion, alcohol and drug abuse, attempted suicide (Stets & Straus, 1990); and general emotional well-being including posttraumatic stress disorder (PTSD) resulting from severe stress (Campbell & Soeken, 1999). The impact of these problems is profound. The rates of suicide of battered women are almost 5 times as high as in nonbattered populations (Stark, 1984). Furthermore, it appears that many of these problems begin *after* the abuse, not as a cluster of which abuse is merely one factor (Holtzworth-Munroe, Smutzler, & Sandin, 1997; Stark, 1984; Woods, 1999). The emotional toll of domestic violence may also be greatly increased if a psychological assault is part of the pattern of abuse. Some researchers have reported that many women find psychological, verbal, and emotional abuse more

harmful and of far greater duration than physical abuse (DeKeseredy & MacLeod, 1997; Fitzpatrick & Halliday, 1992).

Sexual assault as a component of domestic violence is also quite common, but it is not frequently discussed (Mahoney & Williams, 1998), in part because of the lack of empirical data. Although it may occur in isolation from physical and other forms of abuse, it is often seen in cases in which there is also severe physical abuse (Gordon, 2000; Painter & Farrington, 1998). This form of victimization can be particularly harmful for victims and lead to chronic mental health problems (Foa & Riggs, 1994; Riggs, Kilpatrick, & Resnick, 1992).

The severity and extent of abuse is highly related to the victims showing symptoms of PTSD (Barnett, 2000; Follette, Polusny, Bechtle, & Naugle, 1996). In fact, not only do high proportions of victims of sexual, physical, and psychological assault suffer from PTSD, these individuals also constitute a significant proportion of the total number of people who experience these symptoms (Kemp, Green, Hovanitz, & Rawlings, 1995; Riggs et al., 1992).

The Impact of Domestic Violence on Children and Adolescents

Children in abusive families appear to be the most susceptible to the impact of domestic violence. First, it is significant that large numbers of this especially vulnerable group regularly witness violence in the family. One estimate (using data derived from total instances of domestic violence and "adjusted" for the number of children in the household) is that approximately 3.3 million children witness acts of domestic violence each year (Carlson, 1984). Straus and Gelles (1990), using the 1985 national victim survey, suggested an even higher figure. They stated that

10 million teenagers every year witnessed violence between parents and that collectively, "at least 1/3 of American children have witnessed violence between their parents, and most have endured repeated instances" (Straus & Gelles, 1990).

More recent studies confirm the prevalence of children witnessing violence. Edelson et al. (2000) reported that in a group of 114 battered women, 45% stated that their children entered situations in which abuse was occurring at least "occasionally," 18% responded that this occurred "frequently"; only 23% said that this "never" occurred. Even these data may underestimate the extent of child witnessing of adult violence because another study found that 77% of children whose parents said their children did not witness violence did, in fact, do so (O'Brien, John, Margolin, & Erel, 1994). Despite the victim's or even the offender's trying to hide acts of violence from the children, their witnessing of such acts clearly puts them at risk for becoming the "hidden victims" of domestic abuse.

What impact does witnessing violence have on children? Could such an impact manifest itself in the context of general behavioral problems or in a tendency to be a victim or a victimizer? These questions are important in the context of theories of the generation of long-term social and behavioral problems and the possible intergenerational transfer of violence. Edleson (2001) in a recently published research article, noted that there was now an extensive body of literature of more than 100 studies trying to determine the impact of family violence on children, with about one third dealing solely with children witnessing violence as opposed to being battered themselves (Edleson, 2001). Edelson reported that several studies found that "externalized" behaviors such as aggression and antisocial behavior were more common in children, especially boys, exposed to domestic violence; "internalized" behaviors such as unusual fears

and inhibitions were also common, especially among girls (Fantuzzo, DePaola, Lamberg, Martino, Anderson, & Sutton, 1991; see also Carlson, 1991; Hughes, 1988; Hughes, Parkinson, & Vargo, 1989; Stagg, Wills, & Howell, 1989). Other studies have reported a variety of adverse effects with children who have witnessed domestic violence, including that, in general, they score lower on tests of social competency and higher on depression, anxiety, aggression, shyness, and school-related problems (Adamson & Thompson, 1998; Fantuzzo et al., 1991; Silvern et al., 1995; Wolfe, Jaffe, Wilson, & Zak, 1985). Another study indicates that children score lower on tests of cognitive functioning (Rossman, 1998).

These attitudes can potentially result in a series of behavioral problems. One study of violent teenage boys reported that exposure to family violence apparently was associated with the development of positive feelings toward using violence to "solve" problems and hence indirectly to violent offending (Spaccerelli, Coatworth, & Bowden, 1995). In addition—and perhaps this is the most chilling prospect—witnessing parental violence is highly correlated with subsequent suicide attempts of children. One study found that 65% of children who had attempted suicide had previously witnessed family violence (Kosky, 1983). Although Edleson (2001) correctly noted that solely using this factor to predict individual attitudes or behavior would be wrong, he also noted that within the highly variable individual experiences and reactions, most studies show group trends in which adverse impact may be seen.

Can such exposure also be related to the well-known trend of intergenerational transmission of violence? This might be based on "social learning theory," the proponents of which hypothesize that witnessing violence, especially repetitively and in the emotionally laden context of the family, would predispose children to learn to use violence. There is evidence for this effect both outside and within the family. Short-term effects were recently found in one study in which recent exposure to violence in the home was significant in predicting children's and adolescents' violent behavior outside the home (Adamson & Thompson, 1998).

Some children and teens are more affected by exposure to violence than others. Resilience may be due to several factors. First, a child's relationship with a caring adult, usually a parent, may reduce the negative impact of exposure. Second, characteristics of the victim have been found to be of significance. Children with average or above average intelligence and strong interpersonal skills are more likely to have increased resilience. Additional factors include self-esteem and other personality traits, socioeconomic background, religion, and contact with supportive people (Osofsky, 1999).

It is somewhat more difficult to design reliable longitudinal studies measuring the long-term effects of witnessing violence. What evidence there is suggests that, based on retrospective analysis, there is at least some impact on future patterns of behavior—either as an enactor or, more paradoxically, as a victim of future violence. For example, battered women were found to be 6 times as likely to have been subjected to violence as a child than other women. Similarly, adult batterers have been found to originate largely in abusive homes (Kalmuss, 1984; Star, 1978). One national study graphically demonstrated how a tendency toward violence might be expressed against a variety of targets. Abused women were 150 times more likely to abuse their children, and sons who witnessed battering were 10 times as likely to become abusive to their domestic partners (Straus, Gelles, & Steinmetz, 1980).

There are problems with research examining the impact of witnessing or experiencing family violence on children and adolescents, however. Children and teens exposed to this violence are also at greater risk for exposure to other types of violence. Often, they reside in communities with high rates of community violence. Youth growing up in such neighborhoods are regularly exposed to the use of drugs, guns and other weapons, and random acts of violence. One report states that children in urban schools who have not received such exposure are the exception, not the norm (Osofsky, 1999).

Although research regarding the impact of childhood and adolescent exposure to violence is now emerging, findings still need further development. We still lack an understanding of what the link is between witnessing violence and subsequent victimization and offending. Many witnesses of early violence do not become either victims or offenders as adults. Others become offenders, and still others become victims. There are also children who become both victims and offenders. A better understanding of how these behaviors evolve is needed. We also need an increased understanding of how to successfully intervene with children and adolescents to decrease the likelihood of negative consequences. At this point in time, we simply know we need to intervene, but we lack an empirical understanding of how best to provide assistance.

The Impact of Stalking

There are significant difficulties in determining the rates of stalking. The percentage of stalking incidents reported to police is even lower than is the case when an actual assault or an assault involving an injury has occurred. As a result, recent survey research that is not dependent on police reports has revealed prevalence rates for stalking that are far higher than previously considered. The NVAWS reported that almost 5% of surveyed women and .6% of surveyed men reported being stalked by a current or former spouse, cohabitating partner, or date during their lifetime. In addition, .5% of the women and .2% of the men were stalked within the last 12 months. They extrapolated these figures to result in approximately 504,000 women and 185,000 men being stalked annually by intimate partners in the United States (Tjaden & Thoennes, 2000).

As mentioned earlier, stalking is part of the definition of domestic violence, either in the context of being part of an ongoing pattern of a variety of types of abuse, of becoming an alternative to earlier physical abuse, or as the only type of behavior the offender displays. In the case of its becoming an alternative form of abuse, the methods chosen continue at long range the control tactics that had been finely honed previously. Stalking has been concisely described as "psychological war" (Geberth, 1992), and it instills tremendous terror in victims. Tactics vary enormously. Some stalkers simply trail their victims continuously. Others destroy or vandalize property; send packages or deliveries (often of inappropriate or bizarre items); poison or kill pets; use phone threats; and contact employers, neighbors, and relatives, making normal life impossible.

Danger in stalking is an ever-present threat. In this context, the behavior of O. J. Simpson in stalking his ex-wife Nicole Brown Simpson is a typical pattern, even if the outcome was extreme. Although research in this field is in its infancy, we know that stalking by itself is a strong predictor of subsequent, often uncontrolled, violence against the victim, her (or his) family, bystanders, and even the offender. Mass murder and suicidal rage are not uncommon although difficult to predict. The public is familiar with headlines in which both celebrities and others have been stalked and sometimes killed. Others have been attacked and permanently injured or disfigured. In the context of the psychopathological stalker, this is explainable; he seeks to retain control. Such violence may be used as either a tactic (to keep control) or a spasmodic response to the realization that he has utterly "lost it," perhaps when the victim finally rebuffs him (or her) or becomes involved with another. The best evidence of this is the often-expressed stalker statement, "If I can't have her, no one else will."

In addition, stalking affects the mental health of victims. The NVAWS reported that one third of female stalking victims sought psychological counseling. More than a quarter of the victims reported losing time from their current employment because of stalking, and 7% gave up their job altogether (Tjaden & Thoennes, 1998).

IS STALKING THE PROTOTYPICAL OFFENSE IN DATING RELATIONSHIPS?

Although the rate of domestic violence in marital settings has basically reached a plateau for a number of years, domestic violence in the context of dating relationships appears to have escalated sharply since 1976 ("Studies Find," 1992). This may represent a real increase in the number of cases or simply be related to the growing unwillingness of women to tolerate physical aggression in dating. Also, by personal preference, many women now merely stay at an "open" relationship level, dating numerous people and refusing to accede to demands to "go steady." This type of dating relationship is highly threatening to many men ("Studies Find," 1992). Men with psychopathological control tendencies are faced with intolerable feelings of rejection. As such, even after being arrested for stalking or even assaulting or murdering a former lover, they perceive themselves as victims, not victimizers. The "crime of choice" for these offenders is stalking, because they simply are not live-in intimates.

Stalking on college campuses has also become a source of concern. Not surprisingly, research has suggested that college women may be at increased risk for victimization compared with the general population (Fisher, Cullen, & Turner, 2002; Schwartz , Schwartz & DeKeseredy, 1997). Fisher et al. (2002) conducted a national telephone survey of 4,446 women attending 2- and 4-year colleges and universities in 1997. They reported that 13.1% of women were stalked during a 7-month period, a figure considerably higher than the national average. Of those women, 12.7% experienced two incidents, and 2.3% experienced three or more incidents. Victims were threatened or an assault was attempted in 15.3% of the cases.

It has been suggested that routine activities theory may be relevant for explaining why college women might be at increased risk of being stalked; for example, the lifestyle of female college students is likely to put them in situations in which they are more likely to come in contact with potential stalkers (Mustaine & Tewksbury, 1999). Potential stalkers are more likely to be in regular contact with students because of living arrangements as well as regular contact in classes and social activities. This helps them familiarize themselves with the behavior patterns of a potential victim (Fisher et al., 2002).

When is stalking likely to escalate into violence? Empirical research on the causes and patterns of the escalation of stalking is now becoming available. One relatively early research project by Dietz et al. (1991) reported on the incidence of threatening and inappropriate letters to celebrities. The authors attempted to correlate features of such letters with subsequent physical encounters with the targets of the letters—a vast escalation and somewhat similar to the escalation to violence of a domestic violence stalker.

The pattern showed some surprising correlations that underscore the difficulty in predicting future behavior of stalkers. Specifically, whether the writer made explicit threats to the recipient was not at all correlated with the likelihood of subsequent violence.

The authors did find, however, that the number of letters written, the duration of such attention-seeking behavior, expressions of desire for face-to-face contact, and use of multiple avenues of conduct (telephone, mailboxes, fax) were highly predictive of a subsequent physical attack. Dietz and colleagues concisely summarized their findings from their and other studies as follows:

> We have disproved the myth that only threats count. Nearly everyone makes the mistake of assuming that unless there is a threat, you can safely ignore "nut mail," "kook calls," and weird visitors. This false assumption is the source of more misguided policy and decision-making than any other error in this field. (p. 208)

This finding may be of direct relevance to domestic violence stalking in that these factors are all present in the typical highly intensive stalking campaign launched by former physical abusers. As a result, the police, the courts, and probation officers should consider domestic violence stalkers as presenting a profile highly predictive of future assaults.

The real danger is, of course, that we simply lack sufficient knowledge regarding stalking and its relationship to future violence. Although the behavior may well lead to violence, it is difficult, if not impossible, to determine if or when violence will break out in any particular case. At that point, the knowledge is too late because stalkers appear to realize that they may have only "one shot" at their victim and act accordingly. Consequently, it is incumbent on police, courts, and social welfare agencies to treat all stalking incidents as representing a serious threat of injury or death.

We believe this chapter highlights the considerable operational difficulties in terms of defining and measuring the crime of domestic violence and the closely related crime of stalking. The unassailable fact remains, however, that these crimes collectively present a major challenge to society and warrant full, aggressive involvement of the criminal justice system.

NOTES

1. We do not include violence among same-sex partners in this book. Although such violence clearly exists and is significant, there are unique features—regarding victims, offenders, their interaction, and criminal justice interventions—that cannot be adequately addressed here. For those interested in the subject, we particularly suggest the research of Claire Renzetti (1999).

2. *Incidence* refers to the count of new incidents (usually expressed per 100,000 or some appropriate unit of the population). Incidence rates are most appropriate for one-time occurrences, but not for ongoing acts, which are often typical in domestic violence relationships. Therefore, it is difficult to collect data because it is unclear if a victim is a new case of violence (e.g., not counted by other sources such as victim services, social service agencies, or health systems). Furthermore, it is unknown whether the same person was reported as a victim of a previous domestic assault.

3. According to the Reiss and Roth (1993), for example, on average, 100 persons are victimized in every 80 aggravated assault events and in every 90 simple assault events.

4. Nonetheless, currently only 7% of the U.S. population resides in jurisdictions certified by the FBI as capable of reporting incident-based data. Many more departments are "NIBRS compliant," meaning that their internal reporting procedure follows NIBRS format but that data are not collected by the FBI and are available only on a jurisdictional basis.

5. The CTS appears to be an appropriate strategy for determining the frequency of physical and psychological violence in the general population. Although the instrument has been criticized for failing to measure all abusive behaviors, the amount of serious violence in the general population is relatively low. Its value would lie in its ability to monitor abusive acts, changes in the number of couples engaging in such acts, or changes in the severity of violence (Gordon, 2000).

CHAPTER 3

Risk Markers for
Offenders and Victims

As the preceding chapter discussed, estimates of both the incidence and prevalence of domestic violence vary widely. Although we explained the methodological reasons for these variations, we did not address the differences within populations that might differentially place them at risk for violence. Simply looking at an entire population of victims without understanding the diversity within that population may blur efforts to understand risk variation. Although many victims and offenders share characteristics and behaviors that are similar to those not exposed to violence in the general population, it is the context of the interaction among these characteristics and behaviors that is crucial to identifying people at risk.

This chapter highlights the research regarding risk markers for batterers and victims, but it is difficult—if not impossible—to establish conclusive causal relationships. Frankly, we may never identify definitive causes of domestic violence because there may be too many interacting factors that have a differential impact on the individuals involved. Furthermore, as discussed in Chapter 2, it should be recognized that a victim–offender dichotomy is not necessarily an accurate portrayal of an individual over

his or her life span nor of the nature of a given relationship. Nonetheless, there is now a body of research that can help us better understand characteristics, behaviors, and relationships that increase the probability of battering or victimization.

RISK MARKERS FOR BATTERERS

There is a rich body of both empirical and theoretical literature that has examined why some men batter or stalk their victims. This may loosely be divided into research that emphasizes the psychological characteristics and life experiences associated with known batterers, the family structures and interactions that appear to promote battering, and feminist approaches to what these researchers see as social structures and norms that endorse (or, at a minimum, tacitly tolerate) violence against women. Because we are focused on batterers and victims in the context of their reaction to aggressive criminal justice intervention, a detailed study of all approaches would be beyond the scope of this book. Our primary focus instead is the interaction of the criminal justice system with offenders and victims, as well as the system's potential ability to modify offenders' physical aggression.

We must understand that if the criminal justice system simply had a single goal—punishing offenders—an understanding of why men batter would be immaterial; however, as we have noted, its goals are far more complex, encompassing not just punishment, but crime suppression through deterrence, rehabilitation, and victim empowerment. Critically important to many of these goals is determining the reasons a particular person becomes abusive and how the criminal justice system's actions might interact with these reasons. Certainly, the criminal justice system's goal of rehabilitating or at least deterring batterers depends on an understanding of what makes someone batter. Without this, reforms may easily miss the mark, and serious unintended consequences may ensue.

Similarly, the ability to identify key markers in an offender's prior history, such as past criminal record or when an individual's criminal activity was first reported, may prove useful for administrators in determining on which offenders to concentrate their limited resources. Although the list of factors associated with the impulse to abuse is admittedly complex, we briefly highlight the most salient factors.

Psychological Perspectives

The oldest and still most widely adopted perspective is psychologically based (Gelles & Loseke, 1993), which focuses on personality disorders and early experiences that increase the risk of violent behavior. As a result, research on the effects of legal sanctions for batterers has usually been based on psychological typologies or profiling (Andrews & Brewin, 1990; Holtzworth-Munroe & Stuart, 1994). This is a popular perspective both for its commonsense explanatory power and because our society generally believes an

individual can, or at least should, be able to control his or her conduct.

Psychologists understandably have long studied factors that predispose a particular individual to batter. Unfortunately, it is typically true that a single predisposing personality attribute cannot explain psychological dimensions of battering. Instead, a complex constellation of factors is thought to predispose someone to batter. This is important because the genesis of a particular problem affects the likelihood that it might be easily remedied by societal intervention, including sanctions directly imposed by the criminal justice system as well as prospects for rehabilitation through court-ordered counseling.

Strong relationships between domestic violence and a wide variety of mental illness and personality disorders have been reported. Although the claim has been disputed, some studies have suggested that a majority of the male batterers have deeply rooted mental and personality disorders (Hamberger & Hastings, 1989). Hence, difficult-to-treat domestic violence has been correlated with a number of conditions, including depression, schizophrenia, and severe personality disorders (Steinmetz, 1980) as well as other cognitive or profound behavioral abnormalities (Coates, Leong, & Lindsey, 1987; Dutton, 1998; Hamberger & Hastings, 1986, 1993; Hotaling & Sugarman, 1986; Maiuro, Cahn, & Vitaliano, 1986; Margolin, John, & Gleberman, 1988; Rosenbaum & O'Leary, 1981). Of particular significance are the findings of the Dunedin Multidisciplinary Health and Development Study (Mofitt & Caspi, 1999). Researchers investigated a representative birth cohort starting as infants over a 21-year period with periodic reassessments. Eighty-eight percent of male perpetrators of severe physical abuse met the criteria for disorders listed by the American Psychiatric Association (1987; DSM-III-R). Male offenders were 13 times more likely than nonoffenders to be mentally ill. Illnesses included depression, anxiety disorders, substance abuse, antisocial personality disorder, and schizophrenia.

Although this study did report a significant correlation between mental illness and abuse, at least one other study of the psychological characteristics of batterers has failed to disclose truly singular profiles of men who batter (Koss et al., 1994). For this reason, a generalized list of personality traits that are widely displayed by batterers may fail to provide the specific insight we need. Instead, it may be more helpful to focus on the actual behavioral correlates that tend to coincide with domestic violence. What specific areas of mental conditions have we observed to date?

Low Self-Esteem

One of the most frequently observed characteristics of batterers is a pattern of low self-esteem, which is often compounded by a perceived or real power imbalance in relationships (Barnett, Lee, & Thelen, 1997; Green, 1984; Hamberger, Lohr, Bunge & Tolin, 1997).

The negative impact of low self-esteem may actually intensify as growing numbers of women and minorities have entered the work force and assumed management and professional positions. Men with low self-esteem may feel threatened with a relative loss of position compared with women who historically could not aspire to equality in the work force, let alone to management authority. Such a "power loss" by men with initially low levels of self-esteem and little self-control may invite physical retaliation against any target of opportunity in an effort to maintain the appearance of control, especially if the abuser is unable, as a viable alternative, to express himself verbally. The easiest targets of opportunity are typically intimates or children because public displays of violence

or violence in the workplace are far more likely to be sanctioned immediately.

Some research indirectly confirms this theory; domestic violence has been reported to increase when measurable attributes of "power" between the couple are more evenly balanced (D. H. Coleman & Straus, 1986; Kahn, 1984; Yllö, 1984) or when the man feels psychologically threatened by his spouse's career or income success. Not surprisingly, subjectively feeling "powerless" in a relationship may serve as a precursor to violence (Goodman et al., 1993). Similarly, loss of self-esteem may be a key intermediate step in some batterers' decision to retaliate against a victim, either directly by physical attack or passive-aggressively through stalking, after a woman has left the abuser or has used criminal justice intervention to restrain actual physical abuse.

Anger Control Issues

Perhaps the greatest single marker for the potential of abuse is the presence of generalized anger and hostility. Although studies on batterers are not always conclusive (see Sellers, 1999), it appears that generalized feelings of anger or lack of self control (or both) do constitute common precursors to subsequent violence (Barnett, Fagan, & Booker, 1991; Maiuro, Cahn, Vitaliano, Wagner, & Zegree, 1988; Prince & Arias, 1994). This can also be true for offenders who express anger and violence toward children (Saunders, 1995; Straus, 1983). Naturally, if the anger is specifically triggered by the victim's real or perceived acts of rejection (Dutton & Strachan, 1987), abandonment (Holtzworth-Munroe & Hutchison, 1993), or jealousy (Pagelow, 1981), the likelihood that the man will target his intimate partner greatly increases.

Moffit, Robins, and Caspi (2001) aggregated several personality traits that we might define as "anger" or "hostility" into a more generalized construct that they defined as "negative emotionality." This includes negative reactions to stress, how a person experiences emotions, a person's expectations of other people's attitudes and behaviors, and his or her attitudes toward the use of aggression to achieve certain ends. They confirm earlier research that these attributes are more prevalent among batterers (Dutton, 1998; Fincham & Beach, 1999). Individuals who scored high on negative emotionality

> described themselves as nervous, vulnerable, prone to worry, emotionally volatile, and unable to cope with stress; . . . [having a] low threshold for feeling tense, fearful, hostile, and angry; they feel callous and suspicious, expect mistreatment, and see the world as being peopled with potential enemies; they admit they seek revenge for slights, could enjoy frightening others, and would remorselessly take advantage of others. (Moffit et al., 1991, p. 7)

In this context, violence against an intimate partner may be a substitute for the individual's ability to work through anger control issues without resorting to violence.

The interaction between anger control issues and the overall process of male socialization during and after puberty may explain much of the tendency for male violence. In many subcultures within the United States, the ability to identify and creatively express anger in a constructive manner is not generally stressed among male teenagers, or, for that matter, is it even highly valued in boys during their formative years (Dutton, 1998; Hamby, Poindexter, & Gray-Little, 1996; O'Neil & Nadeau, 1999).

In contrast, women traditionally have been socialized to value communication and "sharing" and to work through conflicts. Although the point can be overgeneralized, especially in light of recent research showing that female-on-male violence is far from uncommon, gender role socialization may make women as a group more comfortable with handling loss of control and anger without physical violence. Therefore, they may be more skilled at using and expressing emotions and feelings to shape and indirectly control interpersonal relations. They also may be more adept at the use of verbal and even psychological aggression as an alternative to physical aggression during partner conflicts. In this context, many batterers have stated that they fear the woman's "feminine" capabilities of "twisting words" and manipulation. Susceptible men may inappropriately express this fear through violence (O'Donovan, 1988; O'Neil, 1981).

Conflict Resolution Capabilities

Obviously, most adults frequently confront circumstances that evoke anger without resorting to physical acts of aggression. Why do some individuals become violent, whereas others resolve conflicts through alternative strategies? One possibility is that batterers have poor conflict resolution strategies (Hastings & Hamberger, 1988; Holtzworth-Munroe & Anglin, 1991). In fact, there is a growing body of evidence that batterers generally are less capable or adept at argumentative self-expression (Dutton, 1987; Hotaling & Sugarman, 1986), or tend to grossly misperceive a partner's efforts at communication as constituting an outright verbal attack (Barnett et al., 1997; Holtzworth-Munroe & Hutchison, 1993; Langhinrichsen-Rohling et al., 1994).

The interaction of poor conflict resolution capabilities, fear, frustration, and an inability to control or even readily express feelings may increase the propensity of physical aggressions toward a "threatening" intimate in times of stress or anger. From this perspective, the act of violence for some batterers may relieve otherwise unacceptable stress and forestall emasculation of self-image. Of course, the paradox is that the manifestations of such insecurity are violent acts that from an outside perspective often appear as "controlling" tendencies.

A partial, but nevertheless intriguing, confirmation has been reported in one study in which certain batterers unexpectedly demonstrated a *decrease* in heart rates during extremely belligerent verbal behaviors such as yelling, threatening, and demeaning their partners. This finding indicates that expressions of verbal attack served to provide a calming effect for these individuals. As expected, this contrasts with "normal" individuals who, in the midst of similar behavior, typically experience increased heart rates, evidencing a strong emotional reaction. It even differed from a third, far more dangerous group that was diagnosed as having "antisocial personality disorders," for whom virtually no heart rate variation was seen after they expressed "verbal violence" (Hare, 1993). This provides tantalizing, albeit indirect, evidence that violence and aggression relieves or resolves anger control issues on a physical as well as psychological level for many batterers.

"Immature" Personality

Batterers often display classic aspects of immature personalities. This includes a well-developed propensity to shift blame or to minimize the impact for their criminal actions. Many assailants immaturely externalize blame for violence to the victim with comments such as "She provoked me," thereby rationalizing otherwise inexcusable conduct (Dobash & Dobash, 1979; O'Leary, 1993; Star, 1978). Blame shifting is common with many assailants, who cite assorted victim provocations such as "I told her I wanted a hot meal," "She knew she was not supposed to mouth off to me," "She was casting eyes

on another man" (see Byrne, Arias, & Lyons, 1993; Dutton, 1986).

When the offender cannot sufficiently blame the victim, he may provoke a "minor provocation," which in reality may involve considerable violence; however, he will often minimize the impact of his violence. There is considerable empirical evidence that victims and offenders do not agree on the frequency and severity of violent tactics that male partners use, and this discrepancy is a result of the offender profoundly underestimating the frequency of his violent conduct (Edelson & Brygger, 1986; Sonkin, Martin, & Walker, 1985; Szinovacz, 1983; Wetzel & Ross, 1983). Polling results from one study published in 1997 show a tendency for abusers to understate the extent of abuse (Klein, Campbell, Soler, & Ghez, 1997). Perhaps this may be best understood as a maladaptive effort to reduce the cognitive dissonance of perceiving himself or herself as a victim although, in reality, acting as the aggressor.

Why are these personality traits important? Their existence may indicate that individualized psychological counseling may be needed to accommodate the criminal justice system's goal of rehabilitation. At the present time, such efforts appear far beyond the capabilities and goals of even the most aggressive general batterer treatment programs. Typically, batterer treatment relies on group treatment with generic program content. These types of programs may not be successful for offenders with specific psychological problems who display patterns of generalized violence rather than intimate-only violence.

Childhood Experiences With Parental Aggression

Becoming a batterer perhaps may be best predicted by past familial experiences with violence. One theory is that childhood acceptance of aggression as "normal" within a family interacts with an individual's personality traits (such as impulsive and immature behavior, self-esteem issues, a tendency to take offense easily, and anger control issues) to increase a tendency toward battering (Hotaling & Sugarman, 1986; Riggs & O'Leary, 1989, 1992; Straus, 1980). Not surprisingly, Straus observed that batterers appear to have developed a long-time association between "love" and violence, perhaps caused by physical punishment from caregivers or others in the family starting in infancy (Straus, 1980). In addition, parental violence appears to be closely related to repetitive spousal aggression (Simons, Wu, & Conger, 1995). Specific exposure to childhood violence has consistently been found to be associated with becoming a batterer (Bennett, Tolman, Rogalski, & Srinivasaraghavan, 1994; Howell & Pugliesi, 1988; Roberts, 1987; Rouse, 1984). A number of studies have reported a powerful association between childhood observations of violence, particularly parental violence, and the potential to batter. Some even maintain that witnessing violence better predicts future violence than direct victimization (c.f. Barnett et al., 1991; Hotaling & Sugarman, 1986; Caesar et al., 1989; Seltzer et al., 1988; Widom, 1989, 1992; Widom & Maxfield, 2001).

Nonetheless, although there are clearly adverse effects to witnessing violence, the relationship is not clearly established. It is certainly the case that many children witness violence in the family. Of those children, only a minority actually become abusers themselves. Others in the same situation seek and achieve nonviolent relationships throughout their lives. Recent research has suggested numerous methodological reasons that conclusions cannot be easily made from available data. First, what constitutes exposure, both in terms of frequency and severity? It appears likely that a one-time exposure to one parent slapping another might differ

from witnessing regular severe beatings in terms of long-term consequences.

Second, how are these events affected by specific characteristics of the child such as his or her age, personality, and other risk factors in their life including poverty, parental substance abuse, and exposure to violence in other settings (Corvo, 1992; Fantuzzo & Mohr, 1999). These interactions are frequent and likely to be complex. For example, children exposed to parental violence are also far more likely to be physically abused and neglected, with estimates as high as 15 times the national average (Osofsky, 1999). They are also more likely to be at greater risk for exposure to sibling violence, violence in the schools, and street violence (Osofsky, 1999). To date, research cannot definitively identify the role of these and other factors in subsequent violence.

Other aspects of maladaptive family structure have also been implicated, including separation and loss events (Corvo, 1992), aggressive parental "shaming" and guilt inducement (Dutton, 1998), and socialization into accepting male entitlement to power and the use of physical dominance to achieve control (DeKeseredy et al., 1997). As discussed in Chapter 2, not all children exposed to violence become batterers (or victims). Research suggests that a child's individual characteristics determine his or her resiliency and include traits such as intellectual development and interpersonal skills. These protective factors are further linked to availability of outside support systems (Osofsky, 1999).

Family history issues, regardless of type, appear to create deep-seated behavioral patterns in many batterers. These are not likely to be amenable to the "quick fix" implicitly proffered by the criminal justice system. In reality, determining the existence and extent of the role of these risk markers may facilitate and assist in a more effective, individualistic response to a batterer. To the extent that the formulation of sentencing dispositions consider familial pathology, if there were sufficient resources, courts could provide for individualized psychological interventions rather than (or as an adjunct to) a more generic, behaviorally based offender treatment program.

Substance Abuse

Substance abuse has long been known to lower inhibitions to committing violence. Most researchers have reported that high numbers of domestic violence offenders use illegal drugs or consume excessive quantities of alcohol, at rates far beyond the general population (D. H. Coleman & Straus, 1986; Kantor & Straus, 1987; Scott, Schafer, & Greenfield, 1999; Tolman & Bennett, 1990). In fact, Kantor and Straus (1987) reported that alcohol and drug abuse were among the most important variables that predicted female intimate violence. In several studies that statistically controlled for a number of sociodemographic variables and for hostility and marital satisfaction, the relationship of alcohol to violence remained highly significant (H. Johnson, 2000; Kaufman Kantor & Straus, 1990; Leonard, 1993; Tolman & Bennett, 1990).

It has been suggested that individuals who have a pattern of consuming excessive amounts of alcohol at one time but not on a consistent basis ("binge drinking") are far more likely to engage in domestic violence than individuals who engage in other patterns of sustained alcohol consumption (heavy drinkers). Specifically, Kaufman Kantor and Straus (1990) reported that domestic violence rates for "high moderate" drinkers were twice as high and the rates for binge drinkers were 3 times as high compared with nondrinkers. The National Family Violence Survey and National Violence Against Women Survey estimate that binge drinkers are 3 to 5 times more likely to be violent against a female partner than those who do not drink.

Moreover, the time of the use of the alcohol and drugs appears closely related to the assault. One in-depth study of the correlates of domestic violence in the city of Memphis reported an overwhelming concurrency of substance abuse and domestic violence. This research reported that almost all offenders had used drugs or alcohol the day of the assault; two-thirds had used

> a dangerous combination of cocaine and alcohol . . . the vast majority of those assaulted were repeat victims of the current assailants. . . . victims and family members reported that 92% of assailants used drugs or alcohol during the day of the assault. They also reported that 67% had used a combination of cocaine and alcohol, which forms cocaethylene, a substance that produces heightened and prolonged intoxication. Nearly half of all assailants (45%) were described by families as using drugs, alcohol, or both daily to the point of intoxication for the past month. (Brookoff, 1997, p. 1)

Another study found that 70% of the abusers at the time of attack were under the influence of drugs, alcohol, or both, with 32% using only drugs, 17% only alcohol, and 22% using both (Roberts, 1988). Willson et al. (2000) cited a number of more recent studies reporting even higher correlations between drug and alcohol abuse on the day of assault. At this time, the reason for the correlation in time between alcohol and substance abuse and battering is not totally clear. It is possible that batterers' inhibitions are reduced, although this has not received strong or consistent support in the research (S. L. Miller & Wellford, 1997; Wallace, 1996).

The use of alcohol and drugs appears to be even more common among those committing more serious acts of violence. For example, one study found that more than half of prison inmates convicted of violent crimes against intimates were drinking or using drugs at the time of the offense; the same study found that about 40% of intimate partner homicide offenders reportedly were drinking at the time of the incident (Greenfeld et al., 1998; Willson et al., 2000).

Meanwhile, other studies have maintained that the evidence to date does not provide adequate empirical support that alcohol and drug use are causally related to domestic violence (H. Johnson, 2000; Mears et al., 2001; S. L. Miller & Wellford, 1997; Schwartz & DeKeseredy, 1997). In fact, one recent study in Canada reported that if all attitudinal and behavioral measures that might otherwise predict violence against women were controlled, the simple correlation with alcohol abuse would largely disappear (H. Johnson, 2001).

In support of this position, Stith and Farley (1993) suggested that the relationship between alcohol and domestic abuse is indirect and a function of attitudes supporting the use of violence. Kaufman Kantor and Straus (1990) reported that rates of domestic abuse by men who intellectually support the idea of hitting a partner but who rarely consumed alcohol had higher rates of actual violence than men who were heavy drinkers but did not approve of violence toward a partner. The highest rates of violence, however, were among men with attitudes supportive of violence against women who were also heavy drinkers. This indicates that at least the attitudes toward violence strongly mediated any effect that the consumption of alcohol might have on committing violent acts. Perhaps alcohol simply acts to reduce inhibitions in people who are already attitudinally prone to violence but who in a sober state are able to control such behaviors.

Some evidence supports this belief. A recent study by Holly Johnson (2000) attempts to examine the role of alcohol abuse relative to male attitudes supporting domestic abuse and other sociodemographic variables. She reported that half of assaulted women said the man had been or usually was drinking at the time of assault. Furthermore, 29% of these women believed alcohol was the precipitating factor. Johnson's research did not however find that alcohol and violence were causally related. In fact, when controlling for attitudes toward the acceptability of male dominance and violence toward women, alcohol abuse was not significantly related to violence. Nonetheless, at present most research has reported that there is a fairly tight correlation between alcohol abuse and the perpetration of domestic abuse.

It is possible that the two phenomena, that is, substance abuse and partner abuse, may spring from a personality disorder or physiological factor, such as a chemical imbalance in the pleasure centers of the brain that have a tendency to lead to enhanced misuse of alcohol or illegal substances *and* the inability to control violent tendencies or elevated testosterone levels in males (Scott et al., 1999). Hence, although Holly Johnson (2000) and others have not reported a causal relationship, the fact remains that the two phenomena are closely related.

For this reason, the best we can say at present is that substance abuse is highly correlated with intimate partner violence among batterers. In addition, it is closely associated with higher rates of recurrent battering. In any event, the impact on treatment may be that offenders with substance abuse problems need concomitant help with longstanding issues of substance abuse, as well as behavior modification therapy to address abusive tendencies. Similarly, victim's who have substance abuse problems may need to address them to help protect against future revictimization. Unfortunately, we find that many court-ordered batterer treatment programs do not provide such a sustained, two-pronged treatment approach or even disqualify substance abuse offenders from treatment. Similarly, victims of violence may need substance abuse assistance to successfully avoid being revictimized.

The pernicious effects of substance abuse and other patterns supporting abuse are not totally equal throughout the population. For a variety of reasons, African American, Latino, and Native American populations have been found to be at increased risk for heavy drinking. This dramatically increases the likelihood of their experiencing domestic violence (Bachman, 1992; Hampton, 1987; Kaufman Kantor, 1996; West, 1998). The same holds true for victims from minority populations. Binge drinking by either the offender or the victim virtually always places victims at increased risk. For example, one study reported that Latinas with partners who were binge drinkers were 10 times more likely to be assaulted than those with low to moderate drinking partners (Kaufman Kantor & Straus, 1990).

Biology and Abuse

Biologically based theories of domestic violence have long been asserted. As discussed in Chapter 2, it has been empirically established that although both genders commit acts of domestic violence, men commit far more serious violence than do women. As described in detail in Chapter 4, much of the reason for this is culturally and historically based; however, it also appears that higher natural levels of testosterone contribute to a general latent predisposition to male aggression and violence. Although men as a group naturally have higher levels of testosterone, it has been shown that even among men, higher levels of testosterone are associated with higher rates of violent crimes.

Differential results based on testosterone levels can be striking. For example, in one study relating types of crimes committed by male juvenile offenders with tested testosterone levels, more than 80% of the offenders with high testosterone levels committed violent crimes, whereas more than 90% of juvenile offenders with lower testosterone committed nonviolent crimes (Dabbs, Frady, Carr, & Beach, 1987; Dabbs, Jurkovic, & Frady, 1991). Similar disparities in testosterone levels and rates of violence were also found among women (Dabbs, Ruback, Frady, & Hopper, 1988), and another study found that testosterone levels were higher among violent sex offenders than others (Bradford & Bourget, 1986).

The testosterone link is perhaps the most researched and proven biological link to violent behavior; however, other associations, although not expressly linked to testosterone levels, appear genetically based. For example, a series of studies of adopted male children whose biological fathers were convicted of crimes found these children to be far more likely to commit crimes themselves than in cases where their adoptive parents had been convicted (Mednick, Gabrielli, & Hutchison, 1987). Although the strength of the genetic component has not yet been explained and has been debated, both theoretical (Wilson & Hernstein, 1985) and analytic studies (Walters, 1992) conclude that such a relationship exists. It is unclear at present whether this relationship is due to similar levels of testosterone among biological fathers and their offspring or whether there are other more subtle factors at play.

In a somewhat more speculative vein, even physical trauma to the head, ranging from trauma at birth to childhood and adolescent head injuries (Rosenbaum & Hoge, 1989; Warnken, Rosenbaum, Fletcher, Hoge, & Adelman, 1994) appear to be related to a subsequent history of violence. These results are also difficult to interpret. Although the data suggest a possible theoretical model relating head injury to low impulse control or attention-deficit disorder, which in turn mediates subsequent impulsive violence, such prior head injuries and, even to a lesser extent, birth trauma may be spurious in nature and simply related to familial child abuse, parental substance abuse, or numerous other factors originating in the family environment risk markers already known to be reliable predictors of subsequent levels of violence in offspring.

Sociodemographic Predictors of Violence and Underserved Populations

Poverty as a Predictor of Violence

Many activists and organizations concerned with developing overall domestic violence control policies have noted that domestic violence crosses all boundaries of economic class, ethnicity, and race (Bassett, 1980; Coates & Leong, 1980; Ferraro, 1989a; Hart, 1988; U.S. Attorney General's Task Force on Family Violence, 1984). In reality, literature inferring that batterers are drawn from all socioeconomic classes and ethnic groups has all too often been based on ideological beliefs and the desire to push universal policy changes rather than on empirical research rigorously examining known demographics correlates to criminal history.

Such literature may to some extent rely on unrepresentative samples of middle- and upper-middle-class suburban White women. Many of these women have become spokespersons for battered women or were the focus of the press, perhaps because the media finds their plight more newsworthy than that of more representative, abused women (i.e., those who are poor, minority, and disempowered).

In contrast, most empirically based survey research consistently reports that although domestic violence is present in all social strata and ethnic groups, it is disproportionately concentrated in population subgroups that are stressed by poverty (Kaufman Kantor & Jasinski, 1997; Moore, 1997; Straus & Smith, 1990; Yllö & Straus, 1990).

Certainly it is true that women with less income appear to have higher rates of victimization. For example, National Crime Victimization Survey data reported that women in households with annual incomes of less than $7,500 reported a rate of nonlethal violence committed against them at a rate 10 times higher than those with an income of $75,000 or more. Women who have experienced domestic violence are prominent among Aid to Families With Dependent Children (AFDC) caseloads. For example, a Massachusetts study of 40 welfare offices found that 64.9% had experienced physical abuse by a male adult intimate, and New Jersey found 57.3% of an AFDC Job Readiness program sample reported having experienced physical abuse by an intimate male partner as adults. These women are also more likely than others to have a variety of physical and mental health problems, to have partners who oppose or interfere with school or employment, and to have more frequent periods of unemployment and welfare receipts (Lyon, 1997, for the National Resource Center on Domestic Violence).

There are many groups of women who have not routinely had special needs recognized nor been given the opportunity to receive culturally appropriate interventions and services. Certainly, one of the goals of the Violence Against Women Act (VAWA) was to create and improve both the availability of such services as well as their quality (Burt, Newmark, Jacobs, & Harrell, 1998). Because the United States has rapidly been increasing in ethnic diversity in recent years, we believe a discussion of *additional* risk markers would be incomplete without addressing these factors and special challenges facing these groups as victims of domestic violence. Unfortunately, research is still in its early stages and is often preliminary in nature.

Ethnicity and Domestic Violence

Coker (2000) discussed how research has tended to overly simplify the diverse experience of women in the country. She observed that studies purporting to examine "women of color" have relied primarily on African American women and that research on White women in many studies becomes the surrogate for all women. Even when such studies try to expand their scope, the results are sometimes difficult to interpret. For example, Coker noted that in perhaps the largest study examining domestic violence rates among Latino women, the study only included women who spoke English (Coker, 2000). The following sections attempt to highlight what we know about some of the additional risk markers that each of these groups faces.

Black Americans. Certain minority groups, including African Americans, appear to be at increased risk for abuse. One study reported that each year between 1992 and 1996, an average of about 12 per 1,000 Black women experienced violence by an intimate, compared with fewer than 8 per 1,000 White women (Greenfeld et al., 1998). Rennison and Welchans (2000), who like Greenfeld and colleagues used Bureau of Justice Statistics data, reported that African Americans "were victimized by intimate partners at significantly higher rates than persons of any other race between 1993 and 1998" (p. 4). To some extent, the higher observed rates of domestic violence between some ethnic and racial minority groups are, of course, attributable to poverty. The impact of poverty as well as other associated variables becomes clear by the finding that these differences diminish (but are not totally absent) when other sociodemographic and relationship variables are controlled (Tjaden & Thoennes, 2000).

The impact of race and ethnicity on domestic violence is not simple reductionism of rates of substance abuse. In fact, substance abuse may simply be a component of the differences in domestic abuse rates among different ethnic and racial groups. Bent-Goodley (2001) pointed out that research reports a greater likelihood of sustained serious and lethal injuries as a resolute of domestic violence among African Americans. As such, they are victimized by violent partners at rates significantly higher than any other group (Bent-Goodley, 2001; Rennison & Welchans, 2000).

Despite national surveys that consistently report rates of Black domestic violence as double that of Whites (Straus & Gelles, 1986), it would be overly simplistic to state that this is due to some inherent features of the African American family. Instead, it appears that both environmental stress and family pathologies—including poverty, social dislocation, unemployment, and population density—all have a role (Bent-Goodley, 2001).

One can argue that domestic violence in the Black community is simply maladaptive behavior to societal oppression, racism, and discrimination (Oliver, 1999; Williams, 1999). This argument appears to have credibility, given that rates of domestic violence in West African communities are apparently not high (Bent-Goodley, 2001). Instead, it is the experience of powerlessness, anger, and distrust of a dominant community that may have increased the potential for abuse between intimates (Bent-Goodley, 2001; Franklin, 2000).

In fact, Franklin (2000) posed the intriguing hypothesis that American society has allowed Black men to become the "head" of the household and given him authority over Black women in exchange for their avoiding confrontations with the White power structure. A rationale for why domestic violence might have increased in the African American community during the 1960s and 1970s may be that minority women began to economically and politically challenge this position of African American men in the community (West, 1999). The development of a strong Black political culture in the 1980s and 1990s meant that minority women—even those who knew of extensive domestic violence problems in their community—might otherwise be silent to support their community as a whole and challenge the stereotypes of Black men in society (Bent-Goodley, 2001).

The purpose of this discussion is not to suggest that increasing rates of domestic violence in any racial or ethnic group is inevitable, but rather that it may be a risk marker, increasing its likelihood compared with the population as a whole.

The impact of income inequality and social structure may also create more domestic violence among Blacks. As noted earlier, men's unemployment or part-time employment has been associated with increased rates of domestic violence, particularly severe violence (Gelles & Straus, 1979; Jasinski, 1996). For example, Holly Johnson's (2000) recent study found that unemployment was a significant predictor of violence. She suggested that some men might perceive employment as a critical component of their masculine identity and resort to violence as an effort to regain lost status.

Similarly, relationships in which the partners are cohabitants rather than married are at increased risk for both domestic violence and domestic homicides (Makepeace, 1997; Stets, 1991; Yllö & Straus, 1981). This may disproportionately affect specific population groups like African Americans; there has been an increase in overall rates of cohabitation among all couples, but this increase is greater among African Americans (Bent-Goodley, 2001). It has been suggested that partners in cohabiting relationships have greater ambivalence toward commitment and perceive less stability in the relationship, increasing the likelihood of violence in cases of conflict (Makepeace, 1997). An additional possibility is that these couples experience greater social isolation (Bent-Goodley, 2001).

In addition, urban poverty differentially affects African American women, who are more likely than White women to live in neighborhoods with high rates of poverty overall (Coker, 2000). Research in New York City suggested that 70% of poor Blacks, compared with only 30% of poor Whites, living in New York City resided in predominantly poverty stricken neighborhoods (Sampson & Wilson, 1995). This is likely to have a disproportionate impact on the availability of services for Black victims of domestic violence (Coker, 2000).

It is also interesting, however, that some studies report that middle-class African American women are more likely to experience domestic violence than White middle-class women (Hampton, Carrillo, & Kim, 1998). Clearly, the higher observed rates of domestic violence among some ethnic and racial minority groups are attributable in part to poverty. The impact of poverty, as well as other associated variables, becomes evident from the finding that these differences diminish (but are not totally absent) when other sociodemographic and relationship variables are controlled (Tjaden & Thoennes, 2000).

This may be a result of social class transitions from lower socioeconomic classes to middle class; it has been suggested that former lifestyle behaviors or traditional cultural values encouraging maintenance of relationships are continued (Bell & Mattis, 2000; Bent-Goodley, 2001).

It may be that employment may still be a factor in middle-class Black households.

Some research has suggested that the discrepancy between employment and income places a woman at risk. When women earn more than men or have a higher employment status, many men feel psychologically threatened, and some use violence to reassert power in their relationship (Yllö & Straus, 1990). This may also partially account for the higher rates of domestic violence among middle-class African American women, who may more often partner with men with lower status, or at least lower paid jobs, than their female partners.

Immigrant Populations. There are many cultural differences and ideologies that can place women at greater risk of intimate partner violence. In Asian and Middle Eastern immigrant communities, role expectations for women are often far more rigid, and the right of men to physically "discipline" their wives is often culturally acceptable (Raj & Silverman, 2002). Research has suggested that these women are often more easily acculturated than their male partners and more willing (if not eager) to adopt American expectations for their behavior (Bui & Morash, 1999; Kulwicki & Miller, 1999; Raj & Silverman, 2002). The result of this conflict in role expectations increases the woman's risk of violence because their partners attempt to maintain the type of control their culture has allowed them. This has been supported by research finding that intimate partner violence is more likely in relationships in which the partner holds culturally traditional role expectations for women (Bui & Morash, 1999; Morash, Bui, & Santiago, 2000).

In addition, many immigrant victims of domestic violence are more likely to be socially isolated. They often do not have the traditional family supports available or may actually be isolated from contact by the offender (Abraham, 2000; Raj & Silverman, 2002). As such these victims may be less likely

to receive emotional support because of cultural expectations (Raj & Silverman, 2002). They are also often deterred by their lack of familiarity with the legal system and fear that they will be deported, especially if they report their abuse. Some abusers even take advantage of this situation; it has been reported that many batterers deliberately fail to file the necessary immigration papers to legalize the victim's status (Teran, 1999). Research on Latina victims of domestic violence also reports the high levels of fear by undocumented women. These victims are often afraid that police involvement will lead to their deportation and to possible separation from children (Coker, 2000).

Native Americans. Given the long and ignominious history of White–Native American relations, it is not surprising that social problems that are closely associated with widespread social disorganization emerged shortly after tribal relocation. It is almost redundant to comment on the miserable conditions in which Native Americans live on many reservations. The numbers and statistics pertaining to poverty levels, unemployment, and infant mortality—to name but a few of the social problems Native Americans on reservations face—clearly demonstrate the dire circumstances under which ancient cultures fight to survive. This is compounded by relatively high rates of substance abuse, a factor discussed earlier in this chapter. For these reasons, it is not surprising that American Indian and Alaska Native women report far higher rates of intimate partner violence than women of other racial background (Tjaden & Thoennes, 2000).

Cultural Ideologies

Cultural ideologies often define the appropriate treatment of women by male intimates. Although a true definition of culture is ambiguous, referring to a group's social doctrines varying by gender, class, religion, race, ethnicity, and other variables, we do know that there are often clashes with expected behavior according to our legal system. As is generally known, many of these ideologies marginalize, if not totally eliminate, women's power in a relationship that places them at increased risk for victimization (Raj & Silverman, 2002). Often, the use of physical force to control or discipline women is acceptable or encouraged (Kulwicki & Miller, 1999; Raj & Silverman, 2002).

Schwartz and DeKeseredy (1997) examined the significance of a male peer-support model as a factor that may coexist in the context of traditionally male-dominated environments (e.g., bars, athletic events) with cultural norms supportive of male control of women. This model suggests that the link between alcohol and violence is a result of perceptions of masculinity linking drinking and violence with a masculine or "macho" self-image (Schwartz & DeKeredy, 1997).

Similarly, Bowker (1983) suggested that male peers justify violence against partners and accept, if not outwardly approve of, such conduct. He found that the frequency of contact and interaction with male peers was related to both the frequency and seriousness of domestic assault.

Domestic Violence and the Commission of Violence in General

A link between violence in general and spousal abuse is not unexpected. With minor exception, the previously explored literature on the etiology of a batterer could be an accurate profile of all those who perpetrate violent crimes.

The development of an antisocial personality may be the key linkage between batterers and the somewhat overlapping group of the generally violent. Research on batterer behavior has increasingly used research and insights from those offenders who are generally violent (Barnett & Hamberger, 1992; Dunford et al., 1990; Fagan & Browne, 1994; Fagan et al., 1983; also see discussion by Barnett, Miller-Perrin, & Perrin, 1997). For example, it is known that many if not most family batterers also assault in other settings. In support of this, Hotaling and Straus (with Lincoln, 1989) noted that batterers typically did not limit the use of violence to family members. They reported that men who assaulted children or spouses were 5 times more likely than other men to have been generally violent and to have assaulted nonfamily members.

Although batterers as a population have been extensively studied, subvariations in assaults are less well known; however, implicit assumptions of a monolithic class of "batterers" who respond predictably to the same type of intervention have been increasingly challenged (Edleson, 1996; Gondolf, 1999; Holtzworth-Munroe & Stuart, 1994; Saunders, 1993). Most of this research uses typologies based on measurable psychological and social attributes (Edleson, 1996). This suggests that effective interventions may need to vary based on defined offender risk factors.

Research has demonstrated that some batterers have a generalized history of violence. This occurs when violence is not perpetrated on just one victim or even on a single class of victims. The National Family Violence Survey studied a large sample (2,291 cases), identifying 311 (15%) that had been violent during the preceding 12 months. Of those, 208 (67%) were only violent toward their wives, whereas 71 (23%) were violent against nonfamily members, and 32 (10%) were violent toward both their wife and nonfamily members.

Fagan et al. (1983) reported that roughly half of all batterers in their sample were arrested previously for violence against other victims. They refer to those batterers as being "generally violent." Similarly, Barnett et al. (1997) referred to these offenders as being "panviolent," that is, violent both within and apart from a family setting. Fagan et al. (1983) found that 80% of those reported to be violent with nonpartners had prior experience with the criminal justice system, having been arrested for such violence.

This kind of history is shown among those who receive intervention by the criminal justice system as well as those seen by other service providers. For example, Dunford et al. (1990) found that most abusers of women in shelters had serious criminal records. Klein (1994a) also reported that a majority of men brought to Quincy District Court (Massachusetts) in 1990 for civil restraining orders had prior criminal records for assaults. When the sex of prior victims was reported, men were twice as likely as women to have been victimized previously.

Similarly, frequency of abuse among batterers greatly varies, suggesting the existence of at least several typologies of batterers. Straus et al. (1980) reported that about two thirds of batterers repeat their assault within 1 year, averaging about six new assaults. Similarly, violence appears to be quite concentrated. Jaffe, Wolfe, Telford, and Austin (1986) reported somewhat lower levels of reabuse, finding that 19% to 25% of abusers will be violent again within 6 to 12 months after arrest. Variations in the commission of violent acts are apparent even among batterers. For example, Sherman (1992) found that 20% of abusive couples generated half of all incidents.

Research in the Quincy District Court found graphic evidence of early offender involvement in the criminal justice system (Buzawa et al., 1999). Although this research was limited to offenders reaching court, they found that at least 25% had juvenile records, and an additional 36% began offending by

the age of 20. In all, more than 60% had drawn criminal charges before the age of 21 years; 90% of this sample had a first offense by age 35.

Research in different courts serving other Massachusetts communities also studied by Buzawa and Hotaling (2000) found that the suspect had at least one prior criminal charge at the time of the incident in most cases (58% overall). In fact, the average number of prior criminal charges of suspects was 5.9 per offender. The number of crimes ranged from 0 to 96 incidents per offender. Crimes against the person averaged 1, with a range of 0 to 10; property crimes averaged 1.7, with a range of 0 to 41; public order crimes averaged .7, with a range of 0 to 15; drug and alcohol offenses averaged .5, with a range of 0 to 11; motor vehicle offenses with substance abuse averaged .5, with a range of 0 to 8; and motor vehicle offenses without substance abuse averaged 1.3, with a range of 0 to 41. The only prior criminal areas not heavily represented by the suspects were prior sex offenses, averaging only 1 per person, with a range of 0 to 6, and restraining order violations, averaging .1, with a range of 0 to 5.

The Buzawa and Hotaling research also examined reoffending of abusers for an 11-month period following the study incident. Reoffenders of domestic violence against female partners in this sample were more likely to be young, unmarried, unemployed men with long and extensive criminal histories of personal offending. Their profile matches that of the criminal offender in general that is developed in the criminological literature.

The most important predictor of future offending against female partners was the most recent pattern of offending against female partners: The past served as a good predictor of the future. Male domestic violence offenders who were involved in two or more domestic violence incidents with the same victim during our 4- to 5-month study period were more than 8 times more likely than others to have reoffended during the 11-month period following the 4- to 5-month study frame. Reoffending in this context appears to be another instance of offending in a continuing pattern of multiple incidents within a short period of time that was not deterred by arrest.

Reoffenders of domestic violence were also more likely to be persons with extensive personal crime histories. Reoffenders with four or more personal crime charges were more than 3 times more likely than the less criminally active to have reoffended. The dangerousness of this group does not appear to be directed at only one victim. Reoffenders were almost 4 times more likely to have had multiple individuals take out restraining orders against them over the years. The importance of this is difficult to overstate. Current criminal justice polices and practices tend to treat every batterer monolithically—in many jurisdictions with neglect, in others quite aggressively so.

The literature suggests at least two distinct groups of domestic violence offenders. One subgroup, the majority according to most researchers, primarily uses violence situationally against partners or dependants (children and elderly parents); this violence may occur in response to a variety of situational factors, typically linked with substance abuse, stress, or a desire to maintain control (Straus, 1996). Typically, they do not otherwise have extensive histories of other generalized anti-social behavior. This subgroup is more likely to be employed, have other vested community ties (Sherman, 1990), and have had few adversarial contacts with law enforcement.

In contrast, there is a minority of batterers who have a history of violence, often with multiple targets—the "panviolent." These individuals have far less commitment to a law-abiding lifestyle and consequently tend not to fear criminal justice intervention or

sanctions (Sherman, 1990; Straus, 1996). Although a minority of abusers by number, the Quincy data covered earlier demonstrates how the recurrent patterns of violence in high-risk offenders can lead to their dominating court dockets

Estimates of the relative size of each group vary depending on the population being studied and the criteria used for defining "high risk." Straus, for example, uses two criteria to separate high-risk batterers from the general population of batterers: the repetitive nature of violence in the previous year and certain behavioral characteristics. He reported that only 10% of batterers in general fit this high-risk profile. Despite this, criminal justice agencies see their actions far more frequently because these offenders attacked their partners a staggering average of 60 times per year, compared with 5 assaults per year in the general population of batterers (Straus, 1996).

RISK MARKERS FOR FAMILIES AND SOCIOLOGICALLY BASED THEORIES OF THE INCIDENCE OF DOMESTIC VIOLENCE

Family Violence Theories and the Control of Domestic Violence

Sociological theories may, if properly used, provide a powerful tool for controlling domestic violence. When the general public begins to understand the familial and social conditions that breed violence, society may decide that such conditions are both intolerable and changeable. As such, prevention efforts may be targeted to those families and subcultures in which violence is likely to erupt. Furthermore, the efficacy as well as the potential ethical and legal issues surrounding a nonpunitive, rehabilitation-oriented intervention before the eruption of violence should be further explored. The problem is that resources are severely limited. As such, we can focus in-depth intervention on relatively few families. Sociological theorists help both in identifying those with the potential to commit violence and suggesting which factors we can change to prevent future violence—or at least keep the violence from being duplicated by the next generation.

Family-oriented research, often conducted by sociologists, uses many of the "individual" variables to explain why a particular family unit might explode into violent behavior. Although they are cognizant of the insight of psychology in explaining some acts of domestic violence, they believe it is not the sole or even the primary factor in domestic violence. For example, Gelles (1993) stated that only 10% of abusive incidents might be labeled as primarily caused by mental illness, whereas 90% are not amenable to merely psychopathological explanations (Steele, 1976; Straus, 1980). Part of the argument may be definition. Many personality dysfunctions, such as low impulse control, are not considered pathological but rather a personality disorder. Nonetheless, by concentrating on certain psychologically disturbed individuals, the foregoing approach, by definition, is considered grossly inadequate. Gelles (1993b) argued that by broadening the framework to encompass social and family structure, the sociologist or family theorist neither excludes nor diminishes the contributions of psychological or social psychological variables; instead, it places these variables within a wider explanatory framework that considers the impact of social institutions and social structures on social behavior (p. 43).

Sociologists also provide insight as to when and where admittedly aggressive tendencies are likely to be expressed as violence rather than being directed into socially acceptable activities such as sports. Few individuals are "walking time bombs," potentially exploding at any passerby. Instead, most individuals prone to violence carry out their aggression in settings where they are likely to escape serious repercussions for violence. Gelles (1983) termed this the exchange/social control theory. At the risk of oversimplification, he stated that violence and abuse may occur when the rewards (largely psychologically driven) are greater than the costs, including social approbation or the prospect for social sanctions. For many years, domestic violence, being a private crime not subject to social intervention, was a low-risk place for people to express violent tendencies. Also, even those highly susceptible to violent tendencies because of psychological makeup simply never need to commit acts of physical violence if they have the economic or political resources to impose their will without such action. Following this perspective, those without economic, social, or personal resources should be more likely to carry out violence than those who have the same tendencies but can express them in more socially acceptable ways.

Therefore, family-oriented theorists place their primary research focus on the determination of characteristics of the family structure that lead to high levels of domestic violence. In this regard, the family is viewed as a unique social grouping with a high potential for frustration and violence (Farrington, 1980; Straus & Hotaling, 1980).

These researchers often comment on the irony of a family model that tends to generate conflict and violence while being, at least theoretically, designed to maximize nurturing love and support. This may be due in part to the assignment of family responsibilities and obligations based on age and gender rather than competency or interest.

Researchers have also cited societal trends of family structure as contributing to increasing levels of domestic violence. For example, the increased social isolation of families in today's society is said to neutralize those inhibitive and supportive agents that might otherwise counteract violent tendencies. Therefore, those families who most lack close personal friendships, typifying a stable relationship, are considered at greater risk of domestic violence (Steinmetz, 1980).

Specific characteristics of a family also have been studied as a predictor of future violence. Straus (1973) and Giles-Sims (1983) examined how particular family structures recurrently lead to suppressed or alternatively elevated levels of violence. Families in which violence is taught at a young age are likely to have children emulating this pattern, including domestic violence. Indeed, one study reported that 45% of male batterers had witnessed their father beating their mother (Finkelhor, Hotaling, & Yllö, 1988; Sonkin et al., 1985). From this perspective, family violence becomes the focus of research; for example, under which conditions violence will occur and how severe it will be in particular families. The importance of this is that it is gender neutral, encompassing violence against women by their intimates and reverse violence by women. The extent of familial violence within a family is typically measured by well-designed, neutrally applied conflict tactics scales designed to empirically rate the conditions under which family violence was likely.

Is Domestic Violence an Intergenerational Problem?

Sociological theorists have long reported that there are pockets of groups within most societies that develop a "subculture of violence" with reinforcing values and norms that make violence much more likely. This insight may be applied to explain why domestic violence may be concentrated in some communities and why different subcultures within a particular society have different overall rates of violence (Wolfang & Ferracuti, 1967, 1982). It also serves as a

basis for exploring why family violence appears to be transmitted across generations.

Consequently, the experience of violence in childhood and children's witnessing of violence both within and outside the family have been explored as factors in predicting subsequent violence in later adult intimate relationships. In fact, several studies have found that the impact of witnessing violence in childhood is a stronger predictor of violence in adulthood than the direct experience of childhood violence (Hotaling & Sugarman, 1986, 1990; Pagelow, 1984; Sugarman & Hotaling, 1989; Widom, 1992). The process of learning a power abusive interactional style in which the only strategy for handling negative feelings and anger is for the more powerful to act aggressively toward the less powerful may be the direct link to why violence travels between generations. Children may learn that relationships consist of two roles: victimizer and victim; other styles of interaction appear frightening, undependable, and insecure (Buzawa & Hotaling, 2000). These findings have raised questions about whether children who witness domestic violence are themselves in need of protection (Jaffe et al., 1986) as well as about the long-term effects of observing parental violence. These children also often experience many of the emotional problems that affect victims, including psychosomatic complaints, depression, and anxiety (Office for Victims of Crime, 1999). Children witnessing violence are also at greater risk for adult victimization (Buzawa et al., 1999; Hotaling & Sugarman, 1986; Short, 2000), mental health problems, educational difficulties, substance abuse problems, and employment problems (Widom, 1992).

The "cycle of violence" or intergenerational transmission of violence thesis has been advanced in many policy arguments for effective intervention in domestic violence. Interventions that limit or curtail domestic violence will also have indirect consequences, limiting the exposure of children to violent role models.

It might initially appear that the diverse range of risk markers for domestic violence offenders are totally fragmented. For example, a comprehensive case can be made that individual psychopathology or biological characteristics are responsible for domestic violence. In contrast, other theories focus on the sociological basis for abuse, including race, ethnicity, and poverty. Still other researchers focus on family characteristics and structure that may create an intergenerational propensity toward violent offending (or victimization). Currently, many researchers are attempting to develop and test batterer typologies in which they group risk factors into categories to provide a more comprehensive understanding of offender behavior and dangerousness.

Traditional approaches to the study of batterer behavior clearly failed to identify patterns of differences in violent relationships. Early writers instead simply reported that much domestic violence may be categorized as a pattern of destructive escalation of violence between "battling spouses." Specifically, they thought that much domestic violence by men may be precipitated by earlier aggression or conflicts by their partners. One researcher noted that often the husband is violent as a response to "provocative antagonistic" behavior of a spouse (Faulk, 1977). The natural difficulty in applying this model to the real world is that virtually all conduct not immediately acceding to the wishes of the other party might be viewed as "provocative" or "antagonistic." In most households this is rarely followed by violence, so this model does not explain those instances in which violence erupts.

Although we are uncomfortable with the concept of a violent household, we can recognize as a general proposition that violence by one party in a relationship may be heavily associated with future violence by the other party. For example, one study has shown that if the husband had not previously assaulted the wife but she had assaulted him (however mild the assault), there was a 15% probability that he would seriously assault her the following year—far higher than normal. Furthermore, increases in recidivism among male offenders have been correlated to the actions of their spouses. A 6% recidivism rate has been reported when the female partner abstained from violence compared with a rate of 23% when the wife used minor violence and 42% when the wife engaged in severe violence (Feld & Straus, 1989).

More current research by M. Johnson (1995, 2000) proposes a typology of violent relationships. He believes that there are distinct causes, developmental dynamics, and probable requirements for different types of interventions. His typology of domestic violence is based on the dimensions of physical aggression and coercive control. *Intimate terrorism* (which he labeled *patriarchal terrorism* in a 1995 publication) is perpetrated by a partner who is both violent and generally controlling and is covered in depth in the preceding sections of this chapter. In contrast, *common couple violence* is committed by partners, either or both of whom may be violent but neither of whom is controlling; the violence may therefore be a product of the couple's behavioral relationship. Hence, the same offender might not be abusive in a different relationship.

Johnson is careful to separate this category from *violent resistance* in which a victim's violent behavior is committed by a "victim" against a partner who is both violent and controlling. In his research Johnson (2000) found that only 11% of violence fit the "terrorism" category. Although we might not agree with the relative importance of a mutually combative family structure, it is clear that at least in some cases the family unit is itself violent.

Holtzworth-Munroe and Stuart (1994) similarly proposed a typology with three types of violent relationships. *Family-only violence* is perpetrated by offenders with little or no psychopathology and who pose the lowest level of risk factors. These offenders tend to use violence as a result of personal or marital stress and typically show remorse following the incident. The second category, *borderline or dysphotic batterers,* are individuals who engage in moderate to severe intimate partner violence with the likelihood of some violence outside the family. These offenders tend to be highly jealous, dependent on their partner, impulsive, and lacking in communication skills. The final category, *generally violent or antisocial batterers*, were involved in moderate to severe partner violence and the highest levels of violence outside the family. They tended to exhibit antisocial personality disorder such as criminal behavior or substance abuse.

Holtzworth-Munroe, Meehan, Herron, Rehman, and Stuart (2000) expanded this typology by adding a fourth category, the *low-level antisocial*, that falls between the family-only and generally violent categories on many of the measures. They also reported that approximately 16% of their sample fell into the generally violent–antisocial category.

Hanson et al. (1997) typologized men into categories of non-physically abusive, moderately abusive, and severely abusive based on the severity of their reported violence as measured by severity of injury and use of weapon. Groups differed on a variety of measures of prior violent behavior, alcohol abuse, marital dissatisfaction, emotional instability, and other negative personality traits. The researchers reported that their measures were best seen as linear, that is, non-physically abusive men were the least deviant, severely abusive men were the most deviant, and moderately abusive batterers fell in the middle.

Clearly, research assessing the validity of these various typologies is still in its infancy (see, e.g., M. Johnson, 2000, Swan & Snow, 2002), and there are numerous problems regarding issues such as appropriate operational definitions of control and violence, as well as the interrelationship between physical aggression and control, that need to be addressed.

At a minimum, we now know that batterers should not be considered a homogeneous group. It appears that life course events and interpersonal dynamics all tend to influence milder forms of physical aggression, whereas more violent batterers are more likely to display significant psychopathological disorders. For some offenders, these violent tendencies may be limited by control of substance abuse, anger control therapy, or other behavioral modification approaches. For others, the problems are personality disorders that are not easily amenable to rehabilitation. This perspective suggests that policies attempting a single, generic approach to controlling domestic violence are grossly unrealistic and inadequate. Instead, societal institutions (police, courts, social welfare, and medical establishments) need the resources (and the willingness) to use appropriately a variety of interventions, both punitive and therapeutic, to control domestic violence.

RISK MARKERS FOR STALKERS—A SPECIALIZED PROFILE

There are obviously many similarities between stalkers and men who batter, but there are enough dissimilarities to warrant treating these as having at least somewhat different risk factors. Most research on stalkers focuses on the characteristics of offenders who have been charged and adjudicated for a stalking offense. This suggests that these offenders may have more obvious mental and psychological disorders or pathologies than those who are not identified. In fact, the National Violence Against Women Survey (NVAWS) demonstrated that high rates of stalking are unreported yet may serve as a prelude to future acts of violence against a current or former intimate partner (Tjaden & Thoennes, 1998). Research has reported that between 25% and 50% of stalkers will become violent toward their victims (Mullen, Pathe, & Purcell, 2000), and yet we are only beginning to understand what characteristics, if any, differentiate violent stalkers from other violent offenders or even violent stalkers from nonviolent stalkers. Prior sexual intimacy with the victim has been reported as the most significant risk factor (Meloy, Davis, & Lovette, 2001), whereas prior criminal history, including nonviolent offenses, and substance abuse also increase the risk of subsequent violence (Mullen et al., 2000). Notably these risk factors have also been identified for nonstalking batterers as well (Buzawa et al., 1999; Tjaden & Thoennes, 1998). Hence, although there is no specific profile of a stalker, we are beginning to increase our knowledge of characteristics that typify most stalkers.

First is the fact that stalking of a current or former intimate partner is often a part of a pattern of domestic violence, that is, a broader pattern of abuse. In other words, it is the "obsessional following" component on the continuum of domestic violence (Albrecht, 2001; F. Coleman, 1997). The National Violence Against Women Survey reported that 81% of women stalked by current or former intimates were also physically abused by the same partner; 31% reported that the same partner sexually assaulted them. In addition, stalking is also highly related to other forms of psychological and emotionally abusive behavior (Tjaden & Thoennes, 1998). In fact, research has suggested the

victims who report higher rates of physical or psychological abuse during a relationship are more likely to be stalked by the partner once the relationship has ended (F. Coleman, 1997).

We are also beginning to identify differences between domestic stalking and other forms of stalking. There is an increased likelihood of violence in relationships in which there was a prior intimate or sexual relationship (Kamphuis & Emmelkamp, 2001; Meloy et al., 2000, 2001; Palarea, Zona, Lane, & Langhinrichsen-Rohling, 1999). As discussed earlier, domestic stalking is more likely to begin at the termination of the relationship (Cupach & Spitzberg, 2000; Tjaden & Thoennes, 1998; Zona, Sharma, & Lane, 1993). In fact, one study reported that in 27.5% of terminated relationships, one party was engaged in behavior that could be defined as stalking. Five percent of this group reported that they had followed, threatened, or injured their ex-partner or their ex-partner's friends, family, or pets (Langhinrichsen-Rohling, Palarea, Cohen, & Rohling, 2000). In addition, domestic stalking is more likely to involve threats and actual violence than other forms of violence (Meloy & Gothard, 1995; Wright et al., 1996).

Stalking tends to be a chronic behavior that often lasts for several months, or even years. Most stalkers already have a history of criminal acts, as well as known substance abuse problems and psychiatric disorders (Meloy, 1996).

Because of the varied nature of stalking, it may be difficult to understand stalkers' motivations or even their behavior patterns. Current research suggests that most stalking is a relational and evolutionary process that appears to progress through stages. Research is still at its preliminary stage and lacks consensus, however. Sheridan, Davies, and Boon (2001) report that 72% of victims believed that the stalker intensified his behavior over time whereas Boon and Sheridan (2001) found that stalkers decreased time spent stalking but became increasingly violent over time. Other researchers have posited possible stages of stalking (e.g., Emerson, 1998; Meloy, 1996); however, none of these frameworks encompass variations in the behavior and responses of the targeted victim and how this impacts stalkers' behavior.

At the risk of oversimplification, it may help to divide stalkers into two archetypical categories: the clearly psychotic and the sociopathological. Psychotic stalkers, who typically do not stalk former intimates, are in the minority and may be either men or women. They operate under the burden of a variety of delusions, often suffering from schizophrenia, paranoia, or other major personality disorders. The majority of psychotic stalkers have been singularly unsuccessful in establishing their own identity. Correspondingly, many have a desire to affiliate with someone they perceive to be very successful but needs them. Their targets may be men or women. Once a target is identified—often a celebrity, but even a coworker or a fellow student—they become obsessed with the individual. Often this fixation is nearly permanent, an unshakable delusional system, because they reinterpret every event and every action and reaction by the target as reinforcing their delusions. They tend to become dangerous when cognitive dissonance can no longer be ignored, that is, when they are rejected by the objects of their affection or the target's behavior is inconsistent with the fantasy, such as if the target marries another person. At this point, unrequited love can turn to uncontrollable rage.

Psychotic stalkers are not likely to be deterred by mental health therapy or criminal justice intervention. This type of stalker is more likely than other stalkers to react to criminal justice sanctions by escalating stalking behavior or committing an act of violence. Fortunately, the majority of stalkers in the context of domestic violence are not psychotic but instead are likely to have issues with substance abuse or personality disorders (i.e., they are sociopathological). Their primary mood disorders are borderline, histrionic, narcissistic, antisocial paranoid, or dependent (Meloy, 1997). Sociopathological stalkers have a need to control victims and lack normal inhibitions about using fear, violence, or other tactics to achieve this end. Stalkers suffering from a personality disorder often react with extreme anger or violence when a victim decides to leave. As Meloy (1997) observed, "Stalking is a pathology of attachment, often driven by the force of fantasy" (p. 178). Meloy theorized that stalkers become "overinvolved" with intimate partners and form abnormally intense attachments. These attachments result in obsessive pursuit of their partners to avoid abandonment. This is more likely to reflect borderline, histrionic, and narcissistic traits rather than the antisocial personality traits more often associated with generally violent batterers who are not also stalkers.

Although profiles for all types of stalkers have not been formulated to date, we can readily believe that many, if not most, of this type of stalker come from abusive homes in which violence was used to settle disputes and determine control over others. They are overwhelmingly men, frequently harboring deep resentment toward women in general. In short, they are obsessed with control and will not easily relinquish domination.

Before a woman leaves an abusive relationship with such an individual, he typically tries to control every aspect of her life, including finances, her friendships, and contacts with relatives. Disobedience is subject to verbal, physical, or emotional retaliation against her and or her children. She may, in turn, react in a manner similar to posttraumatic stress, becoming increasingly passive and more likely to be abused. When a woman leaves an abusive relationship in such a context, her partner interprets this as a loss of control; he is preconditioned to attempt to reassert control through whatever means necessary, including stalking, often coupled with violence. For the psychopath, stalking can be seen as the logical method to reassert control.

RISK MARKERS FOR VICTIMS AND THE PHENOMENON OF REVICTIMIZATION

Researchers of assault have also sought (and to a large extent continue to seek) explanations as to why certain people are victimized. Victimology, a discipline termed by Benjamin Mendelsohn (1956) as the "reverse" of criminology, seeks to determine why certain people or classes of people are at increased risk for victimization. He postulated that the victim in many cases had a certain psychosocial parallel with the offender and that it was the interaction of the victim's traits with the propensity for criminal activity by the perpetrator that led to many crimes, especially crimes of violence. Von Hentig (1948), in *The Criminal and His Victim*, stated that for a large percentage of criminal cases, the victim indirectly shared the responsibility for his or her victimization. Similarly, Henri Ellenberger (1955), a psychoanalyst, urged criminologists to focus on victimogenesis, that is, cases in which the victim, in effect, precipitates the crime. In his classic studies of homicide victims, Marvin Wolfgang (1958; Wolfgang & Ferracuti, 1967) explained that in many of the cases, victims' actions made them "mutual participants" in the homicide.

From this orientation, it was relatively easy to seek to typologize victims of crimes. For example, Mendelsohn in 1956 classified victims into six types based on the relative "culpability of the victim" vis-à-vis the criminal: (1) the completely innocent, (2) the victim with "inner guilt" due to his or her own ignorance, (3) victim as guilty as the offender (the voluntary victim), (4) victim guiltier than the offender (she has encouraged someone to commit a crime), (5) guilty victims (the offender kills in self-defense), and (6) imaginary victims—paranoid, hysterical persons. Such typologies became important in the study of abuse because of some basic misunderstandings by the early and primarily male researchers. Mapes (1917), as quoted in Morris (1987, p. 166), stated with regard to sexual assaults that "no adult female can be forcibly compelled to acquiesce since by anatomic and physiologic reasons the male is incapable of successfully fighting and copulating at the same time."

Although it is beyond the scope of this book to discuss the impact or accuracy of classic victimology literature, it should be recognized that female victims of violent assaults would rarely be seen as "completely innocent" using Mendelsohn's terminology. Instead, victims were easily seen as a member of a dysfunctional dyad, with her (perhaps unconsciously) encouraging the violence (e.g., Shakespeare's *The Taming of the Shrew* and the updated play and film version *Kiss Me Kate*).

In many ways, these attitudes developed naturally from earlier psychoanalytic theories of human sexuality. These originally posited the Freudian belief in the essentially masochistic notion of female sexuality. Under that theory, female masochism is now sublimated into the unconscious betraying itself as the painful longing wish of many (most) women to "suffer" for her lover (Deutsch, 1984, as quoted in Morris, 1987). In this regard, being raped may be termed the "ultimate sexual fantasy" for women and being beaten the essence of subjugation to her husband. Needless to say, such theories have few adherents in modern criminology.

Not surprisingly, subsequent authors have strongly criticized such typologies for contributing to victim blaming. It was also noted that earlier studies purporting to show how victims indirectly encouraged or unknowingly contributed to their victimization suffered problems in conceptualization or poor and missing data and measurement resistance (Fattah, 1984; Laub, 1997).

Concerns about victim blaming also led to many advocates examining victim–offender interactions as dichotomous, that is, a clearly identifiable victim and offender. The possibility of ambiguous situations or the possibility that one party is not entirely "innocent" was not commonly discussed (Best, 1999).

Cultural differences between the researcher and victim as well as the inclination of researchers to inject their own biases on ambiguous data made "postmortem" studies of victim participation tentative and has more recently be seen as wholly arbitrary (Elias, 1993) or politicized (Garland, 2001).

Individual-centered approaches have also examined the profile of a domestic violence victim. It has been theorized that differences exist between victimized women and others. It also assumes a "constant" definition of victimization as defined by the researcher rather than the victim. For example, the suggestion has been made that certain victim attributes distinguish victims who report multiple incidents of domestic violence from single-event victims (Pierce & Deutsch, 1990; Skogan, 1981; Snell, Rosenwald, & Robey, 1964). It has been theorized that although most people modify their behavior to avoid future victimization, repeat victims are, as with offenders, relatively unable to learn from such events by changing behavior patterns. For this reason, victims of repeated acts of domestic violence were, in earlier psychiatric-oriented articles, termed to be *masochistic* (Snell et al., 1964) and in later research were viewed as trapped by perceptions of their role (Pierce & Deutsch, 1990).

For many years, victim-centered theories have been hotly debated. Feminists have argued that this simply is a repeat of male-dominated ideology, blaming the female victim of domestic violence when one would not even consider blaming the victims of stranger assaults, robberies, and thefts. There is some truth to this perspective. Psychologically based theories analyzing victim responses to violence tend to minimize historical traditions condoning familial violence, the superior economic and physical power enjoyed by most men, and the impact of fear of retaliation if a battered woman tries to leave or alter her relationship with the offender. In support of this position, recent research suggests that offender characteristics are more predictive of revictimization than are victim characteristics (Buzawa et al., 1999; Fagan, 1996; Goldkamp, 1996; Hotaling & Buzawa, 2001; Willson et al., 2000).

Analysis of data from the Buzawa and Hotaling (2000) study suggests that victims of violence were not heavily committed to any deviant lifestyle involving criminal activity, unlike the suspects who displayed an extensive and varied criminal career. This suggests that among many offenders, domestic violence is part of a broader lifestyle involving numerous "aspects of deviance."

Many of the same factors that are risk markers for offenders are risk markers for victimization, particularly for victims who are repeatedly victimized by the same or different offenders. One issue reported in the literature for at least the past 20 years is repeat victimization. This research consistently finds that once a person is victimized, he or she is at far increased risk of future victimization (Farrell, 1995; Farrell, Phillips, & Pease; 1995; Pease & Laycock, 1996). This is typical of many crime victims; for example, one study found robbery victims were 9 times more likely and sexual assault victims 35 times more likely to be revictimized than other citizens (DeKeseredy et al., 1997).

This finding has also been observed in the cases of domestic assault victims. Farrell and Pease (1993) reported that victimization risk is greatest in the period soon after the initial victimization. In domestic violence cases, the risk of revictimization was highest within the first 11 days of initial victimization and rapidly declined thereafter (Lloyd, Farrell, & Pease, 1994). Clearly, in cases of some offender–victim dyads—repeat victimization by definition—is occurring. Revictimization also is evident outside the construct of the victim's relationship with any particular offender.

Repeat victimization has, for example, been related to demographic factors. Schwartz (1991) used NCVS data to find differences in repeat victimization by marital status, race, and gender. Some behavior patterns, known as routine activities, significantly relate to repeat victimization (Cohen & Felson, 1979; Maxfield, 1987). For example, It is interesting that the role of alcohol and drugs is also a risk marker for victims of domestic violence. A number of studies have demonstrated that the use of alcohol and drugs by women may place them at increased risk for domestic violence (Kaufman Kantor & Straus, 1990; Kessler et al., 1995; B. Miller et al., 1990). Certainly, many victims use these substances before being attacked.

> According to their own reports or reports of family members, about 42% of victims used alcohol or drugs on the day of the assault; 15% had used cocaine. About half of those using cocaine said that their assailants had forced them to use it. (Brookoff, 1997, p. 1–2)

One study reported that users of hard drugs were 5 times more likely to be assaulted than nonusers. This study, found that alcohol abuse alone did not significantly increase the likelihood of being assaulted, a victim's active drug use did (Kilpatrick, Acierno, Renick, Saunders, & Best, 1997).

This study also reported that women using drugs were almost twice as likely to be revictimized within a 2-year period following the initial assault.

We must be careful using this information because it can easily be twisted to blame the victims' substance abuse for further revictimization. In fact this is not the case. Instead, there appears to be an increased risk for women's use of alcohol and drugs *after* being abused (Kilpatrick et al., 1997). Kilpatrick et al. reported that this relationship was significant even after controlling for a victim's prior substance abuse and assault history. Another study quantified this by reporting that women's drinking was twice as likely to occur *after* the abusive incident compared with the offender (Barnett & Fagan, 1993).

Therefore, observations of a victim's alcohol or drug use may not be a "cause" of domestic violence at all, but merely an effect—that is, it may simply be a reaction or serve as a coping mechanism for abuse (Ireland & Widom, 1994; Kantor & Asdigian, 1997). Unfortunately, such substance use by victims, regardless of the reason, appears to increase the likelihood of revictimization, resulting in the continuance of substance abuse (Kilpatrick et al., 1997) and the creation of a pernicious feedback loop between violence and victim substance abuse.

In general, Fattah (1991) categorized victim risk factors by how susceptible characteristics and behaviors are to change by the victim: (a) factors victims can't change (e.g., demography and personal characteristics such as age, gender, height, handicap, appearance, social class, and race); (b) factors victims can change (e.g., marital status, choice of partner, neighborhood of residence, place of school or employment, hours of employment, modes of travel, physical strength, and assertiveness); and (c) factors that are "possibly" under the victim's control and might therefore be changeable (e.g., use of leisure time such as hours, places, type of activity;

display and securing of property; display of personal opinions; style of dress, alcohol and drug use; sexual activity; antagonism and aggressiveness in interpersonal relations; negligence and carelessness; and level of caution for becoming involved with persons, places, and activities). The concept of revictimization "proneness" is important because active criminal justice systems employ advocates who have an opportunity—and arguably the responsibility—to assist women in seeking more long-term assistance. In addition, a critical aspect of achieving the criminal justice goal of victim empowerment will be to help women develop the capacity to protect them from revictimization. R. C. Davis, Taylor, and Titus (1997) found risk heterogeneity and event dependency as coexplainers of victimization.

Domestic violence victims often find themselves at increased risk of revictimization because of the "secondary effects" of battering, including significantly reduced material resources. The lack of material resources increases the vulnerability of women to abuse (Moore, 1997; Sullivan & Bybee, 1999). Victims who are economically dependent on batterers are less likely to leave, resulting in increased batterer access to victims. In fact, many offenders actively seek women who are economically dependent to increase their ability to control her behavior (Jacobson & Gottman, 1998). In addition, batterers often force or cause women to leave their jobs, terminate their education or career plans, and even use up their financial savings (Coker, 2000). At its extreme, battered women can become homeless to escape revictimization, which only further increases their vulnerability to violence as a result of their subsequent lifestyle.

Many battered women are at increased risk of revictimization because of their increased lack of ability to attain financial resources. For example, lost wages and possible unemployment is often a result of abuse (Cohen, Miller, & Wiersema, 1995; T. R. Miller, Cohen, & Wiersema, 1996), and unemployment has been found to be related to subsequent revictimization (Coker, 2000). Sick time, days off required for court appearances, and the batterer's continued interference with the victim's ability to work can each result in high percentages of battered women becoming unemployed. For example, Shepard and Pence (1988) reported that 24% of abused women reported lost their jobs as a result of domestic violence. Lloyd (1997) found that victims of domestic violence were more likely to be unemployed and recipients of welfare; however, later research by Lloyd and Taluc (1999) used multivariate analyses and did not find support for the earlier findings. Lloyd and Taluc (1999) examined low-income women in Chicago and reported that women who experienced violence by a male intimate partner were as likely to be currently employed as those who did not. They were, however, at increased risk to have had a history of unemployment, health problems, and previous dependence on welfare.

Browne, Salomon, and Bassuk (1999) examined the experiences of battered women during their unemployment and found that they were two thirds less likely than nonvictims to maintain 30-hour workweeks for 6 months or more. It is not clear whether the victims were actually free of violence during the study period, however. It is possible that these victims were at increased risk for abuse because of their employment or possible separation from the batterer. It appears that we still need additional research to obtain a clearer understanding of the impact of employment status on victims of domestic violence.

Although most researchers suggest that victimization increases risk for revictimization, Winkel (1999) reported that for some victims, prior victimization serves as a protective factor. His research further demonstrated that the impact of victimization was predicted by victim psychological processes and incident characteristics.

CHAPTER 4

Societal and Historical Factors in Domestic Violence

DOES SOCIETY CREATE AN ATMOSPHERE CONDUCIVE TO DOMESTIC VIOLENCE?

Why do we care about historical attitudes and precedents toward women? Although powerful, an analysis of risk markers for family violence must also include a macro-level analysis. This helps us to understand the structural violence considered endemic against women in Western society. As we discuss more fully in this chapter, socially sanctioned violence against women has been persistent since ancient times. Christianity, Judaism, and other patriarchal religions simply affirmed male-dominated family structures that were already in existence. The results can be seen in the history of official discrimination and tolerance of domestic violence exemplified by English common law and in the history and practices of the early United States. Although most societies have the same—or even significantly worse—issues with official and tacit tolerance toward domestic violence, our analysis focuses on historical and cultural antecedents that have shaped "traditional" U.S. tolerance of domestic violence.

RELIGIOUS AND HISTORICAL PRECEDENTS

Domestic violence has long been both a feature and a concern of society, varying in both attention paid and responses to it. From earliest record, many if not most societies gave the patriarch of a family the right to use force against women and children under his control.

Ancient Historical Precedents

The basis for patriarchal power often was a deeply held societal belief regarding the maintenance of social order. Roman civil law gave legal guardianship of a wife to her husband. This concept, *patria potestas*, included the largely unfettered ability of the husband to physically beat his wife, who became, in legal effect, his "daughter." Theoretically, such rights were not necessarily for her well-being because they extended to the right to sell a wife into slavery or, under certain circumstances, to put her to death (Pleck, 1989).

In the earliest example of a written marital code from the year 753 BC, Romulus simply stated that wives were "to conform themselves entirely to the temper of their husbands and the husbands to rule their wives as necessary and inseparable possessions" (Pressman, 1984, p. 18). Ancient historical precedents can best be summarized by the concept of the natural inferiority of women and of the "property" rights of the male head of the household.

> Traditions subordinating women have a long history rooted in patriarchy—the institutional rule of men. Women were seen in virtually all societies to be naturally inferior both physically and intellectually. In ancient western societies, women, whether slave, concubine or wife, were under the authority of men. In law, they were treated as property (Anderson and Zinsser, Vol. 1, 1989). As men ruled in government and society, so husbands ruled in the home. (Lentz, 1999, p. 10)

The Biblical Basis for Abuse

When looking at responses to abuse, we need to consider how Ecclesiastical (or religious) law treated domestic violence. Throughout recorded history, deeply held religious beliefs have governed political and social attitudes. In this regard, the impact of the religious experience on domestic violence is significant. Although this subject can be oversimplified, at a minimum we can say that Western religions have reinforced a husband's right to control his wife. Many passages in the Bible repeatedly have been interpreted to justify man's primacy and his right to exercise authority over women. Consider the following examples taken from the revised New Testament: "And the rib that the Lord God had taken from the man he made into a woman" (Genesis 2:22).

Why is this passage important? Because in medieval times God was the center of "all good." Although made in the image of God, mankind was led away from the Garden of Eden ("paradise on earth") by the transgressions of his "wife," Eve. Hence, in early church law, it was explicitly stated that women were at least one step removed from the image of God. Because women had already led to the "fall" of man, it was right that he whom woman led into wrongdoing would have her under his direction so that he might not fail a second time through female levity (Davidson, 1977, p. 11–12).

The concept of woman as subservient to man is quite clear in these Old Testament passage in which God says, "I will greatly multiply thy (woman's) sorrow, and thy conception; in sorrow thou shall bring forth children; and thy desire shall be to thy husband, and he shall rule over thee" (Gen. 3:16). This passage clearly set the tone for much of the later writings and indicates that God deliberately sought to extract special punishment to be used against women. Consider the following:

> When a wife while under her husband's authority, goes astray and defiles herself or when a spirit of jealousy comes on a man and he is jealous of his wife, then he shall set the woman before the Lord and the priest shall apply this entire law to her. (Num. 5:29–30)

This stricture is significant: The husband had the authority to interpret the wife's actions as improper and therefore invoke religious law against her. "Wives be subject to your husbands as you are to the Lord. For the husband is the head of the wife just as Christ is the head of the Church" (Ephesians 5:22–23). This passage interprets the relative rights and obligations of men and women in society, making it clear that women were definitely in a subordinate position to men. As early as the 5th century, St. Augustine wrote of the importance of a man and woman's respective duties.

> for "domestic peace" it was necessary that "they who care for the rest rule-the husband the wife, the parents the children, the masters the servants; and they who are

cared for obey—the women their husbands, the children their parents, the servants their masters." In this Christian family and household, rule was not for a love of power but from a "sense of duty." According to Augustine, "if any member of the family interrupts the domestic peace by disobedience, he is corrected either by word or blow, or some kind of just and legitimate punishment, such as society permits. (Lentz, 1999, p. 11)

Until recently, the overwhelmingly male clergy, seeking to support the natural primacy of men, has interpreted such passages. This attitude did not markedly change between the Catholic writers of the Middle Ages and those of the Protestant Reformation. Martin Luther, although seeking to dispel the primacy of the Catholic Church, had no problem stating in unequivocal terms the man's right to rule over his wife and other members of his family "remains with the husband and the wife is compelled to obey him" (Lentz, 1999, p. 11).

In many religions, such interpretations are coupled with a strong belief that marriage is a sacred institution—even if physical abuse occurs. For example, one of the key tenets in most Christian doctrines is that marriage is permanent and not dissolvable by mankind. Consequently, many of us may remember the traditional wedding ceremony in which the bride was told to "love, honor, and obey" her husband, the groom was told to "love, honor, and cherish" his spouse, and both parties agreed to remain together "for better or for worse until death do us part." In the context of domestic violence, this placed the attacker and victim on a similar moral plane; that is, the fact that a wife was supposed to obey her husband, whereas she was to be cherished (as a prize possession?), clearly implied to women that adversity—perhaps including being beaten—would not justify leaving a marriage. At worst, relaying problems of marital conflict to a priest, pastor, or

rabbi might even invoke stern lectures to the wife as to her biblical responsibility to raise the family and accede to the natural order. Some religions such as the Jewish faith even placed a special responsibility on the wife to "maintain" the home and the marriage at all costs. She was often acculturated to believe that marital failings were automatically her fault.

Barbara Hart noted that abuse in the context of a marriage was not recognized historically as violence at all but, instead, was simply one of the religious duties of the husband. A medieval Christian scholar propagated rules of marriage in the late 15th century, which specified the following:

> When you see your wife commit an offense, don't rush at her with insults and violent blows . . . scold her sharply, bully and terrify her. And if this doesn't work . . . take up a stick and beat her soundly, for it is better to punish the body and correct the soul than to damage the soul and spare the body. . . . Then readily beat her, not in rage, but out of charity and concern for her soul, so that the beating will rebound to your merit and her good. (Hart, 1992, p. 3)

For the past 10 to 20 years, most denominations have undertaken great efforts to eliminate (or at least address) inferences tolerating the domination of married women. This phenomenon, however, does not involve rewriting the scriptures themselves, is of very recent origin, and has not fully penetrated popular culture. As a result, even today's batterers often quote the scriptures as justifying their activity. Andrew Klein, the former chief probation officer of a model domestic violence court, has stated that he has heard batterers defy his state's domestic violence laws claiming that "restraining orders are against God's will because the Bible says a man should control his wife" ("Batterer Is Walking," 1993, p. 1). Victims often further exemplify the impact of such deeply held attitudes. It has also emphasized and reinforced the culture of much "victim blaming" even when women sought help from a natural source—the clergy.

The Contribution of English Common Law

English common law, the predecessor to many U.S. statutes, followed a variant of this well-recognized custom of male control over women. English feudal law reinforced both the concept of male property rights over women and the right of men to beat "their women" if needed. In English society, "property rights" were the key denominator of social status, class-heredity determined was far more important than personal achievement in setting the limits for what a person could potentially attain. Hence, one was either bred into nobility (with numerous rights thereof) or one was a commoner. Each group had clearly defined property rights and behavioral expectations with regard to the other. Within such a charged atmosphere, the characterization of one's rights over property was perhaps the single most important attribute of a person's status. In feudal times, women became "a femme covert" according to common law and were under the protection and control of their husbands; under the law of covertures, husbands were legally responsible for their wives. She lost rights to her property in favor of her husband even if it was inherited from her family (Frey & Morton, 1986; Lentz, 1999; Salmon, 1986).

One rather graphic manifestation of a man's "property rights" and his reaction to the violation of such rights was set forth in the official British judicial reactions to adultery by each gender. English common law differentiated between the "reasonable reactions of a husband to his spouse's adultery and those of a similarly situated wife."

Since the 17th century, British common law has endorsed conceptions of male dominance over women's bodies. Under this conception of dominance, adultery by the wife only constitutes adequate provocation to mitigate murder to manslaughter (a lesser crime not punished by death) regardless of whether a husband kills the wife or her lover. Because adultery was viewed as violating a husband's property rights in his wife's body and in his family name, the common law recognized allegations of infidelity as the most severe form of provocation. As the court opined in *Regina v. Mawgridge* (as cited in Miccio, 2000, p. 161), "Jealousy is the rage of a man, and adultery is the highest invasion of property . . . (A) man cannot receive a higher provocation." The law of adultery was gendered in its application. Until 1946, English courts assumed that wives did not experience rage as men did, and adultery was not available as an excuse to women who killed philandering husbands.

This exemption for killing in deference to a man's honor—and in effect, in defense of his property—was carried forth from common law and widely recognized in the United States as well, both by state statutes (four of which made it a complete defense to criminal charges of killing a wife's lover) and more commonly by judicial notice (Miccio, 2000).

English common law did begin the process of introducing some limits on a man's rights over his wife. The concept of restraint was introduced to place some control on the largely unfettered rights of the husband. Under later English common law, husbands were to "dominate" wives using violence "with restraint" (e.g., the theory of "moderate chastisement"). The power of "life and death" over his wife was taken away—at least officially. In practice, however, few if any restraints were imposed on the husband's ability to chastise his wife (Gamache, Edelson, & Schock, 1988; Oppenlander, 1982; Sigler, 1989; Walker, 1990).

It wasn't until the late 1500s and through the entire 1600s that the English began debating whether there were limits to the theory of "chastisement." Public debate began as to whether God or the state sanctioned physical beatings (Doggett, 1992; Fletcher, 1995; Lentz, 1999). In this regard, courts began to be more concerned about the reasons for the beating and the extent of the physical damage inflicted. Hence, it held the women somehow "responsible" for the beating—if a woman was an "adulteress," or even a "nag," more physical punishment would be permitted. From this perspective, the concept of only allow beating for particular acts and restricting the physical punishment inflicted became key limitations on the common-law right to "chastise" one's wife. Similarly, through the period immediately before the colonial era, "wife beating," although widespread, came to be viewed as a mark of the lower class—at least by members of the upper classes, who increasingly disdained such violence. In reality, what happened in upper-class families became veiled in silence (Fletcher, 1995; Lentz, 1999).

Such rights were perhaps most graphically illustrated by the often-stated, if largely allegorical, concept of the rule of thumb, which expressly allowed husbands to beat their wives with a rod or stick no thicker than his thumb. The probability that such a whipping could cause serious injury illustrated how maintenance of the family unit was more important than stopping violence. As such, one 18th-century ruling gave authority to the husband to punish his wife as long as it was confined to "blows, thumps, kicks or punches in the back which did not leave marks" (Dobash & Dobash, 1979, p. 40).

Other societies adopted similar theories that limited the application of the husband's violence while in effect condoning his right as the family patriarch to engage in violence to promote family values. For example, a 16th-century Russian ordinance expressly listed the methods by which a man could beat his wife (Quinn, 1985). When violence became too serious, laws against assault and battery were typically not invoked. Instead, informal sanctions by family, friends, the church, and perhaps vigilantes were undertaken. Such sanctions included social ostracism, lectures by the clergy, or retaliatory beatings of an offender (Pleck, 1979).

The fact is that in virtually every society we have examined, proverbs, jokes, and laws indicate strong cultural acceptance and even approval of the beating of women by their husbands. Any effort to list them all would be futile, but two examples are illustrative of the extent of such beliefs:

> A wife is not a jug . . . she won't crack if you hit her 10 times. (Russian proverb)

> A spaniel, a woman, and a walnut tree—the more they're beaten, the better they be. (English proverb)

In addition, English comic plays used wife beating as a recurrent comic theme. One obvious example is William Shakespeare's witty comedy, *The Taming of the Shrew*, in which it was the play's primary focus.

Certainly U.S. culture is no less inundated with messages of this nature. Until at least the 1970s, American pop culture often trivialized domestic violence. Consider television programs such as *I Love Lucy*, in which Ricky Ricardo regularly "spanked" Lucille Ball, resulting in considerable audience laughter, or *The Honeymooners*, in which Jackie Gleason's arguments with his wife, Alice, typically ended with his catch phrase, "One of these days, Alice . . . pow, zoom, right to the moon." John Wayne movies similarly used spanking as a staple strategy to "tame" and "win over" independent, strong women—usually in front of the entire town, and such taming did not stop until the woman stopped struggling. Although the spanking may have been seen as trivial, and no injuries ever resulted from them on camera, in effect women were seen to encourage "moderate" violence by taunting the male until he gave her the beating she tacitly appeared to desire. The reality or potential for serious domestic violence was simply never addressed.

THE CONTEXT OF EARLY AMERICAN STRATEGIES AND INTERVENTIONS

The Massachusetts Body of Laws and Liberties, enacted by the Puritans in 1641, were the first laws in the world that expressly made domestic violence illegal. This statute provided that "every married woman shall be free from bodily correction or stripes [lashing] by her husband, unless it be in his own defense upon her assault" (Pleck, 1987, pp. 21–22). Similarly, in 1672, the pilgrims of Plymouth Plantation made wife beating illegal, punishable by fine or a whipping (Pleck, 1987). Over time, practices sanctioned (or tolerated under these statutes) began to evolve into the more definitive boundaries for permissible levels of violence that became the historical antecedents for the criminal justice experience in the United States.

The limitations of this period of societal intervention, however, should be clearly understood. Puritans and pilgrims did not object to moderate violence under religious law. The family patriarch not only retained the responsibility but also the duty to enforce rules of conduct within the family. Therefore, moderate force was necessary and proper to ensure that women, as well as children, followed the correct path to salvation. In effect, the right to use violence was sanctioned, but only if it was for the benefit of the family— and hence of the colony's social stability (Koehler, 1980; Pleck, 1979).

Also, the effect of these laws was largely symbolic, defining acceptable conduct and not often enforced by the public floggings or the other more draconian criminal justice punishments then in vogue. In fact, it appears that from 1633 to 1802 (169 years), only 12 cases of wife abuse were ever brought in Plymouth Colony (Pleck, 1989). In addition, these statutes were confined to the more religious New England colonies and were not extended to the larger and more religiously representative southern and mid-Atlantic settlements. Finally, because these were primarily based on religion, determining the appropriateness of conduct that was "suitable in the Eyes of the Lord" became even more problematic as American society, in common with most of Europe, became more secularized. For these reasons, enforcement of such laws largely disappeared before the American Revolution.

During the period between the late 1700s through the 1850s, there were virtually no initiatives by the criminal justice system to control domestic violence, and a legislative vacuum existed (Pleck, 1989). In fact, in the early 1800s, judges commonly dismissed infrequent criminal charges because a husband was legally permitted to chastise his wife without being prosecuted for assault and battery (Lerman, 1981).

Similarly, although not "U.S. laws," state courts as early as the 1824 Supreme Court of Mississippi decision in *Bradley v. State 1* expressly reiterated the English common law principle that a husband could beat his wife with a rod no thicker than his thumb. Some court decisions of this period, although using extreme language, illustrate the prevailing judicial sentiments toward intervening in domestic matters.

One court clearly focused on how the wife brought punishment down on herself (Hirschel, Hutchison, Dean, Mills, 1992): "The law gives the husband power to use such a degree of force as is necessary to make the wife behave herself and know her place" (p. 251). The same court made it clear that it was even immaterial whether the husband used a whip or another weapon on his wife "if she deserved it," and this gave her no authority to abandon her husband, an offense for which she could be prosecuted (Hirschel et al., 1992, pp. 252–253).

In reality, women could not be viewed as being autonomous or being an "adult" in most popular conceptions of the word; until the start of the 20th century, she had few legal rights. As noted earlier, husbands owned all of a family's property and assets and were allowed to physically chastise their wives. He also had the right to force her to accept his domicile even if this meant uprooting the family. Not surprisingly, in the closely related context of marital rape, legislatures and courts by and large viewed the husband as having a largely unfettered right to the sexual enjoyment of his wife with or without her consent.

In *Oppenheimer v. Kridel* (1923), the court abridged this right, noting that in the past in New York State

The marriage contract vested in husbands a limited property interest in the wife's body with the concomitant right to "the personal enjoyment" of his wife. Consequently, in exchange for shelter and protection from external forms of violence, the wife gave over her body. If wives refused conveyance of the self, husbands enforced compliance by force. Marital status conferred upon husbands the right to violate the bodily integrity of their wives. (Miccio, 2000, p. 157, emphasis added)

Why did a long period of nonenforcement occur? To some extent this was simply a result of the widely held belief that women, with an inferior mind and countenance, simply needed the protection of her spouse, regardless of any harm caused by domestic violence. It is also probable that larger societal trends were at work. Society became more secularized; the enforcement of community moral standards in private conduct became considered improper for the state—an overreaching use of governmental power (Hartog, 1976). Of course, it is always possible that levels of

domestic violence actually declined during this period. There is, however, no evidence that this occurred, and it would intuitively appear unlikely given that rapid social change and economic dislocations, factors consistently associated with higher levels of domestic violence, characterized the period.

More probably the operations of the legal systems of both Great Britain and the new U.S. republic reflected the philosophies and teachings of classic liberal philosophers. For example, John Locke, the British philosopher, strongly believed that society should restrict its concerns to the maintenance of public order and abjure both trying to regulate the private order and to eliminate private vice (Pleck, 1989). Jean-Jacques Rousseau, the French philosopher, had a strong intellectual influence in the United States on the importance of equality and the "role of the state." His beliefs did not extend his concept of equality to women, however, whom he viewed as inferior and as having interests confined to "women's functions" (Miccio, 2000).

In the United States, the second period of criminal justice enforcement against domestic violence occurred in the context of the major societal upheavals of the latter part of the 19th century. Laws passed and cases decided during or immediately after the Civil War imposed new restrictions on the citizenry. Part of this was an enhanced government willingness to regulate families. Some legislation began to erode the husband's unfettered authority over his spouse (Pleck, 1989).

We cannot underestimate the force of society's reaction at that time to the lifestyles and mores of new immigrants and the lower social classes—long a theme of American reformers. At this time, the emerging financial elite, as well as the professional and middle classes, were frightened over their perception of uncontrollable crime waves committed by the "lower classes." This was exacerbated by waves of immigrants with markedly different—and supposedly more brutal—cultural backgrounds (Boyer, 1978).

Finally, in the last decades of the 19th century women began to achieve some modest degree of financial freedom and protection of their property rights. Divorce was becoming at least a theoretical possibility. Although there were legislative "reforms" to "protect women" by limiting their ability to work in difficult but well-paying positions, there was a gradual acceptance of women in the workforce, at least in what we now view as traditional female occupations such as teaching, nursing, and other service related jobs. Also, with the widespread passage of Married Women's Property Acts, even the most restrictive limits on women holding property in their own name were lifted throughout the country. Women thus began the process of accumulating wealth and some degree of economic—and later political—power.

In any event, by 1871, the first U.S. court decision by the Supreme Court of Alabama became the first U.S. appellate court to explicitly rescinded common-law rights of a husband to beat his wife as follows:

> The privilege, ancient though it may be, to beat [one's wife] with a stick, to pull her hair, choke her, spit in her face or kick her about the floor, or to inflict upon her like indignities, is not now acknowledged by our law. . . . In person, the wife is entitled to the same protection of the law that the husband can invoke for himself. (Hart, 1992, p. 22)

In sharp contrast, the North Carolina Supreme Court had rejected a similar case earlier in 1868: "If no permanent injury has been inflicted, nor malice, cruelty nor dangerous violence shown by the husband, it is better to draw the civilian, shut out the public gaze, and leave the parties to forget and forgive" (*State v. Rhodes* 61 N.C.453, 1865; cited in Hart, 1992).

In addition to judicial limits on a husband's authority to chastise his wife, concerns about physical abuse was beginning to be expressed by the nascent women's advocacy movement. Although (women's) temperance leagues saw their primary mission as stamping out the most visible cause of societal problems, "demon rum," especially when used by immigrants and the lower classes, growing numbers of suffragettes organized activities designed to help women more generally. They sought to lift numerous legal restrictions on their freedom, including the right to vote, to own property, and, of more direct import, not to be considered as the legal chattel of their husbands.

These efforts did, indeed, affect official attitudes toward domestic violence. By the end of the 19th century, "chastisement" as an official defense to a charge of assault largely ended. Twelve states considered and three adopted a stronger position containing explicit laws against wife beating. In these three states, Maryland (1882), Delaware (1881), and Oregon (1886), the crime of wife beating became officially punishable at the whipping post.

Although these statutes demonstrated societal concerns, we now believe that they were rarely officially enforced. In a far more problematic manner, vigilantes, including the Ku Klux Klan, supplanted official sanctions by using beatings against alleged offenders, primarily Blacks, to explicitly control such behavior (Pleck, 1989). One can obviously question their real motivation in that such actions naturally had the effect of maintaining their claim as final arbiter of permissible conduct—powers dramatically abused since their formation.

DOES HISTORY STILL MATTER?

Continuing Institutional Evolution and Constraints

Although it would be easy to dismiss the relevance to the present of this early period, several recurrent patterns of interface between domestic violence and the criminal justice system appear to carry over from this period. First, restrictive laws nominally on statute books were not equated with real enforcement policies. Although they might exist, criminal sanctions were infrequently imposed. Instead, they were tacitly deployed to control the fringes of clearly improper conduct. The excess had to become impossible to ignore because of a victim's recurrent severe injuries or public breaches of the peace. Instead, as we discuss later in this chapter, informal methods of control became the primary vehicle for enforcing basic societal norms.

Second, when official punishment was deployed, it was far more extensively used against Blacks, immigrants, vagrants, and other groups without political, economic, or social power. In these cases, it is debatable whether the criminal justice system intervened primarily out of concern to assist the wives or intimates of these men or instead became an additional vehicle for enforcing the existing social order against disfavored minority groups.

Third, the contemplated use of highly visible and emotionally charged punishments such as the whipping post, even though infrequently applied, might be considered an attempt to deter future criminal activity with the prospect of public humiliation. As such, it may have been the logical precursor to modern efforts to use arrests without subsequent conviction as a mechanism for deterrence via public humiliation rather than relying on ultimate exercise of criminal punishment.

In any event, the second great experiment of using the criminal justice system to combat domestic violence had largely ended, and by several accounts domestic violence as an officially punished crime virtually disappeared from public view (Pleck, 1979, 1989; Rothman, 1980). This was probably inevitable. After a series of financial panics in the late 1800s and early 20th century, economic issues became the focal point of concern for middle-class Americans. Also, most female activists were concerned with achieving their primary goals: suffrage and, subsequently, temperance.

In the interim, the criminal justice system rapidly evolved away from enforcing crimes committed in the home. Political theorists instead began to fear the possibility of coercive use of police, a characteristic rapidly increasing in emerging authoritarian states such as Prussian areas of Germany and czarist (and later Soviet) Russia. In turn, this helped develop the rationale for societal respect of family privacy, the traditional rallying cry for those who also negate the role of criminal justice in domestic violence (Rothman, 1980).

In this context, case law and statutory restrictions developed that severely restricted previously largely unfettered powers of the police. In one highly significant development, virtually all states codified and even reinforced common-law requirements that forbade police from making arrests in misdemeanor cases without witnesses. Hence, the reaction to the international growth of police power and abuse was to try to limit the neighborhood involvement of police in situations in which they should have been active.

Similarly, judicial innovations were clearly *away* from criminalizing domestic violence. In the first several decades of the 20th century, the development of family courts were expressly designed to eliminate family troubles from court dockets and instead provide a specialized forum that would deal with family crises. Although these courts could frequently grant divorce, the typically expressed goals of such courts were to assist couples to work out problems within the family structure and seek reconciliation rather than address crimes committed (Pleck, 1987).

These courts, as well as courts of general jurisdiction, also began to be influenced by the nascent social work movement. Although perhaps simplistic, at least in the early years, these professionals might have viewed the criminal prosecution of domestic violence cases as "unprofessional" or largely the result of society's overall preference to coercively stamp its own normative behavioral models onto those of the "lower classes" and minorities. The rehabilitative model used by social workers was viewed as vastly superior in that it tried to help dysfunctional family units or rehabilitate an offender's behavior. These efforts attempted to develop a consistent intervention response for all batterers compared with current approaches that acknowledge differences among batterers and apply criminal sanctions on a large scale (Saunders, 1993).

The last era of dormancy had a profound impact on current criminal justice operational practices. Although less true than we reported in the earlier editions of this book, and despite nearly universal policies to the contrary, many police officers, prosecutors, and judges still privately tell us that society should not intervene in domestic disputes except in cases of dire violence.

As we explore in subsequent chapters, until recently procedural requirements adopted by bureaucratized and highly controlled police forces reinforced the belief in sharply limiting the use of formal sanctions in domestic violence cases. There was a largely unexplored concomitant increase in the tendency of police to mete out "street-level" justice to minor miscreants, such as giving stern lectures, or even an occasional beating, to drunk domestic violence offenders to "teach them a lesson" while avoiding making an actual arrest.

The restrictions on misdemeanor arrests without a warrant were probably the key legal impediment to the use of arrest; however, restrictive policies of prosecutors adopted in the 1900s also made use of criminal sanctions even more problematic. The combined effect of these procedural barriers made the actual intervention of the criminal justice system far more remote than the crime would otherwise warrant based on victim injuries or offender intent and conduct.

A Macrolevel Analysis of History and Its Effects

Some researchers have drawn on the totality of the extensive historical background of violence in families and of societies' seemingly callous disregard for it. As we noted in our definition of domestic violence in Chapter 2, many researchers and advocates for battered women disagree about both the concept of domestic violence and its definition. They reject the concept that it is gender neutral and find it to be a cultural attribute of Western society. These researchers look at the same history and, with quite a bit of evidence, view wife abuse and society's tacit acceptance of male violence as a symptom of the unequal distribution of power and perhaps of the key problem in the relations between the sexes. Furthermore, the concept of domestic violence as primarily concerned with physical attack is rejected in that these researchers view all of society as tacitly condoning the economic deprivation, sexual abuse, isolation, stalking, and terrorism of the under classes, including but not limited to women (Yllö, 1993).

In short, despite a series of studies showing high levels of female-on-male violence many researchers do not consider domestic violence to be gender neutral but merely a vehicle by which society, as an adaptive institution, maintains coercive control over the under classes, such as women, through many generations (A. Jones & Schechter, 1992; Ptacek, 1999; Yllö, Gary, Newberger, Pandolfino, & Schechter, 1992). Myra Marx Ferree concisely stated the position: "Feminists agree that male dominance within families is part of a wider system of male power, is neither natural nor inevitable, and occurs at women's cost" (cited in Yllö, 1993, p. 54).

In this model, law, religion, and even the behavioral sciences historically have endorsed the husband's authority and justified use of violence to punish a disobedient wife (Freeman, 1980; Schechter, 1982; Sonkin et al., 1985). In a real sense, structured gender inequality existed both in the home and in the institutions designed to maintain Western cultural and family values. Furthermore, women were forced into the role of maintaining home and family in a male-dominated society that did not value such occupations. Both the men and women recognized how the economic dependence left women effectively powerless to their partner's whims (Schechter, 1982).

In turn, this was reinforced by the somewhat solitary confinement of housewives in their homes because the privatized family structure made familial violence an individual problem, not a societal one (Schechter, 1982). For such reasons, the United States Commission on Civil Rights (1982) recognized the historical legal and cultural basis for continued high rates of familial violence in our society.

Even today, other critical commentators view American society as being based on "successive domination" of one class over another—that is, men dominate women, Whites dominate minorities, and the upper class dominates all those without resources. In this context, *all* men implicitly use the fear of potential violence to subordinate women (Schechter & Gary, 1988). Although such critiques recognize that most men do not themselves resort to violence, the perception is that men, as the dominant class, have benefited from women's continued fear of the potential violence of rape or assaults by both strangers and intimates.

The link between violence toward women and sexual inequality finds support in some cross-cultural research on domestic violence. In one study of 90 societies worldwide, Levinson (1989) found that violence between family members was rare or nonexistent in 16 societies but prevalent in most others. In his analysis of these cultures, he observed that, in addition to the existence of natural support systems and a societal emphasis on peaceful conflict resolution and marital stability, spouses in these peaceful societies enjoy sexual equality. This equality between men and women was reflected in joint decision making in household and financial matters and in the absence of double standards with regard to premarital sex and other freedoms. In short, feminists have argued that a holistic view of our social structure provides a more complete analysis of why violence occurs than any examination of the individual circumstances of a particular individual offender or characteristics of the family unit.

As a result of this perspective, many feminist researchers have not been tolerant of mainstream psychological and family violence sociological theorists precisely because they do not tend to stress the historical and cultural underpinnings of violence against women. From this perspective and as previously covered in Chapter 3, the study of which particular men or family units succumb to the temptations of using violence is largely irrelevant at best and at worst detracts from "deconstructing" societal institutions and practices, a necessary precondition to eliminating sexism in society. In addition, they often find psychological risk factors for violence to be an excuse for countenancing unacceptable behavior, diverting attention from the real societal dysfunction that encourages violence by susceptible men (Yllö, 1993).

Although efforts have been made to synthesize the learning of domestic violence to encompass all levels of analysis, many researchers believe that structural impediments to a gender-neutral social structure are unjustifiably minimized by a focus on the family unit. In short, by focusing on the other levels of analysis, the opportunity to change society at the structural level has been thwarted. Although we do not necessarily believe the entire social critique implied in the feminist model as described earlier, we need to recognize the significant contributions of feminist research. These works provide a theoretical framework to understand how a society may be predisposed to domestic violence or, more aptly, violence against the less powerful within society. It also provides insight into why particular societal responses occur and why social and legal institutions have tacitly tolerated or at times even perpetuated domestic violence.

The feminists have therefore provided a challenge to working within the context of traditional institutions as currently structured. A great debt is also owed to the feminist movement because they arguably have been the primary impetus for social and legal change. Neither the psychological nor the sociological theories explored in Chapter 3 have provided much analysis as to why society tolerates domestic violence, nor have

they proven to be aggressive agents for change. Although the pioneering work of sociologists such as Gelles (1972) and Steinmetz and Straus (1974) played a major role in making domestic violence a salient public issue, they remain more active in academic circles and not as vocal in advocating institutional or structural changes as a mechanism to address domestic violence.

Fortunately, many of these deep philosophical rifts described earlier were more characteristic of writings in the late 1980s and early 1990s. With regard to the role of inherent sexism in our society, disagreements are now less common among feminist activists and researchers and those from other perspectives who do not believe gender and power to be the overarching features explaining intimate violence.

Instead, a more cooperative spirit exists that seeks to understand the psychological, familial, historical, and societal risk markers for domestic violence. As our knowledge base grows, perhaps we can focus on policy change and implementation rather than on philosophical differences as to the relative contribution of a given approach to the problem of domestic violence.

II

THE EVOLVING
POLICE RESPONSE

She sits upon the floor
Curled up in a bail
Remembering the fight
Her body smashed into the wall

Knowing she must go
Somehow she must leave
But she thinks it's futile
After all, who'll even believe?

So through the years she waits
Trembling, beaten, alone
Needing help but doubting anyone will believe her crying moans

Yearning to tell the police
To all them on the phone
Wanting to tell them all the things he has done,
that by their ignoring they have condoned.

Once sure, determined, and proud
She is now a shadow compared to the past
Now timid, shy, and unsure of how much longer she will last

So she sits upon the floor
Curled up in a ball
Trying to get help
But doubting anyone will care at all

Beaten, bruised, but undefeated
She waits for that one day
When it won't be unsafe to go
And even worse to stay

Laura *Buzawa*

CHAPTER 5

The Traditional Police Response and Early Innovations

THE TRADITIONAL APPROACH: MINIMAL INTERVENTION

Why study the "classic" police reaction to domestic violence if it has changed? One reason is simply to measure the extent of change. In addition, despite wholesale enactment of new statutes and promulgation of modern policies, many police agencies have not dramatically changed street-level behavior from the past. Finally, victims and offenders may not know of police changes. To the extent perceptions influence reality by deterring calls for assistance, they *are* reality.

The classic police response has three characteristics that we discuss in this chapter. First, police formally intervened in relatively few potential domestic violence cases; the majority were "screened" by the victims themselves or by third parties. Second, the police did not want to intervene in family disputes. Third, there was a strong, sometimes overwhelming, bias against making arrests in cases of domestic violence.

Case Screening

Researchers concur that until the new proarrest reform legislation, only a small proportion of intimate assaults resulted in the dispatch of police officers. For a variety of reasons, the majority of cases were diverted out of the system.

Failure to Report Crime: Victim Screening

The process of underreporting starts with substantial "screening" by victims who fail to file reports. Estimates of calls to the police as a percentage of actual domestic violence incidents ranged from 2% (Dobash & Dobash, 1979) to approximately 52% (Langan & Innes, 1986). Kaufman, Kantor, and Straus (1990) estimated that at least 93% of cases were not reported.

Although these studies appear to report widely different results, discrepancies may be partially explainable based on the different methods of data collection. For example, the Bureau of Justice Statistics reports on data collected from the National Crime Victimization Survey (NCVS). This survey, conducted by the Bureau of the Census for the Department of Justice, includes data from biannual interviews with about 80,000 persons in 43,000 households. Until its revision in 1992, respondents were simply asked if they were victims of a crime within the last year. The offender may even have been present at the time of the interview, decreasing the likelihood of an affirmative response. If they answered "no," the interview ended. Many victims of domestic violence, due to societal norms, fear of retaliation, or economic or psychological dependence did not report domestic violence. These cases are perforce screened out of the criminal justice system without even being recorded. Data from the revised instrument during the period between 1993 and 1999 showed that about half of women reported they had notified the police of an incident during the period between 1992 and 1996 (Greenfeld et al., 1998), and Rennison (2001) reported that this NCVS figure increased to 54% in 1998.

In contrast, unofficial but well executed private studies consistently show higher rates of underreporting. In one of the largest such studies, a 1985 sample of more than 6,000 households, the National Family Violence Survey (NFVS) stated that only 6.7% of incidents were reported to the police overall, and only 14% of those experiencing serious violence reported the assault (Kantor & Straus, 1987; see also Dutton, 1988). This figure is typical of the more than 100 studies examining reports to the police of "conflicts" in which the figure of victims reporting a domestic assault is almost always less than 20% (Straus, 2000). In other words, individual definitions of an assault may be dependent on whether the behavior is considered as part of a study on how people resolve conflict, such as the NFVS, as opposed to an individual's experiences with crime, as in the officially sponsored NCVS.

The discrepancy between official estimates showing more than half of cases being reported and private studies showing only a small percentage of reports may at first appear trivial, but actually is significant. If the police truly receive calls from less than 10% of abused women, then these are the

exception, and the criminal justice system, although an important aspect of societal control, might realistically be relegated to the periphery of actual intervention.

Most studies to date have failed to cast much light on differences between those who report crimes and those that do not. One important, yet understudied, area is victims' past experience as a victim with the criminal justice system. Few studies provide data on whether reporting rates differ among first-time victims, repeat victims who have never called the police in the past, and those who have reported earlier offenses.

The lack of detailed victim information has significant implications for understanding victim's decisions to report new offenses. This may represent an important gap in our knowledge of the reasons most victims do not report domestic abuse to the police. Historically, many victims failed to contact police because of police failure to respond appropriately. Police indifference or their refusal to take action have undoubtedly discouraged many victims (Buzawa & Buzawa, 1990; Hamilton & Coates, 1993). This shortcoming has been particularly evident with minority groups for whom conflicts have often characterized interactions with police, resulting in lingering distrust (Bent-Goodley, 2001). This is exacerbated by the possibility that incidents involving such minorities are more likely to come to police attention resulting in disproportionate rates of minority arrests (Buzawa & Buzawa, 1996; Hutchison, Hirschel, & Pesackis, 1994). There also may be community pressures in some subcultures not to involve law enforcement due to cultural norms and expectations (Bent-Goodley, 2001).

Many jurisdictions now aggressively enforce domestic violence statutes. Paradoxically, this may in itself deter some victims from reporting. We know that women often omit information about abuse when disclosing incidents to relatives and friends to control the reaction or response they receive (Dunham & Senn, 2000). This would imply that such victims would be even more reticent to contact police when they have far less control over the outcome. After all, with recent reforms, police now often provide an aggressive response to domestic violence assaults by arresting offenders, taking care of the immediate risk of abuse but also effectively removing much victim control. As we explore in depth later in this book, in the purest form of this trend, a mandatory arrest policy, especially when coupled with a highly publicized policy of aggressive case processing, may deter many victims.

We also know that many victims fear other repercussions of reporting abuse. Many realistically fear physical or economic reprisal if they report an incident (Dobash & Dobash, 1992; Frieze & Browne, 1989; Hanmer et al., 1989b). This may take the form of additional beatings, stalking, threats of loss of income, or even of losing one's children because of retaliatory reporting of child abuse, neglect, or substance abuse. The victim's history with the offender often makes threats of retaliation more credible yet, paradoxically, more difficult for the victim to publicly assert.

Victim characteristics also differentially affect their reaction to criminal justice intervention. Although their experiences with the criminal justice system may provide a "rational" basis for future reporting behavior, other victim characteristics may affect their likelihood to report new offenses. These include their prior history of victimization both as a child and as an adult. Victims may through past experience be prone to accept violence as a routine part of their lifestyle and hence are less likely to report abuse to the police. In addition to negative interactions with the police in the past and the economic effects of filing a report (discussed

later in this chapter), several other factors appear relevant. Some people, especially those raised in families who have experienced domestic violence, do not perceive being beaten as a crime or even as abusive (Straus, 1989). Most domestic assaults are not experienced as a crime or threat to personal safety (Straus, 1999); although acts such as "slapping," "kicking," "pushing," or "shoving" are legally considered assaults, it is unusual for people to consider them worth reporting to the police (Ferraro, 1989a; Langan & Innes, 1986; Straus, 1999).

Even if victims recognize that domestic violence is unacceptable, many believe it is a purely personal or family problem. Results of the NCVS indicated that many victims of domestic violence incidents did not report the incident for this reason. This also helps to explain why a much higher rate of assaults by former partners is reported to police compared with assaults by current partners. For example, the NCVS found former partners reported 25 times more assaults in the previous year compared with current partners (Bachman & Saltzman, 1995). Even this relationship status has resulted in contradictory findings. Felson, Messner, and Hoskin (1999) reported that there was no difference in reporting patterns by relationship with the exception of increased reporting of assaults by ex-spouses compared with spouses. Other research however has failed to find a victim–offender relationship associated with reporting differences (Bachman & Coker, 1995; Hutchison & Hirschel, 1998; I. M. Johnson, 1990). It also is possible that many victims may, in fact, seek assistance—but from sources other than the police. Imposition of law perhaps reflects the most formalistic type of help-seeking behavior. Although this is often coupled with the assumption that it is the preferred or ideal strategy for all domestic violence victims, many may prefer other formal or informal strategies. These can provide important—and often preferred—sources social support for many victims. Research suggests that despite widely adopted reforms, many victims are still unwilling to report their victimization to the police and instead continue to seek assistance from family, relatives, and friends (Hutchison & Hirschel, 1998; Kaukinen, 2002).

For some victims, this may be a function of the victim's financial resources as well. As discussed in Chapter 3, physical abuse is the major reason many women initiate divorce proceedings. This requires some degree of financial autonomy on the part of the victim, which may be less available to socially disadvantaged victims. Hutchison and Hirschel (1998, p. 451) reported that "those at the poverty level were more likely to obtain legal help than are those with higher incomes." They were less likely to meet with an attorney or contact victim assistance organizations, however (Hutchison & Hirschel, 1998). Like victims, third parties may be more likely to view domestic violence as a private matter (Black, 1980); however, Felson et al. (1999) reported that third parties are not less likely to call the police in cases of partner assault compared with other relationships, but they are far less likely to witness such incidents. Furthermore, third parties were more likely to call the police in incidents with a male aggressor and incidents with a male aggressor and female victim (or a female aggressor and male victim) than in female-on-male or male-on-male assaults.

Incident characteristics, especially severity of injury, may also affect victim reporting. The seriousness of an incident may necessitate victims or witnesses to solicit police assistance because of the need for immediate medical assistance or fears of future offender access to the victim (Bachman & Coker, 1995; Felson et al., 1999; I. M. Johnson, 1990; Kaufman Kantor & Straus, 1990). Because injuries requiring medical attention are estimated to occur in less than 3% of domestic assaults on women and .5% of assaults on men, those cases that police do see are disproportionately those involving women as victims. It has of course been argued that because women are at a 7 times greater risk of injury than men (Stets & Straus, 1990), it is appropriate that female victims should make most of the calls for police service (Straus, 1997, 1999).

Many victims realistically fear the physical or economic repercussions of reporting an incident of domestic violence (Dobash & Dobash, 1992; Hanmer et al., 1989a; Pagelow, 1984). Such repercussions may take the form of further beatings, stalking, threats of loss of income, or even threats of losing one's children through retaliatory reports of child abuse, neglect, or substance abuse. Finally, many victims may suffer from posttraumatic stress disorder (PTSD), making rational decisions regarding reporting a crime virtually impossible.

Victims also may take into consideration the various costs—economic and emotional—of legal intervention. They may believe their complaint will not be taken seriously; that family, friends, or relatives may blame them for their victimization; or that they may lose custody of their children—a fear that is not irrational. There are personal costs in terms of victims' time, emotional energy, and stress that are associated with the criminal justice process. In addition, victims may believe it jeopardizes their ability to work on improving an already troubled relationship that they seek to maintain rather than terminate.

Victims' decisions to call the police in domestic violence cases are differentially screened in a disturbing manner. Perhaps the most surprising to nonspecialists is the different economic profile of reporting compared with nonreporting groups. It has long been known that a far greater percentage of unreported violent crimes exist among the middle and upper classes.

For this reason, the police predominantly see domestic violence in lower socioeconomic groups (Black, 1980; Parnas, 1967; Westley, 1970). Although it is difficult to quantitatively determine the extent of such underreporting, one 1979 study reported that minority groups and poorer women in general were more than twice as likely to report abuse to the police as their higher income or White counterparts (Bowker, 1982; Hamberger & Hastings, 1993; Schulman, 1979). Differential levels of reporting may be changing, however, along with the changing ethnic composition of the police and their role in the community. In an earlier study Gondolf, Fisher, and McFerron (1991) reported that Blacks were more likely to call police than Whites. However, Smith (2000) reported that there was no statistical difference in White and non-White victims' willingness to report reabuse. (The findings in this latter study were in the context of a mandatory arrest jurisdiction, a modern innovation covered in Chapter 8.)

Researchers have advanced many explanations for past nonreporting by the middle and upper classes. Black (1976, 1980) stated this was primarily attributable to the economic dependency of middle-class women, which is in sharp contrast to the relative economic independence of women whose direct earnings or welfare payments often were the family's economic mainstay. Black (1980) stated this succinctly:

> [A] Middle class white woman is more likely than a lower class black woman to live in a condition of dependency. . . . She is more likely to live on the earnings of her husband, in a dwelling financed by him . . . "a housewife." . . . Such a woman is not readily able to leave her situation one day and replace it with an equivalent the next. . . . Frederick Engels long ago pointed to the relationship between "male supremacy" and the control of wealth by men: "In the great majority of cases today, at least in the possessing classes, the husband is obliged to earn a living and support his family, and that in itself gives him a position of supremacy without any need for special legal titles and privileges. Within the family he is the bourgeois, and the wife represents the proletariat (Black, 1980, p. 125). (1884, p. 137)."

From this perspective, Black (1980) concluded the following:

> It is therefore almost inconceivable that a totally dependent woman would ask the police to remove her husband from his own house. If he beats her, she is unlikely to invoke the law . . . middle class people are unlikely to call the police about their domestic problems. (p. 125)

Black's observation seems quite insightful; however, recent empirical research has failed to substantiate this finding, at least as a broad generality. Indeed, in one study, I. M. Johnson (1990) found no relationship whatsoever between economic status and calling the police whereas several other studies reported a more complex relationship. In these studies, offender unemployment is shown to increase the likelihood of calling the police, but only for cases in which severe violence occurs. In cases of minor violence, victim unemployment increases the likelihood of contacting the police (Kaufman Kantor & Straus, 1990; cf. Hutchinson & Hirschel, 1998).

Another factor that Parnas (1967) and Westley (1970) noted several decades ago is that although domestic violence existed in all classes, violence in the middle to upper classes was more likely to be diverted to doctors, the clergy, or other family members. They theorized that these victims preferred to bring their problems to "social equals" rather than to the police, who were presumed to be from a lower working class.

For different reasons, including distrust of the motives of the police, community pressure not to involve outsiders, and fear of gaining the attention of immigration authorities, the number of calls may be excessively depressed from various discreet groups ranging from Appalachian Whites to recent immigrants. Such nonreporting appears to persist in many communities. In one example, the Boston Police Department planned to set up a special task force to respond to domestic violence in the Asian community when it realized that, by its own estimates, approximately 13% of domestic violence incidents occurred in the Asian community, yet only approximately 2% of service calls were received from this group (WBUR Boston Special Report, August 15, 1994). Consequently, concerns over career, community image, and confidentiality, particularly in certain ethnic groups and upper-income communities, may still inhibit reporting, leaving a wide segment of the population relatively under served and, therefore, unprotected by police intervention.

As a result of widespread victim screening, calls from nonparticipants, including neighbors, friends, relatives, and bystanders have become one of the primary methods by which the criminal justice system is made aware of domestic violence. Such calls may, however, provide their own differential screening. They are not necessarily motivated by the seriousness of the assault, but rather by the disruption of their own activities due to noise or property damage, or even by morbid curiosity about the incident or to see how the police would react.

Bystanders also implicitly screen cases by ethnic group and class and may explicitly screen them on the basis of marital status, preferring to allow married couples to settle such issues regardless of overheard violence. When outsiders observed disputes, they often wryly observed those involved as the neighborhood "problem family" and the disputes as a simple "family disturbance" or an expected neighborhood occurrence. Such incidents were far less likely to elicit calls to the police than those perceived to be threats to the public order.

In contrast, cases involving girlfriends and boyfriends or former cohabitants appear more likely to involve incidents outside a residence and are more likely to be observed and reported than those cases involving married or currently cohabiting adults. The significance of witnesses and bystanders in reporting acts of domestic assault may also increase the conception of the problem as being concentrated among the lower socioeconomic classes. Because of urban congestion in poor neighborhoods, such cases are more visible to neighbors, are more likely to receive attention, and therefore may be the source of a subsequent call to the police.

The net effects of victim and bystander call screening are threefold. First, for whatever reason, police disproportionately see indigents, especially in certain minority groups and urban neighborhoods. As a result, both they and the public tend to view domestic violence solely as a problem of these groups. This conception makes the problem easier to ignore, as is done with many social pathologies of the poor. If the public realized the extent to which all social classes are to at least some degree affected, a more rigorous police response might be demanded.

Second, the most severe cases of domestic assault may not necessarily be the ones to reach the police. Instead, those most disruptive to public order and thereby known to others outside the family are disproportionately reported. For this reason, disclosure rates do not appear to be closely related to incident severity—at least as measured by injury to the victim. Although Kaufman Kantor and Straus (1990) reported that 14.4% of incidents involving major violence were reported to police compared with 3.2% of minor violence, Pierce and Spaar (1992), based on their study of comparative police and emergency room data, reported that the most severe cases of violence resulted in calls for medical services rather than police referrals. Few of these were subsequently reported to the police. In fact, in one early study, Walker (1979) estimated that less than 10% of cases were reported when serious injury resulted.

Third, regardless of the study it appears that only a share, between 10% to 50% of cases ever reach the police, meaning that a substantial unfilled potential demand exists for police services. Research has produced conflicting results as to whether low rates of victim assault reporting are unique to domestic violence victims. Some researchers have noted reporting rates far lower among domestic violence victims than among victims of other crimes (Buzawa & Austin, 1993; Felson, 1996; Felson, Messner, & Hostin, 1999; Gartner & Macmillan, 1995). Others find no significant differences in reporting behavior (Felson et al., 1999). Felson and colleagues used 1992–1994 NCVS data to suggest that their finding of a lack of significant differences may be due to several factors, noting that victims may have greater need for police protection when they know the offender and are in greater fear of continued assaults, when they cannot escape the offender, and when they can identify the offender. In addition, Felson et al. suggested that a victim of intimate partner assault might be angrier than victims of other violence. It is noteworthy, however, that in their research, victims called the police in only a quarter of the incidents; third parties called in an additional 14.4%.

When discussing victim screening, it is important to emphasize why some victims choose not to call the police. Many women simply prefer alternate, nonlegal response strategies that may be quite successful (Bowker, 1983; Hirschel & Hutchison, 2001; Mills, 1998).

Police Screening

In addition to the failure of victims and bystanders to report domestic violence, police departments as organizations have contributed to the low numbers of reported domestic violence cases. One primary method used to reduce the number of police responses to domestic violence was "call screening." To maximize allocation of scarce resources and to avoid responding to low-priority calls, most modern police departments have made this routine practice. Call screening allows the department to assign priorities to all incoming calls requesting police services. Those with low priorities, usually including simple assaults, did not receive authorization to dispatch a police unit until a unit became available.

The importance of call screening is that it operated as a filter, effectively determining what the criminal justice system viewed as a problem. In an organizational sense, those citizen problems that are screened out do not exist. This action, although appearing unbiased, poses a severe challenge to the treatment of domestic calls. D. Martin (1979) observed that at times call screening operated to eliminate disfavored categories of calls and to prioritize others. This was especially true during peak periods of demand for service, such as weekends and nights, when domestic violence calls were most likely and responses to these calls might be eliminated altogether. In a less overt manner, screening calls had the effect of discouraging certain callers from demanding a police response because such callers were instead referred to social service agencies or told that the police could provide assistance for marital conflicts. If police intervention was still requested, dispatch would occur only when time permitted, often after the offender had left, preventing any chance of an arrest (Manning, 1988).

Call screening might simply be considered an adaptive organizational response to help overworked organizations limit environmental demands, functionally similar to triage in a medical setting. Decisions concerning the immediate dispatch of a unit are primarily predicated on the dispatcher's long-distance determination that commission of a felony is imminent. Although such an explanation appears both rational and unbiased, in practice its impact is neither. When responding to typically ambiguous and volatile domestic violence calls, there is always the possibility of an interaction between the police agency's antipathy toward these calls (described later in this chapter) and the inherent problems of an often poorly trained dispatcher trying to determine deployment of limited resources.

For whatever reason, studies in the 1980s suggested that call screening greatly limited police reaction to domestic violence. Pierce et al. (1988) observed that 50% of the 3.2 million calls for police assistance in Boston were for service calls, including approximately 80,000 for "family troubles." Police dispatchers, however, reported an additional 24,400 calls that could have been included in that category but were reclassified by the police dispatch to a "no response" status.

One study in Great Britain reported a variant on this theme. Officers would be actually dispatched, but if they heard nothing from outside the residence, they would exit the premises and report "all quiet on arrival" or "no call for police action," thereby effectively screening the case from the system with virtually no police commitment of resources. The author of this study reported that fully 60% of all domestic calls were never processed past this point (Sheptycki, 1991).

The negative effect of call screening has also been cited in studies conducted in the United States. Ford (1983) reported that in Marian County, Indiana, between two thirds and three quarters of all domestic violence calls were "solved" without officer dispatch. The reasons for such a high rate of case disposal may be related to the known tendency of police personnel to denigrate a domestic offense. Consequently, a call that appeared to be a serious felony assault with a dangerous weapon could merely be termed a "family trouble" call—afforded very low priority and often effectively screened out.

Clearly, call screening in the past presented serious ramifications. An unbiased method effectively eliminated many domestic violence calls. The department's failure to respond or the delay of an officer's dispatch could be so lengthy that the call's emergent nature became lost, the threatened violence had already occurred, or the offender had left the scene (Ford, 1983). Victims often received no attention from police officers who might have prevented new injuries or officially documented past criminal activity. The failure to respond to complaints denied the victim's status, discouraging her from reporting further abuse and perhaps encouraging an assailant to believe abusive conduct was tacitly condoned.

When police intervention occurred, it was criticized as inappropriate. In the context of domestic violence, police response had long been viewed as being perfunctory in nature, dominated by the officer's overriding goal—to extricate the officer from dangerous and unpleasant duties with as little cost as possible and to quickly reinvolve them in "real" police work.

Why Police Didn't Want to Intervene

Police views of "real policing." To fully understand how police responded when a call was screened "in," it is imperative to know how officers perceive their own role as well as their organizational culture. First, police still clearly prefer law enforcement functions in which prospects for action and resulting arrest are higher. In contrast, they almost uniformly dislike non–law enforcement tasks. As Manning (1978) observed, officers prefer to perceive their job in the legalistic sense: as law enforcer. As a result, although laws and department policies have historically provided the officer with extensive guidance concerning the technical basis for deciding to make an arrest, they generally did not formally address order-maintenance issues. The fact, of course, is that police officers have always had a variety of non–law enforcement tasks in which an arrest clearly would be inappropriate or at least highly unlikely. These duties include traffic control, performing rescues, providing transportation to hospitals, and delivering subpoenas and warrants. Police officers also performed a variety of tasks in low-level dispute resolution such as intervening to tone down loud parties, taking care of the drunk and homeless, and intervening in most family disputes. In these tasks, regardless of whether an assault has been alleged, arrest powers were only infrequently used—a tool of last resort.

Regardless of reality, it has long been noted that police historically were socialized from their earliest occupational training into a culture that did not highly value social-work roles (Bard & Zacker, 1974; Harris, 1973). A new recruit, to be an accepted member of the police—that is "one of the boys"—had to adopt this occupational code (Punch, 1985), including the key elements of protecting other officers, admiring a "good pinch" or a "good collar" by a fellow officer (Van Maanen, 1978), and explicit acceptance of the same normative framework as other officers as to what constitutes "serious crime" (Stanko, 1989). Recent authors have reaffirmed that the bias against social work still is apparent among law enforcement (Gaines, Kappeler, & Vaughn, 1999; Kappeler, Blumberg & Potter, 2000; Manning, 1997).

The dichotomy between the actuality of the police experience and the mythology of the police officer as crime fighter and law enforcer created by the occupational culture has been repeatedly challenged. Researchers note that arrests for any crime are rare (Reiss, 1971; Van Maanen, 1974), even though

symbolically important in an occupation in which the daily activities tend to be dull and repetitive (Berk & Loseke, 1980–1981). The importance of the police self-image, therefore, lay less on the reality than on the efforts made by many police officers to undertake conduct consistent with their self image. As a corollary, most officers judged each other's competence on the basis of performing crime-fighting tasks, such as the apprehension of criminals. They simply do not value highly or even see as positive those instances of successful intervention in "private" disputes (Stanko, 1989). The impact of this occupational code is important to understanding police practices. Obtaining and keeping informal prestige or status with peers was (and still is) imperative to most officers. Manning (1978) stated it in the following manner: "His most meaningful standards of performance are the ideals of his *occupational culture*. The policeman judges himself against the ideal policeman as described in police occupational lore and imagery. What a "good policeman" does is an omnipresent standard" (p. 11).

This attitude was and is still reinforced in many departments where rank-and-file officers have maintained a closed internal culture with strong antipathy toward the public at large, toward politicians, and often even toward their own command (Manning, 1978; Punch, 1985; Radford, 1989).

Using this frame of reference, responding to domestic violence calls had until recently little occupational value to an officer. Many officers trivialized such offenses, and arrests were typically infrequent. Because the offender was known and domestic violence was a "minor" (misdemeanor) offense, any arrest that resulted would be considered a "garbage arrest," not worthy of recognition (Stanko, 1989).

Simply understanding that police believed domestic violence calls did not constitute real policing fails to adequately explain why most police agree that such calls rank among their worst duties. Instead, it is necessary to examine additional factors that have reinforced negative police attitudes.

Organizational disincentives. Police departments award few formal organizational incentives for good officer performance in responding to domestic violence assaults. To the extent civil service and not the whim of superior officers affected an officer's chances for promotion, typical practices measure easily quantifiable skills, including arrest rates and subsequent clearances or convictions. Similarly, written tests for promotion heavily emphasize textbook knowledge of law enforcement tasks such as substantive criminal law, criminal procedure, and departmental policies regarding arrests and case documentation. Meanwhile, at a minimum, officers were expected to incur no blemishes on their record by exposing themselves or the police department to civil suits or citizen complaints.

Perhaps inadvertently, these evaluation criteria provided a major disincentive for performing domestic violence and sexual assault tasks. If an officer spends the necessary time handling a domestic assault case, assists a victim with referrals to shelters, and makes follow-up calls, he or she decreases the chance for responding to a call involving a major felony arrest. In reality, the officer has used his or her time "unproductively." The officer also increased the likelihood that the offender, or at times even the victim, might file a complaint based on claims of overzealous or overbearing police conduct.

Are domestic violence calls extraordinarily dangerous to the police? Officers universally cite the extreme danger risked when responding to domestic violence calls. They often are vaguely aware of statistics that "demonstrate" that officers responding to disturbance and assault calls are often killed or injured. Of more impact are the frequently heard "war stories" circulating in most departments recounting incidents in which a victim, whom officers have sought to help, has turned on and bit, slapped, hit, stabbed, or even shot the officers as they tried to arrest the attacker.

Until the mid-1980s, the Federal Bureau of Investigation (FBI) reinforced such fears by publishing statistics reporting the category of "responding to disturbance calls" as responsible for most officer deaths (Garner & Clemmer, 1986). Not surprisingly, both police and family violence researchers emphasized the potential danger to officers in handling domestic cases (Bard, 1970; Parnas, 1967; Straus et al., 1980). Similarly, police training has certainly emphasized the prospects of danger. With few exceptions, training programs have emphasized the inherent danger of the call to the police. They also make frequent exhortations to the effect that if an officer does not follow standard procedures, he or she dramatically increases the chance of injury or death. As Eigenberg (2001) observed, "police were trained to protect themselves but not to safeguard battered women" (p. 271).

Although important for understanding police perceptions, the reality of injury or death is unclear. Wilt and Bannon (1977) reported that less than 9% of injuries were related to domestic disturbances, and Emerson (1979) reported no officer injury or deaths in a study of 1,446 family disputes. The 1986 Garner and Clemmer study also demonstrated that the methodology used in the composition of the FBI statistics was flawed and thereby overstated by approximately 3 times the real rate of police injuries and deaths related to domestic violence efforts. This was because the category used was "disturbances" that included gang calls, bar fights, and any other general public disturbances, as well as responding to domestic disturbances.

Studies report inconsistent results for officer injuries. Uchida, Brooks and Koper (1987) reported that when data from all disturbances were reexamined, police injuries related to domestic disturbances fell to third place after legal interventions and alcohol problems but concluded that it would be premature to deemphasize the danger of domestic disturbances in police training academies. Stanford and Mowry (1990) reported that domestic violence calls did not result in many assaults but did result in frequent injuries.

Other researchers have found relatively few incidents of officer injury when responding to domestic violence calls (Hirschel, Hutchison, Dean, & Mills 1992). Hirschel, Dean, and Lumb (1994) reported that there were relatively few injuries to police officers compared with other types of police calls and that it was largely a myth that female victims came to the aid of their abusers and attacked responding police officers.

Part of the reason for the high numbers of domestic violence–related officer injuries is that there is simply a staggering and rapidly increasing number of domestic violence calls reaching police attention. Consequently, a high percentage of officer time is spent in responding to domestic calls. It is not surprisingly, then, that such activities *do* constitute one of the highest sources of officer injuries (Uchida et al., 1987). Given the disproportionate amount of time that officers spend responding to domestic violence calls compared with other incidents in the disturbance category, responding to domestic violence calls may not be as intrinsically dangerous as other police activities.

Regardless of reality, the effect of such perceptions is clear: Fear of death or injury reinforces officer dislike of such calls. When officers respond to a domestic violence call, they often have been instructed to emphasize a defensive-reactive strategy, with foremost priority on protecting their own safety. Under such circumstances, it is not surprising that innovations in police responses or a more activist approach were discouraged unless mandated by law.

Structural impediments to police action. Traditionally, there were a number of structural impediments to an appropriate police response. One severe handicap had been long-term statutory restrictions that gave officers the authority to make arrests for misdemeanors only with prior issuance of an arrest warrant. In effect, this required a prior action by a magistrate or justice of the peace or allowed action only in those relatively few cases in which a misdemeanor was committed in the officer's presence. This contrasted with statutory authorization of warrantless arrests in felonies, for which an officer needed only probable cause to believe that the suspect had already committed the crime.

Domestic violence has typically been characterized as simple assault, a misdemeanor. Until laws were first changed in the 1980s, police officers were legally unable to make warrantless arrests unless the violence continued in their presence or a previously existing warrant had been issued. Officers could rarely rely on warrants because, at that time, police information systems were usually nonexistent or at best rudimentary, meaning that officers did not typically know whether there was an outstanding warrant when they responded to a violent family. Information systems and record keeping for dispositions short of a conviction frequently did not exist in any acceptable, readily accessible form. Therefore, when there were new convictions, incidents of family violence or disturbances were not systematically recorded by police departments so that they could track repeat offenders or victims (Hammond, 1977;

Pierce & Deutsch, 1990; Reed, Fischer, Kantor, & Karales, 1983).

Finally, the sheer volume of domestic violence cases has been cited as creating an organizational challenge to chronically under-staffed and overworked departments. Disputes and disturbance calls as a class are the single largest category of calls that police receive. They tend to occur at night or on weekends, when criminal activity and traffic responsi-bilities simultaneously invoke their greatest organizational demands. Apart from other factors we have noted here, it is not surpris-ing that recurrent spouse abuse calls received lower response priority, at least absent of knowledge of past violence or imminent threats to a potential victim's life.

The Classical Bias Against Arrest

One of advocates' greatest concerns for victims of domestic violence has been the perception that the police disproportionately discriminated against domestic violence victims by failing to arrest. Until the 1990s, literature consistently documented that rela-tively few domestic violence incidents result in arrest. Meanwhile, researchers in the past observed few arrests in any cases of non-aggravated assault.

The primary coercive sanction available to police is an arrest, and this power is pred-icated on the officer's belief that there is probable cause to support that a suspect has committed a crime. Therefore, it might be assumed that legal variables, such as the strength of the case, predominate in the arrest decision. In domestic violence cases (if not in all cases of misdemeanor assault), it is apparent that there was, and in some depart-ments remains, a persistent bias against arrest. Within this context, the decision to arrest is problematic, dependent on victim and offender characteristics, situational deter-minants, and patterns of decision making

that are not consistent among individual officers or police organizations.

Legal variables, such as finding probable cause that all elements of a crime have occurred, are prerequisite to all but abusive use of arrest powers. Unlike many other offenses, however, the perpetrator and loca-tion of a domestic assault is known, injuries or potential danger are often obvious, and at least one witness—the victim—is usually available. If one were to view this situation solely as the result of having the officer find probable cause, a high arrest rate would be expected. Yet the observation has been made that the closer the relationship between offender and victim, the less likely there will be an arrest (Bell, 1984; Black, 1980). Empirical measurements of arrest rates have varied depending on the crime's definition and the officer's estimates of probable cause. Regardless of measurement techniques and the definitions of the crime chosen, arrests in incidents of domestic violence were infre-quent until the 1990s, with estimates vary-ing from 3% (Langley & Levy, 1977), 4% (Lawrenz, Lembo, & Schade, 1988), 7.5% (Holmes & Bibel, 1988), and 10% (Roy, 1977), to 13.9% (Bayley, 1986).

The bias against arrest was international at that time. Although most empirical research analyzed U.S. arrest practices, other studies in that time period confirmed similar results. For example, in one Canadian city, London, Ontario, prior to a new mandatory arrest policy, the police charged domestic violence assailants with assault in only 3% of the cases that they encountered. This is despite the fact that in 20% of the cases, victim injuries were sufficient to have police advise the victim to seek medical attention (Burris & Jaffe, 1983). Similarly, studies in Great Britain (Freeman, 1980; Hanmer et al., 1989a), the Netherlands (Zoomer, 1989), Australia (Hatty, 1989), and Northern Ireland (Boyle, 1980) consistently observed and criticized police refusal to make arrests in domestic violence cases. (For a summary of such literature, see Stanko, 1989.)

Officers may be reluctant to arrest for a variety of reasons. First, their department's priorities may effectively discourage arrests, which from the officer's perspective may be unjustified for a low-status misdemeanor with relatively poor chances of conviction (Buzawa & Buzawa, 1990). In this context, officers often believe that victims of domestic assault are inherently unreliable and unpredictable and, as a generality, do not make arrests based merely on complaints of assault (Sanders, 1988). Although Stanko (1985) believed the "unreliability" of victims was simply a self-serving, if pervasive myth, Sanders (1988) argued that such claims do in fact have legitimacy. The evidence of discrimination is not clear, or is at least inconsistent, because at least some early studies of police practice demonstrated that police did not differentiate domestic violence victims from equally problematic complainants for other types of crime (Sanders, 1988; Sheptycki, 1993).

Second, officers perceive physical risks to themselves as dramatically increasing when they abandon neutrality and attempt an arrest. There is, in fact, evidence to suggest that the most dangerous period during a domestic violence call is when the officer attempts arrest.

Third, some have argued that failure to make domestic arrests simply validates the observation that the police culture does not care about victim rights—especially when the victim complained of domestic abuse (Ferraro, 1989a; Stanko, 1985). Supporting this thesis are studies showing that when departmental policy requires officers to adopt presumptive arrest policies, mechanisms appear to develop to circumvent such a policy, even to the extent of implicitly defying orders of the police chief (Ferraro,

1989a). In contrast, many officers whom we have interviewed over the years appear to believe sincerely that arrest is not always the appropriate solution and that threatened violence could increase. Many fear that the victim may be placed in increased danger because of an arrest rather than an informal disposition.

CRISIS MANAGEMENT

Specialized Family Units

The first domestic violence innovation that police departments adopted were family violence crisis intervention teams. First developed by psychologists Morton Bard and Sydney Berkowitz in New York City under a Law Enforcement Assistance Administration (LEAA) grant in 1967, these programs quickly spread. By 1971, many major police departments had crisis intervention training programs, and dozens more had plans to adopt them (Liebman & Schwartz, 1973). Bard had previously employed these tactics for different types of offenses and believed that they had potential to reduce both officer injury and violence resulting from police officers' aggravating existing conflicts. Bard convinced Lou Mayo, who was then division director of the National Institute of Justice (NIJ), to select this as the first project for the NIJ's new Training and Demonstration Program. The program was established in 10 cities, using local resources and establishing procedures to develop departmental trainers.

The operation was to train a cadre of specialized officers in mediation techniques and crisis intervention. Officers were not "law enforcement" but instead were more akin to mental health specialists, whose primary role would be to mediate disputes and make referrals to clinical psychologists. Arrest was only to be used as a last resort.

Psychologists used small-group training techniques for a select number of officers. Innovative at that time, role playing was used extensively as a strategy for police training. Furthermore, correcting a major failing in practices of the time, Bard tracked domestic calls using an admittedly low-tech method of officers maintaining file cabinets in their cars with records and case histories of each call.

The officers became generalist-specialists who were not devoted solely to handling disturbance calls; instead, they performed their regular patrol duties when not covering a domestic call. Of course, to some extent, this was a compromise between the desire for a dedicated trained force and the relative inefficiency of special-purpose units. A common misperception, however, is that Bard intended to restrict crisis intervention training to specialized units. The initial unit was for purposes of the feasibility study only, and it was possible that the entire department would subsequently have to be trained. Another misconception was that these units never made arrests. Although clearly not the preferred intervention, arrests were made as the officer deemed appropriate (Mayo, personal communication, 1990).

The program did recognize the need for the entire department to receive some training because crisis intervention calls were frequent and unpredictable. Furthermore, it was believed that the basic techniques of crisis intervention enhanced all aspects of police performance, particularly with its emphasis on strategies for police safety. Subsequently, the New York City Family Crisis Intervention Unit and the follow-up programs received considerable favorable publicity from New York City and its federal sponsor, the project's funding source. It subsequently became a model for numerous other programs (Liebman & Schwartz, 1973) and received extensive publicity, being cited by the Kerner Report on Civil Disorder as a way to improve police performance of service functions (Parnas, 1993).

Did Crisis Intervention Work?

The efficacy of such units depended on several critical assumptions: (a) that a highly trained cadre of officers could transcend the abysmal performance levels of their department in general; (b) that once a group was trained, their performance would act as a catalyst for change among other officers; and (c) that, in most cases, domestic violence was best treated as a pathology of the family unit, not primarily a crime deserving of punishment.

Bard undertook the only systematic evaluation (if somewhat suspect because he was studying his own work) of these programs. In his final report for LEAA, he found that several favorable results had occurred: (a) Repeat calls to the police increased, reportedly because the victims were satisfied with past police intervention; (b) no officer injuries were sustained in the experimental precinct; (c) a high number of officer referrals were made to social and mental health agencies; and (d) arrests declined. Based on these findings, Bard concluded that the Crisis Intervention Unit appeared to be effective in reducing the rate and severity of domestic violence in the test precinct.

This self-proclaimed success of family crisis units drew skeptical reviews. A highly critical article by Donald Liebman and Jeffrey Schwartz (1973) challenged the basic assumptions of success in the New York City experiment. They noted that even more homicides appeared to occur in the experimental precinct and the total levels of domestic violence also apparently increased. Since the decrease in officer injury was itself not statistically significant, the conclusion was that available evidence did not support using "crisis intervention."

The practice of using crisis intervention teams also had several major operational disadvantages. A primary concern was that the potential volume of domestic violence cases would overwhelm available resources unless much higher funding levels for such specialized units were made available. In an era of constant budgetary pressure, any dedicated unit was subject to departmental critique as being an inefficient use of scarce resources. Here the costs of training and maintaining specialized units were obviously far greater than a "downscaled" general training program administered to all officers.

Second, officer burnout in other specialized units, such as narcotics and vice, suggested that long-term officer burnout and turnover would be a serious problem over time, leading to continually high training costs.

Third, many calls were reported ambiguously to 911 dispatch as "family problems," "loud arguing," or another offense entirely. This meant that, in practice, the specialized crisis intervention team was not even sent to many calls that actually involved assault. Some training, therefore, would be necessary for all patrol officers to facilitate the initial police response and ensure subsequent needed cooperation for intervention by the more experienced crisis intervention program.

Fourth, even Mayo and other proponents of crisis intervention techniques did not deny that there was operational disagreement as to whether the police as an institution would ever be capable of handling a social work type of function. One critique by Langley and Levy (1977) challenged whether police as individuals acting within an otherwise unsympathetic organizational milieu would ever really perform family crisis intervention instead of resorting to traditional law enforcement motifs. In fact, one study of the arrest practices of crisis intervention and mediation suggested that crisis intervention teams made even more arrests than they had

previously (Oppenlander, 1982). Although this fact should be neither surprising nor particularly discouraging given that police had previously made few such arrests even when needed, this was not the change that crisis intervention advocates had anticipated.

Finally, although the crisis intervention model might have limited viability in the case of well-trained officers entering low-intensity conflicts, the model was inherently easy to corrupt. Many departments were able to give cursory instructions in crisis intervention by senior patrol officers, not trained psychologists, and then publicly proclaim that their officers were well trained in "modern" crisis management, subverting the goals of the experiment.

The Abandonment of the Crisis Intervention Model

In the end, pressure from politicians alert to the growing concerns of spouse abuse advocates and the possibility of adverse legal actions made nonpunitive options typified by crisis intervention less attractive. If an incident involved physical violence and had an identifiable victim and perpetrator, it would not appropriately be considered a conflict situation to be managed (Ferraro, 1989b). As such, the conflict resolution model typified by crisis intervention teams did not fundamentally address victims' need for safety nor protect their legitimate right to seek retribution. In other words, techniques useful for verbal altercations or diffusing an impending episode of domestic violence were used even if someone had already perpetrated a serious assault (Loving, 1980).

By 1984, the U.S. Attorney General's Task Force on Family Violence took the position that the criminal justice system should take actions consistent with recognition that acts of domestic violence were *crimes*, not *conflict situations* (see also Victim Services Agency, 1988). As such, it was the responsibility of police to assign to an abuser criminal culpability, not to assume that a crisis had a "value-free" internal dynamic that could be "solved." The failure of police to do so previously now was assumed to preventing the offender from assuming responsibility for his actions or giving him reasons to reform. "Rather than stopping the violence and providing protection for the victim, mediation may inadvertently contribute to a dangerous escalation of violence" (U.S. Department of Justice, 1994, p. 23).

As the result of such criticism and the failure to receive new federal demonstration project funds, most of the departments that had adopted crisis intervention units in the 1970s ultimately abandoned or severely restricted such units at least when responding to domestic violence.

Few police departments currently rely on dedicated police family crisis intervention teams as the primary method of responding to domestic violence calls. Variations of this specialized detail, however, continue to be attempted or advocated sporadically, using police–social worker teams and specialized teams as backup resources for households that regularly report violence outbursts.

Also, despite not being in vogue at present, such teams may have set the stage for current reform efforts. Although the specific attention placed on crisis intervention units has waned, Mayo (1990) believed that these programs were indeed the first to be effective in sensitizing police departments to the issue of domestic violence. In fact, a survey conducted by Bard and NIJ found that more than 50% of the nearly 400 departments attending a nationwide executive training program on crisis intervention said they were actively pursuing increased attention to domestic violence within their agency.

DOES POLICE INTERVENTION HELP?

The View That Police Intervention Worsens Abuse

Early empirical research in the 1970s and research of some feminist scholars even to the present maintain that because police attitudes were hostile and skill levels abysmal police intervention had little positive impact— or even had a negative impact—on violent families. To support this, the observation of earliest reported empirical research, Marie Wilt and James Bannon's (1974) study of Detroit and Kansas City, has often been cited for the finding that the police had been to houses where a felonious assault had occurred five or more times in 50% of the cases and at least one time in 85% of the cases. Consequent research analyzing repeat calls to addresses of homicide and assault participants confirmed that police had previously responded to approximately 90% of homicide addresses (Bannon, 1974; Breedlove, Sandker, Kennish, & Sawtell, 1977; Victim Services Agency, 1988; Wilt & Bannon, 1977). Such figures, to a certain extent, exaggerated the percentage of repeat calls because of family turnover in low-income housing and assaults among or against other family members. The logical conclusion, however, was that inadequate police response either failed to prevent future violence or perhaps even encouraged recidivism.

This premise assumed that when officers perfunctorily intervene and give ineffectual or inappropriate advice to victims to "get a warrant" or warn the couple "not to disturb the peace," the abuser loses concern over criminal justice sanctions and might even feel reinforced about the normalcy of his conduct. Conversely, the victim is led to believe that society offers no recourse and in effect tacitly condones the abuse.

This view was supported by Hanmer et al. (1989b), who noted that "If the police don't offer unconditional protection to women, they are in fact condoning the violence" (p. 6; see also Ford, 1988; Straus, 1980). Finally, poor intervention may increase the risk that the offender will retaliate against the victim if the victim called the police or even, in a warped form of retribution, if the victim's screams indirectly caused the offender the embarrassment of a police encounter.

The View That Even Classic Intervention by the Police May Have Helped

Empirical research suggests a different, more complicated pattern of the effect of police intervention on future rates of domestic violence. Although some early studies reported that battered women dismissed the effectiveness of the police at stopping violence (Binney, Harkell, & Nixon, 1981; Bowker, 1982; Pahl, 1985; Roy, 1977), unfortunately, as noted by Elliott (1989), these studies were small samples that were nonrepresentative and did not differentiate between types of service provided. In addition, such studies did not distinguish between police behavior before and after recent trends toward more aggressive policies.

Victims who called the police have not typically reported that the police performed poorly. In one study conducted in Detroit, Michigan, the exact opposite was reported. Of 98 female victims responding, 95% (93) were in fact satisfied with the police response. The only dissatisfied respondents (as noted earlier) were the male victims, with none of the 12 men satisfied with the response (Buzawa & Austin, 1993).

To determine whether police intervention has had a positive impact, it is appropriate to see if victim goals are met. In the NCVS, composed of 128,000 interviews, 52% of domestic violence incidents were brought to police attention. The primary goal of a plurality (37%) of these women was the prevention of future assaults rather than rehabilitation via arrest or conviction for the activity for which the offender was charged. Of married women who did not call the police, 41% were subsequently assaulted within a 6-month period. In contrast, of those who did call, only 15% were reassaulted (Langan & Innes, 1986).

Intervention, however imperfect, may therefore have accounted for a 62% decline in rates of reassault among married women and a less significant, but still major, reduction of 41% of all women, including spouses, former spouses, and singles. Similarly, the crime survey study suggested that calling the police was associated with reduced risks of reported violence and, further, that there was no evidence that violence escalated as a result of intervention (Langan & Innes, 1986).

As discussed earlier, inappropriate police intervention strategies might have the deleterious effect of increasing the severity of the subsequent assaults due to retaliation or increased frustration. Langan and Innes (1986) in the NCVS, however, found no such result. In fact, they reported a reverse statistical correlation in which 2.9% of the women who called the police had a subsequent incident more serious than the first, compared with 4.5% of the women who did not call the police, translating into an apparent 36% improvement on intervention.

Are We in a Position to Evaluate the Effect of Classic Policing?

Clearly, the actual impact of police intervention is complex and requires additional research. Previous research examined victims whose problems have received police attention. As previously noted, a majority of victims do not call the police. Perhaps the most insidious effect of past poor police practices may be their contribution to the inordinately high rates of victims not calling the police, in other words "victim screening." A critical examination, therefore, needs to be made of those who do not make calls to determine if a significant percentage are deterred because of their past experiences or the "common knowledge" of poor police–victim interactions.

In addition, it cannot automatically be assumed that merely because a plurality of female victims view prevention of future violence as the primary goal of police intervention that this should be the primary goal of intervention in these cases. Typically, a crime has been committed, and traumatized individuals may not be asked to focus solely on preventing further pain without considering long-range implications. Finally, if any type of police intervention leads to lower rates of recidivism, a more effective and disciplined police intervention process could, and should in theory, prevent future violence.

CHAPTER 6

The Push for Criminal Justice Innovation

POLITICAL PRESSURE ON THE CRIMINAL JUSTICE SYSTEM

The modern movement for change in the police response to domestic violence arose from an unusual confluence of political and legal pressure from women's rights and battered women advocates, research, and organizational concerns over the possibility of liability if the police continued past practices of neglecting domestic violence victims.

Political pressure began to mount in the late 1960s and early 1970s over observed inadequacies of criminal justice responses to issues of interest to women. The women's rights and "feminist" movements that emerged or grew in strength at that time raised consciousness about societal neglect toward the unique problems of women. The inability of the criminal justice system to respond to violence against women was initially focused on rape and stranger assaults. Soon, however, concerns broadened, as women's rights activists recognized the severity of the problem of intimate violence.

One source of the pressure was the professionals who assisted battered women through shelters and legal services networks. These were, at first, largely decentralized, assisting battered women through hundreds if not thousands, of local community-based volunteer efforts. Later, such groups were assisted by statewide "coalitions" to prevent violence against women. Whether on their own or through the assistance of umbrella groups, shelters acquired the services of volunteer and paid attorneys, victim advocates, and social workers. These trained professionals in turn realized that the needs of domestic violence victims were not at that time being met by criminal justice agencies.

A pattern variously described as "patriarchal" or "cavalier" began to be used to describe the attitudes and, even more important, the practices of male-dominated police agencies and prosecutors. Concerns grew rapidly when advocates came to believe that police arrested everyone *but* domestic violence assailants (Berk & Loseke, 1980–1981). As a result, advocating more aggressive use of arrest became the natural consensus position among domestic violence activists (Coker, 2000; Ferraro, 1989b; Mills, 1999). This group provided the driving and articulate leadership that promoted enactment of state and federal statutes. This occurred first at the local and state levels and much later at the national level.

As discussed earlier, the reasons for the differences in perspective were explainable, if not adequate. Advocates for battered women were faced with policing that traditionally had emphasized public order and authority without official intervention in "private matters," that is, an organizational commitment to intervene in the family using only informal strategies for resolution. This was also amply reinforced, as Sanders (1988) noted, by police ideology in which protection of the "public order" was paramount, individual rights of secondary importance, and the safety of a particular victim was typically relegated to minimal importance.

The contribution of victim advocates was to argue that, regardless of the reason, police would not or could not adequately respond to the concerns of women. It was simply fact that women were more likely to be raped, murdered, and assaulted by someone they knew in private rather than public places. Conversely, men were more likely to be the victims of public disorder. Responding to public disorder was a role historically considered to be the core of responsibility and authority for police action.

Societal pressures emphasizing a legalistic intervention to long-standing social issues also became significant. To better understand the impetus for the changing role of law enforcement in domestic violence, it is essential to acknowledge the political climate of that era.

Since the widespread riots in the mid-1960s and the proliferation of drug usage at the same time, the "war on crime" became (and still is) a reliable vote winner. This strategy was first used successfully by presidential candidate Richard Nixon in 1968 and reinforced during the 1980 presidential campaign, when candidate Ronald Reagan argued that a "new morning in America" was at least partially dependent on being much "tougher" on criminals. A "tough on crime" or "war on crime" approach has become a consistent and successful political theme both among Republican candidates and, partially as a reaction, among "centrist" Democratic aspirants to higher office.

Although it remains to be seen whether emphasis changes with the new "War on Terrorism," recent decades have been a period marked with the increased societal propensity to use its coercive police powers to "solve" social problems and a relative unwillingness to invest in efforts to attempt to reform miscreants. Not surprisingly, criminal justice agencies have been increasing in budget, size of staff, and numbers of cases processed (Garland, 2001). Manning (1993) argued that the increasing role of law to maintain social control indicates the perceived weakness of informal controls. He stated that the pressure to criminalize domestic conflict—such as prohibition, Mothers Against Drunk Driving, and Students Against Drunk Driving—was more in the nature of a reform movement. Policing disorder and emphasizing misdemeanor arrests were part of and a further extension of this trend.

As might be expected, threats of random street violence and drug abuse were generally viewed as a law enforcement issue justifying a greater punitive response. Placed in this context, it is not surprising that the previously lax treatment of spouse abuse became a political issue.

There are certainly parallels with this period to the earlier reform era of the late 1880s. Key distinctions between the current and earlier reform periods have made the challenges to the system far more powerful. Today's mass media, national feminist and battered women's groups, and the growing ability of special interests to influence legislation have made the movement to increase law enforcement a national rather than regional phenomenon. Similarly the existence of support services to assist women with shelter and legal advocacy, even when not well funded, has given increased national visibility to the tremendous numbers of women injured by intimates. Finally, tantalizing stories of celebrity spouse abuse or death have been accorded enormous media attention, focusing public opinion on domestic violence.

Even after the start of domestic violence reforms, national attention to domestic violence was stoked by periodic instances of celebrity domestic violence. For example, In 1990, the national media was captivated by Carol Stuart's murder. Her husband, Charles Stuart, had frantically reported the crime using a cell phone to call 911 from their vehicle. He described in graphic detail how a Black man had shot both of them in an attempted robbery of their vehicle. This account was nationally broadcast both because of its inherent drama and because it played to White suburban fears about random street crime in urban areas committed by minorities. Many in the Boston Police Department attempted to place responsibility on an innocent Black man and to obtain his confession for the crime. These efforts were derailed by Charles Stuart's suicide, as others within the police department, as well as members of the press, developed leads that indicated Stuart was the killer. This incident was ultimately recognized as reflecting both society's tendency to blame street crime committed by minorities for most violence and police departments' inability to recognize domestic violence.

In 1994, the public allegations about domestic violence among celebrities—for example, Roseanne and Tom Arnold, Axel Rose—was rapidly followed by the national media circus attendant to the domestic violence and stalking involved in the O. J. Simpson–Nicole Simpson case. Not surprisingly, such media attention, including gavel to gavel coverage of the O. J. Simpson trial and repeated cover stories in newspapers and national newsmagazines, led to dramatic increases in calls for service to domestic violence hotlines, shelters, the police, and the courts.

THE ROLE OF RESEARCH IN FORCING CHANGE

Early Research

Research linking the criminal justice system to domestic violence also had a dramatic effect alerting the policy elite to the existence of the problems of domestic violence and legitimizing support for certain proarrest policies. In this regard, the research itself became a factor independent of the adequacy of its design, accuracy of conclusions, or the utility of the particular policy nostrums being promulgated.

Academic interest in family violence first emerged with concerns about child abuse. The seminal article "The Battered Child Syndrome" by Kemp, Silverman, Steele, Droegenmuller, and Silver (1962) focused on the necessity that physicians and other primary caregivers such as social workers recognize and intervene in such cases. This article and subsequent publications, however, focused less on criminal law implications and more on the etiology of the problem and treatment of the victim and offender.

Several years after the Kemp article, Parnas (1967) published "The Police Response to the Domestic Disturbance." This was followed in 1971 by Morton Bard's (as cited in Bard, 1973) "Police Discretion and Diversion of Incidents of Intra-Family Violence," examined in depth in Chapter 5 (Bard, 1967, 1973). This study analyzed the effect of a demonstration project on family crisis intervention, funded by the Law Enforcement Assistance Administration (LEAA). This project, in turn, became the theoretical foundation for many other family crisis intervention projects (Liebman & Schwartz, 1973).

Although the specific tenets and a critique of family crisis intervention as a technique is addressed in Chapter 5, the impact of the Bard study was that it reinforced the concept that changing the police response could dramatically reduce the impact of domestic violence. As a result, Louis Mayo, the former division director for the National Institute of Justice (NIJ), stated that he believed Bard deserved credit for drawing national attention to the police response. In 1967, Bard had approached the LEAA, suggesting that the agency was "unaware" of a major social problem. Although the domestic assault policy at that time was for police to do as little as possible and then leave the situation, Bard convinced LEAA that crisis intervention techniques had significant potential. As a result, the Office for Law Enforcement Assistance funded a feasibility study for a special unit of crisis intervention officers. As the following passage demonstrates, the impact of highly publicized research sponsored by the federal government can be at a scale disproportionate to the relative merits of the research itself. Garner and Maxwell (2000) noted that the political impact of the research was far greater than warranted based on empirical findings:

> Despite the weak design and results that indicated that the program had negative results on officers and victims, Bard's research was, in its day, quite influential. In addition to the visibility in the *New York Times*, between 1971 and 1976, the demonstration and testing divisions of the National Institute of Justice spent millions of dollars paying officers overtime to attend training that encouraged the use of Bard's intervention program in more than a dozen police departments across the United States. Elements of the program were promoted by the International Association of Chiefs of Police and discussed positively in the widely distributed Law Enforcement Bulletin (Mohn and Steblein, 1976). Police Family Crisis Intervention had become a major, if not the dominant, law enforcement approach

> to addressing domestic violence. . . . Despite the evaluation's negative program findings, the evaluators advocated their own untested version of police family violence intervention training (Wylie et al., 1976). *The clear lesson is that the strength of federal financial support for a social intervention does not necessarily mean there is an extensive body of knowledge supporting the efficacy of that approach.* (Garner & Maxwell, 2000, p. 87; emphasis added)

The next important study, Domestic Violence and the Police, was by Marie Wilt and James Bannon (1977). They demonstrated that domestic violence was directly related to homicide; that in 85% of incidents, the police had been called at least once before; and that in 50% of incidents, police had been called five or more times. Although it was concluded that an ineffective police response contributed to the excessive rates of death and injury to victims and the high cost of intervention for police departments, no suggestions were given for exactly how the police could intervene effectively.

This body of domestic violence research was supported by other research criticizing the efficacy of rehabilitation efforts for violent offenders. Lipton, Martinson, and Wilks (1975) famous research on the impact of rehabilitation and their conclusion that "nothing worked" contributed to the temporary eclipse of the influence of researchers. After all, if researchers acknowledged that known approaches to date had been a failure, then clearly more drastic measures were needed. Whereas societal reactions to intervention failures had previously been to question the quality of the intervention or the resources allocated to its implementation, the current political climate was far less tolerant of such "benevolent" explanations.

The cumulative impact of this research, as well as subsequent studies, contributed to developing a consensus among researchers and policymakers regarding the then-current police policies of noninterference. There was widespread agreement that passive police responses further contributed to societal tolerance and high rates of domestic violence and that alternate police strategies could reverse this trend.

The Evolution of Research Supporting the Primacy of Arrest

By the 1970s, there was widespread disillusionment among practitioners, researchers, and some police administrators regarding then-current domestic violence policies and practices. In part, this was a reflection of the general societal movement away from what Garland (2001) referred to as "penal welfares." Among criminologists, major philosophical differences began to surface within the discipline, whereas previously a far more consistent posture had been taken toward policy.

Debates regarding the control of domestic violence as a possible exception to policies of tough enforcement continued to persist, however. One side argued that the dichotomy between aggressive enforcement against street crime and lax enforcement of crimes against intimates was justified in that domestic incidents involved "families" and intimate partners. Still others believed such incidents were more trivial and less likely to incur injury, that victims were less likely to desire police intervention and prosecution, and that therefore, an arrest would not result in conviction, negating the value of such efforts (Myers & Hagan, 1979). Many writers successfully challenged these assumptions and instead maintained that criminal justice institutions were demonstrating sexist behavior by presenting such rationales (Dobash & Dobash, 1979; Matoesian, 1993; Smart, 1986). Over time, there was a

growing concern that the use of formal social controls needed to be increased with an emphasis on legal remedies. These sentiments were highlighted by a National Academy of Sciences report addressing the role of criminal justice sanctions as an effective crime control strategy (Blumstein, Cohen, & Nagin, 1978).

Such concerns gradually permeated practitioners, policymakers and the general attitudes of the public (Garland, 2001). This represented substantial change. Although reliance on the law is often believed to be a result of the failure of informal social controls (Black, 1976), many sociologists initially doubted the ability of laws to effect levels of domestic violence (Straus, 1977). Nonetheless, primary emphasis began shifting to increased police use of arrests as a deterrent to domestic violence. It has long been known that arresting certain domestic violence offenders was both proper and essential, at least in some situations. After all, making an arrest was the only method by which police could ensure separation of the couple and the prevention of violence, at least until the offender was released. Similarly, despite a strong past bias against arrest, arrests for non-domestic-violence–specific charges, such as drunk and disorderly conduct or public intoxication, were often used. Also, arrests were an acknowledged method for the police to regain control from a disrespectful or otherwise threatening assailant and maintain the officer's situational dominance (Bittner, 1967, 1974).

In any event, the early 1980s had shattered the consensus on the historically limited role of arrest. It had been replaced by an expanding debate among policy makers, researchers, practitioners, and advocates about arrest as a mechanism to deter violence and a means to strengthening other traditional criminal justice measures that were clearly inadequate.

Deterrence As a Rationale for Police Acton

The concept of deterrence as a general preference for crime control became a dominant perspective in mainstream academic literature and in policy circles. Theories that now shape official thinking and action are control theories of various kinds. They posit that offenses are not the result of specific unmet individual needs, such as inadequate socialization or deprivations, but rather inadequate societal controls (Garland, 2001). Not surprisingly, the two trends were linked; many researchers and activists increasingly advocated deterrence as a justification for use of arrest (see especially Dobash & Dobash, 1979; D. Martin, 1976). It is in this context that research favoring use of arrests flourished.

Beginning in the 1970s, a series of experiments, involving some of the country's most prominent researchers, were conducted to try to determine whether police actions specifically deterred offenders and, secondarily, to develop the most effective police response to domestic violence. These are worth exploring in depth because of their key importance in stimulating change and the resultant ongoing debates over both the reliability and the validity of their findings, as well as their impact on current policies.

The Minneapolis Domestic Violence Experiment

Sherman and Berk (1984a, 1984b) conducted the Minneapolis Domestic Violence Experiment (MDVE), reported as "The Specific Deterrent Effects of Arrest for Domestic Assault," in the early 1980s. This report had a virtually unprecedented impact in changing then-current police practices. The research was initially funded by the NIJ to study application of deterrence theory and

arose from a National Academy of Sciences Report titled *Deterrence and Incapacitation: Estimating the Effects of Criminal Sanctions on Crime Rates*, edited by Blumstein et al. (1978).

The MDVE asked 51 volunteer patrol officers in two precincts to adopt one of three possible responses to situations in which there was probable cause to believe that domestic violence had occurred. Officers were randomly assigned one of three choices: to separate the parties by ordering one of them to leave, to advise them of alternatives (possibly including mediating disputes), or simply to arrest the abuser. Over a period of approximately 17 months, 330 cases were generated. The authors then evaluated the possible success of these various "treatments" in deterring recidivism. Recidivism was measured both by official arrest statistics, such as arrest reports and, when available, by victim interviews. The researchers later reported that 10% of those arrested, 19% of those advised of alternatives, and 24% of those merely removed repeated violence (Sherman & Berk, 1984a). From this, they concluded that arrest provided the strongest deterrent to future violence and consequently was the preferred police response.

It is important to realize that the MDVE was a limited experimental design that did not purport to definitely answer or even necessarily address the question of the "proper" police response to domestic violence.

Methodological Concerns of the MDVE

In fact, the Minneapolis study was strongly critiqued both for its methodology and for its conclusions. Severe criticism was raised in several areas. Responding officers apparently had advance knowledge of the response they were to make. As such, they had opportunity to reclassify offenses to fall outside the parameters of the experiment (Mederer & Gelles, 1989). They might do so if an arrest was assigned despite the officers not desiring to do so—either because of police traditions or possibly to avoid extra paperwork. Even in official statistics of the experiment, a number of cases (17) were dropped from the experiment, and in fully 56 of 330 cases (17%), the officers gave a treatment different than that required.

Unionized, rank-and-file police officers have never been committed to honoring an experiment by academic outsiders (not exactly their favorite group). There is, in fact, considerable evidence that the MDVE experiment did not control the officers. Three of the fifty-one officers assigned to participate in the study made most of the arrests, suggesting that the other officers assigned to participate may have actively or passively subverted randomization techniques. Furthermore, the study only used volunteer officers. This, plus anecdotal evidence, strongly suggests that most officers simply acted the way they thought the situation demanded, indirectly sabotaging the project's validity. Similarly, 5% (16) of the 314 cases were excluded (Sherman & Berk, 1984a).

The victim measurements were also questionable. Only 49% responded in the 6 months following interviews, leaving conclusions based on the database innately suspect. Binder and Meeker (1988) and Lempert (1987, 1989) provided a thorough critique of the MDVE, including these as well as additional concerns. Gartin (1991) attempted to address many of the methodological concerns by a reanalysis of the archived data from the MDVE and found that statistical significance depended on which data sources were used and how the data were analyzed. Gartin concluded that arrest did not have as great a specific deterrent effect as the original research had suggested.

The external validity or generalizability of the conclusions in this study was also suspect. The actions of the officers were, by the nature of the experiment, treated in a vacuum largely independent of the downstream effect of other criminal justice actors. In our view, it is difficult to determine the effect of any police action without explaining how domestic violence prosecutors, courts, probation officers, or social service agencies subsequently handle the cases.

Despite initial disclaimers to the contrary, the Sherman and Berk study immediately became the most cited study in the field. Findings were reported in the *New York Times* (Boffey, 1983), in a Police Foundation report (Sherman & Berk, 1984a), in numerous academic journals (Berk & Sherman, 1988; Sherman & Berk, 1984b), and were widely publicized across the country as a whole. Hundreds of newspapers and nationally syndicated columnists discussed these findings, and several major television networks provided prime-time news coverage, often with special documentaries (Fagan, 1988; Sherman & Cohn, 1989). The 1984 Attorney General's Task Force on Family Violence even cited the MDVE findings as a basis for recommending that all law enforcement agencies should develop policies requiring arrest as the preferred response for domestic violence incidents (U.S. Attorney General's Task Force on Family Violence, 1984).

In their summary of the significance of the MDVE, Maxwell, Garner, and Fagan (2001) stated that "a 1989 survey of local police departments concluded that the published results of MDVE may have substantially influenced over one-third of the police departments responding to their survey to adopt a proarrest policy" (p. 4).

The Role of Publicity in Research

Part of the reason for the profound impact of the Minneapolis Domestic Violence Experiment was the promotional campaign that followed. At least one of the authors, Professor Sherman, stated that he believed it was the "obligation" of social scientists to solicit publicity (Sherman & Cohn, 1989). He recounted how he and his colleagues made decisions about how to manage the story, including persuading local television to feature documentaries or "action" tapes, for national news shows (even before the results of the experiment were known). Efforts to continue to manage the press continued even to the extent of releasing the final results on the Sunday before Memorial Day, assuming that there would have less competition on a slow news day (Sherman & Cohn, 1989) and notifying the *MacNeil/Lehrer NewsHour* of the study's release well in advance.

Such publicity efforts, extraordinary for social science research, were justified as an attempt to "get the attention of key audiences effecting police department policies" (Sherman & Cohn, 1989, p. 121). As Sherman remarked, he also "wanted the audiences to be influenced by the recommendations and be more willing to control replications and random experiments in general" (p. 122). The NIJ did not release any publications on the study, hold any meetings or conferences, nor fund any demonstration programs testing the use of arrest, however. The massive publicity generated by this research was almost entirely due to the efforts of individuals (Garner and Maxwell, 2000).

In any event, the impact of the Minneapolis study was certainly due in part to the extreme publicity it received and the impression that its conclusions, however tentative, were federally funded and supported. Under such conditions, administrative debates on the relative merits of arrest compared with

other potential avenues of reform became nearly irrelevant. In fact, despite its acknowledged limitations, by the mid-1980s the study reinforced to the point of orthodoxy the view among feminists that police should arrest and a mandatory arrest policy should be instituted when possible.

For this reason, the research and policy implications of the MDVE and the attendant publicity campaign clearly deserve extensive study. An interesting dialogue between proponents and opponents of such research was published in several articles (Binder & Meeker, 1988; Sherman & Cohn, 1989) and became the topic of a widely attended debate at the 1990 Academy of Criminal Justice Sciences Annual Meeting in Denver. Echoes of these debates have continued over the years as reanalyses and discussions of the findings continue to be conducted (Maxwell et al., 2001).

All parties acknowledged that widely reported research, although preliminary in nature, might dramatically affect social policy. As might be expected, the differences among the participants was are in the perception of the duty of researchers. Binder found it more responsible to wait until final research was available before publicizing preliminary findings. In contrast, Sherman stated that researchers had a duty to try to effect change in response to a critical problem. He believed this duty existed despite his knowledge of research limitations and the concern of others that prematurely basing policy on a preliminary study that is extensively publicized might cause adoption of a policy that would do more harm than good (Lempert, 1987).

Although we commend Sherman's sense of public responsibility, we believe the concerns expressed by Binder and Meeker (1992) greatly outweigh claims of civic duty. Premature publication and reliance on preliminary research may lead to the adoption of faulty policies, which could scarcely be imagined in the context of experiments on new drugs or proposed medical interventions. Certainly, it is unrealistic to assume that agencies will simply change their methods of operation when future research provides different conclusions or finds unanticipated consequences (cf. Mastrofski & Uchida, 1993).

Finally, there are practical dilemmas to this approach. Stated succinctly, "Sherman's take-the-best-evidence-and-run-with-it approach to policy making . . . will inevitably generate a policy zigzagging that requires of police departments and policymakers a much greater flexibility than is evident in most communities" (Mastrofski & Uchida, 1993, p. 265). It also implies a willingness to subject social policies to the uncertainties of preliminary social science. We believe this is inherently arrogant and potentially harmful. When policies about the application of criminal sanctions change, they do so principally because they respond to substantial potential shifts in the degree of moral outrage or tolerance toward a given crime and the prospects of a particular reform to address that crime. Ultimately, the risk is that police may become less likely to respond to accurate scientific evidence about the impact of proposed policies, a major defeat for social science research in general. This perhaps contributes to the decline in the influence of social science research recently noted by Garland (2001).

The extensive publicity given to this study—and to many of the subsequent "policy-oriented" studies that followed—should be placed in context. Could this be considered the inevitable result of the growing predominance of "professional" experts and researchers who now move freely from "think tanks" to semiautonomous university centers, depending on which administration is in charge? For these researchers, the sponsorship of their research and, in some cases, even for the bulk of their compensation, was primarily dependent not on excellence in teaching but on successfully appealing for federal funds from "activist" government agencies.

Logically, to continue to attract funding, the inherent bias of such research would be to show that "reforms" positively affected policy. The result may arguably have been better, more policy-specific research; undoubtedly, it did result in a huge increase in the influence of preliminary "research" into the development of national policies in many areas, including domestic violence.

The Impact of the MDVE

Although the Minneapolis experiment might best be referred to as being merely a "pilot study," few now deny its great policy impact. This occurred directly on policymakers and indirectly via researchers. Often, other researchers or the policy-making elite unrealistically assumed that the study demonstrated that arrest was always the best policy (Humphreys & Humphreys, 1985). Similarly, as we review later in this chapter, federally funded research on the proper role of the criminal justice response to domestic violence was dominated by the six replications of the Minneapolis experiment. As a result of funding limitations, virtually no alternatives to arrests were explored in federally funded research projects.

In any event, within 1 year of the study's first publication, almost two thirds of major police departments had heard of the Minneapolis experiment, and three quarters of the departments correctly remembered its general conclusion that arrest was the preferable police response. Similarly, the number of police departments encouraging arrests for domestic violence tripled in 1 year from only 10% to 31%—a figure that increased again to 46% by 1986 (with more than 30% of all such departments stating they had changed their position at least partially due to the

Minneapolis study). This impact was immense. The fact that it generated wide-scale abandonment of police doctrine that had remained static for decades is still probably an understatement of its importance in changing policy. The study served as a catalyst for ongoing politically based efforts at change, being favorably cited by other influential researchers and policymakers who were then considering implementing state domestic violence laws (Cohn & Sherman, 1987).

Deterrence Theory and the MDVE

Apart from concerted efforts to publicize the findings, why did the MDVE so resonate with policymakers? In part, it was due to the emergence of the predominance of the theory of deterrence. As indicated earlier, advocates and battered women's support groups seized Sherman and Berk's conclusions. For years, their advocacy and litigation had little visible effect on convincing police departments of the seriousness of domestic violence and the need for greater victim respect. Therefore, the attention placed on the study was fortuitous, supporting an agenda favored by a significant policy elite. Under such conditions, research disclaimers were predictably ignored.

In addition, the belief that arrest would actually stop domestic violence offenders from reoffending had a great deal of intuitive appeal. Arrest or the potential for arrest would provide a deterrent to potential offenders. At that point in time, consideration was not given to the criminal justice response once an arrest had been made. As we discuss in Chapter 11, the likelihood of a case continuing in the criminal justice system was highly unlikely; however, at the time, arrest itself was thought to provide an end point in the cycle of victimization for women.

Indeed, this could be seen as part of a trend among "crime control" proponents to advocate deterrence as a mechanism to prevent future criminal behavior. Von Hirsch (1985) noted the radical shift from a "treatment model" favoring offender rehabilitation predominant during the 1960s and early 1970s to one that implicitly conceded that rehabilitation had little effect. The increased challenge to the treatment model left a void that deterrence theorists happily filled. Economists began to apply their disciplines to criminal justice policy development, an area that had been the province of sociologists, psychologists, and political scientists. They theorized that "crime could effectively be reduced . . . through sentencing policies aimed at *intimidating* potential offenders" (Von Hirsch, 1985, p. 7).

The Replication Studies

Part of the reason for the extensive publicity campaign discussed earlier was to pressure the NIJ to replicate the study in additional cities instead of using its scarce resources to focus research on victims or other aspects of the response to domestic violence. Certainly Sherman and Berk (1984a, 1984b) encouraged replication. In addition, questions, criticisms, and concerns were escalating in the research community, and support for replications became widespread. In deciding to replicate the MDVE, the researchers probably realized that it was not in the political interests of the NIJ to support replication studies because their earlier findings were in accordance with the political preferences and ideologies of the federal government at that time (Garner & Maxwell, 2000).

In any event, the NIJ decided to expend most of its limited research funds on domestic violence on six experimental replications of the MDVE study. It is interesting that a concern among other researchers was the huge expenditure of funds to employ essentially the same type of research methodology. Their concerns, which were not addressed by the NIJ, focused more on victims' needs and employing designs that encompassed more qualitative components, seeking input from victims directly. This became a source of controversy among other researchers, although, according to Joel Garner (who was at that point an NIJ program manager), arguments against funding experimental research designs were not persuasive (Garner, 1990).

In any event, the NIJ subsequently funded six additional experiments. These experiments were collectively known as the "Replication Studies," and their results were revealing.

Omaha, Nebraska

Dunford, Huizinga, and Elliott (1989) conducted the first replication study in Omaha, Nebraska. When both victim and offender were present (330 cases), the officers were explicitly instructed at the time of their initial response as to which of the three options they should use, that is, to arrest, to separate the parties by removing the offender from the household, or to use mediation. Compared with the MDVE, greatly improved methodology, including matching ethnic backgrounds of the victims to female interviewers, was used to attain victim cooperation and to categorize resultant input. Not surprisingly, far more victims cooperated (73% at 6 months).

Dunford and his colleagues (1989) reported that arrested offenders were more likely to reoffend based on official police data but less likely to reoffend based on victim interviews. These findings were not statistically significant, however, leading the researchers to conclude that the relative impact of arrest versus other treatments was not profound because arrest by itself did not appear to deter further assaults any more than separation or mediation. Although this did not appear to provide any rationale for making arrests—the preferred plan—the

study also did not find that using arrests increased subsequent assaults. From this, Dunford et al. concluded the following: "It is clear, however, that arrest, by itself, was not effective in reducing or preventing continuing domestic conflict in Omaha, and that a dependence on arrest to reduce such conflict is unwarranted, perhaps erroneous and even counterproductive" (p. 67).

A second component (247 cases) involved offenders who had already vacated the premises. Offenders in this group were randomly assigned to issuance of a warrant or to no further police action. This data set provided the surprising result that more than 40% of the officers were not present when the police arrived. This was significant because little attention had been paid to the fact that a large percentage of offenders left before police arrived, and it led future researchers to question whether, in fact, there were differences between offenders who remained and those who stayed (Buzawa et al., 1999; Dunford, 1990; Dunford, Huizinga, & Elliott, 1989, 1990).

There were also clear differences based on the treatment chosen when the offender was absent. Absent offenders who were the subject of an arrest warrant were less than half as likely to recidivate than others—5.4% versus 11.9% (Dunford et al., 1989). Therefore, this experiment provided tentative evidence that the issuance of a pending arrest warrant appeared to deter prospective offenses.

In addition to the more structured experimental approach, the researchers also reviewed police records for 45 months after the survey began. They found that although victims were at most risk for repeat violence immediately after the first incident, almost 25% were significantly reabused after the first anniversary of their prior contact with the criminal justice system. This finding presented interesting policy implications about whether contact with the criminal justice system does, in fact, deter offenders and whether as a routine basis probationary supervision of assailants should be extended.

Milwaukee, Wisconsin

A second replication study, by Sherman, Schmidt et al. (1992), was conducted in Milwaukee, Wisconsin. Many of the earlier methodological problems of the MDVE were expressly addressed by this research design. These researchers chose to study four police districts containing high concentrations of minorities and compare the results of offenders who were merely warned by the police with those who were arrested and held for a short period of time (3 hours) and those arrested and held for 12 hours. The duration of holding was tested to see if a "short arrest and hold" might merely provoke an offender.

It was true that when repeat violence was measured after 6 months, arrest deterred more than by the mere issuance of a warning, whereas the duration of the hold period did not significantly effect outcome. This result, however, did not continue. Outcomes of arrest versus warning groups became roughly equal up to 11 months. After that time period, the arrested group showed even higher levels of recidivism. The report concluded that arrests appeared to deter the employed offender but not the unemployed (Sherman, Smith, Schmidt, & Rogan, 1992).

Perhaps this result should not have been surprising. Less self-promoted research such as that of Dutton (1987) had long reported that being arrested appeared only to have an effect for 6 months, a relatively short period. Within 30 months, there was a 40% recidivism rate despite arrest. In short, Dutton had already concluded that any contact with the criminal justice system, unless reinforced by long-term counseling or other activities, might simply cause a relatively short-term

behavioral change. Hirschel, Hutchson, & Dean (1992) reported that offenders might not be concerned about the impact of arrest because many have a long history or arrests or are aware of the fact that arrest seldom leads to prosecution.

In addition, the research strongly suggested that deterrence occurred among many of those arrested. Specifically, arrest appeared to deter White offenders with a reduction rate of approximately 39% over those offenders who were merely warned—versus a modest increase among Black offenders. Unemployed offenders, both Black and White, appeared to be least deterred by arrest, being the group most likely to recidivate in general and most likely, statistically, to appear to show a long-term negative effect after arrest.

These results have received considerable, if perhaps unwarranted, speculation as to their meaning and importance. It is not surprising that blacks who may have a history of negative experiences with many police departments, including that of Milwaukee, might react adversely to arrest, especially if the arrest is not sensitively carried out or if the victim is not supplied with information as to how she can obtain support services. Although difficult to quantify in the context of a mass experiment, it may be the result of the behavioral interaction between the officer and Black citizens that partially or even primarily accounts for part of the variance between racial groups not explained by disparate employment status.

The results of the unemployed offenders are even more intriguing. Logically, if an offender has had significant past experience with the police, he might not be as deterred as someone who has not and thus the experience with police intervention is a shock. This may not necessarily mean, however, that arrest was the wrong strategy to pursue with this group. Instead, it may signify that police and courts should implement complementary actions after an arrest. Unfortunately, because of the somewhat artificial strictures of this experimental design, this thesis could not be tested.

Charlotte, North Carolina

Hirschel, Hutchison, Dean, Kelley, and Pesackis (1991) conducted the third replication study in Charlotte, North Carolina. Charlotte has a relatively high crime rate and high unemployment. In addition, at the time of the study, the city had about a 70% minority population allowing the researchers to address the police response to this subpopulation. The Charlotte experiment focused on misdemeanor-level violence committed in that city during a 23-month period (August 1987 to June 1989). Cases were randomly assigned to three categories of responses: (a) advising or separation of couples, (b) issuing a citation for the offender to appear in court, and (c) arresting the offender at the scene. In addition, all officers were instructed to advise each victim of the availability of shelters and victim assistance programs.

According to official statistics, arrest was associated with increased reoffending. This contrasted with the findings from victim interviews in which arrest was associated with reduced reoffending. Neither finding was statistically significant, however, and the researchers concluded that the data did not support arrest as being more effective in deterring subsequent assaults. Subsequently Garner and Maxwell (2000) suggested that the research designs used may not have been capable of detecting differences that could have existed due to the number of interviews (338) in this case.

The group and jurisdiction selected in Charlotte may have contributed to an especially "tough" test of the effects of arrest. Almost 70% of the offenders had previous criminal histories. It had been hypothesized

that this group is among the least likely to be deterred by yet another arrest (Sherman, Schmidt et al., 1992). Of even greater importance, only 35.5% of those arrested or who had received a citation were ever prosecuted, and less than 1% ever spent time in jail beyond the initial arrest. Simply put, arrest used in an administrative vacuum appeared unlikely to be a significant deterrent to a group of offenders already inured by past experiences with the criminal justice system.

Finally, we believe that excluding those victims who wanted an arrest from the study, comprising 68% of all misdemeanor arrests, ignored the victim-empowering feature of following her preferences. Frankly, we believe a much better measure would have been recidivism in the group that was *excluded* from the experiment because the victims wanted arrest.

Colorado Springs, Colorado

Berk, Campbell, Klap, and Western (1992) conducted the fourth replication study for a 2-year period in Colorado Springs, Colorado. They drew a large sample—1,658 incidents of misdemeanor violence. The study was unusual in several ways. It involved a highly unrepresentative proportion of military personnel (more than 24% of the offenders and 7% of the victims). Also, only 38% of the cases involved an assault, whereas others were claims of "harassment," "menacing," and other related offenses.

This study assigned respondents to one of four options: (a) an emergency order of protection alone, (b) the protective order coupled with arrest, (c) the protective order coupled with crisis counseling, and (d) the officer's response limited to merely restoring order (Berk et al., 1992). Although victim interviews found a deterrent effect, this was not reflected by the official data.

Of equal or greater importance, the study appeared to show only a limited effect of a case being assigned to the Safe Streets Unit; 18.8% of those who received their services reported further violence compared with 22.4% of those who had not. This 3.6% difference was not statistically significant nor was the frequency of reported abuse markedly different.

Miami, Florida

Pate and Hamilton (1992) conducted a fifth replication from August 1987 to July 1989 in the Metro-Dade Police Department. The study involved 907 cases in which the officers had arrest discretion. The sample was somewhat unusual in that it only involved male offenders due to then-current Florida law.

Two interventions were tested—arrest versus nonarrest as an initial action and whether there was a follow-up assignment to the Safe Streets Unit. This specialized unit consisted of a number of detectives, supervisors and support staff all whom had received an intensive 150-hour training course in handling domestic violence. The unit established case histories and interviewed the couple. They tried to assist parties to reach acceptable solutions to their problems. Referrals to appropriate agencies and outside resources were also made. Although updated in its approach, this unit shared the same orientation that the Family Crisis Intervention Teams first used in New York City, which we discuss later in this chapter.

Based on victim interviews and police records, this study reported significant differences between those offenders who were arrested and those who were not. Using the common 6-month follow-up, 14.6% of arrested abusers had reabused their victims compared with 26.9% of those who were not arrested. In addition, the frequency of violence

was greater among those who had not been arrested. Victim's reports, however, indicated that there was no significant effect of treatment chosen on the 29% that were unemployed offenders (Pate & Hamilton, 1992).

A second experiment with this data involved the provision of follow-up police services. The authors reported that there were no significant differences in revictimization rates for those victims receiving follow-up services based both on official police data and victim interviews (Pate, Hamilton, & Annan, 1991).

A New Analysis of the Data

The Atlanta Police Department was intended to be the seventh site of a replication study, but the researchers never submitted a report to the NIJ nor did they ever publish the findings. Maxwell, Garner, and Fagan (2001) recently reported a new analysis of the data from the replication studies with the exception of Omaha, and, of course, Atlanta. Their analysis attempted to address the concern that none of the replication studies employed the same outcome measures, measurement strategies, or the methodologies as the MDVE. They determined that the only analyses possible were based on prevalence, frequency, and time to failure in official records and prevalence and frequency of reoffending in victim interviews. Although they did report that overall arrest decreased the likelihood of reoffending, the findings were not statistically significant when using official data but were significant when analyzing victim report data.

It can be argued that victims only report a small percentage of reoffending, however, and that those who are willing to be interviewed or could be located may be those who were most likely *not* to be revictimized. In research involving several data sets, Buzawa & Hotaling found that victims only reported about half of new offenses. Those dissatisfied with the police response and who believed that the police either overreacted or increased the danger of the situation were unwilling—and, in fact, feared—disclosing new assaults (Buzawa et al., 1999; Buzawa & Hotaling, 2000; Hotaling & Buzawa, 2001). Also, the research protocol in how follow-up interviews were conducted in the replication studies might easily have affected the willingness of victims to disclose an unreported assault to a researcher out of fear that the offender would be arrested.

In addition, we now have research suggesting that many offenders find new victims once a victim is unwilling to tolerate violence or reports it to the police (Buzawa et al., 1999). Therefore, although it is possible for revictimization to be reduced, reoffending rates may remain stable.

The Reaction to the Replication Studies

Reaction to the replication studies and their failure to confirm the earlier MDVE findings were predictable. Feminists and battered women advocates severely criticized their methodology, their sensitivity to policy implications, and their conclusions (Bowman, 1992; Zorza, 1994; Zorza & Woods, 1994). Bowman wrote the following:

Quantitative research has often elicited a good deal of criticism from feminists. Quantitative methods are considered suspect because they place a greater value on "objective" and quantifiable information than on other sources of knowledge. Relying solely on such data assumes a separation—indeed, a distance—between the researcher and the object of study since they isolate the factors under study from their socio-economic and historical context. Further, there is a failure to hear directly from the victim herself and include data as to how *she* interprets the situation. In the domestic violence field, moreover, survey research is greeted with particular mistrust

because of early studies, which were perceived as both insensitive in their design and biased in their results. (p. 201)

An especially telling critique has been leveled at the heart of the experimental approach—isolating one individual variable (in this case, arrest) from all other factors and then assuming that this factor may truly be studied independent of its organizational and societal milieu. Zorza and Wood's (1994) overall analysis of the replication studies best summarizes this position:

The problem inherent in police replication studies is that they isolate the initial police response from any other possible responses to domestic abuse and fail to realize that the effect of arrest on domestic abuse is only one of potentially dozens of issues, which should be studied. Although the experimenters occasionally reported the rarity of conviction and especially imprisonment, they failed to evaluate what steps prosecutors and the courts took and why, what sentences the offenders received, what type of batterer treatment programs were utilized and for how long, how batterers were monitored for attendance . . . were orders of protection issued, or what assistance was provided to the victims . . . In the absence of answers to all these questions, one cannot properly assess whether some other part of the system supported or completely undermined police efforts. (p. 972)

Deterrence theorists may simply treat these studies as a failure to confirm the deterrence hypothesis without providing any exceptionally insightful views of the necessary role of the police and the rest of the criminal justice system on the control of domestic violence. Schmidt, Smith, et al. (1992) state it in following manner:

A policy of not arresting at all may erode the general deterrent effect of arrest on potential spouse abusers. Yet a policy of arresting all offenders may simply produce more violence among suspects who have a low stake in conformity. (p. 688)

We believe that there is a middle ground. Regardless of their individual and collective methodological shortcomings, the replication studies collectively suggest that the role of arrest as a monolithic response for responding to all cases of domestic violence is problematic. Deterrence may exist for some but not all offenders. Furthermore, although not addressed by the replication studies, what is of at least equal significance is the differential impact of arrest on victims. Nonetheless, arrest clearly is an essential tool even if it does not deter certain types of offenders. As we have seen with the MDVE, extensively published research does not guarantee that the results will remain constant in other settings and at other times. Although some offenders may not be deterred, others (both those arrested and those who might otherwise batter in the future) may be so dissuaded.

In any event, such a conclusion would place a wholly inappropriate emphasis on the concept of deterrence. Arrest historically has not been used because of its capacity to deter offenders, but to serve as the primary vehicle by which offenders are brought into the criminal justice system. In addition, it is an important reminder to the victim, the offender, and society at large that particular conduct will not be permitted. These issues are discussed further in Chapter 8.

We believe that the replication studies should be considered along with other evidence suggesting the necessity of providing a coordinated criminal justice response. Arrest could then be a useful tool that is part of a coordinated response rather than an end by itself.

Dunford et al. (1989) perhaps best stated this conclusion when discussing the implications of the Omaha replication study:

> Since arresting suspects is expensive and conflicts/assaults do not appear to increase when arrests are not made, one response to these data might be a recommendation to

effect informal dispositions (separate or mediate) in cases of misdemeanor domestic assaults in Omaha. A significant problem with this approach, however, is that it seems ethically inappropriate, it violates the recommendations of the Attorney General's Task Force . . . and it may be illegal . . . to patently ignore the rights of victims. (p. 204)

A policy that encourages, but does not mandate arrest may be useful from several points of view. First, it would allow officers . . . to respond to the wishes of victims who do not want, for a variety of reasons, suspects arrested. . . . Second, when an arrest is seen as an entry point into a coordinated criminal justice system rather than an end point, it may shift the burden of deterrence from a single official police intervention (arrest) to a sequence of other interventions, each of which may have some salutary effect. This view recognizes that suspects chronically involved in domestic violence most frequently do not admit to having a problem in this regard . . . are not easily treated . . . and do not seek help voluntarily . . . to deal with such problems and thus might require sustained long-term interventions to change their ways. It supports arrest in domestic assault instances in which probable cause for an arrest is present and when victims support the arrest of suspects, not because arrest is a panacea for deterring domestic violence, but because of penalties and the leverage that an arrest implicitly facilitates. (pp. 61–77)

LEGAL LIABILITY AS AN AGENT FOR CHANGE

The final major force that changed the police response to domestic violence was that individual officers as well as entire police departments as organizations were exposed to substantive risks of liability awards, fines, and injunctions if they failed to make an arrest for domestic assault. This concern dramatically restricted their freedom to continue with past practices and also contributed to the development of written policies and training regarding domestic violence.

Several lawsuits in the late 1970s claimed that the Oakland, California, and New York City police departments failed to protect battered women (*Bruno v. Codd*, 1977; *Scott v. Hart*, 1992). In both of these cases, trial courts ordered the police to provide better protection to the victims of domestic violence. These cases were important because the courts clearly recognized that the police had not served the class of victims of battered women, resulting in damages. In these early cases, the remedies requested were largely prospective, for example, to force police to treat victims of domestic assault the same as other victims of crimes. Remedies typically were to force the police to adopt more aggressive and proactive policies.

Although these cases laid the legal groundwork to establish that poor police policy and practices could result in a court order, it has generally been recognized that the seminal case forcing police change was *Tracey Thurman et al. v. City of Torrington, Connecticut* (1984). Because this case is a graphic portrayal of police indifference and had a profound impact on police procedures, it is worthwhile to discuss it in detail.

In this case, Ms. Thurman and other relatives had repeatedly called the police, pleading for help to protect her from her estranged husband, but had received virtually no assistance, even after he was convicted and placed on probation for damage to her property. When she asked the police to arrest him for continuing to make threats to shoot her and her son even while still on probation, they told her, without any legal basis, to return 3 weeks later and to get a restraining order in the interim. In any event, she did obtain the court order, but the police then refused to arrest her husband, citing a holiday weekend.

After the weekend, police continued to refuse to assist based on the fact that the only officer who could arrest him was "on vacation." In one final rampage by her husband

following a delayed response to her call for emergency police assistance, Thurman was attacked and suffered multiple stab wounds to the chest and neck, resulting in paralysis below her neck and permanent disfigurement. The responding officer stated that he was at the other side of the house "relieving himself" and thought the screams he heard were from a wounded animal.

Her attorneys argued two major theories for police liability: negligence and breach of constitutional rights. Simply stated, the negligence theory claimed that police, being sworn to protect citizenry, had a duty to take reasonable action when requested to prevent victim injury from a known offender.

The second theory was that the police, as agents of the state, violated her 14th Amendment constitutional rights by failing to provide equal protection under the law. This claim was based on differential treatment accorded by police to largely male victims of nondomestic assault compared with primarily female victims of domestic assault. This was considered sex discrimination because most victims of serious injuries in cases of intimate partner abuse were women.

The court found a clear hidden agenda of the Torrington police department. Police actions were found to constitute deliberate indifference to complaints of married women in general and of Thurman in particular. This was negligent and violated the equal protection of the law guaranteed Thurman. A $2.3 million verdict was awarded to Ms. Thurman and her son. An excellent description of the legal rationale of the judgment is contained in Eppler (1986). The Thurman case was widely reported in the popular press, police publications, research journals and was addressed in a variety of legal seminars nationwide. It graphically confirmed to all parties, including prospective legal counsel, that financial penalties that could be imposed on municipalities that abjectly fail to perform their duties.

The impact of *Thurman* and similar cases was twofold. Fear of liability became a prime factor motivating departmental administration, the least out of self-protection, to require more justification if arrests were not made. In some cases, this actually nudged departments to adopt proarrest policies.

Fear of liability awards was even more important for those departments located in jurisdictions that had adopted, by statute or department policy, mandatory or presumptive arrest. Such statutes could easily be used by plaintiffs' attorneys to establish the standard of care that police owed to victims of domestic violence. In this context, it is noteworthy that one state's mandatory arrest law was cited in a legal advocacy journal as providing a "sound basis" for asserting a legally enforceable right of action to victims hurt by police failure to make arrests (Gundle, 1986; restated by the Victim Services Agency, 1988).

As a result of a number of cases both before and after *Thurman*, there was a proliferation of consent decrees resulting from negotiated settlements of class action lawsuits to stop tacit "no arrest" policies. As a result, a number of police departments operated under consent decrees for many years requiring them to treat domestic violence as a crime, to make arrests when appropriate without consideration of marital status, and to advise victims of their legal rights.

The importance of having these orders in place is twofold: If the order is violated, a clear standard of care has been set—and not met—making liability relatively easy to determine. In addition, if the violation was intentional, the police administrators and the officers in question risk contempt of court, possibly risking personal fines or incarceration. (For a summary of the early cases, see Ferraro, 1989a; Victim Services Agency, 1988; and Woods, 1978. For a discussion of the full breadth of civil litigation and its impact, we recommend Kappeler, 1997.)

Unfortunately, although such consent decrees have been imposed in a number of jurisdictions, including Oakland in *Scott v. Hart* (1992), New York City as a result of *Bruno v. Codd* (1977), and many other locations, there is a lack of empirical research examining the extent to which actual operational practices were changed after such orders were in effect. We can, however, hypothesize that the prospects of paying substantial attorneys' fees (even if ultimately successful), of the drain on management attention, and of the potential for a public relations and financial debacle each applied pressure on police departments to adopt policies that were easy to explain and defend. Such policies, if written clearly and, presumably, applied and enforced, would have the effect of insulating police departments from organizational liability and shifting that risk to the individual officer.

This book does not, of course, purport to describe the latest legal findings on police liability, or lack thereof, but only the influence of litigation as a factor in changing the police response to domestic violence. In that vein, there has been little, if any, rollback of policies simply because the U.S. Supreme Court in *DeShaney v. Winnebago County Dept of Social Services* (1989) made it far more difficult to sue police departments. In this case against a social service agency, the Supreme Court disallowed the action even though the county had seemingly negligently sent a minor child back to his father, who then brutally murdered him. The county was held not liable for damages caused by the private violence of one party against another. This can be contrasted with *Canton v. Harris* (1989), which the Supreme Court decided 6 days after DeShaney. In that case, the Supreme Court found liability against a police department after it determined that the department had not adequately trained an officer to their own policies, resulting in injury to people who should have been protected. *Canton v.*

Harris (1989). Similarly, liability under state law for negligence or even intentional liability may continue to pose potential problems for police departments that fail to deal with domestic assaults in a systematic fashion.

The collective impact of these suits is that, by the early 1980s, there was a highly unusual blend of research, pressure from advocates, and legally based administrative need for change. These factors all operated in one direction—to force the police to increase arrest rates in domestic violence cases.

The irony is that as of the writing of this third edition, two of the three reasons for the change in practices have been severely eroded, with research no longer consistently reporting that arrests are the best method for handling domestic assaults. Similarly, legal liability against the police has been minimal—at least at the federal level and for many states. Nonetheless, there is no apparent relaxation in the push for mandatory arrest, as we discuss in the next several chapters.

CHAPTER 7

The Development of State and Federal Legislation

Waves of unprecedented statutory changes beginning in the 1970s have altered the official response to domestic violence. As we explore in this chapter, such legislation has markedly changed the official approach toward intervention.

Although differing greatly in their scope and limitations, the new statutes strive to make profound structural change in the response of government agencies. Such changes have primarily been concentrated in four areas: (a) the police response to domestic violence, (b) the handling of cases by prosecutors and the judiciary, (c) the increased availability and enforcement of civil restraining orders, and (d) the development of efforts to educate the public and victims about the problem, as well as its prevention and possible solutions. Statutory mandates, both at the state level and through the federal Violence Against Women Act, have also led to funding for shelters and other direct forms of assistance for victims.

DOMESTIC VIOLENCE-RELATED LAWS

Early Changes in Laws

As we noted in our summary of the history of intervention, there were few legislative mandates addressing domestic violence until the last quarter of the 20th century. Explosive change commenced with the 1977 enactment of Pennsylvania's landmark Protection from Abuse Act. Since then, every state has adopted reform legislation. Often, these were tentative measures that simply allowed a police officer to make warrantless arrests for a nonwitnessed domestic violence–related misdemeanor assault.

In addition, many other aspects of societal control of domestic violence began to be explicitly addressed, often for the first time, in comprehensive domestic violence statutes. Topics addressed in such comprehensive statutes included law enforcement responsibilities, the effect of family violence in custody disputes, regulation of mediation and other divorce procedures in the presence of family violence, liability of violent perpetrators for civil damages even if the parties are or, at least were, married, reforms to social and health services, and the impact of spousal violence on the victim's as well as offender's responsibility toward minor children. Perhaps most controversial, some statues also address whether being a victim of domestic violence is a partial defense to a homicide charge. These statutes, especially in their earliest forms were not uniform and often contained significant exceptions or limitations. Furthermore, they rarely allocated funding or other resources needed to ensure that organizational change really occurred. Despite such limitations, these statutes collectively began to provide the first comprehensive legislative framework in this area.

A complete review of all of the substantive provisions of reform legislation would be far beyond the scope of this effort. For those interested, Neil Miller of the Institute for Law and Justice (2000) wrote an excellent compilation of such provisions, which demonstrates the diversity of statutes current at that time along with cogent suggestions for further reform. For the purposes of this monograph, our focus is placed on several key reforms: the removal of warrantless arrest barriers, the expansion of substantive grounds for arrest, the enactment of comprehensive domestic violence criminal codes, and the limits on official discretion.

Statutory Removal of Procedural Barriers to Arrest

Over time, procedural impediments to the use of arrests have been largely eliminated. As discussed earlier, before the late 1970s, most states followed English common law practice and required an officer to witness a misdemeanor before making a warrantless arrest. This was in sharp contrast to the ability of an officer to arrest without a warrant on finding probable cause that a felony had occurred.

Because most acts of domestic violence are apt to be classified as simple assault and battery, a misdemeanor, this was a key limitation. If the act was not repeated in the presence of the officer, no arrest could be made, and a victim either had to initiate and sign a criminal complaint separately—an action rarely undertaken by domestic violence victims or enforced by arrest. Alternately, the police might be forced to arrest for a general-purpose, non–domestic violence charge such as disorderly conduct or public intoxication. These charges, however, rarely connoted the existence of a serious assault. Consequently, they would usually be "flushed" from the system with regularity.

By the mid-1980s, the first wave of statutory enactments had eliminated most of these statutory restrictions. In fact, by 1992, 47 states and the District of Columbia had already enacted statutes authorizing arrest in such cases; in 14 of these states and in the District of Columbia, arrest was even mandated when the officer concluded that domestic violence had occurred.

Expansion of the Substantive Grounds for Arrest: Protective Order Violations

At the same time the procedural restrictions were swept away, the first domestic violence statutes often incorporated other changes to allow greater use of arrests. Civil protective and temporary restraining orders were soon authorized in all 50 states for prior restraint on possible assailants.

Of particular importance to the police, many such statutes expressly provided for enforcement of a protective order by warrantless arrest. In effect, their enforcement was thereby "criminalized" even if no substantive crime was recognized. This was in sharp departure to the older style "peace bonds," in which conduct might have been prohibited by a magistrate but enforcement was via simple forfeiture of the bond itself. This has considerable potential importance in that police, acting at times with extraordinary caution, often refused to find probable cause for a misdemeanor assault arrest. The temporary restraining order could be used, however, to restrain any contact between the suspect and the person under protection, giving police a far more flexible vehicle to find probable cause to make warrantless arrests. The existence and violation of the orders also was much easier to prove in court. This fact has made a victim's lawsuit against the police for failure to enforce much easier to prove.

Domestic Violence–Specific Statutes

Another major change in statutory structure has been enactment of substantive changes to states' criminal laws. A growing number of states have enacted statutes creating a separate criminal offense for domestic or family violence.

At first glance, explicit domestic violence laws may appear superfluous. After all, every state has a lengthy history of laws prohibiting assault and battery. There are, however, several key advantages to a statute specific to domestic violence. First, they direct law enforcement to the elements of a crime specific to domestic violence, not the generalized law of assault and battery. Activities such as harassment, intentional infliction of emotional distress, or threats other than the threat of assault are typically difficult to prosecute under the rubric of general assault and battery statutes. The existence of one centralized statute addressing domestic violence instead serves to focus law enforcement attention. This may occur either because of police officers' enhanced knowledge of the new law applied to domestic violence or, more obliquely, because they now recognize

increased exposure to civil liability for a knowing failure to enforce specific criminal statutes.

Second, as discussed, statutes allowing warrantless misdemeanor arrests often had major procedural limitations. For example, there were often strict limits on the time between the event and the arrest, requirements of evident visible injury, or both. The creation of express domestic violence statutes freed the police from such restrictions.

Third, a domestic violence specific crime made it far easier for the state to retain accurate records of the occurrence of reported domestic violence and case disposition by agencies. When such cases were aggregated into the generic category of "assault and battery," it was difficult to determine critically whether spouse abuse cases were prosecuted with the same vigor as other assaults.

Fourth, because a domestic violence assault violation was more specific, it was assumed that the legislative intent to mete out punishment appropriate to the crime would influence courts as they imposed sentences. Although difficult to prove, the judiciary might be inclined to use more innovative sentences when an assault statute was cited, such as imposing injunction-type conditions on release from jail, continuing threats of deferred prosecution, and forced assignment to counseling programs. Although these sentences were available in the past and might be undertaken at the initiative of an individual judge, they were not always intuitively obvious because sentencing judges typically only rapidly reviewed a plea bargain on a generalized assault charge.

As we discuss in other chapters, although such statutes clearly have great potential for widespread impact, evidence of the extent of change is more problematic. Initially, this may have been partially due to constitutional concerns. The U.S. Commission of Civil Rights (1978) indicated that, at that time, many judges were questioning the basic constitutionality of such statutes on the grounds that they created unwarranted and major distinctions based on gender or marital status. Their report also noted, without specific support, that when judges attempted to aggressively enforce the laws, case backlogs rapidly appeared. In any event, early analysis appeared to show only modest impacts on agency performance (see Quarm & Schwartz, 1985).

In addition, the efficacy of these earlier statutes was challenged because of a lack of coherence. In 1991, after reviewing new statutes in all 50 states, one commentator concluded that their impact was severely eroded and "elements of a well thought out program are missing (perhaps) due to haste in drafting, lack of adequate resources for legislative research, or perhaps out of legislative reluctance" (Zalman, 1991, p. 17).

Recent Statutory Amendments

The initial enactment of domestic violence legislation to a jurisdiction's criminal code has not proven to be the final statutory change. In virtually all states, the first spousal abuse or domestic violence act merely initiated a subsequent wave of related legislation designed to correct inadequacies of past laws or, as in the case of stalking legislation, address previously unknown problems.

The impulse to pass new statutes has not abated. In our second edition (1996), we believed many, if not most, issues were already addressed. We discussed how many new innovations led to growing police, prosecutorial, and judicial powers and mandates. What has continued to surprise us, and perhaps others, is that the volume of new statutes has not diminished, but increased, as of the writing of this book. Miller (2000) reported that 100 new laws had been passed regarding domestic violence in 2000, 160 in 1999, 64 in 1998, and 83 in 1997.

Although research of such statutes would evidently be dated as of the publication of this book, broad trends of these later enactments can be identified. This summary does not include laws designed to expressly assist stalking victims, covered separately later in this chapter, which also during the past few years have been enacted, amended, and typically amended again.

First, statutory gaps, in which certain states had not passed a basic domestic violence statute, have been addressed. In the last 4 years, 13 states passed new criminal statutes on domestic violence. Therefore, as of October 2000, 37 states had such laws (Miller, 2000). As we noted earlier, such statutes should provide a cornerstone for state power against this crime. Included in the passage of new "gap limiting" statutes has been the widespread elimination (or severe limitation on) the "marital exemption" defense to charges of spousal rape. The issue of sexual assault of married parties had not been widely addressed in the past. Now there is a plethora of legislative schemes; as of October 2000, two states had eliminated the exemption but only if the spouse reported rape within 30 days, six states had eliminated it if the parties were not living together, three states had eliminated it if "forcible rape" occurred, and several states enacted separate spousal sexual assault laws (Miller, 2000).

Second, severity of punishment for domestic violence crimes became an open issue, with many legislatures trying to limit the ability of police, prosecutors, and magistrates from turning severe assaults to simple misdemeanors by providing various "aggravating" or "enhancing" aspects of an assault that would make the act of assault a felony. The list of these is broad, but often states now include one or more of the following factors: use of a weapon in an attack, degree of injury to the victim, presence of children witnessing the crime (8 states), a second (7 states) or third act (16 states) of domestic violence, and a second assault occurring within 72 hours of the first (resulting in a 2-year sentence enhancement; per Miller, 2000).

Third, statutes mandating particular police practices have continued to be enacted in many states. These tend to reflect continued concern over the actual services delivered to victims as opposed to merely being promised. Matters formerly left to officer discretion became increasingly matters of statutory mandate. For example, many states have greatly increased reliance on mandatory arrests, at least for certain incidents. Twenty-one states and the District of Columbia now require mandatory arrest for at least some circumstances, often limited to the type of crime (e.g., felonies) or, in 31 states, for violation of protective orders (Miller, 2000). A discussion of the impact of such laws is contained in Chapter 8.

Mandated police behavior was no longer confined to simply an arrest. Instead, specific conduct of the officer is often addressed. This includes requirements such as the following:

- Determining if there is an existing restraining or protective order
- Providing transportation for the victim and her children and attention to any children present (this is now routine in most states)
- Arranging for social services
- Informing victims of the right and procedure to make a citizen's arrest
- So-called victim's rights laws requiring that police inform a victim of the right to demand an arrest and to obtain court protective orders and often to have shelters available to her
- Mandates not to release prematurely offenders who have been arrested for violation of a restraining order
- Developing and implementing written incident report forms identifying the alleged occurrence, the police response, and reasons

for their actions if an arrest was not made (Under the impetus of VAWA, 35 states now require that such incident reports be filed and, even more significantly, mandate that if no arrest is made or if a dual arrest has occurred, reasons be stated explicitly.)

- Removal of any dangerous weapons from the scene of a domestic assault
- Perhaps in the ultimate recognition of the inability to protect victims, a South Carolina statute now "authorizes" officers to take victims of domestic violence into protective custody if the officer believes the victim is in a life-threatening situation (SC S 1287, 1994)

Fourth, legislation to change the operation of courts and prosecutor's offices has also continued, but tended to be somewhat less coercive than laws directed toward the police, displaying greater deference to prosecutors' tasks and the separation of powers. Many simply give more options for prosecutors and courts. These include the following:

- Granting more authority to call a domestic assault a "felony" rather than a misdemeanor
- Allowing courts to sanction uncooperative victims such as those who refuse to testify at subsequent trials (For example, although limiting the grounds, California recognized the court's capability to find a victim in contempt of court for refusing to testify [CA A 363, 1991]. Several years later, a less punitive provision was adopted, allowing the introduction of a victim's videotaped testimony at a preliminary hearing to be admitted into a trial, if otherwise admissible, thereby obviating the need for her further testimony [CA S 178, 1993].)
- Prohibitions of "mutual orders of protection" (This appears to be an attempt to prevent courts from effectively coercing domestic violence victims by treating them in the same way as their aggressors
- Giving the presumably more capable and sympathetic family court exclusive jurisdiction over cases involving any violations of domestic abuse orders [HI H 2712, 1992].)

At the same time, some legislation took tentative (or less aggressive) steps to mandate prosecutorial and judicial action. These include the following:

- Provisions in the "victim rights" statutes discussed earlier mandating that prosecutors offer to meet with victims to discuss offender sentencing or to accept reduced charges
- Requirement of written policies on handling domestic violence cases
- Compulsory "no drop," or at least limits on plea bargaining, statutes in certain instances (e.g., California and Colorado)
- Granting probation to a convicted abuser requiring their participation in a batterer treatment program

Fifth, many states have broadened the original scope and duration of ex parte and other protective orders. Some have extended their duration up to a 1-year ex parte order if the respondent fails to appear at a hearing after notice is given. Similarly, enforcement of violations of court orders has been significantly boosted by enhancement of penalties associated with violation of these orders. In fact, in 48 states, violation of a court order is a separate offense, which therefore means no underlying crime of domestic abuse need be proven (Miller, 2000). Adding teeth to this measure, a growing trend has been to make repeat violations of restraining orders a felony.

Sixth, batterers have also been addressed in this second round of legislation. Not surprisingly, the measures have generally been designed to punish more severely rather than to accelerate rehabilitation. For example, some states limit a batterer's access to diversionary programs. California now requires that defendants charged with misdemeanor domestic violence offenses not be eligible for existing diversionary programs unless the defendant has no conviction for any violent offence and has not been diverted under similar statutes within 10 years (CA A 226, 1993).

Michigan does not specify an express date, but limits by number the instances in which an alleged offender can have domestic charges dropped (MI H 4308, 1994). Noncriminal code statutes affecting batterers have also been enacted. At times, these include preventing batterers from obtaining firearms, or at least handgun licenses. Seventh, types and levels of training of agency personnel and comprehensive standards of conduct have been increasingly specified. These now include a majority of states requiring some level of initial police training on domestic violence. In addition, a small minority now requires in-service domestic violence training.

Miller (2000) noted that 18 states now require local written policies and procedures. The impact of such policies may be threefold. First, they force higher level administrators to focus on this problem and set forth the standards to which they expect their officers to perform. Second, such policies, if communicated widely, will hopefully act to standardize police responses far more than when unfettered discretion was the norm. Third, by providing a standard of care that should be maintained should a victim be injured or killed because the policy was not followed, there is a virtual "roadmap" for litigation against the police department, or at least the responsible officer.

The diversity of the foregoing statutory changes prevents any easy generalization as to their cause and probable effect. In fact, as we more fully detail in the discussion on stalking statutes, the inability of states to establish a fixed legislative set of requirements regarding domestic violence may actually impede effective responses to crimes, at least in the short term, until some consistency between new rules, funding for new mandates, and new training requirements have been widely adopted within the states.

Over the long term, we would expect this cascade of new legislation to diminish, and, after time has passed, it is hoped it will lead to greater organizational adherence to "best practices" regarding the control of domestic violence. Whether such behavioral changes occur because of actual attitudinal change as opposed to concerns with liability due to failure to perform an explicit legislative function is subject to ongoing debate.

SPECIFIC ANTI-STALKING LEGISLATION

Every move you make, every breath you take, I'll be watching you.

From "Every Breath You Take" recorded by The Police on the album *Synchronicity* (A&M Records #3735)

Until he rapes me or kills me, the police can't do anything. When I'm a statistic of some kind, they'll put every man they have on it.

From a Victim of Stalking

Initial Statutes

In many ways the sudden enactment of anti-stalking statutes in the 1990s has mirrored the rapid rise of domestic violence laws in the late 1970s to the 1980s. Before 1990, no state had anti-stalking legislation. Instead, statutes addressed "criminal trespass" and "terrorist threats" and were very specific requiring a particular pattern of behavior. Hence, they were only occasionally used for domestic violence situations. Common "harassment" statutes, of the type now on the books in virtually all states, considered stalking-type behaviors to be low-level misdemeanor offenses. Such omnibus statutes were designed to curtail offensive physical contact, insults, false reports, and other relatively petty offenses. Harassment laws, which are general in nature, were also

severely limited in application by numerous judicial decisions that had held that unless "fighting words" or other speech not protected by the First Amendment were involved, such laws might be unconstitutional. As such, these laws did not prove useful in combating stalking related to domestic violence or other serious predatory behavior.

Similarly, although many local jurisdictions had separable anti-stalking ordinances, such efforts were scattered, could be circumvented if the victim or offender left the jurisdiction, and provided for minimal enforcement or punishment. In this regard, the criminal code for stalking situations largely paralleled the frustrations of policing domestic violence. Here, the police were stymied in that typically no crime was committed before a violent assault.

The nation's first statewide anti-stalking statute was enacted in California in 1990. This statute was passed largely as a response to the stalking and subsequent July 1989 murder of actress Rebecca Schaeffer, who starred on the television show *My Sister Sam*. In addition, five murders the year before had taken place in Orange County, California, in which the victims had actually obtained restraining orders and had reported to authorities that the restraining order "did not work."

The California statute defined stalking in a manner that was quite explicit (*California Penal Code*, 1992, section 646.9). A stalker "willfully, maliciously and repeatedly follows or harasses another person and who makes a credible threat with the intent to place that person in fear of death or great bodily injury." By its terms, the statute required concurrent findings of the following elements: willful malice, repetitive following or harassing, a "credible threat," and "intent" to place the recipient in "reasonable fear of death or great bodily injury."

This statute was obviously limited in that it required finding both behavior and intent, leaving its application severely constrained, in particular because an overt threat and proof of intent to cause fear of the threat were required. In addition, it did not provide for warrantless arrests, increasing penalties for a violating court order, nor for conviction in subsequent offenses. It also had less-than-adequate provisions for victims of domestic violence–related stalking in which the incidents might individually appear trivial (such as going into the same grocery store as the victim right after the victim entered). In an effort to respond to such criticisms, California revised its stalking statute in 1992 to increase the grounds allowed and to increase the attendant penalty for violation.

During the next several years, increasing, although anecdotal, evidence of stalking in most states led to the recognition of obvious statutory gaps. There ensued a virtual deluge of new statutes. For example, unusually tough legislation (potentially imposing up to 4 years in prison for stalking) passed in Illinois after California's law was enacted. In hearings, lawmakers were told that stalkers had killed five victims in Illinois in 1 year. In addition, victims of domestic violence–related stalking recounted how they were terrorized even after restraining orders were imposed and how they continued to receive harassing mail and calls even after the attacker was incarcerated.

Subsequent laws became extraordinarily varied both in their terms and level of enforcement. Specific provisions of such statutes now typically include the following prohibitions: pursuing or following, harassing, nonconsensual communications, surveillance or lying in wait, trespass, approaching or continued presence, disregard of warnings (to leave), and intimidation. In addition, some states that did not expressly state the acts that were proscribed now implicitly leave the courts to judicially create a common law for this crime.

The Model Code Provisions and the Second Wave of Statutes

Later statutes began to adhere to the following tenets of the 1993 Model Anti-Stalking Code for the States (National Criminal Justice Association, 1993), proposed by the National Institute of Justice:

Section 1. For purposes of this code, (a) "Course of conduct" means repeatedly maintaining a visual or physical proximity to a person or repeatedly conveying verbal or written threats or threats implied by conduct or a combination thereof directed at or toward a person (note electronic harassment was not covered); (b) "Repeatedly" means on two or more occasions, and (c) "Immediate family" means a spouse, parent, child, sibling, or any other person who regularly resides in the household or who within the prior six months regularly resided in the household.

Section 2. Any person who
(a) Purposefully engages in a course of conduct directed at a specific person that would cause a reasonable person to fear bodily injury to himself or herself or a member of his or her immediate family or to fear the death of himself or herself or a member of his or her immediate family; and
(b) Has knowledge or should have knowledge that the specific person will be placed in reasonable fear of bodily injury to himself or herself or a member of his or her immediate family or will be placed in reasonable fear of the death of himself or herself or a member of his or her immediate family; and
(c) Whose acts induce fear in the specific person of bodily injury to himself or herself or a member of his or her immediate family or induce fear in the specific person of the death of himself or herself or a member of his or her immediate family is guilty of stalking.

The key components of this code were that (a) an explicit threat would not be required (the proposal recognizes that conduct, even absent a threat, may be just as serious a predictor of future violence); (b) a course of conduct that would cause a reasonable person to have fear was covered, even if the intent to actually cause fear was not present (because many stalkers, especially domestic violence stalkers, may be under delusions that their victims want to reunite with them); and (c) states were encouraged to make violation of the stalking code a felony (to allow greater flexibility in sentencing and to impress on potential offenders and the criminal justice system the seriousness of the crime).

Despite the promulgation of the 1993 Model Code, statutory coverage was quite varied. For example, a threshold issue is what level of threat is required to sustain a conviction. Threat requirements for conviction appeared broken into several groups. The majority followed the Model Code and merely required a threat, or conduct even absent an express threat, that would make a reasonable person fearful. This was the easiest standard for prosecutors to meet because it allowed them to introduce circumstantial and cumulative evidence in place of a "smoking gun"–type of express threat.

In contrast, the remaining states required that an express threat be made and that the threatening person have the apparent ability to carry out the threat or have commenced actions. The weakness in such statutes is evident. Stalkers may seek to operate (barely) out of its statutory confines by not making overt threats even while terrifying victims. This is a potent threat, especially when some observers have commented to the authors that at many batterer treatment groups, conversations take place about "how to get even with the ***** by making her life miserable" yet circumventing the wording of domestic violence and stalking laws.

Thus, a significant limitation existed if proof that the defendant intended to cause and actually did cause a reasonable fear on the part of the person being stalked was required. Although it could theoretically be argued that intentionally frightening behavior should be

the only conduct that is criminalized, such intent is customarily denied by the defendant and is in practice very difficult to prove.

As a result, many states began experimenting with a more flexible statute structure by providing for an "aggravated" or "enhanced" offense on the presence of certain types of stalking. For example, some states have made it a felony to possess or show a weapon in aid of stalking whereas other states treat the use of a weapon, the confinement or restraint of the victim, or the subjection of the victim to bodily harm as an aggravating offense, justifying substantially increased penalties.

Not surprisingly, penalties for violation were also extraordinarily varied. In most states, the basic penalty is a misdemeanor—subjecting those convicted to not more than 1 year in jail (or less) plus a fine. On the other hand, even these states allowed enhancement of the penalties to felony level in cases involving the violation of court orders, prior felonies, possession of weapons, creating a "credible threat," or causing bodily harm.

Although the directives to law enforcement remain somewhat limited, several states have given police the power to make warrantless arrests of stalking subjects on determination of probable cause, even absent witnessing the incidents (similar to domestic violence cases). In addition, several states expressly require law enforcement to provide victim assistance or notification that a defendant has been released before trial. In other states, that duty may be implicitly assumed.

Recent Trends in Stalking Laws

States have been adopting ever more comprehensive statutes. For example, a growing trend is to explicitly recognize the interjurisdictional nature of stalking by allowing "enhancement" (increased sanctions) in a stalking offense based not only on conduct committed in their state, but also on previous violations in other states. In addition, there is no requirement that the second offense justifying sentencing enhancement be against the same victim, demonstrating knowledge that it is not only the behavioral interaction between the offender and a particular victim, but the innate behavior of the offender that accounts for the crime's importance to society. Finally, in some states, there exists a "presumption of ineligibility for bail" in the event of a third stalking offense.

The level and volume of statutory changes make it impossible for a volume of this type to keep current with the restrictions now being set forth in statutes. Indeed, in the second edition of this book, published in 1996, we were able to state that, following the California law in 1990, virtually all states (48 and the District of Columbia) had anti-stalking statutes, often having already been amended to cover apparent loopholes. Since then, the statutory basis has continued to change at an almost dizzying rate. In a March 2001 report, the U.S. Department of Justice reported 11 amended anti-stalking statutes; in 1999, there were 26 new state statutes related to stalking; and by August 2000, there were 27 new amendments to stalking laws (U.S. Department of Justice, 2001, p. 20).

The most recent directions of stalking amendments have been eclectic because there is no unifying authority. New measures include the following:

- Expanding the coverage of stalking laws to differentiate between "normal" stalking and "aggravated" felony stalking, based primarily on the existence of a court injunction or restraining order
- Adding cyber threats to the definition of stalking
- Allowing the courts to compel psychological evaluations
- Compelling statewide data gathering on stalking behaviors
- Authorizing "antiharassment" protective orders

- Expanding the issuance of warrantless arrest misdemeanors from domestic violence only to include stalking
- Prohibiting the purchase or transportation of a firearm or explosives for any person subject to a stalking order of protection
- Requiring employers to provide leave for crime victims (including victims of stalking) to attend court hearings and receive medical or psychological treatment
- Requiring police officer certification training to include instruction in responding to incidents of stalking
- Authorizing preventive detention or electronic monitoring if danger to the victim is demonstrated to the court
- Allowing employees to seek an injunctive order against harassment of employees at the workplace
- Allowing the crime of stalking to be alleged even if it is known the alleged perpetrator is incarcerated
- Creating address confidentiality programs for victims of stalking
- Assessing court fees against the harasser rather than the complainant in successful civil harassment order proceedings

What does this frenzy of state laws indicate? We believe several factors are evident. First, in common with the early statutory experience with domestic violence, the initial statutes did not prevent stalking. If they did, it is doubtful that the majority of states would be changing them on an ongoing basis. Such change indicates a degree of legislative frustration. Second, state statutes are not being amended in any consistent manner. The actions are instead somewhat disjointed and idiosyncratic, indicating perhaps, a response to specific failures (e.g. cases in which a stalker has injured or killed a victim despite an existing statute when the statutory structure was perceived to contain an unacceptable loophole). Third, our review of the constitutionality of these laws is still germane. When legislation is passed quickly and without consistency, it greatly increases the chance that certain provisions will be held unconstitutional. Fourth, this degree of legislative "churn" makes it difficult for police officers and prosecutors and court officials to know the current status of the relevant statutes. Although advocates and researchers will be able to uncover this information, it is nearly impossible to train agency workers when laws change continually. Fifth, until laws standardize and become stable, research on the efficacy of such statutes will be difficult, will become "dated" very quickly, and will not be able to guide policy effectively, as opposed to reacting to anecdotal events or pressure from interest groups.

Are Anti-Stalking Statutes Constitutional?

In the second edition of this text written 6 years ago, we predicted that there would be extensive litigation regarding constitutionality and application of anti-stalking statutes. This has indeed proven true. The May 2001 U.S. Department of Justice publication, *Stalking and Domestic Violence: Report to Congress,* chronicled 464 state and 17 federal stalking and related cases in which challenges to anti-stalking and related laws were addressed. Of these, 157 directly challenged the express stalking statutes (124 largely on constitutional grounds; U.S. Department of Justice, 2001). Defense attorneys have raised constitutional challenges using a multitude of grounds including First Amendment rights and "freedom of expression" as incorporated in the Fourteenth Amendment prohibiting unwarranted state (and local) curtailment of such liberties. They also argued as a factual matter that "stalkers" were merely "expressing their feelings" toward the recipient.

The significance of that argument was that simply because such expressions might place an individual in fear, however reasonable, society should not curtail a citizen's rights to self-expression. They also argued that because the definitions of improper conduct were not clear, they might have a "chilling effect" on permissible communications and hence be challenged as being impermissibly "overly broad" due to their natural tendency to inhibit otherwise protected free speech, or, by being too vague, be unconstitutional for being "void for vagueness."

The reality is, courts have always recognized that the right to free speech has never been considered absolute. Limits have long been set on unprotected speech, such as obscenity, defamation, and imminent threats of illegal activity (see *Miller v. California,* 1973). Similarly, the time, place, and manner of making comments, even if not expressly falling under one of the recognized exceptions to free speech, have long been held to justify reasonable limits (see *Paris Adult Theaters v. Slaton,* 1973). Thus, a balancing of interests was required.

The key to the successful resolution and enforcement of these statutes, as briefly summarized by the Department of Justice, were as follows:

1. Statutes need not (and typically did not) require any proof that the defendant was going to carry out his threats.

2. An intent to knowingly cause a victim's fear must be included in a case, thus giving the trier of fact (ultimately the jury) the ability to decide whether the conduct might be unintentional.

3. Statutes must use careful wording. Terms such as to *annoy* or *alarm* needed limiting definitions to prevent challenges for being too vague.

As a result of litigation and after a series of amendments, virtually all stalking statutes now require a trier of fact to determine that a defendant willfully and intentionally instilled fear in the recipient. The courts have even allowed statutes that sanctioned "reckless behavior" by the offender to be used as proof of intent to cause reasonable fear. After all, it is rare that a perpetrator with knowledge of the existence of an anti-stalking law would say, "Sure, I intended to cause her to fear me." An evasive response is far more typical, citing the repetitions of "coincidence" and "misinterpretation" by the victim.

Gaps in Current Laws

The issue remaining is that some stalking behavior can be so amorphous that, over the years, potential stalkers find ever-changing, repetitive, novel behaviors and hence, at least at first, are difficult to define as illegal even under the most liberal stalking statutes.

The U.S. Department of Justice report best states this as follows:

> Unfortunately, at least two major gaps remain in States' legislative initiatives against stalking and their interpretations by the courts. State legislatures and courts frequently fail to recognize implied or conditional threats in their construction of the stalking crime. Stalkers who follow, repeatedly contact, and otherwise terrorize their victims in a persistent and even obsessive manner may slip through the cracks of the criminal justice system if they refrain from spelling out threats. Such legislative loopholes need to be addressed. (U.S. Department of Justice, 2001, p. 39)

Similarly, new technologies have led to new behavior. For example, the explosive growth of e-mail has inevitably led to cyber stalking. The U.S. Department of Justice report stated that prosecution of such offenses may require specific statutory language prohibiting the use of these media to harass:

> By and large, courts are not interpreting older legislation to cover recently developed communications technologies. Such narrow interpretation of anti-stalking codes does not cover cyberstalking and other modes of high-tech terrorization. Thus, many States may need to enact specific

legislative bans on the use of such media for stalking purposes. (U.S. Department of Justice, 2001, p. 39)

Similarly, no existing statute can adequately cover the full range of activities a stalker might pursue. The hope is that the risk of serious sanctions imposed by stalking legislation deters conduct close to the purposes of the statute.

The dilemma for stalking legislation is that any particular act may not, by itself, comply with narrow categories contained in a statute. As amply demonstrated, however, no one can deny that the failure to restrain stalking places people at risk, especially past victims of domestic violence, in which case the offender's propensity for violence and choice of target are clear. As a matter of practice, judges hearing stalking charges should be fully aware at the bail hearing of the circumstances of the stalking, presumably including all past instances of domestic violence. Conditions for release should specifically include propensity for future violence and targeting of a particular victim.

THE FEDERAL LEGISLATIVE RESPONSE

In our first edition, we observed that there was only an aborted federal response to domestic violence. In our second edition, we discussed the then recently enacted Violence Against Women Act of 1994. This was reauthorized in October 2000, providing us with far greater optimism about the future of the federal role in combating domestic violence.

Initial Efforts

The initial strategy of those advocating change to the federal response to domestic violence was to publicize the failures of the state-based criminal justice system and thereby obtain a federal commitment to force structural change. Indeed, sympathetic congressmen in the late 1970s and early 1980s held numerous hearings on proposed federal legislation. These focused primarily on shelter funding and mass education and training for affected agencies.

These hearings uniformly heard witnesses explaining the widespread nature of the problem, decrying the inability of law enforcement and the judiciary to take effective action and emphasizing the necessity of federal funds to assist in upgrading and standardizing shelters and other victim resources. The U.S. Commission on Civil Rights (1982) ultimately issued a widely cited report. In this report, domestic violence was called "a civil rights problem of overwhelming magnitude." Ironically, before this report was even published, virtually all of the federally funded programs that were positively cited in this report had already been eliminated because of the new Reagan administration's changes in federal priorities.

Indeed, strong conservative opposition kept federal funding of shelters and research on domestic violence prevention and treatment to a minimum. In an example of such a reaction, Senator Jesse Helms critiqued providing any federal support to domestic violence shelters because they constituted "social engineering," challenging the husband's place as the "head of the family" (Congressional Record, 1980).

Despite resistance, several federal agencies including the Attorney General's Office, the National Institute of Justice, the Bureau of Justice Statistics, and the National Institute of Health remained active in funding much-needed research and demonstration projects; these federally funded projects in turn became springboards for evaluation and policy recommendations. Although promising individual projects have been funded, little long-term sustaining effort was in place until the federal government in 1994 passed the Violence Against Women Act. To a large extent, this is due to greatly decreased funding in most federal agencies. It also reflected an unwillingness of the federal government to address such social problems as a valid topic for federal action. For such reasons, despite strong recommendations such as those contained in the 1984 U.S. Attorney General's Task Force on Family Violence, funding to implement recommendations did not materialize for 10 years, forcing state governments and individual communities to address change largely with their own initiatives.

The Violence Against Women Act of 1994 (VAWA)

The VAWA was enacted as Title IV of the Omnibus Crime Control and Law Enforcement Act of 1994. This legislation promised a significant change in the level of federal commitment to the control of violent crimes against women and children. Among other provisions designed to deter sex and hate crimes against women were measures expressly targeting control of domestic violence.

Several key provisions in that statute dramatically affected the federal government's role. First, $120 million was made available from FY (fiscal year) 1996 to FY 1998 for grants to state and local government and Native American tribes to implement mandatory or proarrest policies; improve tracking of domestic violence victims; increase the coordination among police, prosecution, and the judiciary; strengthen local advocacy and service programs for victims of domestic violence; and educate judges about domestic violence. Similarly, VAWA authorized $30 million in grants to rural states, localities, and Native American tribes to improve prosecution of domestic violence and child abuse.

Applicants for assistance (state and local agencies) first had to certify that their laws encouraged or mandated arrests for domestic violence offenders and those violating restraining orders; demonstrate that their laws, policies, and practices discouraged dual arrests of offenders and victims; and demonstrate that the abused person need not pay costs for filing criminal charges or to secure a protection order. Hence, targeted and restrictive funding forced change even when individual police administrators might not have believed all program requirements were needed. This impetus may have led to the proliferation of laws in recent years that we have noted.

Second, VAWA funded the National Domestic Violence Hotline, (NDVH) operational in February 1996. A nonprofit private organization, the Texas Council on Family Violence was selected to establish and operate this toll-free service, including maintenance of a national database of local providers of services as well as those providing local and state hotline services. According to NDVH Web site (www.ndvh.org), it now contains a database of more than 4,000 shelters and service providers throughout the United States and its territories. Since its inception, more than 700,000 telephone calls have been received from victims, family members, and others. Currently, the associated Web site is quite comprehensive, allowing victims and service providers to get answers to frequently asked questions, gain access to resource materials, and find assistance in each state. It also provides specialized materials on domestic violence in the workplace, teens and dating violence, and community and outreach programs. At present the hotline receives more than 13,000 calls per month. More than 70% of these are from victims of domestic violence or family and friends, and nearly 70% of hotline callers are women.

There is a distinct difference between the service population of people who seek help from the hotline versus those who seek help from police. According to NDVH data, for approximately 60% of callers, contacting the

hotline was the first step taken; many callers stated that they were unaware of existing community resources or were afraid to ask for help at local agencies where they might be recognized. This is important because, as described earlier, no matter which measurement is adopted, less than 50% of victims of domestic violence ever contact the police.

The real area of the NDVH's impact may be on the "hard-core offender," given the inability of locally based criminal justice system to protect against a truly determined assailant. As their Web site states,

> Now, with just one phone call, a victim trying to flee an abusive relationship in Wyoming can find out about a shelter in Ohio. Hotline advocates are even capable of setting up conference calls between battered women and the shelter they will go to for help. . . . Bilinigual staff and a lanaguage line are available for every non-English speaking caller. (http://www.ndvh. org)

Third, VAWA created federal criminal penalties for anyone who traveled across state lines with the intent to injure a spouse or intimate partner or to violate the terms of a protective order and then intentionally committed a violent crime that caused injury or violated a protective order. In effect, this provision federalized interstate domestic violence–related stalking laws and may be a useful adjunct to them.

Fourth, federal court proceedings increased their victim orientation by expressly allowing victims of interstate crimes the right to appear in court to speak about the danger of pretrial release of the defendant. At the same time, state courts were required to enforce protection orders issued by the courts of another state. This made it markedly easier for women forced to vacate their homes to evade violence without having to reapply for court protection in a new location (or to reveal their new address to the offender).

Fifth, various provisions of VAWA increased funding for community-based agencies that target domestic violence and stalking. One provision allocated $325 million to be provided to states and Native American tribes. State coalitions against domestic violence and various research centers were to disseminate funds for construction and operational costs for battered women's shelters and other projects designed to "prevent family violence and to provide immediate shelter and related assistance for victims of domestic violence and their defendants" (Violence Against Women Act, 1994). Finally, development of a number of model programs were funded to teach youth about domestic violence and violence among intimate partners; $10 million was given to nonprofit organizations to set up community programs in domestic violence intervention and prevention.

Sixth, more specific interventions were made to federal institutions. For example, the U.S. Post Office was directed to protect the confidentiality of domestic violence shelters and abused person's addresses. Similarly, other various federal agencies were required to collect data and conduct research on domestic violence. Overall responsibility for the development of a research agenda research was given to the National Institute of Justice. The Office of the Attorney General was delegated the role of determining how states might collect centralized databases. Federal crime databases were to be made available by state civil and criminal courts to assist in responding to domestic violence and stalking cases. At the same time, $6 million was provided to assist states and local governments to improve data collection. At the same time, the Centers for Disease Control was directed to study the costs to health care facilities for victims of domestic violence and related issues.

Federal Efforts to Combat Stalking

The federal response to stalking has been unusually swift. In 1993, the U.S. Department of Justice Bureau of Justice Assistance first mandated federal assistance to state and local law enforcement, only three years after passage of the first state statute. One result was that the National Institute of Justice funded a proposal to develop the model state anti-stalking statute described earlier. In 1996, a federal interstate stalking law (18 USC 2261A) was enacted, prohibiting as a federal offense the crossing of state lines (or in U.S. maritime jurisdiction) with the intent to injure or harass another person (provided that) this caused reasonable fear of death or serious bodily injury to that person or to a member of that person's immediate family. Although the original law covered only the intent to injure or harass, VAWA 2000 expanded the definition to cover interstate travel with the intent to *kill*, injure, harass, or intimidate another person, the person's family, *or* the person's *former or current intimate partner* (emphasis added for 2000 statutory additions). Similarly, the law now federalizes the use of mail or cyberstalking via the Internet.

Federal crimes, of course, invoke federal criminal sanctions and federal sentencing. Guidelines dramatically limit the authority of federal judges to change sentences. Of these sentences, penalties ranged from 13 months and supervised release to life imprisonment. Restitution has also been granted. Finally, because of the existence of this relatively new federal statute, extensive federal resources at the U.S. Department of Justice have been committed to develop anti-stalking task forces with state and local law enforcement and the development of multijurisdictional training programs for law enforcement, prosecutors, judges, and victim advocates. Although potentially the most sweeping of all antiharassment statutes, this federal response is limited and, per the U.S. Department of Justice, is not meant to "supplant" state efforts. There simply are not the federal resources to prosecute significant numbers of cases, especially following the terrorist attacks in September of 2001, which have tied up virtually all available resources. Hence, this effort should best be considered as an adjunct when the interstate nature of harassment effectively prevents state prosecution.

Since enactment of the new anti-stalking statutes from 1996 through October 2000, the U.S. Department of Justice had prosecuted 35 cases against 39 stalkers and had won convictions against 39 stalkers (U.S. Department of Justice, 2001) and 25 defendants in 23 years (11 cases were still pending) by 2001. This extraordinarily high conviction rate shows that the statute can be effective but remains selectively used. This is perhaps due to the lack of knowledge of the underlying incidents, because prosecutorial discretion has limited the number of cases brought, or possibly because state and local law enforcement agencies were prosecuting these cases.

The VAWA Re-Authorization Act of 2000

The original VAWA provisions expired in 2000. Extension of the act became the subject of heated congressional debate not only on the amount of money expended, but also because of the philosophical issue of whether the federal government should lead in intervention had never been settled. Despite this doubt and a significant delay to achieve bipartisan support, the legislation passed, and the total amount of money authorized over 5 years was $3.3 billion. Major initiatives included "Services•Training•Officers•Prosecutors" or STOP Grants, with $925 million for distribution to police, prosecutors, courts, and state and local victim service agencies; $875 million to fund communities to develop shelters; and $200 million to fund civil legal assistance to help women obtain civil protective orders. In addition to these relatively highly funded items, there were additional areas that were not well funded, including $25 million transitional housing for victims and their families and $30 million for supervised visitation centers.

It is clear from the type and extent of funding that high priority was given to criminal justice and legal service agency efforts that were, in effect, of indirect benefit to victims, with less money directly channeled to victims themselves. If we were more cynical, we could surmise that this was due to a bureaucratic compromise in which funding for such agencies was the chief goal of the federal government—or at least that the lobbying by state and local agencies was more effective then that of the national women's groups who also supported the law.

Nonetheless, when federal money was not an issue and simple policy declarations could demonstrate legislative concerns for victims, the new legislation clearly broke new ground. Included were requirements that states give full faith and credit to each other's protective orders; that immigrant women subjected to threats of domestic violence, even those illegally in the country, would be protected and might even get permanent legal status; and that studies would be conducted to determine if victims of domestic violence had equal access to insurance, unemployment compensation, and if employers were adequately dealing with the problem.

CHAPTER 8

The Increased Policy Preference for Arrest

THE EVOLUTION OF ARREST PREFERENCES

By the early 1980s, there was widespread disillusionment with crisis intervention training. In part, this was a reflection of the general societal movement away from what Garland (2001) referred to as "penal welfarism" and toward the increased use of formal social controls. As noted in Chapter 6, Lipton, Martinson, and Wilks (1975) had already reported that "nothing works" as far as rehabilitation for many offenders. Policies favoring punitive rather than rehabilitative responses gradually permeated practitioner, policymaker, and general public attitudes (Garland, 2001).

Whereas reliance on the law is often believed to be a result of the failure of informal social controls (Black, 1976), many sociologists had long doubted the ability of the criminal justice system to substantially reduce domestic violence (Straus, 1977). Nonetheless, primary emphasis began shifting to the increased use of arrests. It had long been known that arresting certain domestic violence offenders was both proper and essential. After all, making an arrest was the only method by which police could ensure separation of the couple and prevent violence, at least until the offender has been released. Similarly, despite a strong past bias against arrest, police had made arrests for charges not specific to domestic violence. As we have discussed, the consensus on the historically limited role of arrest had been shattered by the early 1980s, followed by an expanding debate among police administrators, advocates for battered women, feminist allies, and researchers. The new proarrest consensus emerged when the traditional policy of nonintervention lost credibility and when the first reform, "crisis intervention," lost adherents. The concept of deterrence as a general preference for crime control was set to become the dominant perspective in mainstream academic literature and in policy circles. Not surprisingly, the two trends were linked; deterrence as a justification for use of arrest began to be regarded as the only possible reform. The line between researchers and activists often began to blur, with both vehemently advocating this perspective despite that fact (discussed later in this chapter) that research was inconclusive.

As explained in Chapter 6, these changes were the result of the unusual confluence of the acknowledged failure of past approaches combined with political pressures, legal liability, and highly publicized research. In Chapter 7, we discussed how a wave of state and federal legislation resulted in arrest becoming the focus for criminal justice intervention. It is now valuable to explore the theoretical basis for this perspective particularly because it is nearly unique in criminal justice. For most offenses, an arrest without commitment to subsequent prosecution and conviction or "plea bargain" would be regarded as a "failure." For example, the police would never define the mere apprehension of a burglar without prosecution as a success.

THE DEVELOPMENT OF MANDATORY ARREST POLICIES

In recent years, the increased policy preference toward arrest has been coupled with a growing desire to limit police discretion in the decision of whether to make an arrest. The result has been the widespread implementation of mandatory "arrest policies," whether adopted by statute or by administrative edict.

Why has this become true for domestic violence? What led researchers to believe that a domestic violence offense presented a unique criminal profile justifying different expectations for the use of arrest? In reality, it was assumed that the impact on victims, offenders, and society were behind this shift in policy. The following discussion focuses on the trend to limit discretion by imposing mandatory arrest policies.

The distinction between mandatory and preferred (or presumptive) arrest policies is quite significant in that a mandatory policy directs action and limits discretion, whereas a presumptive arrest policy simply services to guide, albeit strongly, officers' use of discretion in the direction of making an arrest. In Chapter 10, we discuss what, if any, operational differences arise between the two types of policies.

The Theoretical Basis for Mandatory Arrest

The adoption of a mandatory arrest policy has been based on the belief that enactment of such policies is necessary to actually change street-level justice. The premise also assumes that administratively eliminating officer discretion will actually lead to change in officers' behavior on the street.

The proponents of such a policy do not necessarily believe that *abuse of discretion* is the only, or even the primary, problem with normal police practices. Instead, they may believe that the basic problem is the inherent ambiguity of the police–citizen encounter in the context of domestic violence. The assumption is that the normal, even proper, use of discretion requires that an officer act on his or her values and experiences to make rapid interpretations of ambiguous facts, determine legal requirements, and analyze the consequences of possible actions. Only then is discretion applied to decide the proper course to follow. In cases involving domestic violence, officers must decide whether to arrest, separate, or merely warn. Although theoretically an independent decision for each intervention, police actions in normal domestic calls will almost inevitably be colored and bounded by the officer's "common knowledge" of the futility of police intervention. Consequently, the use of discretion itself, not the actual abuse, is the justification for preferring a mandatory policy.

Proponents of mandatory legislation and administrative policies also recognize that most officers either do not have adequate knowledge to handle domestic violence cases effectively or actively disapprove of police intervention. Implementing rigid proarrest policies, therefore, tries to force change in behavior without necessarily changing officer attitudes. Attitudinal change, although apparently considered less important, would then occur at some later point, if at all, by training officers on the rationale of the policy and by conversion due to their immersion into the procedure.

It is also hoped that implementation of an arrest policy collaterally increases the likelihood that the arrested offenders will be prosecuted. Arrests signify that the officer believes there is probable cause that a crime has occurred and that the defendant perpetrated it. It is hoped that this will influence the prosecutors and court to take such cases seriously. In contrast, prosecutors and judges in general, and in domestic violence cases in particular, disfavor victim-initiated actions. One early study reported that such cases were taken less seriously and were far more frequently dropped than those cases brought by the police (Burris & Jaffe, 1983). The accuracy of this observation has, however, been questioned (Ford, 1987). It is unclear whether it is an artifact of the sample studied or may instead be generalized to other jurisdictions. The relevance of this point to mandatory arrests may, of course, be questioned. The arrest of a domestic violence offender in a mandatory arrest jurisdiction might be treated as similar to those brought in by private complaints since, for this specific crime, a prosecutor would not have to face a potentially irate police officer asking why his case was not filed.

Proponents for both victims and offenders have also predicted positive effects of a mandatory arrest policy. One article theorized that without such a policy, women have become disillusioned with the police, feeling they cannot be protected and, as a result, do not even call them (Burris & Jaffe, 1983). Similarly, if one accepts the premise that arrest does deter further violence, then adoption of a mandatory arrest policy should provide an even higher level of deterrence (Burris & Jaffe, 1983).

Advantages for Victims

The specialized treatment of domestic violence was partially based on a theoretical model that explained how arrest itself might benefit domestic assault victims and confirm their status as victims of crime rather than as "guilty participants" in a "battling relationship." The opposite effect was feared when the parties were simply admonished to "keep the peace" or an assailant was merely arrested for being drunk or for disorderly conduct or disturbing the peace. The label of being a victim was also believed to increase victims' confidence in assessing their legal rights (Burris & Jaffe, 1983). In addition, police intervention (although not necessarily arrest) might be a vehicle for a victim to gain access to support services (Stark, 1993).

By placing the burden of an arrest fully on police, the theory was that less pressure would be placed on already-traumatized victims. They also may have suffered from situational stress reactions, including symptoms of posttraumatic stress disorder or "battered woman syndrome," which produce panic attacks, depression, and high levels of anxiety. When the police aggressively respond by arresting an offender, the victim might be greatly relieved, because both the immediate source of the terror and the responsibility for coercive actions taken against the offender has been removed.

Finally, such a policy fulfilled perceived victim needs of obtaining retribution. The underlying rationale of retribution is that, given similar factors, victims of interpersonal violence deserve the same societal reaction as victims of stranger violence. Although many researchers discredit the legitimacy of retribution, it is a well-recognized goal of criminal justice intervention—institutionalizing retribution and obviating the need for vigilantism.

Positive Effects on Offenders

Although the foregoing paragraphs discussed the impact of arrests on victims, most of the attention on the impact of arrest clearly has focused on current and potential offenders. For the past 15 years, deterrence-based theories of offending and reoffending have largely shaped criminal justice as well as overall societal responses to domestic violence. Certainty of apprehension and deterrence via arrest, aggressive prosecution, forced attendance in batterer treatment programs, and "target hardening" via issuance of restraining orders has therefore become a focus of the criminal justice system with arrests serving as the typical entry point for intervention.

Specific Deterrence

The theory of specific deterrence relies on the belief that individuals consider the benefits of a particular behavior against its potential consequences. Furthermore, once an offender is punished by means of an arrest or other criminal justice sanction, resulting threats of future punishment become more credible. The fear of punishment would then inhibit further violence (Ford, 1988).

Some researchers have argued that domestic violence is an ideal setting for the application of deterrence. Williams and Hawkins (1989) noted that although classic deterrence theory focused on formal punishments or "the intrinsic consequences of legal sanctions" (Gibbs, 1985), this analysis was inadequate. Instead, in domestic violence cases, it was the act of being publicly labeled as a "wife beater" and the attendant fear of adverse publicity that deterred possible recidivists. The shock of an arrest, especially to a man who does not often confront the police, was said to greatly deter future violence.

Applying deterrence theory to domestic violence was also consistent with psychological theory, which posited that the best time to attempt to correct deviant behavior was immediately after it occurred. When promptly administered, the punishment prevented reinforcement of deviant behavior that might otherwise recur if unnoticed and unpunished. Indeed, if, as Williams and Hawkins (1989) stated, the arrest is itself punishment, deterrence

would be enhanced because the punishment would be administered almost immediately after the incident, as opposed to waiting months for a slow and inconsistent criminal justice system.

General Deterrence

Specific deterrence is not the only method by which arrest may deter further acts of domestic violence. In addition to deterring existing offenders, arrest has long been claimed to be an effective deterrent for potential offenders (D. Martin, 1978). This is based on the theory that potential offenders weigh the benefits and costs of a crime. Hence, "general deterrence" may occur as well as the "specific deterrence" of past offenders (Nagin, 1998; Zimring & Hawkins, 1973).

This appears theoretically plausible. Men generally believe that arrest poses serious consequences (Carmody & Williams, 1987; Dutton, 1988; Williams & Hawkins, 1989). In one study of anticipated indirect effects of an arrest for domestic violence, 63% of men stated they would lose self-respect if arrested. Most men also feared family stigma and social disapproval. Consequently, although the possible ultimate costs of an arrest such as time in jail or loss of a job might be severe, they were correctly perceived as being unlikely (Williams & Hawkins, 1989).

Deterrence theorists believe this is predictable because although conviction and sentencing for a domestic violence–related offense would be far more serious than simple arrest, the chances of conviction are so low that the threat is simply not credible. In contrast, public perception of the likelihood of an arrest may be effective as a deterrent.

Apart from the Minneapolis Domestic Violence Experiment (MDVE) and its replications (discussed in Chapter 6), further tests of deterrence in the context of prevention of domestic violence were problematic.

Advantages for Society

A policy favoring arrest may have an additional indirect societal impact. As set forth in chapters 1 and 4, some victim advocates believe that our culture implicitly uses domestic violence as a method of reinforcing the societal domination of the more powerful members of society. From this perspective, the failure to arrest batterers tacitly condones such conduct, thereby impinging on the social equality of women. A policy favoring domestic violence arrest, then, has the potential of undermining one of the pillars of sexism in society—the implicit right of men to physically dominate women and children within his patriarchal family unit without fear of government intervention.

We need not fully subscribe to this belief to realize that the increased role of arrest benefits society for a variety of reasons. For example, arrests may well serve a boundary-maintenance function. If police enforce existing laws against domestic violence, societal tolerance for abusive behavior in general may gradually dissipate as the behavior is labeled and actually *treated as a crime*. The direct analogy is to the increased enforcement of drunk driving laws in the past several years. By many accounts, this first resulted in less toleration of drunk drivers by the public, and over time, in a reduction in the number of drunk drivers and resultant accidents.

This indirect potential for societal change has not really been explored in mainstream criminal justice literature and may, at least at this time, be more of a hope than reality. Empirical research and writings as well as funding of feminist academicians have not been as evident in mainstream academia. Similarly, until the enactment of VAWA, there was little funding to enable practitioners to gather data. This was perhaps an unintended consequence of the almost exclusive focus of funding agencies on deterrence and experimental research. Feminist research also may not have been widely publicized because of barriers in academia toward such approaches. Although we do not judge ability of researchers by their gender, it is noteworthy that funding for the MDVE, as well as all of the replication studies, was given virtually exclusively to male researchers, many—if not most—inexperienced with domestic violence research. Furthermore, it is questionable if the entire topic of domestic violence as presented in the initial MDVE would have been directly funded had the proposal not addressed the topic as a "case study" for broader deterrence theory.

For some time, there has been a body of researchers that have argued for the need to hear directly from victims about their experiences, both with violence and the criminal justice system. Fortunately, this research is now beginning to proliferate and emerge.

THE LIMITS AND COSTS OF MANDATORY ARREST

Although the impact of arrest sanctions on victims, offenders, and society may provide a cogent argument for its enhanced use, we continue to believe that the negative consequences of total removal of police arrest discretion and mandatory arrest presents severe costs to society in general and victims in particular. As we discuss later in greater detail, we believe such approaches fail to adequately address victim preferences or *their* perspectives.

The Controversy Over Mandatory Arrest

Policy mandates and pressures to mandate arrest in the case of a specific offense result in a shift from the traditional police role in which the organization had to display an overriding "commitment to maintaining the collective good, serving with honor and loyalty, and observing tradition," even if certain categories of citizens were not adequately served. In fact, it can be argued that policy mandates such as mandatory arrest for domestic violence are in direct contradiction with the traditional mandate (Manning, 1993).

If we assume that resources are made available and a policy of mandatory arrest is actually implemented at the street level, the merits of such a policy and its costs and drawbacks need to be carefully considered. To start, we need to consider critically the supposed major benefits. A primary argument for increased use of arrest is its deterrent value.

Can Arrest Really Serve As a Deterrent?

As we described earlier in this chapter, in the context of a domestic violence arrest, deterrence depends on the accuracy of a string of assumptions about the attitudes and behavior of offenders: (a) an offender can consciously change deeply rooted, noneconomically driven abusive behavior if an arrest is threatened; (b) an offender believes the police will actually be called; (c) the offender believes that police will respond and make an arrest; and (d) an offender will be inhibited by the prospects of an arrest, often without any realistic probability of a conviction or jail time.

The theory of an arrest having such an impact on domestic violence offenders is somewhat inconsistent with other studies on deterrence. Researchers who have examined offender conduct have reported that real deterrence depends on the offender consciously weighing the prospects of a negative response to a particular act. Therefore, the behavior is rationally calculated in light of the long-term risks of arrest compared with the shorter term "gain" from committing physical abuse. Unfortunately, reality is somewhat more complicated.

It is difficult to discern which form of deterrence will occur from the coercive exercise of police authority in the presence of oftentimes "uncontrollable" or irrational rages typically exacerbated by substance use. Certainly, any exposure to the criminal justice system will affect many offenders, and there may be short-term behavior modifications for most batterers. Moreover, the extent to which such an effect is long-term or how many offenders find new victims when a prior victim no longer tolerates violence is unknown.

As we cover in detail in Chapter 15, perhaps the best long-term result that might be expected occurs when arrest is simply part of an integrated holistic approach to partner and family violence. A more modest achievement of arrest may be that fear of future punishment will facilitate compliance, at least to the point of attendance, with rehabilitation efforts. If this is the limited and indirect deterrent value of an arrest, however, perhaps the goal could be accomplished by aggressively prosecuting and publicizing fewer but more severe cases of domestic violence.

We also question the underlying goal of a mechanistic application of deterrence theory. If arrest serves as a deterrent to spousal assault without ending the underlying tendency of an assailant toward violent outbursts, the ultimate effect may be merely to displace these tendencies. The offender might then perceive that he can batter others—perhaps children, aged relatives, or people in barroom brawls—with less police interference.

Because researchers typically have focused on reoffending against the same victim, many might view this as a victory; however, if the potential for displacement is also considered, it is entirely possible that the offender may simply target a new victim. This is not an unlikely outcome for an offender who does not change his attitudes toward assaulting victims yet perceives an increased cost for reabusing a particular victim (Reiss, 1986, cited in Elliott, 1989).

There is evidence to suggest this occurs. Buzawa et al. (1999) found that those offenders with the greatest prior criminal history and greatest number of prior restraining orders were, in fact, those most likely to find new victims rather than reoffend against the same victim. In a modification of this pattern, it has been posited that if the victim finds that arrest does not deter subsequent assault, she may leave. This creates a strong possibility that an offender, whose attitudes remain largely unchanged, will simply abuse a different victim (Elliott, 1989). Under either of these scenarios, deterrence without rehabilitation does not of itself justify increased arrests.

Clearly, the primary problem with relying on arrest to deter intimate violence is the limitations inherent in the practical application of deterrence theory to domestic abuse. Illicit activities that are economically motivated or require careful planning would intuitively seem to be more amenable to deterrence than acts viewed by most people as spontaneous or arising in the context of serious mental health or substance abuse. Indeed, it is more likely that noneconomic crimes in general and the impulsive explosive use of violence, often coupled with substance abuse or other mental health concerns that are typical in domestic assaults, are the least apt to be deterred. In this regard, Ford (1988) pointed out that domestic violence is usually an impulsive act drawn from a limited repertoire of responses to stress, attacks on self-esteem, or frustration by those who have few inhibitions against using violence in angered states. Under such circumstances, it is difficult to argue that violence will reoccur unless underlying issues are satisfactorily addressed.

In stating this, we recognize that many believe violent men really can control their aggression. These men use violence as a weapon to establish dominance in settings where they are least likely to be punished—typically the home—and can control the degree of violence that they use. Therefore, men who beat their wives and children, despite alcoholic rages, are said to somehow continue when the police have arrived or when they are in public. This may indeed be true for some assailants, but it is overly simplistic, to generalize the ability to control violence among all batterers. In fact, Buzawa et al. (1999) and the domestic violence replication studies consistently reported that the most violent domestic abusers are the most violent criminals in general, arguing fairly persuasively that no level of deterrence can be assumed based simply on arrest or even conviction.

Deterrence of the remaining batterers also was more likely to have had greater credibility when the police rarely, if ever, arrested domestic violence offenders. At the present time, with the well-publicized (if somewhat overstated) emphasis on police use of arrests, it is plausible that many, if not most, of the remaining offenders cannot be easily deterred.

There are several reasons deterrence-based principles appear to be overly simplistic when addressing likely variations in batterer responses to criminal justice sanctions. Of primary importance are the anticipated variations in batterer responses to criminal justice sanctions. This diversity is evident even when considering the impact of arrest on relatively low-risk offenders such as the occasional "domestic violence only" offenders, generally considered "capable" of controlling their behavior. Such offenders may indeed batter because they perceive they "can get away with it," are under significant stress, or have consumed excessive alcohol or drugs. This group is less likely to reoffend even if no arrest is made. Consequently, arrest as a deterrent appears to have the most value in the group needing it the least.

Although some of these types of batterers may suffer remorse, still others in this group may believe their conduct did not justify arrest (Dutton, 1987). This may mean that even for some "low-risk" offenders, the consequences of arrest may be the retaliation that victims so often express as a concern.

Therefore, the argument that Williams and Hawkins (1989) advanced of the "humiliation" of an arrest as a deterrent may apply only to certain groups. For many, the fear of an arrest and its indirect effects do serve as an effective deterrent, but many may instead react by further rejecting societal norms in an effort to protect self-esteem and justify their behavior. Furthermore, the social stigma that could result in job loss or other negative consequences may also negate the deterrent effect of arrest.

Hard-core deviants and those that have already been arrested for domestic violence or other charges are unlikely to be markedly deterred by another arrest (Buzawa et al., 1999; Ferraro, 1989a). As stated earlier, research has found that the latter group of hard-core abusers accounts for most numerous and severe acts of domestic violence (Buzawa et al., 1999; Pierce et al., 1988; Sherman, 1992; Straus, 1996). This may be especially true in cases of serious repetitive offenders—those who are widely regarded as being the most likely to pose serious, long-term risk to victims. Second, even if accompanied by a night in jail, the minimal costs of arrest alone may sometimes actually serve as a reinforcement of the crime's benefits. In jurisdictions without a comprehensive strategy for domestic violence intervention, offenders will rapidly learn that there are no further sanctions imposed beyond the arrest itself. They may conclude that the "cost" of an arrest is considered acceptable (Dutton, 1987; Fagan, 1988; Maxwell et al., 2001), especially because many of the offenders are already experienced with the criminal justice system (Buzawa et al., 1999).

Even if a conviction occurs, it is unlikely that an offender will be incarcerated. Probation is the typical outcome for a misdemeanor assault, and if jail sentences are imposed, they tend to be of short duration. Domestic violence offenses are primarily processed as misdemeanors rather than felonies in many states. In Massachusetts, for example, domestic violence legislation included an enhanced sentence for a misdemeanor assaults to 2.5 years in the House of Corrections. This change from the 1-year limitation for a misdemeanor offense was considered necessary given the gravity of many assaults; it may more cynically be observed that this is an alternative to charging an offender for conduct that meets the legal definition of a felonious assault. For example, more than 98% of domestic violence charges in the Quincy District Court (QDC), in Massachusetts were for misdemeanor assault (Supreme Judicial Court, 1996).

Using interview data, Ford (1992) found that more than 95% of those arrested had previously battered the same victim, 94% in the previous 6 months. Therefore, repeat offenders are likely to be driven by factors that are not easily controlled or changed. Klein (1994a) confirmed this, finding that such offenders to fit profiles similar to other serious violent offenders. In addition, one study in a model court found that 84% of offenders reaching court for domestic assaults had prior criminal records, 54% had five or more prior criminal charges, and 59% had prior histories of crimes against persons with an average of 3.1 charges per defendant. For this group, arrest only served to enrage these offenders, resulting in increased victim danger rather than as a deterrent (Buzawa et al., 1999; see also Sherman et al., 1992b).

Has the Increase in Arrests Led to a Corresponding Decrease in Offenses?

We have noted that overall rates for serious domestic violence offenses appear to have been decreasing since 1990, but not at a rate greater than for other violent crime. Indeed, data for domestic homicides and the impact of criminal justice intervention are inconsistent at best (Dugan et al., 2001), suggesting that the impact of the increased use of sanctions has been of limited impact.

To the extent that there has been a recent decrease in domestic violence, this may suggest that the current increased likelihood of arrest has deterred many former or potential offenders who are able to control violent tendencies when there is a high risk of arrest; however, it is too early to conclude that arrest itself was the key factor leading to the decrease in the rate of domestic violence assaults. It is important to acknowledge the overall societal context in which trends are analyzed. In this case, the underlying trend is unclear. According to recent National Crime Victimization Survey (NCVS) data, violence overall, including nondomestic assault, has decreased at greater rates than domestic violence.

It can be argued that observed declines in assaults are merely a function of current demographics with the high violence age cohorts (aged 20–29) decreasing as a percentage of society. This analysis also is too simplistic because the increased number of police and the increased rates and length of incarceration, particularly for minority offenders, have affected violent crime rates. One researcher, using statistics from the Bureau of Justice Statistics, reported that on any given day, 42% of Black men between the ages of 18 and 35 in Washington, DC, and 56% of the Black men in Baltimore were in prison, jail, or on probation or parole (Walker, 2001). In all likelihood, this factor has contributed to the decreasing rates of domestic assault against Black women.

While this may not appear relevant, this point is actually of great importance. Recent research suggests that those offenders

reaching the criminal justice system who continue to reoffend despite increased sanctions also tend to be generally violent. If increasingly severe jail and prison terms incapacitate such people for lengthy periods of time, the overall societal problem of domestic violence may diminish regardless of whether arrest itself, or any other domestic violence specific action, is effective. If not, society may simply be waiting for a new cohort of young men to appear for the rates of domestic violence to increase to previous levels.

In any event, as we discuss in subsequent chapters, the current thinking is that researchers need to typologize offenders and acknowledge that these variations have an impact on the effect of any type of intervention. Unfortunately, it would be conceptually and legally difficult to divide use of arrests between groups of offenders. In fact, merely articulating a policy favoring arrest for a first time or "normal" offender but to ignore the "hard-core" abuser graphically demonstrates its folly. Instead, such a policy can only be implemented as part of an overall framework heavily favoring arrests while providing alternative intervention strategies for an occasional batterer committing minor assaults. Indeed, we believe it necessary to focus on differing approaches to different types of offenders, just as we should acknowledge differential victim needs and priorities. Certainly criminal justice has adopted this perspective with other types of offenders—that is, recognizing the difference between a kleptomaniac and a career larcenist or incorporating "criminal history" as an important part of the federal sentencing guidelines.

THE COSTS AND UNINTENDED EFFECTS OF ARREST

For more than 20 years, researchers have examined police arrest practices and their impact. This research has resulted in a diverse range of organizational, attitudinal, situational, and sociodemographic variables affecting the outcome. Nonetheless, although there has been a plethora of studies examining whether the intended outcomes of policy mandates have been achieved, there has been a paucity of research on the costs and unintended consequences of such policies. Over the years, we have suggested a variety of known costs and unanticipated consequences of arrest.

Costs of Arrest

There are a variety of ways to measure the impact of an agency's actions. One of the primary ways in which any agency action is judged is by its cost-effectiveness. In the police world, this translates relatively directly into a calculation of the costs of an action such as arrest as a function of prevention or apprehension of criminal activity. It cannot be disputed that an arrest, especially if coupled with temporary incarceration, is costly to the law enforcement agency, to the offender, and often to the victim.

In addition to the rather obvious direct costs of time and effort to the responding agency and the victim and offender, an arrest of a family member, including an abusive spouse, is likely to traumatize other family members. Children, already affected by the abuse, may be affected by the arrest itself or the stigma associated with the incident. Of course, this concern may be countered by believing it beneficial for children to witness a parental arrest as confirmation of the unacceptability of assaulting a family member; however, in many, if not most, cases, a child closely identifies with his or her parent and typically would not benefit from seeing him or her led out of the house in handcuffs. This does not mean arrest should not be used when indicated, merely that all ramifications should be considered.

There may be indirect effects on an offender beyond the obvious criminal justice intervention. Although Sherman and Berk (1984a) and the replication studies did not really find a serious problem in "secondary deviance," it is possible that, over time, arrested assailants may begin identifying themselves as generalized deviants and experience a reverse spillover effect (e.g., committing more forms of deviance) from being labeled as a batterer.

The victim also may feel the effects of an arrest. She may justifiably fear physical or economic retaliation or other acts committed by the assailant or by his family, relatives, or friends that are designed to intimidate and prevent her from pressing charges. If already severely physically or emotionally traumatized by abuse, she may find the additional demands attendant to supporting arrest beyond her capabilities. Although the arrest alone may not have a serious financial impact on the family, it may affect an offender's current or future employment thereby indirectly affecting the offender's ability to maintain child support or other payments.

For such reasons, the prospects of arrest may deter many women from reporting abuse. This may be especially true in some minority communities. African Americans have long protested that they are disproportionately subject to arrests and police brutality. Furthermore, African American women are more likely to have their children taken away from them because of domestic violence (Bent-Goodley, 2001). In fact, one study reported that African American Women were 1.5 times less likely to call the police compared with white women (Joseph, 1997). It is possible that many African American women currently believe racism is more serious than sexism, even when the latter involves personal risk (Bent-Goodley, 2001). This is extremely significant because domestic violence is more likely to be known by police among urban, lower socioeconomic classes in general and minority communities in particular.

It is likely that the increased use of arrest will strengthen the number (and validity) of claims of disproportionate use of arrests and physical force on Black men (Forrell, 1990–1991; Zorza & Woods, 1994). Therefore, it is necessary to determine if other less intrusive measures would be of similar effectiveness with far fewer negative consequences. As noted earlier, virtually any police intervention in domestic violence, even if flawed, has some deterrent effect for many batterers (Carmody & Williams, 1987; Feld & Straus, 1989; Ford, 1988; Pierce & Deutsch, 1990). If this is true, should the "default position" be the routine resort to arrest, the police action most likely to focus increased tensions and dissatisfaction with the minority community?

Can We Determine a Valid Reason for Arrest Without Conviction?

We admit to a transcending philosophical concern over the use of an arrest as a "punishment." Arrest used for its deterrent value appears to be a subversion of the legitimate but limited arrest powers constitutionally given to police. Police have never constitutionally been given power to inflict pain and humiliation to effect social goals, no matter how laudable. Instead, there has been a recognition that no agency, especially the police, has this authority, independent of established legal procedures to adjudicate guilt.

Although it would be simplistic to ignore the daily informality inherent in dispensing street-level justice and previous police inaction, making an arrest without an attendant commitment to prosecute those arrested establishes a dangerous precedent. We recognize that the goal of deterrence of spousal assaults is sound and has been frustrated by past police behavior; however, we are concerned that if a policy of "automatic" or mandatory arrest is started, checks on police abuse of power will become absent. This is a realistic concern.

It has long been theorized that the "exclusionary rule" forbidding the introduction of illegally obtained evidence has been a key factor limiting improper police conduct in searches and seizures, making arrests and obtaining confessions. What restrains improper police conduct when arrests are simply a tool to "punish" an offender? If the police have the organizational "mandate" to punish via arrest, why shouldn't they also feel the right to "rough up" the offender while they are at it? After all, it could be argued this will strengthen deterrence and "even the score." The fact is that as a society, we have never trusted police with such power. The theory of deterrence as a simple result of an arrest may ultimately push society toward such an end point.

Is Dual Arrest a Likely Outcome of the Push for Arrest?

A further consequence of nationwide efforts to enforce mandatory arrest policies in intimate partner cases has been a distinct rise in the number of women arrested for intimate partner violence. This often occurs in the context of a dual arrest, in which *both* the male and the female partners are arrested. Along with the general increase in arrests has been a rise in the number of cases in which the police have arrested both the victim and the offender after the implementation of a preferred or mandatory arrest law (see, e.g., S. Epstein, 1987; M. Martin, 1997; Pirro, 1997; Saunders, 1995; Victim Services Agency, 1988). In one study, women were arrested in 50% of cases in which an arrest was made for domestic violence (S. Epstein, 1987).

More recently, when New York enacted its mandatory arrest law in 1995, dual arrests were reported to have had similar increases (Pirro, 1997). In her seminal work on dual arrests, Martin (1997) examined the disposition of domestic abuse cases handled by the criminal courts in Connecticut just after implementation of a 1988 mandatory arrest policy. She found a dual arrest rate of 33% in adult intimate partner violence cases. Compared with incidents resulting in single arrest, dual arrest cases were more likely to involve young White women who were unmarried and living with the codefendant. Drugs and alcohol were more likely to be involved in dual arrest cases, although there was no information on which partner was actually under the influence.

Subsequent research has shown wide variations in dual arrest rates. According to available data, dual arrest rates are as high as 23% in Connecticut (Connecticut State Police, 2000) and as low as 5.5% in adjacent Rhode Island (Rhode Island Domestic Violence and Reporting Unit, 2000), and 9% in Arizona (Governor's Commission on Violence Against Women, 2000). The rate of women arrested for domestic violence also varies. In these three jurisdictions, it is 19.8%, 16.7%, and 27%, respectively.

To date, there has been a lack of comprehensive research conducted on dual arrests, although it is currently an issue receiving considerable attention among policymakers and practitioners. What research does exist suggests that dual arrest rates have often increased after the implementation of a preferred or mandatory arrest law and that the rates vary greatly throughout the nation (Hirschel & Buzawa, in press). It is unknown whether the differences in dual arrest rates are the result of variations in state laws, police training, organizational culture, or incident, offender, and victim characteristics (or a combination of these factors).

Clearly the police are required to rely on the criminal code as the basis for arrest decisions. Criminal codes focus on an individual act (usually physical harm or threat of physical harm) for which an individual is held responsible. As a result of applying "legalistic definitions" that emphasize violence rather than a continuing pattern of psychological and physical abuse, the police typically force a diverse range of incidents into one of a fixed set of formal categories, preventing them from dealing with the complexities and unique aspects of each case (Manning, 1996).

For example, a woman who has been the victim in an ongoing pattern of violence may find that the police arrive only to misinterpret an act of self-defense on her part out of context, resulting in her arrest. The inability or refusal of police to distinguish victims from offenders is one possible explanation for the existence of high dual arrest rates. To address this concern, some states, beginning with Washington in 1985, started enacting "primary" or "predominant aggressor" laws. Currently, 22 states have such laws.

Primary aggressor statutes have attempted to reduce dual arrests by recognizing that people can legitimately commit acts of violence in self-defense. In practice, however, such laws do not always help. The true aggressor may not have struck a physical blow at the particular time that would allow the police to use a primary aggressor provision. As discussed earlier, the criminal justice system implicitly requires the identification of a crime with a defined victim and offender. Long-term abuse resulting in victim retaliatory violence is likely to be treated as domestic violence.

In Chapter 3, we discussed how violence in some families may be mutual, forcing police to judge who initiated a particular violent incident, rather than who is generally the primary aggressor. Even when it is clear that one party is at fault, this victim–offender dichotomy precludes one from seeing domestic assault as a type of interaction that, in some cases, may be a response to conflict. A person's status may not only be difficult to identify but not remain constant in across incidents. We know there are some violent relationships in which partners may be both violent and victimized at various points in their lives (H. Johnson, 2001; Straus, 1999). M. Johnson (1995) reported that in situations with "common couple violence,"—so-called battling couples—there are low but recurrent acts of minor violence initiated by either party, but the type of violence generally seen by police (and in shelter and clinical samples) is more likely to involve serious and frequent beatings, as well as the terrorizing of women.

Unfortunately, police typically do not (or are not allowed) to consider these factors when determining which party is a victim. They are forced to identify a "victim" and an "offender." Although this might involve identifying the person with the most serious injury as the victim, research by Buzawa and Hotaling (2000) indicates that this is not always true, with more insidious factors entering into decision making. This research found that women involved in partner violence were the category of victim most likely to be seriously injured, and they also were the "preferred" victims regardless of injury. This might appear to be explainable in adult male–female partner violence; however, what is surprising is that Buzawa and Hotaling also found that minors to be 6 times more likely to be arrested compared with either men or women and that despite child abuse laws covering juveniles until the age of 18, an arrest is far less likely to be made when a minor is the victim of domestic assault.

Many researchers and advocates believe that dual arrest typically discriminates against women as the primary victims of domestic assault. This belief is fostered by research clearly showing both that offenders seen by the criminal justice system are likely

to represent the more serious of the batterers (who are predominantly male) and that women's physical violence is far less likely to cause injury or to be motivated by attempts to terrorize the partner (Kaufman Kantor & Straus, 1990; Stets & Straus, 1990). A high proportion of male batterers engage in systematic victimization of women. Currently, there is no comparable evidence of this type of victimization by women (Kantor & Jasinski, 1998). Therefore, as an aggregate, women's violence may be more likely to be an act of self-defense because the cases police see are less likely to reflect the (usually) more minor cases in which there are mutually violent relationships.

In some cases, dual arrests may be a result of insufficient police training in identifying the primary aggressor. Alternatively, some advocates argue that such arrests may constitute a tacit mechanism to further punish women that burden the police with domestic "problems." There are, however, additional explanations for high dual arrest rates. It has also been suggested that officers, who are prone to assume that adult male-against-female violence involves a male primary aggressor, find that they are in a situation in which the female (according to both parties' admissions and to evidence on arrival) is the primary aggressor.

In some jurisdictions, current political or organizational pressure may discourage officers from arresting women as aggressors. This observation is supported by extant research. D. A. Jones and Belknap (1999, pp. 265–666) found in their Boulder, Colorado, study that "those identified as male victims were more than three times as likely to be part of a dual arrest couple than those individuals identified as female victims." Likewise, Buzawa and Hotaling (2000) found that even when a man was a victim, the woman was 5 times less likely to be arrested than a man in a similar situation. In addition, current organizational and political pressures may discourage officers from dual arrest when the incident could in fact be defined as mutually violent. For example, if a woman initiated violence by throwing an object at her partner, resulting in a bruise or cut, and the man retaliated violently, causing similar bruising, officers were found to make no arrest or simply to arrest the man (Buzawa & Hotaling, 2000).

As stated earlier, there are some jurisdictions that do not have high dual arrest rates. In these jurisdictions, again for organizational or political reasons, officers may be discouraged both from arresting women and from making dual arrests. Furthermore, the likelihood of prosecution in such cases is likely to affect officer behavior, with both formal and informal knowledge of the prospects of prosecution affecting their actions (Manning, 1997). Research conducted in three Massachusetts towns found that only three (less than 1%) of 319 domestic assault cases produced dual arrests and that none of these dual arrests involved a female against male intimate partner. Although these towns did not have high dual arrest rates, many domestic assaults that could have been defined as mutually violent appeared to be redefined so as not to merit even a preferred arrest response. This occurred even though in 18.8% of nonarrest cases, in which both parties acted violently, one of the parties was injured (Buzawa & Hotaling, 2000).

A fundamental question is, when, if ever, is dual arrest appropriate? There is no easy answer to this question, particularly because there is no empirical data suggesting that some families involve two violent partners, and sometimes violent children (M. Johnson, 1995, 2000; Straus, 1999). To date, there has been little detailed research conducted on dual arrests. Certainly a contextual understanding of exactly what occurs in dual arrest cases and an empirical analysis distinguishing

them from other domestic assault cases is totally absent. The research that has been performed, such as M. Martin (1997), has been limited to a single site or single jurisdiction with a limited set of variables (Hirschel & Buzawa, in press).

THE DIVERSITY OF VICTIM NEEDS AND DIVERGENT AFFECTS OF MANDATORY ARREST

The primary goal of all domestic violence legislation is to prevent further violence, but its implementation may further disempower victims and possibly work against their best interests. In many cases, the goals of assisting and empowering domestic violence victims is not as straight forward as in other settings. Even among violent crimes, victims of domestic violence may differ from other victims if only based on their intimate knowledge of the offender and their relationship.

To understand the impact of mandatory arrest on victims, it is important to realize that victims as well as offenders are not a monolithic group but are a highly diverse population (Hirschel et al., 1992). Many victims are trapped by dependency on the offender, believing that they must remain in an abusive situation for economic, physical, or even emotional survival (Barnett, 2000). The victim's goals are similarly diverse. Some may wish to salvage a flawed relationship in which aggressive behavior is now customary, whereas other victims may have already terminated contact with the offender. Victims may believe that an arrest will make a bad situation worse, or as described earlier, they may have had negative experiences with police interventions in the past. Victims also vary in their perceptions of the level of danger, threat, and harm that an offender presents. Obviously, not all offenders present the same degree of danger; some victims are threatened or assaulted by a first-time offender, and others find themselves the target of a serial batterer.

Jurisdictions with mandatory arrest policies cannot incorporate the complexity of these victim needs and preferences into policies and practices. Clearly, victim situations are not all alike, and yet such policies perceive them to be. Unfortunately, it can even be said that many practitioners consider this largely irrelevant because the goal of the criminal justice system is to address the offenders behavior rather than the victim's preferences and needs. Still others acknowledge that victims have preferences but believe that victims are incapable of judging what is in their interests and that "professionals" should make these decisions. For many racial and ethnic minorities, the risks of arrest may outweigh potential benefits. These groups of women are more likely to perceive or actually be the recipients of police mistreatment—or at best are more vulnerable to state control. They have greater fears than other victims that their children might be taken away from them, especially in states mandating investigation of all domestic assault cases in which children are present. Furthermore, they are at greater risk of having their own criminal activities uncovered (e.g., drug-addicted victims); the likelihood of their arrest increases with proactive or mandatory arrest policies (Coker, 2000).

Differential rates of domestic violence among certain population subgroups compound this lack of trust. Rates of domestic violence are the highest among racial and ethnic minorities and the poor in general (Fagan, 1996). As discussed earlier, research has found minorities to be less likely to trust the criminal justice system (Bent-Goodley, 2001; Black, 1980; Coker, 2000; Robinson & Chandek, 2000). In the African American community, the label of victim or offender may create an unwanted stigma. Many African American women perceive domestic violence as a concept of "white feminism and male bashing" (Bent-Goodley, 2001, p. 321). Many domestic violence victims may simply want "restoration" or redress, not vengeance or absolute punishment. They may be far less concerned with the abusers' punishment than using the criminal justice system to achieve these purposes (Lerman, 1992).

Ambivalence, as discussed in detail in the chapters regarding prosecution, often translates into a victim's failure to support cases. Domestic violence victims are far more likely than other victims to be motivated by self-protection and less on vengeance in calling police and pursuing prosecution (R. C. Davis & Smith, 1982, Lerman, 1992). Although many people who are victimized by someone with whom their relationship has ended may want aggressive prosecution, others simply seek an end to immediate abuse.

Victim Preferences

The previous discussion is not intended to suggest that victims do not want police intervention; the vast majority of victims do. Recent research in western Massachusetts by Hotaling and Buzawa (2001) found that victims consistently wanted the police to respond to incidents, even if arrest was not always desired. More than 84% of all assault victims wanted a police response, with no real difference between domestic assaults (83%) compared with nondomestic assaults (88%). A follow-up question asking the victim's first choice for who should handle the incident (e.g., the police, themselves, medical or counseling personnel, family neighbors, or family members) found that for both domestic and nondomestic assault cases, more than two thirds (67% and 68%, respectively) wanted the police to handle assaults.

Interesting data were uncovered in terms of the primary action that the victim wanted the police to take. Choices given were arrest, control the offender, do nothing, or don't know. The overall result showed that 47% wanted an arrest, 39% control, 9% do nothing, and 5% don't know; however, this conceals data that reveal a major difference in the two populations. In domestic assault cases only 33% wanted an arrest made compared with 52% who wanted the offender controlled but not arrested. In nondomestic assault cases, 76% wanted the offender arrested, and only 12% wanted the offender controlled.

This data show, as reported in many other jurisdictions, that most victims of domestic assault do not prefer arrest as their first option. Given the current policy preferences for domestic violence arrests, data also show that police refuse to follow the victim's request more frequently in domestic assault cases (25%) than nondomestic assault cases (4%). The victim disagreed with arrests made in 60% of domestic assaults compared with only 12% of nondomestic assaults; situations in which the suspect was not arrested but the victim disagreed occurred in 4% of domestic assaults and 44% in nondomestic assaults. Clearly, the police in the jurisdictions studied determined the need for arrest independently of victim preferences in cases of domestic assault.

In contrast, the areas of agreement in which the suspect was arrested and the victim agreed with the arrest were lower (29%) for domestic and higher (36%) for nondomestic assaults or when the suspect was not arrested and the victim agreed (8% in both domestic and nondomestic assaults).

Mandatory arrest statutes or policies may therefore lead to adverse consequences in which victims are at the least disempowered and, at worst, deterred from calling the police in the future because unwanted arrests are made. These data strongly suggest that the significant numbers (60%) of domestic assault cases in which the offender was arrested and the victim disagreed dramatically increasing the potential of adverse consequences. This finding shows that victims are either very satisfied or somewhat satisfied in 70% of cases. Of even greater significance, they were more satisfied in cases of domestic assault (75%) compared with nondomestic assault (60%). Similarly, when victims were asked if they would call the police again in a similar situation, the data suggest that a high percentage of people would do so. Overall, 61% would definitely call the police (62% domestic, 60% nondomestic), and 14% would probably call the police (12% domestic, 20% nondomestic); however, 25% overall would probably not, definitely not, or were unsure of whether they would call the police again. This was higher in cases of domestic assault for which 27% said they would not or might not call the police compared with 20% of nondomestic assault victims.

The Limitations of Police Response to Stalking

As covered in Chapter 7, anti-stalking legislation, beginning with the 1990 California anti-stalking statute, has now been enacted in every state. The proper police response to stalking is, however, even more difficult to determine than in cases of domestic assault. The issue posed here is typically not simply whether to make an arrest, but what constitutes an offense for which an arrest may be made. The actual effect of an arrest on a stalker's propensity to continue stalking as opposed to other possible law enforcement actions has not, to the best of our knowledge, been empirically examined to date. Unless stalking occurs as part of an overall mixed pattern of violence, harassment, and threats, stalking may simply be a precursor offense to other, more traditional criminal activity. As such, although there are now criminal statutes on the books, realistically it is difficult to expect police to be able to arrest someone for what may initially perceive as random or relatively minor occurrences. In some states, it may be impossible to make arrests because of statutory restrictions allowing arrest only for cases of actual threats. Unfortunately, we know that subsequent violence cannot be easily predicted based on the specific harassment activity.

In such cases, the only realistic police intervention strategy may to support stalking victims by helping them seek and enforce restraining orders, the violation of which can justify an arrest. The responding officer should assist a stalking victim in developing sustainable evidence of such behavior. For example, the victim's first impulse may be to remove or destroy obscene messages from the stalker. As J. Reid Meloy, a noted forensic psychologist stated,

> In all cases of relational intrusion, both before and after the behavior has passed the threshold of criminal stalking, the victim should thoroughly document each incident (date, time, place, event) in a daily log, and keep any tangible proof of its occurrence. This may include but is not limited to, photos, audio tapes, videotapes, letters, notes, facsimile transmissions, printing of e-mail messages, unwanted gifts, and suspicious, inappropriate, or frightening items (one perpetrator scratched the name of his victim on a bullet cartridge and mailed it to her). Evidence such as this establishes a course of conduct in stalking cases and may be central to convincing the trier of fact that the victim was in reasonable fear. (Meloy, 1997, pp. 176–177)

Activity of this nature would need to be coordinated closely between a specific police officer knowledgeable about the circumstances (who has investigated prior criminal activity of the alleged perpetrator) and a prosecutor willing to maintain a case despite lack of physical violence. In addition, either that officer or other crime prevention officers should assist the victim in target hardening as well as documenting any incident. The types of such evidence may be extremely varied.

CHAPTER 9

Factors Affecting Police Response

Police can take a variety of actions in cases of domestic violence, including making an arrest. In many jurisdictions in which arrest remains highly variable even if a "proarrest" policy has been implemented, researchers have focused on identifying those factors on which the decision to arrest is based. Some research has suggested that even in jurisdictions with nominally proarrest policies, little congruence exists between laws that mandate arrest for domestic assault and the police enforcement of those laws (Buzawa & Austin, 1993).

The issue of the extent to which police honor policy preferences to make arrests is covered in Chapter 11. Here, we consider the factors under which an arrest actually occurs. The purpose is to see which arrests are predictable and to provide insight as to when new proarrest policies are most likely to meet resistance.

It has long been known that police usually do not arrest in cases of both of domestic and nondomestic assaults; arrest has generally been infrequent and considered a last resort (Bittner, 1974; Black, 1976; Elliott, 1989; Manning, 1997; Parnas, 1967; Skolnick, 1975; Wilson, 1968). In fact it is become widely felt that police act situationally, that is, they treat all cases that share the same characteristics in a similar manner (Elliot, 1989; Faragher, 1985; Sanders, 1988;

Sherman, 1992). The differential impact of these situational factors on domestic versus nondomestic assaults are explored in the next chapter.

Certainly the concept that police base arrest decisions on the situational characteristics of an interaction is not new, nor is the topic of much dispute. It is well known that police rely on many factors unrelated to the crime itself. This, of course, leads to several critical questions for this text: What are the situational characteristics of the police–citizen encounter that are most likely to lead to arrest? Perhaps equally important, how do the use of these "nondiscriminatory" factors affect police performance in domestic violence cases?

In analyzing these questions, we note that most police officers appear to share a common reference regarding when to make an arrest. For example, in one 1980 study of officers from 17 departments, more than 90% identified the following factors in their decisions to arrest: (a) commission of a felony, (b) serious victim injury, (c) use of a weapon, (d) violence against the police, and (e) likelihood of future violence. In contrast, prior calls from a household and victim preference were not nearly as important (Loving, 1980).

How might these and other policy preferences affect the decision to arrest batterers and other assailants? First, in the context of professionally accepted roles and missions, most police officers believe that arrest priority should be given to cases in which public order and authority have been challenged, attaching only secondary importance to the protection of individual victims (Sanders, 1988). Because most domestic violence cases are not public in nature, they would be relegated to positions of less importance (Sanders, 1988; Sherman, 1992). It is only in recent years that proarrest policies may, in many departments, have skewed arrest decisions in domestic assaults versus nondomestic cases.

In recent years, there has been a proliferation of research on arrests in domestic and nondomestic assault cases, with varied findings apparently affected by a huge number of variables. The conclusion to be drawn may simply be that these observed variations are real; there is no one set of variables that works as a constant among all departments (Buzawa & Hotaling, 1999). Clearly, there have been major administrative pressures to increase the role of arrest in cases of domestic assault. Despite these laws and official policies in most jurisdictions, arrest remains nonroutine in most places when officers respond to a domestic call. This is not surprising. In some cases, police may be called "proactively" before any violence or even a threat of violence, and in keeping with the problem-oriented approach to policing, a variety of alternatives are considered. In other cases, the true status of "victim" and "offender" cannot reasonably be determined or probable cause to arrest is insufficient. In still other cases, for which arrest is not mandated, officers may follow a victim preference not to arrest. Even within a particular police department, a variety of organizational, attitudinal, situational, and sociodemographic variables involving victims, offenders, and police affect the decision to arrest even when circumstances of the crime committed would suggest similar treatment.

Two major problems stand in the way of trying to fully understand arrest decisions in domestic violence. First, as with all decisions, a web of factors that are not well understood influences arrest. These include jurisdictional and community requirements and expectations, organizational policies and culture, and officers' individual characteristics and belief systems. This is further affected by characteristics of the incident, the victim, and the offender. Complicating the matter further are common strategies pursued by one or both parties in an incident to negotiate the meaning of the situation to counter the police definition (i.e. "he/she initiated it," "we both got physical," "it's a one-time thing," "we're both under a lot of stress," etc.). Second, researchers (similar to police officers) rarely have access to all relevant data that have bearing on arrest. In addition to police incident and arrest reports, accounts from victims, offenders, and law enforcement are needed to fully understand arrest in domestic violence.

Perhaps the most important question to ask is what are the "proper" discriminators of the decision to arrest and to what extent do police follow them? We recognize that most police officers believe they should, and do, arrest when the incident indicates a high degree of potential future danger or that an obvious criminal assault has already occurred. Police need to focus on cases in which there is potential for violence or a past history of assaults (or both). It is for this area of police discretion that the study of arrest behavior becomes critical. Three major factors appear as consistent themes in this literature: (1) situational or incident characteristics; (2) victim traits and attitudes toward the police; and (3) suspect traits and behavioral interactions between the perpetrator and the police. Of necessity, this discussion is generalized in nature and hence may not properly reflect many less common variables, but in the following sections, we examine available data to determine the primary factors that appear to account for variation in police arrest practices.

SITUATIONAL AND INCIDENT CHARACTERISTICS

Offender Absent Upon Police Arrival

A key situational- or incident-related factor in the decision to arrest is whether the suspect leaves the scene of the offense (Buzawa & Hotaling, 2000; Eigenberg et al., 1996; Feder, 1996; Robinson, 2000). In fact, some researchers have found it to be the most significant predictor of arrest (Robinson, 2000). Clearly an actual arrest is more difficult if the offender has left the scene; however, police typically are not confronted with the key problem of stranger domestic assaults—who did it and where can the perpetrator be located? By questioning victims and witnesses, police should be able to easily locate most domestic assault offenders, making this less of a proper discriminator.

Discrepancies in arrest rates between offenders who are present versus those who are absent at the time of police arrival are an important factor in the police response to domestic violence. Estimates are that more than 50% of intimate abusers leave the scene before police arrival (Berk & Loseke, 1980–1981; Buzawa et al., 1999, Dunford, 1990; Feder, 1996; Hirschel & Hutchison, 1992; Robinson, 2000). Any distinction in treatment of these offenders is not only often unwarranted in terms of police ability to locate perpetrators, it also appears to perversely impact offenders less likely to be "experienced" or repeat offenders.

In the limited studies of offenders who left the scene before police arrival, Dunford (1990) reported that, on average, their victims are far more fearful than those whose offenders remained. In another study, offenders who left the scene were twice as likely to reoffend within the next year as those who stayed (Buzawa et al., 1999). Despite this, most police agencies do not aggressively pursue or even issue warrants for those offenders who have left the scene. Robinson (2000) reported that of 55% of offenders at the scene were arrested compared with only 2% when the suspect was absent. These differences may be due to the perception that domestic violence does not warrant real policing, especially the additional time required to locate offenders. Officers may assume that once an offender is no longer in the presence of a victim, she is safe.

Who Called the Police?

Police as a group appear to differentiate domestic violence cases based on who initiated the call for service. We would normally expect police to be more responsive if the victim initiated the call. After all, this indicates a degree of commitment to stopping the assaults on the victim's part and thus seemingly increases the likelihood of successful case prosecution. Research suggests the reverse, however (Berk & Loseke, 1981; Berk & Newton, 1985; Buzawa & Hotaling, 2000; Stanko, 1985). For example, Berk and Loseke (1980–1981) found that when the victim alerted the police as opposed to a third party, probability of an arrest declined significantly. The reasons apparently related to the police mission of protecting public order more aggressively than seeking to stop private crimes. From this perspective, when a bystander has become involved to the extent of calling the police, the conflict is no longer confined to its principals, but becomes a matter affecting the public order. When a bystander calls, the initial police characterization of the call would be as a "disorderly conduct" or a "disturbance," a classic mission for police concerned with public order maintenance. The classic touchstone of police intervention in domestic violence cases has been whether the activities constituted a public disturbance versus a private dispute.

Presence of Weapons and Officer Perceptions of Risk

As expected, when incidents appear to have greater potential to have serious consequences, likelihood of arrest increases. Several authors have reported that if an assailant uses or threatens to use a weapon, threatens to kill, or (at least in some departments) violates a restraining order (Isaac, 1994), the odds of an arrest increase dramatically (Kane, 1999; Loving, 1980). Use of weapons can be a factor the officer considers in determining risk to the victim. Kane (1999) reported that officer perceptions of the situation's overall risk to the victim risk was the single most important factor in the police decision to arrest.

We readily agree that presence or use of a weapon should affect considerations of danger and hence potential risk; however, the officer's determination of risk is itself the product of an interaction of a variety of factors that involve not only the incident, victim, and offender, but also the officer's attitudes, training, socialization, and departmental policies and practices. Hence, an officer's predictive construct of an offender—that is, how the officer perceives a given offender will behave—will vary. For example, a White police officer may incorrectly believe a young Black man is far more likely to be a risk than if an older White man who is clearly under the influence of alcohol committed the same offense. Decisions that appear seemingly obvious, such as determining a victim's safety, may be conditioned by underlying beliefs of which neither party can agree or even at times articulate. Furthermore, even relatively straightforward analyses such as presence or use of a weapon to determine degree of potential injury involve a surprising amount of subjectivity.

Kane (1999) reported that subgroup differences among offenders interacted to determine how police determined "risk." Also, when considering weapons, only guns, not knives or other objects, were perceived as a threat. Kane reported that only if the officer determined there was no immediate threat to the victim, then other variables determined an arrest. These included presence of a restraining order, the victim's employment status (i.e., arrest was less likely for those who were unemployed), and presence of children (i.e., arrest was less likely despite the potential risk of psychological or physical harm; see discussion below).

Injuries and the Threat of Injury

The impact of victim injury has generated varied findings. Some research has found that victim injuries are positively related to the arrest decision (Berk & Sherman, 1988; Black, 1980; Buzawa & Austin, 1993; Buzawa & Hotaling, 2000; Eigenberg, 2001; Feder, 1996; Ferraro, 1989a; Hotaling & Buzawa, 2001). Other studies have however failed to report such a relationship (Berk & Loseke, 1980–1981; Eigenberg et al., 1996; Feder, 1998; D. A. Jones & Belknap, 1999; Klinger, 1995; Worden & Pollitz, 1984). Most research, however, has been consistent in concluding that the degree of violence or threat of violence to the victim is often of only minimal significance in the arrest decision. Even when victims were in danger and requested an arrest, numerous studies report that most officers consistently refused to make arrests unless other factors favoring arrest were present (Black, 1980; Brown, 1984; Berk & Loseke, 1980–1981; Buzawa & Buzawa, 1990; Davis, 1983).

We continue to be perplexed with this finding. The degree of injury to a victim clearly should be considered as a legitimate discriminator for police action and even subsequent prosecutorial and judicial decision making. Taken to the extreme, the punishment for "attempted murder" is far less than that of "murder," even if the motive, intent, and method of attack are the same. Similarly, the distinction between "felonious" larceny and a "misdemeanor" level of the same crime is primarily based on the property stolen. Nonetheless, in the case of domestic violence, the degree of harm to victims is not apparently a major factor in the decision to arrest.

Presence of Children

Most researchers have reported a greater likelihood of arrest if an offense is committed in the presence of children or children appear at risk of abuse or neglect, either from the commission of the crime itself or from situational factors at the home (Buzawa & Austin, 1993; Eigenberg et al., 1996). Kane (1999), however, reported a much lower arrest rate when children were present. This finding, if it presents a new reality, would be a troubling fact, given the now widely known potential that witnessing domestic violence has for causing psychological damage to children. At this point, the extent of this anomaly it is unclear because Kane's study was limited to incidents with no explicit risk to the victim and no violation of a restraining order.

Victim–Offender Relationship

Some studies, especially early research, have reported that offenders who were married to the victim were less likely to be arrested regardless of victim preference (Bachman & Coker, 1995; Dobash & Dobash, 1979; Ferraro, 1989b; D. Martin, 1976; Worden & Pollitz, 1984). The consensus was that the relational distance between the offender and the victim indeed affected probability of arrest. The apparent rationale was that when police perceive a continuing relationship between the victim and offender, the likelihood would be lessened that the victim will ultimately cooperate with the police and that prosecutors will secure a conviction,

a factor described previously as being of great import to these agencies (Black, 1976).

It is now less common to have officers overtly blame victims. It is, however, probable that some officers still believe it legitimate for a husband to physically chastise his wife "with moderation" at least in some circumstances. Some police in the not-too-distant past agreed that moderate violence is a legitimate response to marital infidelity (Saunders & Size, 1986). Even if one adopts this regressive perspective, however, the "right" may not extend to boyfriends or casual acquaintances. In fact, the probable real effect of this attitude is at the largely unconscious margins of the decision to arrest. More recent research has found marital status unrelated to arrest, however (Buzawa & Austin, 1993; Feder, 1997).

Normative Ambiguities

There is some evidence that arrest practices are influenced by normative ambiguities in family and relationship issues (Buzawa & Hotaling, 2000). Research in several Massachusetts communities suggested that in some departments, the likelihood of arrest for domestic assaults involving the use of force is low for those parties who can provide the police with a plausible rationale for the incident that involves the offender experiencing of a major life event. Actual violence "explained" by a crisis such as an impending divorce or separation, the birth or impending birth of a child, a child about to be removed from the household, or a serious mental health problem of the offender resulted in arrest in only 1 of 5 instances. For example, the presence of a single factor, the prospect of divorce, had a profound effect. The authors reported that a claim of a recent or impending divorce among parties in the incident reduced the likelihood of arrest to less than half of other offenders.

In contrast, offenders who offered the police more pedestrian excuses for violence citing "everyday conflicts" (e.g., problems with drinking, fights over money and sexual jealousy, time spent at work, and child custody issues) as the reason for their violent behavior were anywhere from 3 to 5 times more likely (depending on the police department) to be arrested than those with a major life crisis (Buzawa & Hotaling, 2000).

We are concerned that, in some departments, police appear less willing to protect victims when offenders simply provide a certain rationale for their conduct. A significant question is why such distinctions are important. For reasons we discuss later, if such distinctions relate to victim preferences, they might be appropriate; however, if they reflect on officers' personal beliefs or their identification with the offender's behavior, then the implications are far more insidious.

Victim Preferences for Arrest

Victim preference has long been termed an important determinant of arrest (Black, 1980; Eigenberg et al., 1996; Feder, 1996; Sheptycki, 1993). In all but mandatory arrest jurisdictions, an informal operational requirement for a domestic assault arrest is the victim's desire for the arrest. Without victim concurrence, most jurisdictions in the recent past had policies or at the least standard operating procedures actively discouraging arrest (Bell, 1984). Studies have confirmed that the probability of an arrest increases by 25% to 30% if the woman agrees to sign a complaint and decreases by a similar amount if she refuses. Not surprisingly, Berk and Loseke (1980–1981) and Worden and Pollitz (1984) stated that victim preferences accounted for the largest variance in arrest rates in every study examined.

Some studies have reported that victim preferences or injuries are only of limited importance in the decision to arrest, however. In these studies decisions instead are far more influenced by other factors. For example, Bayley (1986) reported that assailant arrest was not even correlated with victim wishes. In another study sampling certain Massachusetts police departments, the police could not have been strongly affected by victim preferences as evidenced by their inability even to report the victim's arrest preferences in more than 75% of the cases (Buzawa & Austin, 1993).

Similarly another study suggested that mandatory arrest practices may, in some departments, drastically limit "deference" to victim desires. Hotaling and Buzawa (2001) compared domestic versus nondomestic assaults in two communities with mandatory arrest policies but only for domestic violence assaults. As discussed more extensively in the last chapter, the result was apparent—an overall arrest rate of 77% for domestic assaults compared with 36% for nondomestic assaults.

Although differences in arrest practices in the departments studied apparently reflected officer compliance with mandatory arrest policies, it is possible that the ability to make a warrantless misdemeanor arrest in cases of domestic assault (now common in all 50 states) was the reason for the low arrest rate for nondomestic assault cases. In misdemeanor cases involving nondomestic assaults, at least in Massachusetts, officers are still required to witness an assault to make an arrest on the spot.

POLICE EVALUATION OF VICTIM TRAITS AND CONDUCT

Another factor in the decision to arrest is the officer's overall reaction to the traits and conduct of the victim. If, for example, the officer judges the victim to have a "deviant" lifestyle, arrests are less likely to be made. The category of victim apparently also has an impact on the decision to arrest. Research finds that those victims who conform to societal expectations (such as in cases discussed later involving woman victims compared to male victims) are more likely to have their assailant arrested. (Buzawa & Hotaling, 2000). In fact, police officers inevitably view conduct of any party through the prism of their own beliefs. Certainly, if an officer is biased against helping domestic violence victims, arrests are less likely. Some research has found that biased officer attitudes toward certain types of victims disproportionately influence their response to domestic violence incidents compared with other types of assaults for which arrest is more predictable (Feder, 1998).

This is not unexpected. A necessary component of police decision making is to make rapid value judgments in circumstances in which reality is unclear. In the face of ambiguous facts, research on police responses to the disfavored categories of rape, sexual assault, and domestic violence has long noted that officers make judgments based on their inherent assumptions regarding proper victim conduct (Manning, 1978; Skolnick, 1975). In such cases, the nature of the relationship between the parties may be considered by police as a valid factor in evaluating criminal behavior of either party. Not only do officers scrutinize the victim's behavior as well as that of the assailant, it also may affect who is actually identified as "victim" and "offender." Often, police do not find either party to be "guilt free" (Stanko, 1989). In this context, the victim's demeanor toward the officer may be as significant as her degree of injury. If she is rational, undemanding, and deferential toward the police, her story may evoke more sympathy and attention, probably because it is assumed that within the context of the relationship the woman had retained those same

characteristics (Ford, 1983; Pepinsky, 1976). Buzawa and Hotaling (2000) found strong correlations between the victim appearing upset and trembling and the likelihood of arrest. In fact, they reported that "victim trembling" was more strongly related to arrest than injury.

Other victim actions at the scene clearly influence the police. For example, victim "cooperation" with the officer influences arrest decisions (Belknap, 1995; Berk & Loseke, 1980–1981; Buzawa & Austin, 1993; Ferraro, 1989a; Smith, 1987). In general, police stereotype domestic violence victims as providing little support or dropping complaints, ostensibly because they reconciled with their abusers. In police parlance, they are perceived as "fickle." Of course, officers know that without victim cooperation, there is an increased likelihood for case dismissal or acquittal at trial because of lack of evidence. They may also believe that if the victim is unwilling to extend the effort to initiate a complaint, the seriousness of the injury may not warrant disrupting their own schedules.

Research on victim cooperation has, until recently, largely measured victim cooperation solely by their preference for arrest. Using a different approach, Robinson (2000) asked officers to report a "global rating" of victim cooperativeness. She reported that cooperation globally defined in this manner did not have a significant impact on the arrest decision; however, she did report four variables that significantly predicted an officer's rating of victim cooperativeness: whether the officer believed the victim had a substance use problem, whether drugs or alcohol were present at the scene, whether the suspect was present at the scene, and the officer's length of service. In contrast, if the woman is abusive, disorderly, or drunk, officers rarely make arrests or, at least, fail to follow victim preferences. For example, after conducting extensive field observations in

Detroit, it was noted that when officers did not follow preferences of female victims, it was often because she was not "liked" by the responding officers who would label her as being too "aggressive," "obnoxious," or otherwise causing problems for the officer (Buzawa & Austin, 1993).

A totally different dimension of the officer's reaction to a victim may be because the victim does not conform to societal norms. The special case of male victims, although not a primary subject of this book, is instructive. It has been well documented that male victims are less likely to report a domestic assault (Langley & Levy, 1977; McLeod, 1984; Steinmetz, 1980; Straus, 1977–1978). A contributing factor to their reluctance to report assaults is a realistic expectation of limited police understanding. Officers may incorrectly assume that a male victim should be capable of preventing violence by his partner or that he initiated the exchange. When he does not, he no longer conforms to accepted standards and perhaps renders his account of events suspect. In any event, a decision to arrest his partner is rarely made. Unfortunately, we cannot determine if this critique is solid. Although significant research attention has been focused on the impact of traditional male views on the police treatment of female victims, similar research has not yet been extended to encompass the effect of the traditional views of "proper conduct" effect the police response to male victims.

It has been reported that male victims believe that even when severely injured, the police did not respect their desire for arrest of a female abuser. For example, one man required hospitalization for treatment of a stab wound that just missed puncturing his lungs. Despite his request to have the offending woman removed (not even arrested), the officers simply called an ambulance and refused formal sanctions against the woman,

including her removal. Indeed, all the male victims who were interviewed consistently reported having the incident trivialized and being belittled by officers (Buzawa & Austin, 1993). This was contradicted in more recent research, however, which reported that female against male intimate partner assault was more likely to result in the arrest of the female than the converse (Hotaling & Buzawa, 2001).

Another victim-oriented criterion is the officer's subjective perception that violence may be a "normal" way of life for a particular victim and offender (Black, 1980; i.e., "battling spouses"). As discussed by Ferraro (1989b), when officers observe a regularly recurring pattern of violence, they may believe it is part of the social fabric of the couple's lives. Consequently, they are less likely to believe that any police response, including arrest, will be successful in deterring future violence. Many may dichotomize between "normal citizens," similar to themselves, and "deviants," perhaps seen to use excessive alcohol, not to speak fluent English, to belong to minority groups, or to participate in an interracial relationship. For these groups, many officers perceive battering as merely a part of overall family pathology and, therefore, not amenable to any effective intervention (Ferraro, 1989b).

One characteristic deserves special note. Various researchers have also observed that, at least in the past, police have responded with less of a service orientation to Blacks and other minorities. They are therefore less likely to use arrest powers in cases of domestic assault for these groups (Black, 1980; Stanko, 1989). Of course, it is possible that assuming officers react directly to race and ethnicity is an insufficient and perhaps stereotypical analysis of a complex phenomenon. In this regard, Ferraro (1989b) reported that the key variable appears to be the typology of the victim as belonging to a "deviant" population group, which might in turn partially be based on race or other problematic criteria. Although this differential may exist in certain departments, in others it is clearly not seen. For example, in the Buzawa and Austin study of Massachusetts departments, no disparity based on race of the victim or offender was found (Buzawa & Austin, 1993).

It is hoped that patterns of differential enforcement for different racial groups have diminished as the cultural diversity and training in departments have increased in the last decade. For example, Buzawa and Buzawa (1990) examined attitudes within the Detroit Police Department and reported that Black and female officers present markedly different operational arrest patterns than their White male counterparts, the subjects of traditional analysis of police behavior. This distinction, which we discuss later, in this chapter may become more important as the number of minority officers increases.

ASSAILANT BEHAVIOR AND DEMEANOR

General research on police use of arrest in situations in which the officer has the discretion to arrest or not repeatedly has found that officers are often guided by their reaction to the offender and his demeanor (Black & Reiss, 1967; Buzawa & Hotaling, 2000; Mastrofski, Worden, & Snipes, 1995; Worden & Shepard, 1996). Hence, if the potential arrestee appears argumentative, still ready to behave aggressively toward the victim, or otherwise challenges the police authority, an arrest is likely to be made, as much to establish control of the situation as a response to the incident.

Similarly, past domestic violence research suggests that an offender's criminal history or demeanor dramatically affect chances of arrest. Some of the key factors include (a) past history of offenses reported to the police (Buzawa & Hotaling, 2000; Gondolf, Fisher, & McFerron, 1988; Hotaling & Buzawa, 2001; Klinger, 1995; Smith & Klein, 1984; Waaland & Keeley, 1985; Worden & Shepard, 1996;); (b) use of drugs or alcohol (Berk, Fenstermaker, & Newton, 1990; Jones & Belknap, 1999; D. A. Smith & Klein, 1984; Worden & Pollitz, 1984); (c) lack of offender civility toward the police (Bayley, 1996; Dolon, Hendricks, & Meagher, 1986; Smith & Klein, 1984; Worden & Pollitz, 1984).

Assailant demeanor clearly appears to affect the arrest decision. For example, it has long been known that an arrest nearly always occurs if an assailant remains violent in the officer's presence (Ferraro, 1989a). Perhaps because of the implied threat to the officer's authority or a lack of respect, an arrest is likely if the offender is perceived to constitute a direct threat to the officer even independent of the strength of the case (Black, 1980). Similarly, when police respond to gang locations or other places where they feel threatened, they tend to act more aggressively and use their powers far more frequently (Ferraro, 1989a).

It has also been observed that arrests are quite likely when the suspected abuser is belligerent or drunk. In one early study, Bayley (1986) found that two thirds of offenders who were hostile were arrested, whereas none who were civil toward the police were arrested. Buzawa and Austin (1993) tried to put this factor in perspective. They noted that victim injury was not as predictive of arrest as offender demeanor. In one case, an uninjured victim who had called the police cut the assailant with a butcher knife near his eye, requiring several stitches. No arrest was made because the assailant was drunk; in fact, the officers were not sure if he could have been potentially dangerous to the victim.

DIFFERENCES IN ARRESTS AMONG POLICE OFFICERS

Officer characteristics constitute a critical set of variables affecting the arrest decision. Not surprisingly, different officers have far different propensities to make arrests. For this reason, many studies have concluded that the police–citizen encounter is profoundly unpredictable from the viewpoint of the victim and offender. The response depends heavily on the officer's orientation toward domestic violence, skill level, and time constraints. Although difficult to quantify or predict, these factors are evident in practice.

Some relate to legally irrelevant but organizationally significant facts. For example, if an intervention occurs at the end of the officer's shift, an arrest may be less likely because the crime is not considered worthy enough to justify the officer's staying late (Berk & Loseke, 1980–1981; Ferraro, 1989b; Stanko, 1989; Worden & Pollitz, 1984).

It appears that both attitudinal factors and demographic variables add to variance among officers. Certainly in the absence of specific enforced mandatory arrest domestic violence policies, individual attitudes of officers toward domestic violence cases appear to dramatically affect arrest preferences. When confronted with a report of serious injury to a victim, one study found that approximately 50% of the officers would regularly arrest, whereas the remaining 50% would not do so on any consistent basis (Waaland & Keeley, 1985).

The reasons for this difference are not clear. Officers often have different role expectations. Some see their mission as being a crime fighter or maintaining public order; others are more service oriented, concerned with assisting victims. From this, one might expect that those oriented toward a service approach would make arrests at a higher rate than those viewing their mission as crime fighting. Although this may be of some help

in determining which offenders might be arrested, the overall rates of arrest for both groups appeared in the past to be equally low, consistent with an overall bias by those departments against using their arrest powers. Therefore, in the 1980s, one study of departments with proarrest policies nominally in place reported that "service-oriented" officers had an approximately 10% arrest rate compared with 8.5% for "crime fighters," hardly an overwhelming difference (Worden & Pollitz, 1984).

Differences in the use of arrest powers have also been attributed to officer demographic characteristics. Male–female distinctions have most frequently been examined in this regard. The preponderance of research suggests that female officers, although not necessarily more likely to arrest, are reported by victims as being more understanding, showing more concern, and providing more information about legal rights and shelters for victims. In one survey, 40% of a male and female officer sample stated that the two groups handled domestic violence situations differently. Male officers perceived female officers as "softer," "more uncertain," "weaker," "more passive," "slower," and "lazier," whereas female officers saw themselves as "feminine," "nonviolent," and agreed that they tended to be more "passive" (Homant & Kennedy, 1984). Also, many of the female officers stated they were more concerned with domestic violence than male officers (Homant & Kennedy, 1985). The extent of a male–female dichotomy has been questioned by several feminist authors (Ferraro, 1989a; Radford, 1989; Stanko, 1989) who believe that to work in a male-dominated organization, female officers behave similarly to men because of occupational socialization or simply to fit in. This theory is still generally unproven by empirical research. Other researchers have more recently reported that female officers actually made fewer arrests than their male counterpart (S. E. Martin, 1993; Robinson, 2000). Although perhaps unexpected, the decreased rate of arrests by female officers is not necessarily a negative response. It is possible that female officers are more likely to follow victim preferences not to arrest (Robinson, 2000). Female officers may not be as likely to follow department policies regardless of whether they believe it would serve the interests of the victim and her family.

Other officer demographic features have been considered to affect arrest rate and the overall officer response. Buzawa and Buzawa (1990) found variations on the basis of officer age. This result held even when controlling for exposure to domestic violence training. Older officers were probably exposed to departmental socialization, training, policies and practices that in the past were clearly not supportive of aggressive responses to domestic assaults. Some research has indeed reported that older and "more experienced" officers make fewer arrests than younger officers (Bittner, 1990; Stalans & Finn, 1995). It also may be important to put these findings in the context of the overall likelihood of older officers making arrests because research examining police socialization argues that older officers are simply less aggressive and less likely to make arrests than younger, more motivated officers (Van Maanen, 1978). In contrast, other researchers did not find arrest differences based on age, despite the fact that these officers had attitudes less supportive of victims then their younger compatriots (Robinson, 2000; Worden, 1993).

Officer's race also has been examined. On the one hand, White officers have been seen in some contexts to be more coercive toward Black suspects. Alternatively, they may be more biased about "endemic" violence in Black communities and therefore less likely to want to intervene. Black officers may not share these stereotypes regarding normal behavior in Black families. In one classic study, however, Black (1980) noted that the arrest practices of Black officers in some contexts often involve more coercive behavior toward Black citizenry, compared with their White cohorts who seek to enforce the law impartially. In any event, to date research provides no consistent empirical support for major racial differences for domestic violence arrests (Walker, Spohn, & DeLone, 1996).

ORGANIZATIONAL VARIATIONS AMONG POLICE DEPARTMENTS

We can safely state that research on the actual response of the criminal justice system to domestic assault shows highly inconsistent results. Although many individual police departments have recently instituted proactive arrest oriented policies in response to statutory instructions or administrative directives, often such efforts receive little encouragement or reinforcement from prosecutors or the judiciary. Even today, truly integrated responses to domestic violence offenders are more the exception rather than the rule.

Clearly, research on arrests in domestic violence cases with varied findings apparently have been affected by a huge number of variables. The conclusion to be drawn may simply be that these observed variations are real; there is no one set of variables that work as a constant among all departments (Buzawa & Hotaling, 1999). In fact, some research has reported little variation within departments, but significant variation *between* departments. Little attention has been focused on organizational commitment to change and what structural changes are made to ensure compliance. For example, in one recent research project working with several departments, the departments and researchers jointly developed a common domestic violence incident report form. One department was successful in having all officers complete these reports, another somewhat successful, and a third totally unsuccessful. The difference? The department that succeeded in gaining compliance simply designated a sergeant to review all officer reports and ensure that the supplementary form for every domestic assault was included (Hotaling & Buzawa, 2000).

Unfortunately, as we describe in the next chapter, many police departments still have minimal domestic violence policies, despite state legislative requirements. Still others are not in compliance with state reporting requirements. Although many police administrators try to aggressively respond to this problem, others display varying levels of commitment to domestic violence through their efforts at monitoring policy implementation. For example, some administrators simply file these policies in their office. Others distribute the policies at rapid-fire roll calls. Still others discuss them in detail at roll call. Finally, there are departments that mandate high effort to ensure that all officers receive in-service training both on the new policy and on their role in intervention. Differences in observed arrest rates may therefore largely reflect different implementation practices and implicitly its overall importance in the departments studied.

From these data, we can conclude that although changes may occur after initiation of new policies, these may be inconsistent among departments and do not always comply with the "ideal" contemplated arrest profile. Also, we tend to dismiss the "global" conclusions of researchers who either try to generalize their results from a limited number of departments or who rely on aggregate data from many departments—or national data—that mask departmental variations.

Obviously, many departments have recently instituted proarrest policies, which have the potential to better predict officer behavior; however, past circumstances suggest that new policies may not override an organization's past practices and culture. These departmental differences may be based on organizational attributes or possibly the general orientation of the department toward calls for assistance and the community in which it operates. Although there is little empirical research in the context of departmental responses to domestic violence, a number of researchers have differentiated between "service" versus law enforcement–oriented agencies.

Similarly, the characteristics of a department's service community have been shown to affect police practices. In one study of suburban departments in the 1980s, suburban police departments recorded higher rates of domestic violence, less likely due to a real crime wave in these communities than because suburban residents tended to report complaints to police as a matter of course. Despite this, the suburban police departments initiated criminal complaints at lower rates than rural and urban departments (Bell, 1984). Bell concluded that the three types of departments—urban, rural, and suburban—had markedly different policy orientations toward domestic violence. In addition to such generalized variation, specific features of a department and its organizational milieu have been shown to have a dramatic impact on arrests and other behavior in cases involving domestic assault.

Second, organizational imperatives at the individual officer and departmental levels drive police officers to spend time on cases that are likely to lead to convictions. The effectiveness of police officers, a key aspect of promotion, is partially determined by the number of major felony arrests leading to conviction. Similarly, police departments seek to prove their efficacy by emphasizing the number of felony arrests and the percentage of convictions. Because most domestic violence cases are organizationally termed misdemeanors, time spent on such cases may not be justified, considered a "waste of time" both by officers trying to advance their careers and departments trying to justify budget requests and maintain high performance ratings. Of course, we emphasize that many police departments have created this dilemma because their officers unofficially downgrade domestics to misdemeanor assaults even though these cases would otherwise fit the textbook definition of a felonious assault (Buzawa & Buzawa, 1990; Kemp et al., 1962).

Still other studies have focused on unrelated attributes of the criminal justice system to determine if they affect arrest rates. At least one study reported that extraneous conditions such as overcrowded jails or lockups appear to reduce domestic violence arrest rates (Dolon et al., 1986), as do inconvenient court hours or court locations (Ford, 1990).

Profound differences in arrest rates and other attributes of performance have also been found between different police departments. This is not altogether surprising. It would be expected that arrest rates would increase in departments with extensive domestic violence training that emphasizes a proactive approach or those department with policies that require an increased role for arrest.

THE IMPORTANCE OF TRAINING

Training is a primary vehicle for reinforcing existing and planned practices reflective of the goals of an organization's leadership. In the context of policing, training becomes decisive because methods and practices of police training have historically been instrumental in either implementing change or, conversely, thwarting implementation of progressive policies. Manning and Van Maanen (1978) discussed the overriding importance of the academy in the police socialization process in which police occupational perspectives are transferred to new recruits and course content is presented in such a way as to ensure its continuance.

Before conferring arrest powers, police departments rely on an extensive routinized training program of at least 8 weeks to impart basic knowledge of substantive criminal law, criminal procedure, and departmental regulations to recruits. Even after the formal training program, officers maintain "rookie" or probationary status. In most departments, rookies are assigned to experienced patrol officers until they are considered sufficiently familiar with required tasks and departmental practices.

For a variety of reasons, classic police training programs made the response to domestic violence less effective. In the past, every component of the training process—time allocation, instructor selection, content, and in-service traineeship—tended to reinforce existing negative stereotypes against domestic violence cases. Harris (1973) observed that in classic police academies, great emphasis was placed on the "ethic of masculinity" and development of the officer's identity as "first and foremost . . . a man" (p. 291).

Before the 1960s, there typically was little or no specific training on domestic violence. In the 1960s and, in some departments for years thereafter, officers were instructed simply to quiet tense situations, advise on social welfare agencies that might provide assistance, and quickly extricate themselves (Bard, 1970; Berk & Loseke, 1980–1981; Loving, 1980).

In the late 1970s, when assisting the Detroit Police Department in the development of a new training program, one of the authors of this book conducted a nationwide review of existing domestic violence programs. At that time, in virtually all police training programs, the training component related to domestic violence was perfunctory and typically composed of a single 4- to 8-hour lecture segment under the general rubric of handling "disturbed persons" (Buzawa, 1978). The content was not restricted to, nor did it even necessarily address, the topic of domestic assault. Instead, it included proper techniques for handling hostage situations, potential suicides, mentally disturbed individuals, violent alcoholics and addicts, and child abuse, with brief mention of domestic disturbance calls. To the extent that they were addressed as a separate topic, domestic calls were explained to the recruits as a largely unproductive use of time, ineffective in resolving a family problem, and potentially dangerous for the responding officer. Recruits were told that the desired outcome was to restore peace and maintain control as a vehicle of restoring the public order and self-protection. Arrests were actively discouraged as a waste of time. The only exception was if disrespect or threats by an offender or victim indicated that the officer might lose situational control. Recruits were trained that arrest, therefore, was primarily to assert authority rather than to respond to prior criminal action.

Departmental choice of training staff did not usually result in interested or qualified instructors in the field of domestic violence. Except for those relatively few larger departments with dedicated permanent training sections, police academies traditionally used senior line personnel. Frequently, the basis for their selection as trainers was "temporary disability" or other special duty restrictions, such as having been involved in a prior shooting or other incident requiring a departmental investigation prior to being placed back on active duty. These instructors had little interest in training itself, generally lacked instructional background, and had little substantive expertise or affinity for the topic of domestic violence.

As a result, it is not surprising that the primary mode of instruction was an explanation of official policies of nonintervention

accompanied by colorful (if not totally accurate) stories about their own personal experiences. Few if any, training materials or multimedia aids were available or used, and outside expertise was rarely sought.

Formal in-service training in this area also rarely existed before the early 1980s. During the initial entry period, a recruit relied on the perceptions of relevant teachers such as experienced officers to develop his or her own views toward proper organizational practices and objectives. The trainee, after all, had few, if any, relevant experiences to guide his or her behavior during the often-frightening immersion into the reality of policing (Van Maanen, 1975). The field training process, in which the rookie was assigned to learn under the direction of an experienced officer, usually reinforced prejudices against domestic violence cases. In fact, this experience often served to undermine an academy's instruction in those few cases in which the academy might have attempted to promote a more activist police response (Van Maanen, 1973).

For these reasons, it was acknowledged by both senior police officials (Bannon, 1974) and researchers (Loving & Quirk, 1982) that traditional police training failed to provide police officers with any rudimentary skills required for successful domestic violence intervention. In one study based on research conducted in the mid 1980s, 50% of the officers in a department were not even aware of the elements of probable cause for domestic violence assault (Ford, 1987). As Bannon (1974) observed, "the real reason that police avoid domestic violence situations to the greatest extent possible is because they do not know how to cope with them" (p. 4).

Until relatively recently classic patterns of training may therefore be seen to have reinforced prevailing occupational ideology toward domestic violence. The net effect of such a training process was to enhance the likelihood that officers would attempt either to avoid a response or rapidly complete domestic violence calls to devote energy to the more "appropriate" police work. In summary, the training process thereby in the 1970s, the 1980s, and, in some jurisdictions, even today remains an important and largely unrecognized factor impeding the implementation of actual change even when "officially" desired by departmental leadership.

Current Training

More recently, many departments, either through their own initiative or following training curricula recommended by organizations such as the International Association of Chiefs of Police (IACP) have transformed training from a factor blocking arrests to one that supports stated proarrest objectives. In this regard, these organizations have been leaders in trying to institute change. This has been especially true from the first IACP policy pronouncement in 1967 advocating crisis intervention (relying on the most current theories of intervention of the day, advocated by Morton Bard) to the most recent training policy promulgated in 1999. Their latest policy on domestic violence is exceptionally detailed, describing issues such as the proper role of police, making referrals, promoting officer safety, and providing for extra training for command officials; it appears to require a considerable commitment of departmental resources to ensure implementation.

Aspects of this type of comprehensive training include emphasizing the role of domestic violence intervention by police (Buchanan & Perry, 1985; Pearce & Snortum, 1983), arrests in the context of domestic violence strategy (Buzawa, 1982), and training that focuses not only on the law but also attitudinal change (Kinports & Fischer, 1993). Innovative teaching methods such as role playing, especially of instances in which the officer is placed in an unusual position (acting as the victim or offender), may also prove beneficial (Malefyt, Little, & Walker, 1998).

It would be wrong, however, to assume that training has been transformed nationwide into a source spreading the new gospel of aggressive police intervention. In most departments, basic training has not increased in duration. Officer candidates still spend an overwhelming, perhaps inordinate, amount of time on physical fitness and firearms techniques (Eigenberg, 2001). In sharp contrast, the amount of time devoted to domestic violence varies considerably from 2 to 30 hours, with an average of 10 hours. Nonetheless, 29 states now mandate extensive domestic violence training, with 21 of these actually setting forth minimum training standards that simply could not be covered in the allocated time (N. Miller, 1997).

Equally problematic is the continuing reliance on "unofficial training" that rookies have with experienced officers. To date, we are not aware of any official training programs in the country that rotate new officers to tours of duty with experienced domestic violence officers to demonstrate the preferred strategies and effective techniques for intervention. Instead, the typical pattern is a rotation with an experienced patrol officer who may or may not be particularly responsive to domestic violence incidents or be able to impart the skills needed to new recruits.

In-service police training is equally problematic. In-service domestic violence training is now routine in many departments and in fact mandated under some state domestic violence statutes; however, the extent and quality of such training varies enormously from a brief roll call or video (not very effective) too much more formal, and far more likely to be effective, formal departmental or offsite training programs (Gaines, Kappeler, & Vaughn, 1999). Because such programs cost considerable funds in the form of overtime for other officers to replace those receiving training, there are strong organizational disincentives for departments to allocate resources to for these purposes (see Eigenberg, 2001, pp. 277–281, for a review of why training continues to have a problematic impact).

As a result, the uneven status of training may explain a great deal of the variation in arrest practices among departments, despite the fact that approximately 20 years have passed since proarrest policies were widely adopted and publicized.

DOMESTIC VIOLENCE IN THE CONTEXT OF COMMUNITY POLICING

Over the last 30 years, critics of the criminal justice system have increasingly acknowledged limitations in its capacity to control crime. For this reason, the emphasis of criminal justice agencies, researchers, and activists has been to shift ultimate crime control responsibility to the community and its social processes. A corollary theme of policing is that police cannot be responsible for preventing and controlling crime.

Community policing has become the predominant motif for police operations. Currently, more than 50% of municipal police agencies, including most of the largest departments, have developed comprehensive community policing plans (Reaves & Hart, 2000). The U.S. Department of Justice has advocated this movement and many police departments across the country have adopted such programs, at least officially. The 1994 Crime Act provided for $8.8 billion to support community policing; currently, community policing officers service approximately 90% of communities (U.S. Department of Justice, 1999).

A major premise of community policing is that primary police responsibility should focus on dealing with community problems by order maintenance, problem solving, and service-oriented activities (Goldstein, 1990; Kelling & Cole 1997). In short, current police expectations are for their role to expand disposition decisions beyond primarily arresting offenders to encompass a variety of social service functions. This approach focuses on the role of police as problem solvers rather than crime fighters. Consequently, attempts to mobilize all relevant agencies to address community problems replaces the previous focus on police simply making arrests. Departments are making an effort to develop police "partnerships" with agencies, including public welfare, social service, and private- and community-based groups, to establish a more holistic approach to policing than the conventional paramilitary model.

In addition, a key tenet of community policing is community involvement, that is, collaboration between citizens and the police (Skolnick & Bayley, 1986) as well as an expectation for the police to respond to community concerns (Manning, 1997). As organizations, many police departments no longer view their primary role as "crime fighters" but rather to be responsive to community priorities for law enforcement activities focusing on reducing the fear, disorder, and incivility that some argue create conditions that breed crime. Tremendous variations exist among various communities. In fact, Garland (2001, p. 124) argued that community policing has become the "all pervasive rhetoric . . . used to describe any and every policing practice, however conventional."

Many models of behavior now fall under the term *community policing* (Maguire, Kuhns, Uchida, & Cox, 1997). One initial model, still followed in most jurisdictions, is what has been termed *broken windows*. This approach focuses on "alien" threats and attempts to strengthen the community's immunity from strangers. There is a further assumption that signs of urban decay and disorder contribute disproportionately to citizen fear, and although efforts at its control may not really affect crime rates, it will affect citizen perceptions of crime (Wilson & Kelling, 1982). Therefore, police are encouraged to use discretion and selective enforcement of the law to reduce citizen fears (Goldstein, 1997).

The administrative focus in this model was placed on "cleaning up streets" and signs of community disorder believed to generate fear of crime as well as actual crime. Massive federal funding on so-called weed-and-seed programs reflected this organizational paradigm.

In recent years under the same rubric of community policing, the response of some departments has been to shift focus developing strategies to put officers into closer contact with citizens (e.g., through the use of bicycle, foot, and mounted patrols; by attending community meetings and similar activities). Perhaps the best way to phrase the changing emphasis is that in community policing, the police focus on their role as problem solvers rather than crime fighters (Goldstein, 1997).

In community policing, public involvement is used to define both police priorities and their appropriate response to problems. Not surprisingly, because the concept is not as driven by the organizations as in the past, there has been considerable controversy over what the term *public* actually means. It is a mistake to assume the existence of a monolithic, homogeneous community and a single consensus of what is in the public's interest (Manning, 1997). Who defines the community in terms of how it affects police behavior—the general public, the victims of crimes, the offenders, policymakers, politicians, criminal justice administrators, or experts?

Typically, in community policing the focus on making arrests is replaced by attempts to mobilize relevant agencies to be responsible for, and solve, community problems. It is therefore a more holistic approach to policing than the conventional paramilitary model. As a consequence, community policing often prioritizes publicly visible nonemergency services over crime control, emergency assistance, and law enforcement activities (Rosenbaum & Lurigio, 1998). This is a result of how the notion of "public" used for this particular frame of reference typically defines public priorities as noncriminal, nonemergency problems (Skogan & Hartnett, 1997). It is now virtually a maxim in the literature on community policing that the "community" perceives disorder as the most serious problem (Rosenbaum & Lurigio, 1994; Kelling & Cole, 1997; Skogan, 1990). We believe this is potentially harmful to large segments of the population because many at greatest risk of victimization often are socially disadvantaged and as victims are never going to be the predominant "public." Their voices and needs are therefore often lost.

Here, however, we focus on the impact of these ongoing initiatives on the police response to domestic violence. To do so, we have to assume that police resources are "set"—that is, wishing for more officers to perform the increased tasks created by community policing as well as the traditional tasks of policing is ultimately quixotic at best. At worst, it may condemn police initiatives to partial funding resulting in ineffectiveness (at least after any initial federal grant funds are spent). As a result, the focus of community policing strategies on public disorder may even further reduce protection for women and children. Their victimization is most likely to be the result of a "private" crime rather than publicly visible offenses.

Tactics used to implement community policing may also have a problematic effect on domestic violence both for philosophical reasons and resource concerns. Virtually all such programs emphasize increases in foot patrol in highly populated areas and officer efforts to mingle with the population. To the extent that a department has no additional resources it simply reallocates existing patrol officers, often detracting from the police ability to respond rapidly to victim calls for service—and this means that domestic violence and other crime victims may be affected. This impact may not yet be evident in that many of the current community policing programs receive additional funds through other sources of federal funding. Ultimately, the burden will shift back to the individual departments. Without the reduction of administrative and support services, the only source for such funds is likely to be other patrol operations.

Placing officers "on the street" has therefore indirectly increased the response time to citizen calls in many jurisdictions. Similarly, the percent of patrol available for responding to calls has steadily decreased. The only mitigating factor is the huge increase in the number of patrol officers hired in recent years. The majority of these funds were provided by the U.S. Department of Justice's Community Oriented Policing program as an incentive for departments to support community-policing initiatives. The resulting increase in personnel may simply hide the actual police prioritization of citizen calls, however.

A cursory review of media stories on community policing is illustrative. Numerous police chiefs have claimed success in "cleaning up rowdy bars," as well as dispersing public and disorderly drunks, homeless people, and congregating teens. They claim that their efforts ensure that these "problem regulars" will no longer frequent public locations. The underlying assumption is that these problem individuals posing a "community problem" no longer exist.

We believe this is unduly optimistic. Merely forcing these individuals out of public places such as bars and the street may reduce a variety of public offenses, but although the community problem may no longer exist, the people, in fact, do. It cannot simply be assumed that because certain men no longer

frequent public bars, they are not drinking. In all likelihood, individuals who previously congregated in bars and were involved in public fights still drink and behave inappropriately. They may, however, do so at home, or at least in private settings, putting women and children at greater risk as targets than strangers are in a public setting.

Although not widely discussed, an examination of community policing data reporting "success" typically does not include or separate out domestic assaults and violence against children in their data. However, a study reporting the decrease in many types of offenses noted that the one category for which there was an increase was domestic assaults (Braga et al., 1999).

Yet another example is the efforts to divert calls from the police to other sources. In fact, cities such as New York have been attempting to "demarket" 911 with billboards suggesting alternative places to call for assistance. Our concern is that this may inappropriately impact victims of domestic violence. Victims most likely to respond to such demarketing efforts are those who are already hesitant to request assistance for fear that requests are or will be trivialized. Given the disproportionate underrepresentation of calls for assistance by female victims of both domestic and sexual abuse, the addition of still another barrier even if psychological, may deter reporting of such calls.

A final concern is that many departments have included domestic violence as a "priority" under community policing initiatives. We believe these claims are highly misleading. How do departments operationalize their "community policing" response to domestic assault? In other contexts, police are instructed to expand their actions beyond arrest and creatively respond to citizen preferences and needs. Often, these are situations in which arrest would previously have been the routine response. Paradoxically, in cases of domestic assault, community policing initiatives typically involve mandatory arrest of offenders. Officers working in departments or states with mandatory arrest policies or laws are allowed no arrest discretion. Victim preferences and needs are generally not solicited and if so, are ignored by departments with such policies. Some critics have already raised the question of how a zero-tolerance approach conforms to the "problem-solving" approach of community policing (e.g., Manning, 2000). We believe the inclusion (and federal funding) of domestic violence programs that remove all police arrest discretion, especially when no concurrent or subsequent victim support services are provided, do not properly fit under the rubric of "community policing."

In summary, we recognize that there is considerable value to the philosophy of community policing, as well as its potential as a means of better integrating the police with the community. Nonetheless, we are concerned about the impact of current strategies on abuse victims. We hope research will address the extent to which community policing initiatives actually do "problem solve" and receive support form community agencies to better service domestic violence victims.

CHAPTER 10

Variations in Police Response to Domestic and Nondomestic Assaults

HAVE THERE BEEN CHANGES IN STREET-LEVEL BEHAVIOR?

Given the removal of structural barriers to arrest in the later 1970s and early 1980s, coupled with the convergence of academic, political, and administrative pressures favoring arrest, many researchers and policymakers expected rapid increases in arrests. For a variety of reasons, actual change has occurred sporadically without any consistency. For example, in Massachusetts, after 10 years of broadening police powers and heavy administrative pressure from state agencies and advocacy groups, in 1990, few police encounters with domestic violence resulted in arrest (Buzawa & Buzawa, 1990).

It is also possible that the effects of proarrest policies may be transitory. Research conducted by one of the authors in Detroit, Michigan, after the start of a mandatory arrest program in 1976 initially showed a noticeable decrease in incidents reported to the police during the 12 months after enactment of new legislation removing procedural barriers to arrest (Buzawa, 1982). This occurred despite the fact that the economy of Detroit was declining at the time and domestic violence shelter workers believed domestic violence was increasing.

Officer interviews taken after the policy was implemented stated that when an officer warned victims that an arrest would be made if the police were called again, the "problem families" seemed to "quiet down," as measured by a decrease of their demands for police service. One comment told to the author was that some police simply stated, "If we come back, everyone goes to jail." This would obviously be an effective way to reduce repeat calls because victims risked jail if they called again. In effect, such practices virtually invited batterers to continue offending with a reduced risk of interference. Thus, there is the theoretical possibility that a proarrest policy might perversely have actually led to less victim protection.

The record of the acceptance and honoring of such policies still remains fragmented. A political firestorm in New York City is illustrative. In 1995, the police response to domestic disturbance calls and the lack of arrests that followed became an issue between the largely Democratic city council and the Republican administration of Mayor Rudolf Giuliani over whether the New York Police Department actually enforced its own domestic violence policies. The city council officially charged the department with failure to make arrests in conformity with a must arrest policy (Firestone, 1995).

The mayor's office contended that felony arrests increased by 37.5% and misdemeanor arrests increased by 75.5% after the April 1994 initiation of the new policy. City council members sharply challenged the adequacy of these statistics, however, noting that the prepolicy baseline had an extremely low combined arrest rate—only 7% of 911 domestic violence calls—and that the subsequent increase to approximately 10% was meager at best. New York City's performance was also adversely compared with the records of cities in New Jersey, in which a 35% arrest rate resulted, and Dallas, with a rate of 39% of 911 calls resulting in arrest.

Not surprisingly, victim advocates, victims, and assistant district attorneys all told the New York City Council that the "must arrest" policy was not being honored despite the conditions of the consent decree agreed on by the city as a settlement of earlier class action litigation. The conclusion of the city council, as expressed by a formal report of its public safety committee, was that crimes of domestic violence were still not being treated as seriously as other kinds of crimes (Firestone, 1995). We assume that after the political profile of the arrest data was raised, administrative attention to making arrests was enhanced and, at least for a short period, the number of arrests dramatically increased; however, it is an open question whether previous practices reappeared when the funding period ended.

We believe that the foregoing simply illustrates the lack of consistency among departments over the proportion of arrests. Can the fault be one of a failure to issue supportive policies? The answer appears, quite definitively, to be no. One comprehensive 1998 study collected data from the official records of research and planning offices of most of the largest police departments in the country (more than 100 officers and greater than 5% minority population). Figures from these studies suggested little variation among departments. The data found that almost 99% of officers made arrests as "the usual response" to violence occurring in the officer's presence, almost 81% if violence had occurred before the officer's arrival, and 28% if violence had been threatened but had not yet occurred (Chaney & Saltzstein, 1998). Although no question was apparently asked in their study about restraining order violations, arrest would likely be listed as the outcome in virtually all mandatory arrest jurisdictions. It has also been our experience that most state laws, policies, and announced practices also make this a subject of mandatory arrest.

Despite the apparent good faith of the research and planning staffs, we simply do not believe that arrest behavior actually follows such policies, at least to the extent stated. We do acknowledge that arrest rates appear to have risen dramatically in many, if not most, police departments despite variations in measurement and definitions. This does not rise to the level expected for full enforcement of domestic violence statutes, however.

As cited in our earlier chapters, arrest rates for domestic violence crimes in the 1970s and 1980s varied from 3% (Langley & Levy, 1977), 4% (Lawrenz et al., 1988), 10% (Roy, 1977), 7.5% (Holmes & Bibel, 1988) to 13.9% (Bayley, 1986). More recently, reported arrest rates have increased. Recent research has found rates of 30% (Robinson & Chandek, 2000) and 34% (Hotaling & Buzawa, 2000). The question that still remains unanswered is, how can such relatively low arrest rates continue when departments now have a policy that either "presumes" or even "mandates" arrest in the case of observed domestic violence?

The study that Buzawa and Hotaling (2000) conducted in several Massachusetts communities suggests several possible explanations for the variance between "mandated" and "actual" police behavior. Police officers may simply view mandatory policies as being "too restrictive" and not in correspondence to the complexities of real life, in which the status of victim–offender may not be clear-cut. In addition, the decision to arrest may be considered an overreaction to a situation that "technically" meets the requirements of arrest. The towns studied did not have high dual arrests. Instead, the problem was simply "defined" away. For assaults in which arrests were not made, the incident was redefined to a category not mandating arrest (e.g., a case of "involved parties" rather than assault). In fact, the percent of cases classified as "involved parties" in the departments studied ranged from 26% to 56% of incidents of cases, despite the fact that in 18.8% of these "involved parties" cases, one of the parties was actually injured.

The context of the gap between policy and street practices can be better understood when examining how departments incorporate other contradictory "demands" into their daily practices. There is now a well-established procedure for evaluating police based on measures of cost-effectiveness. Police organizations, lacking sufficient resources, are forced to develop standard operating practices or express strategies targeting limited resources on "hot spots," career criminals, repeat victims, and high-risk offenders. At the same time, they use a variety of techniques to screen out low-risk or trivial cases unless linked to some other serious public safety concern. Of course, concerns for cost-effectiveness may be seen at the street level as a contradiction to policies demanding increased rates of arrest for domestic assault or any other type of offense for which there is deemed to be "zero tolerance." Screening out certain categories of victims is also seen as contradictory to other practices focusing on maintaining order because empirical data do not support this practice having an impact on

reducing actual rates of crime (Laub & Sampson, 2001).

HOW CLOSELY DO POLICE FOLLOW PROARREST POLICIES?

Having made an initial inquiry into what factors influence the rate of arrests among assaults, we focus on two related issues: (1) Is there still some discrimination by police officers against using arrest in cases of domestic violence? (2) Have police conformed with proarrest policies of the last 15 years? As explained in earlier chapters, many feminists still maintain that discriminatory police behavior exists and that, far from enforcing proarrest laws, the police actually still discriminate against victims of domestic violence. In contrast, Sanders (1988), Elliott (1989), and Sherman (1992) have argued that the police respond consistently with all cases that share similar characteristics. For example, the relevant factor is not whether the assault is nondomestic or domestic but the circumstance under which the assault occurs (i.e., police act situationally).

In support of this perspective, Elliott (1989) reviewed- studies and concluded that despite the reported findings of other researchers, arrest practices for nonfamily assaults were not significantly different from those for domestic assaults. This was primarily due to the lack of severity in response to nondomestic assaults rather than proarrest practices in cases of domestic assault. Faragher (1985) also reported that nondomestic public violence was treated as lightly as domestic violence. For example, the 1977 Police Services Study was examined by Oppenlander (1982), who reported that the rate of arrests for assaults within a family was 22% compared with only 13% for assaults outside the family. This disparity disappeared, however, when injury was controlled as an intervening variable.

Oppenlander also found that in the family cases, the arrest was often for drunk and disorderly conduct rather than an arrest for the assault itself, but this claim appeared to be based on the author's impressions rather than quantifiable data (Elliott, 1989).

The strong inference among these researchers is that the focus should be on the situational characteristics of incidents, with the assumption that these adequately explain arrest decisions. If followed to its logical conclusion, failure to arrest in domestic violence cases does not reflect bias, but is merely a result of routinized police behavior (Sherman, 1992).

D. A. Smith (1986), using the same database as Oppenlander (1982), reported virtually no difference in arrest rates between family and nonfamily assaults (28% vs. 30%). Smith found that when assaults involved only men (typical of assaults among strangers), arrest was substantially higher than when male–female assaults occurred. This may explain the disparity in domestic assaults cases, which are composed of more than 94% of male assaults on females (National Crime Victimization Survey [NCVS], 1994). This was not directly addressed in Smith's study, however, leading Elliott (1989) to conclude that there was no research directly comparing differences between arrests involving male and female victims.

The Oppenlander and Smith studies are, however, only tangentially relevant to determine disparity between domestic and nondomestic assaults. They dealt with family versus nonfamily assaults rather than domestics (husband–wife, girlfriend–boyfriend) versus stranger assaults and failed to separate misdemeanors and felonies. The latter may be crucial because officers may exercise discretion with a felony assault other than that used with misdemeanors. Furthermore, nonfamily assaults frequently involve friends, relatives, or acquaintances, which may invoke a response different from those including domestic or stranger cases.

To show how important this type of analytic detail is, Sheptycki (1993) reported that although family versus nonfamily calls revealed little differences in arrest practices, when he separated out cases of husband–wife assaults, arrests were far less likely for the latter group.

We also have examined this issue but have reached markedly different conclusions from Elliott. Although we admit that past studies often are not directly on point or have certain methodological limitations, they do support the thesis that police differentially respond to family assaults in two ways: (1) a reluctance of some officers to enforce laws with regard to domestic assaults and (2) the slow, uneven implementation of domestic violence proarrest laws and policies. This resistance to policy simply does not exist in other types of offenses.

What is the empirical evidence for finding differences in performance? It starts with classic studies. In 1971, Black reported that rates of arrest for felonies involving strangers were far higher than those among family members (88% to 45%), with somewhat smaller differences for misdemeanor assaults (57% to 47%). Black then concluded that there was a continuum of responses to assault cases, with sanctions becoming more formal (i.e., arrest) as social distance between the victim and assailant increased. Black's findings probably cannot be generalized to current police practices. In common with much research of the time that relied on a relatively small sample size for felony and misdemeanor family assaults, he failed to differentiate between violence among intimates from other familial disputes, and the study had no control for the level of injury involved.

Nonetheless, current research continues to find variation in actual practices among different types of assaults, even within the context of an overall rise in arrest rates. Fyfe, Klinger, and Flavin (1997) reported that men who assault their wives were treated more leniently than men who commit other assaults. Other data continue to suggest intriguing, but difficult to quantify, differences in policing between domestic and stranger assaults. For example, according to the U.S. Department of Justice (1994) in a Report on Violence Between Intimates (long after proarrest policies were in effect throughout the country), there was a small but consistent trend toward more aggressive policing in stranger assault cases when compared with intimate assault cases. According to this study, police responded within 5 minutes in 36% of the cases when the offender was a stranger but only in 24% of cases in which the offender was an intimate. Similarly, police were more likely to take a formal report if the victim was a stranger (77%) rather than an intimate (69%).Other recent studies have confirmed that despite stated policies to the contrary, many police departments continue to discriminate against making arrests in cases of domestic violence, at least compared with similar nondomestic assaults. For example, Eigenberg et al. (2001) did a meta-analysis of numerous other studies and reported that police were less willing to arrest in battering cases, having restricted their arrests primarily to cases in which additional witnesses were present. Even victim injury and the use of a weapon by the offender had little effect on these noted discrepancies. Similarly, Fyfe et al. (1997) reported that officers treated domestic violence incidents less severely than assaults.

A recently published analysis of NCVS data also found that a suspect's relationship to an assault victim continued to have dramatic impact on arrest; however, according to the researchers, such a relationship did not appear to be "improper" and instead attributed it to situational factors of the incidents. These included the inability of many victims in stranger assaults to identify the assailant, the greater presence of witnesses in stranger assaults, and the reluctance of many victims in

intimate assaults to sign complaints (Felson & Ackerman, 2001). This study used NCVS data collected from the latter part of 1992 through the first half of 1998, encompassing a period well after all states had enacted domestic violence reform legislation promoting a policy proactive intervention, including aggressive use of arrest. The results were that in cases of minor assaults, police were less likely to make arrests if the suspect was an intimate partner of the victim compared with an identifiable stranger. As might be expected, their conclusion was fairly complex:

> our research suggests that the suspect's relation to the victim affects police arrest decisions in a variety of ways. The police are less likely to arrest strangers than nonstrangers for assault because they are often unable to identify them. On the other hand, *when the police are able to identify the suspect, they show leniency when the suspect knows the victim.* Their leniency is not due to a tolerance for intimate violence or violence against women; they are more likely to make an arrest in incidents involving intimate violence than in incidents involving other nonstrangers. Rather, *leniency in nonstranger incidents is due to the reluctance of victims to sign complaints, the absence of witnesses, and the unwillingness of the police to arrest suspects for minor acts of violence against people they know.* (Felson & Ackerman, 2001, p. 673, our emphasis)

We believe that while the Felson & Ackerman study encompasses the large NCVS database, it has several key shortcomings: First, the data set relies on the victim's recollection of events. It is not illogical to assume that a victim whose offender is not arrested and receives a "reasonable" explanation for nonaction from the police may have internalized that explanation and therefore no longer considers the event as having been appropriate for an arrest. Second, a study based on the NCVS national data in fact hides potentially vast real differences in behavior between various departments. As we have seen in

Chapters 5 and 6, departments display markedly different policies and practices, both stated and unstated.

In fact, we believe that the researcher's use of NCVS data as an aggregate may mask two contradictory trends. Specifically, most of the studies of a single jurisdiction find either a policy that increases the number of arrests in cases of domestic assault (following express preferences of the legislature and police policies), or alternatively, that fewer arrests are made in cases of intimate partner assault. Of course, these two trends may offset each other at an aggregate level allowing for a misrepresentation of police reluctance to arrest in cases of domestic assault.

One study (Buzawa, Austin, & Buzawa, 1995) of which we have detailed knowledge unfortunately illustrates why actual police practices within different departments need to be studied in depth , not as part of a "national aggregate." A study of all 376 domestic and stranger assaults in a 10-month period was taken from official records of a Midwestern police department. In this study, we tested the hypothesis that an inverse relationship characterized the association between level of intimacy and arrest.[1]

We ensured that police accurately categorized incidents as domestic violence or assault by individually reviewing every single police incident report during the time period. In fact, police classified many domestic violence cases as disorderly conduct, disturbing the peace, destruction of property, or family dispute. After identifying all cases of assault, cases were again individually reviewed to include only cases of male-against-female intimate partner assaults as "domestic." Other domestic relationships were not included in the data set.

We (Buzawa et al., 1995) found that, notwithstanding relevant elements of probable cause such as the presence of weapons, witnesses, injury, and the offender, results confirmed that in the department studied,

there was a measurable difference in how domestic violence cases were treated compared to similar nondomestic assaults. Specifically, although overall police arrest rates for minor assaults were, as elsewhere reported, quite low, we tested in that department whether domestic violence cases resulted in lower rates of arrest compared with similar crimes. We controlled key potentially intervening variables. Despite the relatively low percentage of arrests made overall (26%), it became clear that officers in the police department studied did not make as many arrests for cases involving domestic assaults as stranger assaults. This distinction was magnified when relevant factors, for example, offender presence at the scene and victim preference, were controlled. Of equal importance, victim preferences for arrest were ignored in 75% of the domestic cases compared with just slightly more than 40% of stranger assaults.

Our research did find that, regardless of type of assault, offender presence at the scene increased the probability of arrest, whereas the extent of injury to the victim had no effect on arrest in any of the types of assaults. Both the type of force or weapon used and the presence of witnesses, however, affected the decision to arrest in domestic incidents but not in acquaintance or stranger cases. In domestic cases, when witnesses were present or the weapon used was more deadly, an arrest was more likely.

This suggests that a higher standard or level of probable cause was needed for an arrest in domestic incidents. The finding that victim preference did not affect the decision to arrest in domestic assaults but did affect it in cases involving acquaintances and strangers reinforced this tentative conclusion. More weight appeared to be given to the victim's request in the decision to arrest when the parties were less intimately acquainted. The latter two findings support the idea of specification and suggest why arrest in less intimate incidents is more likely. Assaults involving strangers appeared to be viewed by the police in this department as more genuine, thus not requiring corroboration by outside sources. Conversely, police appeared to view domestic incidents as "family matters" and required, by their very nature, independent verification.

To determine whether these observable differences in arrest practices were a reflection of policies and practices, Buzawa and Austin (1993) reviewed policies, procedures, and incident reports in these departments to see if they displayed a differential (less favorable) response to handling domestic violence. These measures were used either to confirm the analysis of official arrest data or to cast doubt on relationships found therein. This also helped answer whether observed practices were likely due to individual officer preferences or the result of official or unofficial policy preferences. We started with the premise that departmental policies would best demonstrate the relative attention accorded to an offense, which in turn would be reflect administrative priorities.

A review of this department's policy manual indicated a low level of interest in domestic violence. An initial observation was that this police department relied on numerous exhaustive written policies. As a result, the department's policy manual was several hundred pages in length. Police department administrators apparently believed that without such policies, officers might not act appropriately; the administrators also used such policies as a vehicle to develop consistent practices and as an officer training guide.

In this context, several observations were striking. First, despite statutory guidance, there was no policy on handling or complying with the new domestic violence proarrest statute. Second, there was no policy addressing how to respond to protective orders, an

important vehicle for protecting victims. There was merely a one-line reference to ex parte orders—far too vague to provide officer guidance.

Within the policy for "assaults" was a call for exceptionally passive police responses. Officers were instructed to "stand by" a short distance away until arrival of the second officer rather than respond immediately to the scene unless the officer determines that an emergency exists. The obvious question was how officers might even ascertain such an emergency existed when waiting in patrol cars. This dilemma was verified in reports. For example, in one situation, an officer waited for backup, noting that all was quiet inside. As soon as his partner arrived, they entered the premises; however, there were five people seriously injured requiring emergency medical treatment.

Domestic assault cases were the only cases singled out for such a cautious response. Such a policy appears to conform to the observations of other researchers that officers in many departments delay their arrival, hoping the call will "go away" (Sheptycki, 1993). In contrast, in cases of shoplifting or minors attempting to purchase intoxicants, officers were instructed to respond immediately because the suspect might resist or attempt to flee from a merchant before the officers arrive.

Although this may be true, the priority of these calls cannot possibly be compared with calls from battered women whose lives (or the lives of their children) may be endangered by a policy to deliberately wait until backup arrived. Although the organizational goal ideally may be (although in this case, it was not stated) to protect victims and arrest batterers when appropriate, the policy's primary focus was the officer's—not the victim's—personal safety. The emphasis in the policy manual was on the response to "disturbances" that need to be "quelled," not investigated to determine whether a crime had occurred or an offender should be arrested. As Wilson (1989) noted, officers were taught to define their job, at least in the case of domestic violence, as "handling the situation" rather than enforcing the law.

This policy statement also demonstrated that handling tasks such as domestic violence were not really valued by the department. In a 14-page, exhaustively detailed description of knowledge an officer needs for career development and reimbursement, there was only a one-line reference to any knowledge arguably of interest to domestic violence. Of the approximately 120 items required, there was a place to put a "check mark" on his or her knowledge of family crisis intervention. By the number of references, this was the same as checked-off knowledge of "calculators," "cameras," or "public speaking."

Finally, although the department had a progressive, six-page "posttrauma procedure" on how to ascertain that all of its members were aware of posttraumatic stress disorder (PTSD) and how to cope with stress, this was not at all in reference to PTSD in victims. Rather, officers were instructed to present a good attitude, showing personal concern for other officers who were involved in a fatal shooting or other trauma. Similar sensitivity toward victims was totally absent. This once again reflected a police department that appeared to be far more sensitive to the feelings of its members than to those of the general public.

In summary, the department studied appeared to be striving to be professional with multipage policies on diverse topics deemed important to its mission. Policies evidenced a desire to conform and control officer conduct even to the extent of personal grooming (wherein female officers were expected to keep their hair in "a condition befitting their sex"). In this context, the lack of a specific and detailed policy on the proper handling of domestic assault cases was incongruous, seemingly graphically demon-

strating that such cases were not important to the department's mission.

Finally, a content analysis of 1,000 consecutively numbered incidents was conducted to obtain a general understanding of how domestic assault reports were written compared with other calls. Initially, it seemed reasonable to assume that officer time in report preparation and detail given to describing the event were reflective of the perceived relative importance of such incidents. Several observations were obvious. Of the 1,000 incidents to which officers responded, only 564 reports were actually written. Although there was no way of determining with certainty if domestic cases were more likely to be screened out, a reading of the reports certainly suggests this possibility. Criminal traffic offenses were typically a minimum of two to three typed pages, with careful attention to detail. It appeared that officers thought convictions likely or were concerned about the possibility of impacting civil liability of participants. As a result, narratives were fully documented. Conversely, domestic assaults were far more abbreviated, making subsequent successful prosecution less likely.

Because arrests actually were rarely made at the scene, it appeared that when officers thought an arrest necessary, they simply would note that they had "advised" the victim to see the prosecutor. This notation was seldom placed in stranger assaults for which arrests were far more typical. In addition, the domestic assault victims were frequently described as "hysterical" and were told to see the prosecutor when they "calmed down." The victim's story was described as "alleged" rather than as "fact," which did not typify police reporting of stranger assaults. Again, this designation and admonition was absent in cases of stranger assaults. Although such reported results are impressionistic, it seems reasonable to assume that the officer's time in report preparation and the detail given to describing the event reflect the perceived relative importance of such incidents.

Sheptycki (1993) made similar observations with regard to domestic abuse cases in London, where he observed police using phrases such as "victim claims," "it seems that," and "victim alleges" in domestic assaults 3 times as frequently as in nondomestic assaults. Police were found to be far more likely to discourage such victims from pressing charges (Faragher, 1985; Sheptycki, 1993). Not surprisingly, this had considerable impact. Victims frequently interpret poor police attitudes as a lack of interest, which can affect subsequent pursuit of criminal charges (Radford, 1987; Sheptycki, 1993).

In sharp contrast, Hotaling and Buzawa (2001) analyzed all assaults that came to the attention of law enforcement in two communities in western Massachusetts over 6 years: 1990, 1991, 1994, 1995, the last 6 months of 1997, 1998, and the last 6 months of 1999 (n = 1,639). They examined all incident and arrest reports in police files and reproduced all reports that met the study definition of assault.[2] The research found that there appeared to be far higher rates of overall arrest for domestic assaults (77%) compared to nondomestic assaults (36%). This was true both for assaults involving physical force (39% vs. 52%) and even for assaults when there was a threat only (59% vs. 26%).

Hotaling and Buzawa (2001) suggested three alternate explanations for these differences in arrest behavior. The first was that the police were trained or socialized to treat assailants of domestic assault more punitively, at least in terms of arrest when they were toward nondomestic assailants. Second, the behaviors of the officers could simply reflect police compliance with the department's proarrest policies. To some extent, the police here reacted positively to such policies. In theory, an officer finding probable cause for domestic assault is required to arrest. It is evident that these police departments took this mandate seriously. In 75% of the domestic cases in which the victim preferred no arrest, an arrest was made. In contrast, in cases of nondomestic assaults, not a single arrest was made when the victim did not want one. Finally, Massachusetts domestic violence statutes, in common with all 50 states, have made warrantless misdemeanor arrests possible in the context of domestic assaults whether or not the officer has seen the assault. In contrast, cases involving nondomestic assaults still require the officer to witness the assault (Hotaling & Buzawa, 2001).

There was also relative consistency in who reported cases. In 60% of cases, the victim reported domestic assaults compared with 52% of nondomestic assaults. This suggested that victims of domestic assault were not more reticent about reporting assaults than victims of other types of assaults.

Finally, Hotaling and Buzawa's (2001) findings reported a robust police response that did not demonstrate apathy toward the problem being addressed or lack of attention being paid. In fact, the data examined 16 categories of police actions taken when responding to an assault, and significant differences were found in 10 categories. In every category in which the difference was significant, it was in favor of domestic assaults. Hence, police did not treat domestic assaults less seriously than nondomestic assaults.

One finding of note, however, is the police response to children present at the scene. In these cases, police may not have followed all requirements of the statute. In overall cases, they checked on the child's safety in 17% of cases and talked to children present in 40% of domestic assault incidents compared with 100% of nondomestic assaults incidents. It should be noted, however, that children who were present in domestic assaults were, on average, much younger than children who witnessed nondomestic assaults, possibly accounting for the difference (Hotaling & Buzawa, 2001).

The key is that not all police departments act as cavalierly toward domestic assault cases as shown in the Buzawa and Austin study or the Sheptycki study in London. In addition, the studies examining differences between domestic and nondomestic assault described here suggest that the real unit of analysis should be at the department level. It would be inappropriate to artificially aggregate results from these into any "national" study that attempted to state definitively that police either did or did not discriminate against victims of domestic assaults.

THE IMPACT OF DIFFERENTIAL POLICE INTERVENTIONS

Indeed, perhaps the cause of lower rates of arrest for domestic cases is less important than its effect. Most victims of domestic assault are women, and most victims of crimes of public disorder are men; therefore, the system in many locations effectively offers greater protection to men. In that context, it is less important whether the criminal justice system considers domestic cases more trivial because they are less likely to result in conviction (Myers & Hagan, 1979) or because the system is inherently sexist (Dobash & Dobash, 1979; Matoesian, 1993; Smart, 1986).

Regardless of the reason, if situational factors disparately affect the enforcement of laws when a largely identifiable class of victims is involved, then further public attention is merited. In short, it may be true that a lack of aggressive law enforcement may typify cases in which people who are powerless, whether victims of domestic violence or otherwise, may not receive the same degree of police action as others (Dobash & Dobash, 1992; Edwards, 1989; Hanmer et al., 1989; Skolnick, 1975).In addition, warrantless

misdemeanor arrests (e.g., arrest with probable cause) are only allowed in cases of domestic assault rather than nondomestic assault. Because most domestic assaults are charged as misdemeanors (Buzawa et al., 1999), this suggests that the proportion of domestic assaults resulting in arrest should be higher than nondomestic (although witnesses may be more likely at nondomestic assaults).

Although a situational analysis helps us explain why police do not make many domestic violence arrests, the factors cited earlier are not relevant to determining probable cause. It is therefore facile simply to dismiss differential impact as being merely situational. Furthermore, there is an element of de facto discrimination. Although it may be conceivable that arrest rates would also decline in situations in which "nonintimates" are cohabiting, most of these cases brought to the attention of police are domestic violence incidents, and the vast majority (estimates ranging as high as 95%) involve men assaulting their female partners or ex-partners. Clearly, in some cases, police may simply be acting situationally in a manner that favors aggressive responses to public disorder and downplays aggressive responses to interpersonal crimes. Although perhaps not overtly discriminatory, this should still unacceptable. Women are most likely to become victims of homicides, assaults, and rapes behind closed doors in private settings, whereas men are victimized in more public settings. As a consequence, the concept of police limiting active intervention to public order violence must be challenged.

Elliott (1989), Sanders (1988), and Sherman (1992) apparently favored the situational view of comparative arrest practices and found little differences in behavior. This ignores the fact that in the last 15 years, every state in the country has passed reform legislation stating the express policy of state (and formal) governments to aggressively respond to domestic violence cases including arrest. No such policy has ever been considered or even articulated for handling cases of stranger assaults.

Therefore, making the case that similar situational factors are used in arrests in domestic and stranger assaults implicitly concedes that many police officers simply ignore the statutory policy favoring domestic assault arrests, hardly a nondiscriminatory policy. It is precisely the gap between stated policies favoring arrest in domestic assault cases and actual practices that needs further explanation. For this reason, it is legitimate to critique the failure of police departments to follow goals that are mandated or at least preferred by statute. Although we have our own concerns with overuse of arrest, we believe that arrests should be made when appropriate and that statutory and official policies should be honored.

We must disclose our own bias in this matter. We believe that variables such as the public setting of a dispute versus a family nature and the presence or absence of witnesses should not affect arrest decisions or act to void statutory policies. Such decisions should instead be based on probable cause determinations of violation of the particular statutes involved including those demanding a more aggressive arrest practice in cases of domestic violence. The proper role of arrests in the case of domestic violence should be settled in the legislatures across the country, not by police officers who may decide individually whether to follow specific statutes. At a minimum, even if the officers discard statutory directives in certain police departments, arrest decisions should reflect their honest and well-founded assessment of prospective violence, not a "situationally" based construct having little to do with the offense committed or the likelihood of future attacks against a victim. For this reason, we fundamentally differ from the recent conclusion reached by Felson and Ackerman, as well as earlier by Elliott, Sherman, and others,

that situational variables "logically" and in an "unbiased" method differentiate between arrest practices in cases of domestic versus stranger assaults.

How Police Changed in Response to Proarrest Policies

The reality of how police organizations actually respond to proarrest statutes and policy directives remains problematic and, at times, unpredictable. Before we examine the possible negative impacts of enhanced arrest, we need to explore the extent to which actual change has occurred in arrest practices in street-level behavior of law enforcement. The process of implementing organizational change rarely received adequate attention from policymakers. As a result, a pattern of state-mandated changes in law enforcement practices have been decoupled from the administrative detail sufficient to ensure actual change. A failure to critically focus on strategies to effectively implement change results in inadequate or even simplistic solutions. The result may be that policies fail to change actual practices or street-level behavior. Alternatively, policies may become so transformed in practice that the problem not only remains, but new problems are created (e.g., the phenomenon of "dual arrests" described later in this chapter).

Because administrative or legal pronouncements and statutory changes do not automatically translate into effective operational behavior, this section concentrates not only on the mandate of changes but also on an assessment, even if preliminary, of the impact of such mandates on actual service delivery.

What do we know about implementation issues in this area? Researchers have long been aware of the difficulties in successfully implementing politically mandated changes on "independent" agencies (Bardach, 1977). Since the 1970s, concerns have been raised that bureaucratic institutions may transform policy mandates with their own standard operating procedures and their own mechanisms for rewarding and punishing behavior (Salamon & Wamsley, 1975). There is a recognition that bureaucratic discretion coexists with the exercise of political control (Ringquist, 1995) and even a frank admission that we often do not know about the determinants of political control, or even at times the causal mechanisms of control (Wood & Waterman 1991, 1994). As a result, there is a wide variety of responsiveness depending on the type of agency and the type of directive involved (Gruber, 1987; Moe, 1987).

Such issues are in turn compounded by the structure and traditions of the criminal justice system. Police departments, despite their reputation as paramilitary "command and control" bureaucracies, are known to be remarkably resistant to change. This is partially due to the inability of command officers to observe officer behavior directly, to ingrained "respect" and deference for officer discretion from commanders who were former line officers, and to training systems for which formal academic instruction is limited and in-service training often nonexistent. Rookie as well as more experienced officers who are often resistant to change coupled with strong police unions further contribute

to difficulties in implementing change. Such structural bases for resistance to change are often supplemented and reinforced by a widely recognized feature of the police culture: a highly insular and self-reinforcing organization in which both civilians in general and civilian control over police practices in particular are regarded suspiciously and perhaps with cynicism or are simply dismissed with outright derision (Crank, 1998; Manning, 1997).

Most police departments we have studied over recent years now have adopted detailed policies about handling a maze of subjects; now these typically include domestic violence (sometimes to an excruciating level). These policies "read well" in that they express institutional commitment to politically correct policies and administrative control. To some extent, the reality of policing is different than these policies suggest. After all, policies may be written in part to insulate the department from legal liability rather than a genuine concern for policy adherence. At times, absolute compliance may not be expected or even desired by department leadership. This makes street-level implementation of any legislation or policy directives problematic at best and, to us, focuses attention on the methods used to facilitate actual behavioral changes.

NOTES

1. This research project was the outgrowth of a study conducted by one of the researchers on behalf of the plaintiffs in a lawsuit. The suit was filed against the police department of a midsize Midwestern city. Although plaintiff's counsel in effect commissioned the study, every effort was made to obtain unbiased data that would fairly test the premise that the department might have disparately treated victims of domestic violence.

2. The assault definition was broad in scope and included all cases of physical violence, sexual assaults (involving the use of violence, threat of violence or force, or the use of luring and other forms of manipulation), face-to-face threats to harm another person, indirect threats to harm another person (through letter writing or telephone), and incidents involving behavior that placed a person in a state of fear, even when no actual force was used or threats issued.

III

WHAT HAPPENS AFTER ARREST? THE ROLE OF THE PROSECUTORS AND THE COURTS

CHAPTER 11

Classic Patterns of Nonintervention by the Prosecutors and Courts

THE VICTIM'S EXPERIENCE

Much has been written about the lack of assistance and support that have historically been provided by prosecutors and the courts to victims of domestic violence. In this section, we briefly describe the victim's experiences and how victims were hindered by their reaction to her issues. We study this now not only—or even primarily—for historical significance, but also because this is the response that victims receive in many jurisdictions when seeking redress.

The importance of the prosecutor and the judiciary is becoming of paramount importance precisely because of the rapid changes happening in the field of law enforcement. As described in previously in earlier chapters, starting in the mid 1980s, there has been a massive and steady increase in the number of arrests made by many police departments. If not carefully managed, the interplay between a police department's new proarrest—and especially mandatory—arrest policy may have unanticipated consequences. Reformed police practices undoubtedly sent more cases to be prosecuted. The prosecutor's office, however, received no additional staffing and was already straining under drug cases. The net result was that such cases competed for the same limited amount of judicial and prosecutorial time (Balos & Trotsky, 1988).

This has created a tremendous number of new cases reaching the prosecutor's office. Their historic response to such cases was similar to that of the police, however—not a sterling endorsement. As described earlier, it has been a long-standing concern that prosecutors in domestic violence cases tend to dramatically limit charges filed after the police present the initial charges. The effect of this screening has been severely criticized as subverting activist policing. Our concern is that even if the police are motivated to make domestic violence arrests a priority, their efforts—and ultimately their commitment—may, unless coordinated, be undermined by inaction on the part of the prosecutors. It is easy to assume that prosecutors do not take domestic violence cases seriously when multiple charges of felony battery and specific domestic violence offenses are reduced to generic simple assaults, which in turn are amenable to judicial dismissal.

Naomi Cahn (1992) noted the dilemma faced by even well-meaning prosecutors who now confront increasing numbers of domestics in their caseload. Proarrest policies, coupled with increasing victim and advocate awareness, have created the necessity of increasing early dismissals to manage caseload or a full-scale commitment to adopt innovative approaches. This was confirmed by data from a large-scale study, conducted by the American Prosecutors Research Institute. It reported that the level of available resources affected how the prosecutors' offices processed cases. Although a select group of local prosecutors' offices have developed innovative programs, a larger group had not, a group the author of the study termed (albeit somewhat optimistically) "desirous to establish such programs" (Rebovich, 1996). To better understand contacts between the prosecutor's office and the victim, it may be important to review features of the prosecutorial organization. We believe several aspects are of significance.

Prosecutorial Autonomy

Prosecutor offices are organizationally committed to maintaining autonomy. When a victim enters a prosecutor's office, she is often confronted with an organization with its own bureaucratic goals and operational norms. She often reluctantly learns that the self-declared primary purpose of this office was to enforce society's rights to sanction activities harmful to the public order by punishing offenders and deterring future misconduct. Because its primary goals are societal in nature, victims may not have a right to insist on prosecution. Conversely, the decision to pursue charges, of which charges to advance, and of which charges to dismiss or settle do not require victim consent.

The foregoing may appear to be intuitively obvious, as prosecutorial discretion—the ability of the state's officer to choose to charge, prosecute, or settle criminal cases—is a key feature of American jurisprudence. It is doubtful, however, that most victims understand this feature, and they erroneously tend to expect that prosecutorial staff members operate primarily to redress their particular grievances, and those of other victims. The potential effect

of this difference is to create barriers between the victim and her nominal allies. Their differing interests, unless carefully managed, provide an environment in which distrust and victim disparagement inevitably lead to high rates of voluntary dismissals. One British study reported that the entire experience was extraordinarily frustrating to them because victims could not understand what was happening or why some cases were dropped, others prosecuted, and still others "continued" without a concrete resolution. This contributed to extremely high rates of voluntary case dismissal (Cretney & Davis 1997). One key result of prosecutorial discretion was the interplay between its negative effects on the victims of abuse and the official's often deeply held views demanding such autonomy.

The Reality of Budgetary Pressures

As with virtually all public service agencies, prosecutors typically operate with fiscal restraints that result in limited budgets. They also are unlikely to have the ability to add resources in response to crises. Clearly, the effect is to force the lead prosecutor to selectively allocate scarce resources. As a result, special attention is reserved for homicides or crimes of a "heinous nature," drug cases, and other high-profile cases such as official corruption, cases involving public figures (e.g., the 1994 Los Angeles, California, murder indictment of O. J. Simpson), and, at least more recently, to terrorist offenses. Other crimes might then be prosecuted, to the extent the prosecutor in his discretion believes appropriate, if they cannot be plea-bargained or otherwise rapidly disposed.

Prioritizing Prosecutorial Efforts to Targeted Offenses

The crisis of excessive caseloads has shaken this uneasy fiscal tightrope, creating the current overriding organizational imperative to dispose of most cases. An unprecedented increase in prosecution targeting highly visible, drug-related crimes has occurred, covering drug dealing and drug use to street crimes and burglaries that support drug dependencies. These have become the single largest related categories of offenses. As a result of political pressure to eliminate drug use, disproportionately large resources are devoted to a single problem. The present drug crisis and resultant budgetary pressures dominate the attention of state and federal judiciary, and, in many areas, more than half of all prosecutions now relate to drug offenses. Some estimates are that as many as 65% of all criminal cases are, in some manner, drug related, with state courts handling more than 95% of such cases (Labaton, 1989). In 1990, the Philadelphia Police Commissioner stated in the *New York Times* that the massive increase in arrests created such a backlog that the criminal courts were close to collapsing.

Is this inevitable? In the 1980s and 1990s, public dismay over drugs and street crime led to the passage of laws and policies for specific drug-related offenses that expressly limited the discretion of the prosecutor's office to plea-bargain and, therefore, rapidly dispose of such cases. By this mechanism, the magnitude of drug cases has, in turn, been compounded by the longer sentences imposed by courts and new federal and state sentencing guidelines removing discretion in judicial sentencing.

An unexpected, but predictable, consequence of such legislation has been that affected defendants have little incentive to plea-bargain because their sentences cannot be substantively reduced. Whatever their other merits, such constraints have diminished the ability of an assembly-line process that previously had rapidly disposed of more than 90% of criminal offenses. In 1989, a report of the Conference of Chief Judges of the nine most populous states commented that lawmakers and officials who had adopted such policies failed to consider the impact of the huge flood of cases on the courts. Conferees warned of either an imminent or existing caseload crisis or of possible "breakdown of the system" if solutions were not found (Labaton, 1989). Unfortunately, in the 12 years since that report, the "drug" caseload has grown even larger, now impacting family courts as well as traditional criminal courtrooms. For example, in one 3-year period, New York State Family Court filings increased by 699% and, in 1989, accounted for up to 532,000 cases annually (Labaton, 1989). Most such of these were juvenile drug-related cases or ones that involved custody of children whose parents were incarcerated or considered incompetent for drug-related reasons. Because of the impact on children, these cases take considerable court resources. Because the total number of judges did not markedly increase (in New York City's Family Court, there was no increase from 1983 to 1989), the average caseload grew tremendously (Labaton, 1989).

We are writing this chapter in early 2002, after the September 11, 2001, terrorist attacks. From this perspective, it could easily be the case that new crimes, perhaps related to breaches of security or other terrorism-related crimes, may now begin to consume disproportionate prosecutorial time.

The Impact of These Constraints on the Prosecutorial Response

A critical problem for prosecution of domestic violence crimes is that until recently, many prosecutors have not perceived that serious deficiencies existed in how domestic violence cases were processed (Belknap et al., 2001; Weisz, 1999; Wills, 1997). Under these circumstances, fiscal crises from an organizational perspective became a justifiable reason to not aggressively respond to domestic violence cases in general.

Under this kind of pressure, it is not surprising that prosecutors and their staffs attempted any possible means to informally reduce caseloads by outright dismissal or other diversion from the criminal justice docket. As described in previous chapters, domestic violence cases are usually characterized as being in the category of less favored misdemeanors or, when felonies are first offenses, are not usually covered by sentencing guidelines. It therefore is not surprising from an organizational perspective that they become disproportionately subject to pressure for settlement or dismissal. Perhaps this can be best summarized by the comments of a West Virginia assistant prosecuting attorney:

> as a one woman, part-time domestic violence "unit" that maintains a "no drop" policy of sorts, I am without the resources to back it up. Many if not most prosecutors share this impediment, to which little attention is given inside or outside the domestic violence community. It takes time to properly prosecute a domestic violence case, more time than those who fund and manage prosecutor offices and law enforcement agencies are willing to pay for. (Hartman, 1999, p. 74)

UNIQUE FACTORS LIMITING EFFECTIVENESS OF PROSECUTORS

Unique characteristics of prosecuting domestic violence and sexual assaults also increased the probability that such crimes would not be treated as seriously as they might otherwise warrant.

The Bias Against Relationship Cases

It has long been surmised that there is a general organizational bias in prosecutor offices against "relationship" cases in which the offender and victim know each other and had some right to interact with the other party (Rebovich, 1996; Stanko, 1982). This attitude arises because of time and resource constraints and the high proportion of such cases in

the system. Cases involving relationships are typically overrepresented in a prosecutor's caseload because, to him or her, they should be comparatively easy for the victim to report and the police to apprehend and should not be repetitive.

The very nature of such cases troubles prosecutors and, if the case passes their screening, the courts. Although a common problem in a civil setting, the complexity of a relationship often negates the simplistic, right-or-wrong dichotomy needed to convict in a criminal tribunal. A relationship case may also be denigrated because it does less violence to the public order and on its surface may appear to be a personal problem, thereby "really" belonging in a civil court. Prosecutors and court personnel may tend to believe that defendants in a relationship case are influenced by the relationship itself. Thus, offenders may not be perceived as being a "hard case" worthy of prosecution, and by the nature of the relationship the offender was less likely to recidivate against others than those responsible for violence, property loss, or theft against strangers or drug addicts who must continue criminal activity to feed a habit (B. E. Smith, 1983).

With sufficient resources, the general bias against relationship cases, and domestic violence cases in particular, would be interesting but not overly significant. Unfortunately, as explained earlier, the system operates without sufficient resources forcing many disfavored cases to be dropped. In addition, the prosecutor's bias against handling "relationship cases" may be in direct conflict with victim expectations.

We believe it fair to state that women are more likely than men to operate from a "culture of relationships." The significance of maintaining personal relationships (i.e., performing obligations within the family structure) often leads many women to make decisions based on compromise or even a known subordination of her own needs to those of her partner, children, elderly relatives, and others. In sharp contrast, criminal justice agencies expect victims to behave more like the stereotypical man, acting autonomously from the offender and the rest of her family, responding "rationally" by maximizing her own gains and concentrating solely on legally germane facts. This conflict and organizational perspective creates enormous potential for misunderstandings that can fatally effect the interaction between the victim and those agencies (Ferraro & Pope, 1993; Weisz, 1999).

The Impact of Domestic Violence Being a "Low-Status" Offense

The organizational imperative in most prosecutors' offices is to achieve high rates of felony convictions. The number and percentage of such cases successfully processed to a guilty plea or conviction are measures for evaluating prosecutors' performance and the efficiency of their offices. In times of budgetary crisis, such measures may prove critical in sustaining or even increasing allocated resources in a zero-sum budgetary game between fiscally strapped agencies.

Domestic violence cases still fail this "real-life" test in most jurisdictions despite the widespread statutory reforms discussed in Chapter 7. Organizationally, there still is a marked distinction in treatment accorded misdemeanor and felony crimes. Most domestic violence cases continue to be classified as misdemeanors, albeit they now named as domestic violence specific crimes. This distinction appears to be another product of the relatively low esteem that is given such cases, not a reflection of the degree of injury caused by the assault. It perhaps also reflects the inherent sexism of the traditional criminal justice system. In most other contexts, the offender's conduct would be termed a felony. For example, in one national crime survey, it was reported that more than one third of misdemeanor domestic violence cases, if committed by strangers, would have been termed rape, robbery, or aggravated assault—all felonies. In 42% of the remaining misdemeanor cases, an injury occurred. This rate of injury for a misdemeanor crime was higher than the combined injury rate of all of the foregoing felonies (Langan & Innes, 1986).

These surprising statistics occur partially because in U.S. jurisprudence, mere injury is not typically determinative of the severity of the crime charged. Unless a homicide occurs, evidence of premeditation and use of a weapon are given far more importance in the charging decision. Because acts of domestic violence are typically treated in isolation, the existence of a persistent pattern of battering a spouse or other family members typically does not constitute evidence of intent. Even a violation of a temporary restraining order, a fairly obvious intentional crime, remains by statute a misdemeanor in most states, merely a cause for civil contempt in many other states, and at the discretion of the court as being either civil or criminal in still others (Finn, 1991). As such, even the creation of new remedies has done little to effectively change organizational incentives to underrespond to matters of apparently low priority.

Some critics have also argued that crimes are downplayed simply because they are crimes against women, historically a disfavored group. We cannot find sufficient evidence to strongly support this conclusion in most jurisdictions; however, regardless of the reason, the effect of the dichotomy is to lessen the willingness of a prosecutor or court to waste its scarce resources to process domestic violence cases (Langan & Innes, 1986).

Case Attrition by Victims

In Chapter 5, we discussed why many victims never call the police. Now because of mandatory or presumptive arrest policies, many such cases now go to the prosecutor's office. What is the result? Perhaps inevitably, in domestic violence cases, victim or attrition dismissal rates are extraordinarily high. This may occur either because the victim drops charges or because she refuses to appear as a witness. A series of studies in different jurisdictions conducted during the early years of reforms demonstrated that, absent unusually aggressive measures, attrition rates for victim-initiated cases hovered between 60% and 80% (Cannavale & Falcon, 1986; Field & Field, 1973; Ford, 1983; Lerman, 1981; Parnas, 1970; Rebovich, 1996; Ursel, 1995; Vera Institute of Justice, 1977; Williams, 1976).

Despite increased societal attention to domestic violence, the rate of prosecution is still limited by the unwillingness of victims to cooperate (Belknap et al., 2001; Hirschel & Hutchison, 2001). In fact, one recent study that controlled for type of evidence, witnesses, and relationship reported that when victims cooperated, prosecutors were 7 times more likely to press charges (Dawson & Dinovitzer, 2001). Why should such high rates of victim-initiated case attrition persist?

Variations in Victims'
Reasons for Prosecution

Once an arrest has occurred, Ford (1991) found that victims were not irrational decision makers, citing instrumental and rational reasons rather than emotional attachments in their decision to cooperate with prosecutors. For example, victims may frankly be far less concerned with deterrence as an esoteric concept than with using the criminal justice system as a whole to accomplish personal goals of enhancing safety, maintaining economic viability, protecting children, or having an opportunity to force participation in batterers' counseling programs (Ford, 1991).

A couple's minor children may present significant issues for those who want to be sure they are protected but still wish to maintain an intact family structure. Financial ties (intensified by recent welfare reforms) may make some victims critically dependent on an abuser's financial support for minor children, a factor at odds with strict punishment models. A simple threat to have a person arrested or to initiate prosecution may terminate an abusive relationship. Pursuing prosecution past that point may not be in the interests of the victim because it may increase the risks of retaliation while forcing her commitment to a process with little direct benefit.

As a result of these factors, although the goal of assisting and empowering victims may be understood in the abstract, it is generally lost. This is especially true when trying to attain larger societal goals of punishing an offender or deterring other potential batterers by arresting and hence making an example of an assailant (Lerman, 1992). In short, the general assumption that mandatory prosecution is in the victim's interests may not be accurate. In fact, at times there may be an irreconcilable dilemma: to assist and empower a victim may not involve the offender's subsequent case processing (Mills, 1997, 1998, 1999).

Several studies have shown that victim preferences were rarely solicited, and when they were known were rarely honored if they contravened policies designed to punish and deter offenders (Buzawa & Buzawa, 1996; Lempert, 1989). Because victim choices normally influence the criminal justice system to some degree (and the quest for restorative justice is pushing this to the forefront), policies that remove or limit victim input into decision making are unusual.

Although victims may not desire arrest, let alone subsequent conviction, we recognize that in reality, they may truly need law enforcement and the courts. In the past, family, church, or friends may have provided such support. In today's society, such assistance is much more problematic making victim reliance on criminal justice agencies more acute. The reality is that victims of domestic abuse often do not find or use social service agencies without support at critical moments. For this reason, criminal justice agencies, especially law enforcement, do not just enforce their own mandates by making an arrest, but also serve as critical gatekeepers to the provision of services of other essential actors.

Attitudes of Agency Personnel

The attitudes of the prosecution and members of the office staff often still tend to influence victims to drop the charges (Belknap et al., 2001; Dawson & Dinovitzer, 2001; Erez & Belknap, 1998). Unlike most nonrelationship cases, court personnel in domestic violence cases have generally made victims feel personally responsible for case outcome. This occurs because, in other contexts, although the victim is considered to have suffered direct harm, public order has also been affected. For this reason, prosecutors often encourage or, less frequently, even require by subpoena victims in nonrelationship cases such as stranger assaults to support resultant prosecutions. In domestic violence incidents, the violation to the public order is apparently not as evident to the prosecutorial staff, leading, at least in the past, to profound ambivalence about intervention. Not unexpectedly, they subtly or even at times overtly may encourage the victim to drop the charges.

Victim Costs in Prosecution

Victims often sustain high costs when prosecution is continued. Available empirical evidence suggests that many victims may be subject to subsequent retaliation or intimidation by offenders to force victims to drop charges. Although retaliation may be unlikely statistically, no one can provide certainty to a frightened victim, particularly if she is with a high-risk offender. Such victims' fears, as we have shown, often have demonstrated validity.

Retaliation has been documented as real in one key study. As reported by Klein (1994b), nearly half of the victims reported that their assailants had physically threatened them if they preceded further and attempted court procedures such as obtaining temporary restraining orders. Nor was this an idle threat. The batterers as a group were demonstrably dangerous. Victims were aware of prior criminal records for 55% of batterers (still others, of course, had hidden criminal records), 2% of the entire group of assailants had firearms of which the victim was aware, and two thirds of those with weapons had already threatened or assaulted the victim with these weapons.

Similarly, there was a fear of retaliation against children. Klein (1994b) noted that 25% directly threatened kidnapping the couple's children if legal action was pursued. Abusers also usually threatened to lie or exaggerate the victim's personal problems as a parental caregiver to child protective services. Thus, victims with their own substance abuse problems or who had perhaps neglected or abused their children (frequently as a consequence and not a precedent to their own abuse; Stark, 1992) were threatened with loss of their family. Although this study focused on incentives for victims to drop restraining orders, there is every reason to believe that such acts of intimidation would occur more frequently when a criminal prosecution was pending, because the stakes for the offender far exceed a court order. In many judicial systems, there has been an utter failure to give victims information about methods to protect themselves via temporary or permanent restraining orders—and how to get these orders enforced.

Although less dramatic, there is also the real possibility that indirect economic harm of continued prosecution may deter victims from prosecution. If the victim continues to cohabitate with the offender, she may fear direct economic loss should the offender lose his job. In other cases, a reduction in alimony or child support may be at risk. Actual out-of-pocket monetary losses often occur in the event of a conviction or if extensive court time is required (Bent-Goodley, 2001; Coker, 2000; Mills, 1999). Direct economic harm to the victim may result if she is required to take time from her own job or arrange for child care to support prosecution by making court appearances. In many cases, scheduling forces her to wait for hours to give a few minutes of testimony or, as often happens, her time is completely wasted when the case is continued to a later date.

The batterer often fans such fears of economic retaliation. Klein (1994b) reported that monetary threats were made by 42% of abusers in his study; 31% of the victims were unemployed, and 67% earned under $10,000, making threatened loss of financial support critical.

Changes in Victim Attitudes Over Time: Self-Doubts and the Complexity of Motivation

The fact is that in many cases, victims' attitude toward the crime and the offender alter over time. Memories of the crime and the perpetrated harm recede after an extended period. Those victims who experience cyclical battering may experience a prolonged "honeymoon," in which the offender seeks to make up with the victim due to atonement or fear of prosecution. Alternately, he might have ceased battering altogether. In time, continued prosecution of the criminal case may become the only event that reminds her (and the offender) of the battering incident and threaten to end the current harmonious period. Finally, the victim may have successfully left the batterer and negotiated acceptable financial support or terms of custody.

She may now justifiably fear that prosecution would simply anger the batterer, jeopardizing this often hard-won status.

Also, even if inappropriate, many victims tend, at least partially, to blame their own behavior for a violent incident. Self-doubt and guilt are even more significant than for other victims of violent crime and may uneasily coexist with the victim's desires for retribution, deterrence, and perhaps rehabilitation that led the victim to initially charge the offender. Feminists would, of course, observe that such a result is predictable given the socialization process reinforced by constant societal pressure. Regardless of reasons, victim self-doubts may result in prosecutors believing these "high dropout" cases are not worth extensive resources.

It is not surprising that the complexity of victim motives inevitably predicts high dropout rates. Ford and Burke (1987) listed five predominant motives for a victim's initiation of prosecution: (1) curiosity over how the system might help, (2) confirmation of her status as a victim (a sort of "coming out" as a battered woman), (3) a promised increase in her own legitimacy as a victim in subsequent police encounters, (4) a matter of principle (i.e., a crime has been committed and should be reported), and (5) revenge for the crime.

An effort to find out how the courts might help may appear to be an unusual motive for the decision to charge a crime. Until recent passage of victim right's laws, the legal system, commencing with the initial police intervention, provided little substantive information to victims. Given the known desire of the criminal justice bureaucracy to get rid of these undesirable cases, one might cynically observe that information on alternatives to prosecution are provided not with the intent to best handle the offender, but because the victim's demands have become a nuisance.

Similarly, Ford (1984, 1991) suggested that prosecution may be the only available alternative for many women to gain control in a relationship. The actual prosecution would then really be of only secondary importance to the control gained as a "power resource" through the threat of prosecution. Thus, the victim is primarily using the criminal justice system as a strategic tool rather than to achieve conviction. If researchers do not wish merely to become advocates of prosecution for its own sake, one must understand that these varied reasons reflect reality. Many domestic violence victims simply are not as deeply committed to continued prosecution as are other victims of criminal behavior.

Case Screening by Agency Personnel

Regardless of the reasons for the attrition rate among domestic violence victims, their failure to assist the prosecutorial process has served to reinforce frustration and cynicism among professionals. Prosecutors' offices typically lack sufficient personnel and simply lack the time, background, or inclination to understand why victims drop charges. They often express cynical thoughts such as, "no real harm must have occurred," "the victim was never serious about the charges," "the victim is a 'masochist' for continuing to live with the man," and "the victim had lied earlier to the police to obtain revenge on an unrelated dispute" or "to influence a pending divorce, custody, or child support proceeding" and was now "scared she would be caught in a lie." Even the more sympathetic personnel believed that the victim might be "trapped" and has now realized that "the criminal justice system can't help."

In the context of an overwhelming lack of prosecutorial resources, a high victim dropout rate reinforces prosecutorial decisions to exercise discretion by refusing to bring or later to dismiss charges. One result has been that both victims and offenders are faced with a prosecutorial office and judicial system that

appears to have little predictability. Cases that would be continued in another context or a different jurisdiction (even against the express wishes of the victim) are dropped, despite clear evidence that would sustain successful prosecution.

How and Why Prosecutors Treat Cases Differentially

The tendency of prosecution to use a number of "extra-legal" variables to differentially screen cases has often been noted (J. W. Ellis, 1984; Hirschel & Hutchinson, 2001; Schmidt & Steury, 1989; Stanko, 1982).

Measuring a Victim's Motivation

Perhaps of greatest significance are those prosecutors who believe they have the right to evaluate a victim's motivation and thereby assess her commitment to continued prosecution. This is considered a legitimate case discriminator independent of the inherent strength of the case. In a position that was otherwise favorable to increasing commitment to domestic violence cases, the National Association of District Attorneys stated in 1980 that, in deciding whether to prosecute, a district attorney should consider whether it is likely that a victim will cooperate, whether the victim agreed to live apart from the defendant, and, in general, to consider "the relationship of the parties" (National District Attorneys Association, 1980). This position was subsequently reversed.

Inherent in such a position is the assumption that a commitment to continue prosecution is a valid case discriminator. We believe this is profoundly incorrect as a basis for the exercise of prosecutorial discretion. If a primary concern is for injuries suffered by the victim and the prevention of future violence, bureaucratic goals of achieving high conviction rates should be subordinated. We hasten to add that the NADA position has been explicitly changed to now understand that the victim may be subject to pressures not to continue prosecution.

Despite this, the reality has been that concern for the victim's misfortune has not in the past been prosecutors' prime motivation. Instead, the critical factors have been whether the injury was of a type and quality that could not be ignored—for example, death or an overwhelmingly vicious and publicized attack—or if the victim stubbornly refused to quietly go away. The prosecutor's office was then forced to confront a complaint. If the charge was filed and abandoned, measurements of their capability to obtain high conviction rates were adversely affected. The possibility that the victim may have achieved her goals in the interim would, of course, be irrelevant in this context.

Frustration With a Victim's Continued Relationship With an Offender

As a result of many prosecutors' attitudes, one study found that the victim's continuing relationship with the offender was a key factor in decisions about whether to continue prosecution (Schmidt & Steury, 1989). Schmidt and Steury reported that charges were far more likely to be filed if the victim claimed to have no continuing sexual intimacy with the offender. Hirschel and Hutchison (2001) analyzed data from the Charlotte Replication Study and reported that previously married or cohabiting couples were more likely than those currently married or cohabiting to have their cases prosecuted. Although these studies contradicted other research by finding little effect of marital status per se, they found a significant negative correlation between prosecution and victim–offender cohabitation. This result could be attributed to organizational concerns over victim's commitment to prosecution or, more charitably, to a victim-oriented concern that

maintaining a prosecution in this context might prove to increase her danger.

The Role of Other Victim Factors in Prosecutorial Assessment

Prosecutorial Assessment of Offender Characteristics

An important factor in deciding to prosecute is whether the prosecutor perceived that the offender is truly recalcitrant or unlikely to recidivate. One study found that a history of prior abuse was strongly related with future charging decisions. Of perhaps greater surprise was that the prior record appeared to influence the prosecutor even more than the evidentiary strength of the case (Schmidt & Steury, 1989).

For many offenses, use of drugs or alcohol has been taken by officials to mitigate the intent and therefore the nature of a crime. In domestic violence cases, the reverse appears to be true in the context of offender sentencing (Schmidt & Steury, 1989). Although this may be a result of a generalized phenomenon of tougher law enforcement against substance abusers, it may also be due to the prosecutor's recognition that drug-induced violence is likely to reoccur at higher rates among addicts than nonaddicts.

Organizational Factors Within Prosecutor's Offices That Limit Effective Responses

Finally, organizational imperatives beyond the knowledge or control of most victims have, at least in the past, affected the decision to initiate or continue prosecution. Perhaps the most significant of these is the tendency of prosecutors to treat police-initiated arrests more seriously than a victim's complaint. This is understandable. Police and prosecutors need mutual support. In this context, prosecution legitimizes officer arrests, whereas the police give prosecutors the evidence that sustains high conviction rates.

If a police officer arrests a suspect and the prosecutor declines to pursue a charge, there is an implicit challenge to this compact. The police officer may be personally affronted or interpret this decision as questioning competency. Also, the attorney might view police-initiated charges as somehow having been screened for content. Whatever the reason, such charges are organizationally considered to be the more legitimate (Cole, 1984; Jacoby, 1980; Schmidt & Steury, 1989). In contrast, citizen-initiated complaints are treated as having no organizational sponsor and no designated bureaucrat having responsibility or accountability for any decisions. Ford, Reichard, Goldsmith, and Regoli (1996) noted, however, that this factor may not necessarily be as significant in the decision-making process as the increased commitment and cooperation in victim-initiated cases.

Another significant factor is the failure of the prosecutor's office to facilitate victim cooperation. For example, one recent study (conducted in Denver, Colorado; Boulder County, Colorado; and Lansing, Michigan) reported that 20% of victims who did not go to court on the scheduled date did not appear because they had not been informed of the court date (Belknap, Fleury, Melton, Sullivan, & Leisenring, 2001). This study also noted that women reported numerous other obstacles affecting the likelihood of their appearance in court, including child-care and transportation difficulties.

Imposing Procedural Barriers to Prosecution

Even if the prosecutor's office does not formally dismiss the charges, requiring the victim to take responsibility for dropping a case, a variety of procedural barriers have often been imposed, either formally or through a process of accretion, to prevent charges from being filed, or if filed, subsequently pursued. For example, Ford (1993) reported that in Marion County, Indiana, a major obstacle was to be overcome before domestic violence–related arrest warrants were issued on a victim's behalf. In nondomestic cases involving violent activity, an arrest warrant was issued within 1 to 2 days of the victim filing a complaint. This rapid response did, in fact, happen in domestic violence complaints when the victim was accompanied by a police officer, thereby showing the prosecutor that the officer had a personal attachment to the matter and demonstrating the officer's appraisal of the case's legitimacy. However, when the complaint was initiated solely by the victim, it took 2 weeks or longer to issue a warrant. Also, after this 2-week period, an arrest warrant often would not be issued at all. Instead, a summons to appear in court would be mailed to an offender. As a result, in only one third of the cases was any arrest made within 1 month after a victim initiated a complaint; in only 62% of cases was an arrest made after 6 months (Ford, 1983). Obviously, the prosecutor's office was not trying to process such complaints nor were the police eager to serve warrants.

Other procedural hurdles have been used to screen out undesirable or frivolous cases. In the Indianapolis study, a mandatory 3-day waiting period existed before the court would receive a domestic violence complaint. This forced a second victim-initiated action before any organizational evaluation of the merits of the case took place (Ford, 1983). This particular procedural hurdle is virtually unheard of outside of domestic violence complaint processing. The net effect was to force the victim to reaffirm what may have been a traumatic initial decision to prosecute before there was evidence that the prosecutor's office would help.

Not surprisingly, this served as an effective mechanism for discarding domestic violence complaints. In the Indianapolis study, Ford noted that 33% of married women filing domestic violence complaints had these placed on hold and 78% of them failed to return. This compared to corresponding figures of 60% and 52%, respectively, for those who had filed for divorce and 46% and 59% of those who actually divorced. In this case, the screening device ostensibly used for organizational reasons to eliminate frivolous domestic violence complaints effectively frustrated approximately two thirds of the small minority of women victims who had already called the police and then taken the further initiative of filing a criminal complaint.

THE IMPACT OF PROARREST PRACTICES: THE DILEMMA OF GROWING CASELOADS

As shown in earlier chapters, proarrest domestic assault policies now in place in many police departments have dramatically increased the number of domestic violence cases referred to prosecution in many jurisdictions.

Have Case Dismissals Simply Been Moved From the Police to the Prosecutor's Office?

In recent years, it is possible that the large increases in police arrests have effectively been offset by corresponding increases in dismissals resulting in approximately the same number of domestic violence cases ultimately reaching judicial attention. The effect of prosecutorial actions of this sort can be said to create a "funnel effect" in which domestic violence cases are channeled out of the criminal justice system by nullifying police charging behavior and, ultimately, undermining proarrest policies.

According to one study, the major effect of the institution of mandatory arrest policies

has been to "simply move discretion from the point of arrest to the point of prosecutorial screening" (Davis & Smith, 1995). This same study, conducted in Milwaukee, Wisconsin, after mandatory arrest policies for domestic violence were implemented, presents data supporting such concerns. These researchers reported case rejection rates of 80% at prosecutors' initial screening. They speculated that the underlying reason for this high rejection rate was to avoid the enormous burden a high number of domestic violence cases would bring to bear on existing resources. Prosecutors, in effect, simply developed adaptive responses to proarrest laws that effectively screened out large numbers of cases. Although such practices have long been suspected, empirical evidence of their existence has only been recently developed (Davis & Smith, 1995).

Case screening by prosecutors is often accomplished through the use of relatively obscure and typically unpublished collateral procedures. For example, in the Davis and Smith (1995) study, the Milwaukee Prosecutor's Office had a policy in which misdemeanor domestic violence offenders were only charged when the victim came to a charging conference the day after arrest. This resulted in only 20% of cases being prosecuted and the remaining 80% of cases screened out. In 1995, when the Milwaukee prosecutor changed this policy to no longer require victims to attend charging conferences, the rate of accepting cases tripled overnight from 20% to 60% of cases. The authors of this report strongly suggested that the analysis of criminal justice impact on the handling of domestic violence should change focus: "Whether this same displacement of discretion from the decision to arrest to the decision to prosecute has occurred elsewhere as a result of mandatory arrest laws is unknown, but it is certainly an important subject for investigation" (Davis & Smith, 1995, p. 546).

What happened when the policy in Milwaukee changed? Did this singular event increase everyone's satisfaction? Unfortunately no. This research also found that after the new charging policies were implemented, case backlog increased greatly; time to disposition doubled, convictions declined, pretrial crime increased, and victim satisfaction with case outcomes and the prosecutor's handling of the case decreased (Davis, Smith, & Nickles, 1998). Hence, the failure to add sufficient resources in effect unintentionally sabotaged the prosecution's efforts.

The degree to which prosecutors face this dilemma is uncertain. Certainly, prosecutor's offices are now aware of the heavy new emphasis on aggressive handling of domestic violence. Often, "no drop" policies (described in the next chapter) which mandate prosecution are instituted, typically with great fanfare. The actual effect is less clear. Rebovich (1996) reported that although two thirds of the prosecutor's offices now had official "no drop" policies regarding the handling of domestic violence cases (generally defined as "flexible" no-drop policies, described in the next chapter), fewer than 20% of these offices admitted that their decision-making policies and plea-bargaining negotiations had actually been affected.

Summary: Why Hasn't the System Worked for Domestic Violence Victims?

It is apparent that, at least in the past, a complex interaction evolved between the motives and actions of the domestic violence victim and prosecutor's office. Each profoundly misunderstood the other's individual and organizational motives and needs. Victims of most crimes assume that once criminal justice processing is commenced, the procedure is straightforward. Few realize at the outset the inherent complexities created by the need for their continued involvement or the uncertainty caused by the requirements of protecting the offender's constitutional rights. Unfulfilled expectations, normal to most victims of criminal conduct, are coupled with the domestic violence victim's often ambiguous or conflicting motives for prosecution and the apathy and even hostility of a bureaucracy nominally dedicated to protecting her interests. Under such circumstances, it would be unrealistic to assume anything other than high rates of victim attrition.

Similarly, the prosecutor and his or her staff often cannot understand why victims refuse to leave abusive partners or fail to rigorously assist prosecution of their abusers. This misunderstanding in turn changes their behavior in a manner that implicitly reinforces these misperceptions—that is, even more women drop charges or fail to appear because of the indifference or cynicism of prosecutors and judges or the erection of Byzantine barriers that "test" her commitment to prosecute. Although, for the reasons we described earlier, some victim-initiated drops may be unrelated to prosecutorial or court behavior, the experiences of the victim with agency personnel do, in fact, influence the rates of the victims' "voluntary" decisions to exit the criminal justice system (Chaudhuri & Daly, 1992; Ford, 1992).

Subsequent victim actions to "voluntarily" drop a case reinforce negative staff attitudes, affecting the whole criminal justice system by greatly increasing the deleterious effect of the "prosecutorial funnel" noted earlier. Furthermore, low rates of prosecution and conviction reinforce and justify often persistent reluctance of police officers to become involved in "no win, no outcome" domestic violence cases. Thus, two negative feedback loops are strengthened by the initial victim–prosecutor misperceptions.

CHAPTER **12**

The Changing Prosecutorial Response

VICTIM SUPPORT AND VICTIM ADVOCACY PROGRAMS WITHIN PROSECUTOR OFFICES

Many prosecutors, especially in larger jurisdictions, have added victim advocates to their staff or as staff to the court system. In addition to victim advocates who are formally affiliated with prosecutor offices, many jurisdictions that have a comprehensive response to domestic violence provide victim advocacy via a protocol that assigns such services to affiliated agencies such as family shelter service agencies, general social welfare programs, or other noncriminal justice agencies. Although we recognize that such programs may have their own agenda separate from the prosecutor's office, in this text we treat their contribution in the same light as if the advocates are formally retained by the prosecutor's office. Another caveat is that although there are literally hundreds of advocacy programs, there is a lack of agreement on what advocacy actually is (Edleson, 1993). The tension that we explore is between advocacy that provides information to the victim within a supportive relationship (Cahn 1992; Lyon & Goth Mace, 1991) and advocacy (as described later in this chapter) that promotes

victim participation and commitment to the criminal justice process (Hart, 1993). Often, those advocacy agencies housed within the prosecutor's office are perceived as acting in the interests of ensuring efficient case processing, whereas those agencies that act autonomously are more likely to prioritize victim needs.

Typically, victim advocates are not attorneys, but highly trained and motivated professionals. The growing use of advocates was supported by the recommendations issued in 1992 by the National Council of Juvenile and Family Court Judges. These recommendations included providing victim assistance in initiation and management of cases and a commitment to pursue prosecution in all instances in which a criminal case could be proven, including, when necessary, proceeding without the active involvement of the victim.

The primary purpose of victim advocates is to assist the victim in coping with the unfamiliar and often threatening process of the criminal justice system. To understand the importance of this, we must realize that being battered often inflicts significant concurrent psychological abuse (Gondolf, 1998; Tolman, 1992). In turn, this pattern of abuse has the residual effect of encouraging self-doubt among survivors (Barnett, Martinez, & Keyson, 1996). As a result, levels of posttraumatic stress disorder (PTSD) are frequently severe (Dutton-Douglas, 1992). As noted in the previous chapter, it is not uncommon for survivors to be disengaged, have difficulty with concentration, and to display a basic inability to make decisions (or when they are able to make a decision to suffer extreme sense of self-doubt; Dutton, 1992).

The suffering that many victims incur is often reinforced by lack of knowledge of the criminal justice system, making it difficult for them to know how to access the police, the prosecutor, and the courts (Fischer & Rose, 1995; Muscat & Iwamoto, 1993; Yegidis & Renzy, 1994; Weisz, 1999). In one study, Jaffe, Hastings, Reitzel, and Austin (1993) reported that the most common suggestion of survivors for improvements to the criminal justice system was to obtain more information on available court proceedings and community services (compare L. V. Davis and Srinivasan, 1995, which reported that one of the most important factors in having women sever abusive relationships was giving them knowledge of the available resources to help them do so.

In an excellent article summarizing legal advocacy for domestic violence survivors, Weisz (1999) reviewed how female victims used advocacy services to fill in basic gaps in knowledge of the operations of the police and the courts and to obtain economic and legal assistance and other services.

A concerted program using victim advocates also has the advantage of sensitizing prosecutors to the problems of prosecuting domestic assaults. The concept of a knowledgeable victim advocate may provide critically needed support to a woman who, with relatively few resources, has to confront an indifferent bureaucracy. Finally, such advocates are expected to explain to the victim the availability of shelters, prior restraints, and the services of other social welfare agencies. Lack of knowledge of such services undoubtedly led to many victim-initiated dismissals in the past.

The Impact of Victim Advocates

A series of articles have appeared describing how advocacy actually helps women learn about legal options in the criminal justice system (Hart, 1993) and how advocates retain a better understanding of battering issues and the realities of the context of battered women as well as a better ability to communicate with victims (Finn, 1991). The ultimate result is that battered women who receive advocacy services, according to one source, are more likely than others to continue processing their case through to conviction (Weisz, 1999).

Victim advocates can graphically demonstrate the system's sensitivity to a victim's needs and provide needed coordination of services both within and apart from the actual prosecution of offenders.[1] In addition, victim advocates can assist victims in gaining a better understanding of the criminal justice process and its capabilities in providing assistance.

There has been empirical evidence to support that such approaches will, at a minimum, increase victim satisfaction. Whetstone (2001), reporting on the impact of a specialized domestic violence unit (which included a victim advocate), found that the majority of victims were "overwhelmingly positive about their experience with the unit" (p. 390). Victims described being satisfied with services received, their understanding of the process, and the belief that their safety was improved by their experiences with the police and victim advocates. Jolin and Moose (1997) reported victim satisfaction and increased feelings of empowerment even if reoffending remained unaffected.

It is even possible that a critical component of widespread victim satisfaction with the criminal justice system may be the support of an effective victim advocate. Although victim advocates can provide victim assistance and support throughout the process, they also provide victims with more realistic expectations of the likely outcomes and information about how to maximize safety and well-being. This is a possible explanation for why some studies report satisfaction with police intervention, regardless of its impact on reoffending (Jolin & Moose, 1997), whereas others only report satisfaction if there is a subsequent impact on their safety (Whetstone, 2001). In general, women who are assisted by victim advocates may believe that they are more likely to achieve their goals than they would be if services had not been provided (Sullivan et al., 1992).

In the Quincy District Court of Massachusetts (QDC) study, Buzawa et al. (1999) reported that a well-developed victim advocacy program engendered high levels of victim satisfaction. Eighty-one percent of recipients of such services were either very satisfied or quite satisfied with the services; 77% said they would use such services again if confronted with a similar problem. Similar findings were found in Orange District Court (Massachusetts). More than 77% of the victim advocates reported being "very" or "somewhat" satisfied with the victim advocates Hotaling & Buzawa, 2001.

Potential Limitations of Victim Advocates

Despite the potential of these programs, they may produce undesirable effects for particular victims. Currently, in a climate of budget austerity for public agencies, virtually every institution must compete with each other for available funds to justify its actions with some "empirical" measures of success.

If a victim advocate program uses simplistic evaluation criteria (as we have at times seen), it may merely measure success of a program through lowered levels of case attrition as opposed to more victim-centered measurements. We are concerned that the primary goal—cessation of battering and victim satisfaction with the criminal justice process—can easily be subverted to serve an organizational goal, such as increasing the rate of convictions regardless of victim needs or desires.

For this reason, prosecution-based programs have the potential to be counterproductive when agencies try to commit victims to the prosecution process and thereafter define success by their own vested interests (Ford & Burke, 1987). This is not an entirely theoretical concern. Prosecutorial organizations, faced with high caseloads and increasing backlogs, may find their interests best served by having fewer total cases but with a higher percentage of convictions. This, of course, directly conflicts with the desires of victims to have easy access to a judicial system staffed with helpful, but not domineering personnel.

This role conflict may perpetuate misunderstanding between victim advocates and victims, reflected in complaints we have heard from many committed personnel, such as, "Look what we've tried to do without any success or gratitude," which are met with responses such as, "They don't understand me and my family and are trying to run my life." Ultimately, a system that strictly measures success by the reduction of case attrition may actually diminish victims' access to justice by deterring them from pursuing otherwise available alternatives. Further research should be conducted to determine if this concern is theoretical or real.

It is possible that victim advocacy services when provided outside a prosecutor's office (or a court) may limit such a negative interaction. At its best, as Hart (1993) noted, the victim advocacy is supportive, helping the woman learn about her legal options. If the legal advocates are not necessarily bound by organizational imperatives to achieve high levels of conviction, it is certainly possible that advocacy may be more tailored to the needs of the particular victim, which may or may not involve prosecution through conviction. Of course, if such victim services are privately funded, it may be the case that there is less control over the quality of services. Some may be exceptional in terms of their commitment to victims and their knowledge of the system. Others, especially if they are part-time volunteers, may simply not have the level of training or the detailed knowledge of how the prosecutor's office and the courts work to best assist victims.

NO-DROP POLICIES

Description of No-Drop Policies

Advocates for domestic violence victims have long pointed out that traditional prosecution policies dependant on victim actions have been ineffective. Even in the most aggressive courts where victims of domestic assault are less likely to prefer prosecutorial involvement with their cases, the importance of this can be shown. In one case, researchers found that domestic assault victims were more than 9 times more likely than non-domestic assault victims to report that they wanted the prosecutor to drop their cases (Hotaling & Buzawa, 2001).

Concern over excessive case attrition has led many jurisdictions to limit the freedom of both victims and prosecutors to drop the continued prosecution of cases. Such practices start with strict limitations on prosecutorial discretion to drop charges except for a demonstrated and documented failure to find evidence of commission of a crime. Policies implicitly requiring prosecutors to follow a victim's desires to prosecute have been

adopted in many jurisdictions. A controversial addition to such policies has been to impose restrictions on victims that effectively prevent them from freely dropping charges—that is, a "no-drop policy" (Lerman, 1981). At its most coercive, this policy may compel a victim to serve as a witness. When carried to its logical conclusion, she may be subpoenaed, and if recalcitrant, held for contempt of court. Some courts sporadically do indeed issue contempt of court citations to victims (Pleck, 1987).

It is important to recognize that no-drop policies vary considerably in different jurisdictions. So-called hard no-drop policies never follow victim preferences to drop charges unless certain criteria are met; soft no-drop policies permit victims to drop charges under certain limited circumstances, such as if the victim has left the batterer. In fact, a recent study of no-drop policies in four jurisdictions (San Diego, California, the first jurisdiction with such policies; Omaha, Nebraska; Everett, Washington; and Klamath Falls, Oregon) suggested that "no drop" really did not mean "no drop" per se. Instead, it was more of a philosophy rather than a strict policy—at least in these sites—with none of the jurisdictions prosecuting every case filed. What did they do to put teeth in the policy? The jurisdictions each required a coordinated intake process to determine which cases should be screened out before the imposition of a "no-drop" policy; provided for coordination with the judges, who would then relax the rules of evidence; and, perhaps equally important, made available additional resources to make the policy feasible (B. E. Smith, Davis, Nickles, & Davies, 2001).

Extent of No-Drop Policies

Officially at least, no-drop policies have been widely instituted in large jurisdictions. Rebovich (1996) noted that fully 66% of a sample of local prosecutors in jurisdictions with populations of over 250,000 had no-drop policies, with 83% stating it made no difference whether the police or victim initiated the complaint. Of these, however, 90% reported "some flexibility" in the application of these policies.

The widespread nature of such official policies was partially due to federally funded demonstration programs in Cleveland, Los Angeles, Miami, Santa Barbara, Seattle, and Westchester County, New York (Lerman, 1981).

Rationale for a No-Drop Policy

The theoretical underpinnings of this approach derive from the belief that unless abusers are adequately prosecuted, their violence usually will continue, causing further physical and emotional damage to victims, their children, or even other victims (Cahn & Lerman, 1991; Waits, 1985, Wills, 1997).

Such policies also implicitly rely on the concept that domestic violence is a crime against the public order of the state, not just the individual victim whose interests could be "purely" protected by civil action, by protective order, or a victim's decision of whether to initiate prosecution of a crime. At its root, the state interest is said to center on the theory that even if victims successfully terminate being battered, there remains a state interest in aggressive enforcement to deter this.

No-drop polices are said to encourage a higher level of specific and general deterrence as the perceptions and reality of a conviction after a domestic violence arrest is increased—a fact that will rapidly become known to current and potential batterers. Many prosecutors believe that the goal of prosecution supercedes the victim's interests. As one prosecutor noted,

> The prosecutor's client is the State, not the victim. Accordingly, prosecutorial agencies that have opted for aggressive prosecution have concluded that their client's interest in protecting the safety and well-being of all its citizens overrides the individual victim's desire to dictate whether and when criminal charges are filed.
>
> Aggressive prosecution is the appropriate response to domestic violence cases for several reasons. First, domestic violence affects more than just the individual victim; it is a public safety issue that affects all of society. Second, prosecutors cannot rely upon domestic violence victims to appropriately vindicate the State's interests in holding batterers responsible for the crime they commit because victims often decline to press charges. (Wills, 1997, pp. 173–174)

In addition to state-oriented goals, a domestic violence victim is also expected to benefit from such polices. The implicit rational advantage of a no-drop policy is that these batterers will be identified and then "treated" or sanctioned by the criminal justice system. They will be incarcerated if deemed appropriate and, at the least, placed into rehabilitation programs, thereby reducing the likelihood of future battering incidents, letting future potential victims know that they are consorting with a batterer, and increasing the likelihood for heavier sentencing in the event that a second prosecution occurs. Although we may not agree with the policy they favor, supporters of such no-drop polices may have a solid understanding of the realities of batterer behavior and how they can pervert the normal operation of the criminal justice system.

> Batterers are "master manipulators." They will do anything to convince their victims to get the prosecution to drop the charges. They call from jail threatening retaliation. They cajole their victim with promises of reform. They remind her that they may lose their jobs and, hence, the family income. They send love letters, pledging future bliss and happiness. They have their family members turn off the victim's electricity and threaten to kick the victim and her children out into the street. They pay for the victim to leave town so that she will not be subpoenaed. . . . They prey on the victim's personal weaknesses, especially drug and alcohol

abuse, physical and mental disabilities, and her love for their children. They negotiate financial and property incentives that cause acute memories of terror and pain to fade dramatically. Prosecutors watch with practiced patience as these vulnerable victims succumb to their batterers' intimidation and manipulation. Then, "no drop" prosecutors try to hold the batterers responsible regardless of the victims' lack of cooperation by using creative legal maneuvering.

Supporters of "no drop" domestic violence policies realize that empowering victims by giving them the discretion to prosecute, or even to threaten to prosecute, in actuality only empowers batterers to further manipulate and endanger their victims' lives, the children's lives, and the safety and well-being of the entire community. By proceeding with the prosecution with or without victim cooperation, the prosecutor minimizes the victim's value to the batterers as an ally to defeat criminal prosecution. A "no drop" policy means prosecutors will not allow batterers to control the system of justice through their victims. (Wills, 1997, pp. 179–180)

Although the interests of the state may appear somewhat esoteric compared with the concrete needs of the victim, there are other clear victims of violence, such as children, whose interests may not be able to be adequately protected by the victim without forced prosecution of an abuser. Again, as stated by Wills:

> Most notably, children are secondary victims of violence in the home. The link between domestic violence and child abuse, both emotional and physical, cannot be ignored. Each year, between three and ten million children are forced to witness the emotional devastation of one parent abusing or killing the other. Many are injured in the "crossfire" while trying to protect the assaulted parent, or are used as pawns or shields and are harmed by blows intended for someone else. Some are born with birth defects because their mothers were battered during pregnancy. Children of domestic violence are silent victims who suffer without the options available to adults. Thus, aggressive prosecution furthers the State's goal of protecting not only the victim, but

also the children in homes where domestic violence occurs. (Wills, 1997, pp. 175)

Limiting discretion also alleviates the problems of victims with uncooperative agencies relying on often-unsympathetic court personnel by forcing these officials to justify dismissals only by insufficiency of available evidence.

Finally, although obviously rarely stated as a justification for a no-drop policy from an organizational perspective, such policies are "productive." At an organizational, more than at a societal, level no-drop policies limit unproductive dropped cases, thereby increasing clearance rates through convictions.

Evidence That "No-Drop" Policies Are Effective

There is some evidence that the institution of "no-drop" policies can provide marked improvement, at least from past practices where domestic violence cases were systematically screened out of the system. In San Diego under the older policy, it was reported that abusers were not deterred by the criminal justice system as they grew to associate the system with lack of enforcement.

> In San Diego, for example, officials found that under the old policy, when abusers learned that a case would be dismissed if the victim refused to cooperate, levels of violence increased. In 1985, the city implemented a no-drop policy. Domestic homicides fell from 30 in 1985 to 20 in 1990, to 7 in 1994. No drop polices also appear to lower recidivism and strengthen the message that intimate abuse will not be tolerated. (D. Epstein, 1999, p. 15)

Similarly, Deborah Epstein, director of the Domestic Violence Clinic at the Georgetown University Law Center and co-director of the Washington, D.C., Superior Court's Intake Center, noted a similar type of improvement in Washington, DC. She stated that in 1989, the prosecutor's office prosecuted fewer than 40 misdemeanor cases out of 19,000 emergency calls reporting family abuse. By1995, the rates had not changed markedly. The charging rate for prosecutors was only approximately 15% of those arrested, and few of those cases ever proceeded to a plea or trial. She attributed the low numbers of successful prosecutions to "special" policies of applicability only to domestic violence. Chief among those was a policy by which charges would be dropped at the victim's request at any time with no questions asked.

In 1996, Washington, D.C., instituted a "no-drop" policy with a domestic violence unit. That unit filed approximately 6,000 misdemeanor cases in the first year and 8,000 the following year. Even more interesting is the case disposition. Fully two thirds of those arrested faced prosecution. According to Epstein (1999), this is exactly the same rate as for stranger violence. In addition, the rates of convictions in domestic cases—69%—closely approximated those for other misdemeanor, nonjury trials. Clearly, policy in this court with these committed prosecutors resulted in an overwhelming change from an ineffective regime.

Drawbacks of "No-Drop" Policies

We believe no-drop policies constitute the functional equivalent of police mandatory arrest policies. Although a policy of limited victim and prosecutor discretion certainly has some merit in the context of the pressures placed on domestic violence victims to dismiss cases, we believe they often are operationally impractical. This poses several relevant policy questions. Is the state interest actually served by such policies? Second, what is the impact on the victim? Is it best in actual practice for societal interests to triumph over victim interests?

State Interests

The state interests in "no-drop" polices are not nearly as clear as advocates would believe. For example, there is a need to address the reality of limited available prosecutorial resources. We believe it safe to assume that in most cases resources will not increase merely because a new policy mandating prosecution of one specific class of crimes is adopted. Therefore, any increase in time demand from this type of crime must be offset by a diminished capacity of the organization to perform other tasks related either to domestic violence or other issues.

Limiting prosecutorial discretion may be justifiable in domestic violence cases given past tendencies of many prosecutorial bureaucracies to downplay the importance of domestic violence. It is difficult to argue persuasively, however, that a district attorney should not have the resources to prosecute, and a court should subsequently be unable to try, other contested criminal cases (perhaps even felonies), merely because prosecutors are mandated to try all misdemeanor domestic violence cases, even if a victim does not want the case to be prosecuted. We believe that the advocates of no-drop policies should expressly explain why the displacement of limited resources attendant to such a policy is justified and explicitly state what tasks now being performed by prosecutors with limited ability to increase resources should be foregone to implement a true no-drop policy. If this is not done, then difficult choices are simply dismissed and the true impact of policy is not fairly debated.

Alternatively, it may be the case that no-drop policies become discretionary policies in reality. Several prosecutors have noted that even those offices widely publicized as being "no drop" develop procedures that, in effect, screen cases. For example, an analysis of the practices of the San Diego City

Attorney's Office noted that it refused to prosecute one third of all domestic violence cases; essentially, they did not prosecute if there was a lack of independent corroborating evidence when the victim declined to cooperate.

It is easy to see why even the most committed office would develop such screening techniques. As one prosecutor explained, if the victim recants, the proper prosecution for domestic abuse cases is similar to a homicide in that independent corroborating evidence has to be used in place of the victim's testimony (Hartman, 1999).

> However, except for the relatively rare occurrence of a federal grant, no additional resources are typically received. The reality is that misdemeanor cases are typically tried by the most overworked and least experienced district attorneys. If they must try cases of such complexity without additional resources, the burden may be overwhelming.
>
> Taking iffy misdemeanors to trial in my jurisdiction is seen as wasteful, not unethical. As along as I do my trial preparation on the weekends at home, so far, I am allowed my idiosyncrasy. However, if I want the help of another prosecutor for misdemeanors, I am shown the door not only by my own prosecutorial kinds, but also by legislative bodies that persist in passing statutes which amount to unfounded mandates (making the prosecution of most domestic crimes more time-consuming and intricate). . . . We've gotten tough enough already; the only real solution . . . is putting our money where our mandates are. So long as the domestic violence equivalent of MADD [Mothers Against Drunk Driving] encourages their elected representatives to add more "politically correct" but fiscally ignored burdens on those of us who try to prosecute these cases, we're never going to get there. (Hartman, 1999, p. 74)

To some extent, the expressed societal interest is only achieved if high conviction rates result. Indeed, some jurisdictions, such as the County of Los Angeles, have very high conviction rates (Wills, 1997); however, the actual impact on conviction rates of no-drop policies in other jurisdictions is unclear. Some recent research reports that when victims do not support prosecution or are unconvincing witnesses, the result is far lower conviction rates despite the increase in committed resources (R. C. Davis et al., 1998). This is not a hypothetical concern. Consider the following:

> the problem is that the policies backfire. When we force arrest and prosecution on battered women, they often recant and lie. One prosecutor in Los Angeles, who will remain anonymous, estimated that most battered women are reluctant witnesses who are willing to perjure themselves when they are put on the stand against their will. (Wills, 1997, p. 190)

The extent of this problem is difficult to overstate. Despite being an advocate for mandatory prosecution, Wills, head deputy of the Family Violence Unit of the Los Angeles County District Attorney's Office noted that victims in Los Angeles County recanted in more than 50% of cases (Wills, 1997). Such findings are not unusual. A study using Canadian data found that, according to prosecutors, almost 60% of all decisions not to prosecute were due to victim's noncooperation, including refusal to testify, recanting, or retracting testimony or failing to appear in court (Dawson & Dinovitzer, 2001; Ursel, 1995). As such, even an advocate for mandatory prosecution had to recognize obvious practical problems with implementation of such a policy, and Wills acknowledged the real conflict between prosecutors and victims:

> Prosecutors and the courts have taken a long time to accept that a domestic violence victim's "refusal to press charges" is the norm in domestic violence prosecutions. Indeed, prosecutors traditionally are reluctant to charge batterers because victims frequently change their minds and later drop the charges. Faced with having to testify in court, domestic violence victims, especially battered women, routinely recant, minimize the abuse, or fail to appear. (Wills, 1997, p. 177)

From this it is evident why, for reasons of practicality, such a policy is almost never forced for other misdemeanor offenses.

Society's interest in a no-drop policy implicitly depends on no reaction by victims to the behavior of the criminal justice system. This is paradoxical in that to have any real long-term impact on rates of abuse, domestic violence advocates tacitly, or even at times explicitly, assume that batterers will desist from battering as a reaction to the threat of future prosecution. When the majority of victims are forced into prosecuting cases against their will, however, advocates do no appear to expect an adverse victim reaction. We believe this to be highly simplistic and somewhat patronizing. It is highly likely that a no-drop policy may deter victims from reporting crimes. Victims often are faced with the realization that once a case enters the court process, they lose control to what seems to them an impersonal and overbearing bureaucracy.

After all, disempowering victims is the antithesis of the goal of most abused women and advocates. Those supporting this type of control are probably unaware that they may often be further reinforcing the belief that the "helpless" or "fickle" victim is the primary reason for the system's lack of responsiveness, rather than the system's inability to flexibly address individual victim needs.

Data in the QDC study gave support for this concern, reporting that a latent outcome of aggressive policies dismissing victim preferences appeared to discourage the future utilization of the system by those victims who feared for their safety. Victim interviews found that these women were more than 2.5 times less likely than other victims to report revictimization in a 1-year period following the initial study incident Buzawa et al., 1999).

Implicit in many of the arguments raised in favor of "no-drop" policies, such as victim intimidation by batterers, batterers as master manipulators, and prosecutors as "guardians" of the rights of victims, is that the victims are, as a class, incapable of assessing their peril. This lacks empirical support. In fact, the QDC study found that the victims' preferences and perceptions of dangerousness were generally very good predictors of subsequent revictimization. Women who did not experience revictimization within a 12-month period were more than twice as likely as those who were revictimized to have preferred no criminal justice involvement. A greater number of women who felt that going to court would decrease their safety were accurate in their assessment. Women who were "forced" to prosecute and who felt that going to court reduced their ability to bargain with the offender were also more likely to be revictimized (Buzawa et al., 1999).

Impact on Victims

Although there may be limited positive impact of such policies on state interests, the effects on victims can be quite dramatic. As discussed in Chapter 11, not all prosecutors have an understanding of the myriad factors that may motivate a victim seeking to discontinue case processing. Even the basic tenet that prosecution of domestic violence offenders typically helps victims has been criticized. A recently published National Institute of Justice study of homicide data in 48 states reported that increased prosecution rates for domestic assault (even when controlling for a number of variables) were associated with increased levels of homicides among White married couples, Black unmarried intimates, and White unmarried women—hardly the positive result anticipated (Dugan et al., 2001). A no-drop policy that forces prosecution certainly restricts victim autonomy. This is not an idle concern. Even an advocate of "no-drop" policies such as Professor Epstein observed the following:

> as police and prosecutors escalate their response to domestic violence cases, survivors increasingly confront a criminal justice system that can perpetuate the kinds of power and control dynamics that exist in

the battering relationship itself. In many cases, prosecutors take complete control over the case, functioning as the sole decision maker and ignoring the victim's voice. If a victim changes her mind mid-way through the litigation and seeks to drop charges so that the father of her children can continue to work and provide financial support, a prosecutor may refuse to do so, on the ground that this would not serve the interests of the state in punishing violations of the social contract. Such re-victimization can thwart the survivor's efforts to regain control over her life and move past the abusive experience.

Thus, where the bulk of control was ceded to the perpetrator under the old automatic drop system, it is now ceded to the prosecutor. Although battered women have a far greater influence over the criminal justice process today than ever before, the system's responsiveness to their individual needs remains limited. (D. Epstein, 1999, pp. 16–17)

The extent of conflicts between victims and prosecutors driven to prosecute with victim support should not be underestimated. On one hand, at least one researcher has reported that even those women who did not want intervention beyond arrest, regarded the prosecution of the offender as "beneficial" (B. E. Smith et al., 2001). Prosecutors certainly are aware of the reality of this problem, however; conflicts appear quite frequently when no-drop policies are adopted.

Rebovich (1996) confirmed Will's earlier cited observation that more than 50% of victims refused to testify. He reported that many of the larger prosecutor's offices had considerable problems with uncooperative victims. For example, 33% of the prosecutors who responded claimed that more than 55% of their cases involved uncooperative witnesses; 16% claimed the number to be between 41% and 55%; and 27% estimated that it was between 26% and 40%. Only 27% reported a 0% to 25% lack of cooperation (Rebovich, 1996).

Not surprisingly, to accomplish their own organizational goals, Rebovich (1996) reported that prosecutors became coercive with victims, and fully 92% of such officials used their subpoena power to require victim testimony. Surprisingly, the least coercive methods to overcome a lack of victim cooperation—use of victim advocate testimony and videotapes of initial victim interviews—were used the least (10% and 6%, respectively), and relatively few used expert witnesses who could testify on such issues as why victims often refuse to cooperate (Rebovich, 1996).

No-drop policies that are coupled with a strong victim advocacy program may also have an additional adverse impact. Victim advocates housed within the prosecutor's office may not be perceived as true "victim" advocates. There is the potential for a clear conflict of interest between the victim, who might not be interested in pursuing a charge, and the victim advocate, whose task as defined by the prosecutor's office is to ensure victim cooperation. Unfortunately, this may cause the victim to lose trust and be less communicative with the advocate, her nominal ally. She may even find her fears of adverse consequences minimized as her case is "pushed" through the system.

The promotion of simplistic views of victim needs ignores the complex nature of a victim's decision to desist prosecution. Many advocates for battered women are now better understanding that there are, in fact, unanticipated consequences to such policies. Linda Mills, an early advocate for victim empowerment, may have best stated this concern:

A small but growing number of feminists are beginning to worry that universally applied strategies, such as mandatory prosecution, cannot take into account the reasons women stay in abusive relationships or the reasons for their denial. These feminists fear that the State's indifference to this contingent of battered women is harmful, even violent. . . . By violent, I refer to the institutional violence inflicted through the competitive dynamic that dominates the relationships between the State, the survivor, and the batterer. The State, in its obsession to punish the batterer, often uses the battered women as a pawn for winning the competition. This destructive dynamic is abusive in itself to the woman. (Mills, 1997, p. 188)

Not surprisingly, Mills persuasively argued for what she described as "tailored service" for victims rather than mandatory policies that fixate on offender conviction (Mills, 1998).

As noted in an earlier chapter, a victim may drop charges after she has been successful in achieving her primary goal of exercising increased power in a continuing relationship with the offender, at least to the extent of deterring future physical abuse. The failure to allow her to use this power resource may in fact erode the utility of a prosecution. One study of towns in western Massachusetts found that of those victims not wanting the case to go forward, 27% reported they had already obtained what they wanted from the offender or worked things out, and an additional 23% had already ended the relationship with the offender and felt no further need to prosecute (Hotaling & Buzawa, 2001).

It has been noted that a victim may be safest if she retains the power to drop charges at her discretion. This gives her the ability to manipulate the system to work toward her ends with the threat of continued prosecution as a "victim power resource" (Ford & Regoli, 1993; Hotaling & Buzawa, 2001).

The reality of the process of prosecution is that most victims wait 6 to 9 months from the time of complaint to the time of trial. During this period, significant changes frequently occur. Many victims, often with the support of family, friends, acquaintances, service agencies, or formal and informal mediators, are able to successfully negotiate factors such as separation, child custody, and

visitation rights. They legitimately may fear that prosecution would jeopardize such arrangements. As the trial date approaches, many batterers begin to harass the victim, create obstacles with visitation, and jeopardize the negotiated arrangements she has already achieved.

Under these circumstances, it is not always in a victim's interest to continue prosecution. In this regard, our perspective directly challenges the assumption of other writers (Cahn & Lerman, 1991; Waits, 1985), who have maintained that prosecution must be completed to achieve long-term cessation of violence. Perhaps the dilemma may be resolved by understanding that many women may be safer if they can freely drop actions but ultimately may be less safe if they do. The implication of this insight may be that victims need to be treated as full partners in the prosecution of the case. This necessitates that the victim be given full disclosure of the long-term trends of familial violence, including the tendency to escalate attacks, the potential of effective prosecution to end such a cycle, and a realistic assessment of the costs and delays that she will likely incur if there is a full prosecution of a case.

The negative effects of enforced prosecution may disproportionately impact racial and ethnic minority victims—those who might most need the assistance of the criminal justice system. It has become increasingly clear that the impact of prosecutorial and judicial intervention may be affected by race, socioeconomic status, ethnicity, and cultural norms (Dobash & Dobash, 2000; Thiselthwaite, Woolredge, & Gibbs, 1998).

For example, immigrants, especially those whose husbands are in the country illegally, may strongly wish to avoid prosecution for fear that it may lead to job loss or even deportation of the family's source of financial support. This is not uncommon. Recent "reforms" in U.S. immigration statutes mandate that even lawfully registered permanent resident immigrants convicted of virtually any major crimes, including domestic violence and stalking, may be deported. Conviction for a domestic assault may be totally devastating in situations in which a woman needs the batterer's financial assistance. Similarly, many immigrant communities may be somewhat insular, and women held responsible for deportation of a fellow immigrant may find themselves and their families subjected to severe ostracism, or perhaps even violent retaliation, within their communities (D. Epstein, 1999).

Similarly, Bui and Morash (1999) reported that Vietnamese immigrant women who were victims of batterers feared that new laws would lead to the deportation of their husbands upon arrest and conviction of a domestic violence offense. This has resulted in decreased levels of reporting abuse—directly contrary to the goals of most domestic violence advocates.

Many additional minority group members, even if native born, belong to a class that have had a long, uneasy relationship with police and prosecutors that has been characterized by harsh treatment of suspects and the widespread scapegoating of the entire community for the crime of a minority. Not surprisingly, many minority women may not want to draw attention of these agencies, let alone be told how and when their cases will be prosecuted. They are also aware that many minority community leaders feel that convictions for such "minor" offenses perpetuate the stereotype of criminal behavior. Prosecutors and courts also need to be aware of the fact that certain subpopulations of women, including minority women and those of lower socioeconomic status, are at greater risk of revictimization or retaliation and might therefore be more reticent about cooperation (Mills, 1998).

Empirical Research

What has empirical evidence shown about the adoption of rigorous "no drop" policies?

The classic study of mandatory prosecution was conducted in Indianapolis, Indiana (Ford & Regoli, 1992). This was an experimental assignment of 480 men charged with misdemeanor assaults on their domestic partners. They were assigned to one of three tracks: diversion, prosecution with a recommendation of counseling, or prosecution with a presumptive sentence. The study did found that the prosecution policy could affect batterer behavior. Although they found that victims who chose not to prosecute were at greatest risk of reabuse, they did not find the lowest levels of reabuse in the "no-drop prosecution" category. Instead, they concluded that victim complainants were best off when they were permitted to drop charges but, in fact, were persuaded to follow-up with them. In fact, they reported that this was the only policy with a preventive impact, significantly more effective than traditional processing (Ford & Regoli, 1993).

In short, enhancing the empowerment of the victim, rather than the actual prosecution, may be a key factor, despite the ideal situation in which the victim and prosecutor cooperate with each other to convict the abuser. Ford and Regoli's ultimate conclusion is instructive:

> The Indianapolis experiment, however, offers the surprising finding that, contrary to popular advocacy, permitting victims to drop charges significantly reduces their risk of further violence after a suspect has been arrested on a victim-initiated warrant, when compared with usual policies. We believe that under a drop-permitted policy, women are empowered to take control of events in their relationship. Some are empowered through prosecution such that they can use the possibility of abandoning prosecution as a power resource in bargaining for their security. . . . Others are empowered by the alliance they form with more powerful others, such as police, prosecutors and judges. (Ford & Regoli, 1993, p. 157)

In a second study conducted in Milwaukee, an analysis of an aggressive policy of having prosecutors charge virtually all domestic violence crimes demonstrated a variety of negative factors. Specifically:

- Case backlog increased greatly.
- Cases filed with the court contained a higher proportion of victims who did not want their cases prosecuted.
- Time to disposition doubled.
- Convictions declined.
- Pretrial crime increased.
- Victim satisfaction with case outcomes and with the prosecutor's handling of the case declined. (R. C. Davis et al., 1998, p. 71)

From this, the overall conclusion of the researchers was quite negative:

The district attorney's policy to prosecute a larger proportion of domestic violence arrests had several effects, none of them positive, which may have been due in part to insufficient allocation of resources. One effect of the new policy was to bring into the court system a larger proportion of cases with victims who were not interested in seeing the defendant prosecuted. Victim satisfaction with prosecutors and with court outcomes declined after the new screening policy. As the special court became overwhelmed with cases, case-processing time increased back to the level that had existed prior to the start of the specialized court [thus, in effect, sabotaging the effect of a different reform, a dedicated domestic violence court]. (R. C. Davis et al., 1998, pp. 71–72)

VICTIMS CHARGED WITH CHILD ENDANGERMENT

Reforms are also exposing latent tensions between the needs of two seemingly aligned groups—victims of domestic violence and their children and their respective advocates. All too often, female victims of domestic violence are aware, or perhaps more accurately, they should be aware of physical or sexual abuse of minor children. Not surprisingly, abused women who bring their assailants to the attention of the police are frequently

subject to criminal claims that they have "failed to protect" their children. Many have had their children removed from their custody for such reasons or have been prosecuted. In some cases, the "failure to protect" charges appear to be a thinly veiled attempt by prosecutors to retain leverage over the victim, in effect coercing her to support criminal charges against her attacker (D. Epstein, 1999).

Of course, the problem is that few advocates for child welfare consider the precarious nature of the female victim of domestic violence—a person traumatized by a man and by physical violence who, for financial, emotional, and communal reasons, often cannot realistically leave her abuser. Similarly, domestic violence victim advocates often fail to comprehend the ongoing damage to children caused by the exposure to relentless acts of violence in the family, whether or not those acts are committed against children directly. The fact of the matter is that many women, perhaps due to their own psychological issues including anger displacement or profound substance abuse, may neglect or physically mistreat their children.

In addition, in many instances, continued drug or alcohol abuse really results in severe impact on the mother's continuous ability to care for minor children—a fact often cited by abusive fathers in custody hearings. The impact of such intervention on domestic violence case handling, however, is quite clear: If victims calling the police for assistance are themselves subject to prosecution for child abuse or neglect charges or are at serious risk or losing child custody, they may simply not make such calls. This problem is likely to worsen as women become increasingly aware the child protective status and services may affect them.

One recent commentator noted that in New York State, the legal system has become a source of implicit danger to battered mothers rather than a source of assistance. This came from a recent trend to hold mothers

Table 12.1   Prosecutors' Responses to Scenarios Involving Children and Abuse

Scenario	Would Report at Least Sometimes	Would Prosecute at Least Sometimes
Mom abuses children	94%	100%
Mom fails to protect from abuse	83%	77.5%
Mom fails to protect from exposure	40%	25%

Note. From Whitcomb (2002), p. 5.

strictly accountable for their actions and the actions of their spouse toward their children (e.g., it was common for mothers filing for a civil protective order to face a criminal charge of child neglect for "exposing their children to domestic violence"; Lemon, 2000). In other words, even if the child had not been victimized, the mere exposure of violence toward the mother allegedly constituted a crime committed by the mother. A recently published NIJ report (Whitcomb, 2002) described how prosecutors nationwide have been responding to changing statutes designed to protect children from the effects of violence in the family. The researcher conducted a survey of 128 prosecutors who worked in 93 offices in 49 states. They had jurisdiction over both felony and misdemeanor cases involving family violence and/or child maltreatment cases. She described a pattern in which children witnessing acts of domestic violence were used as a power resource by many prosecutors to increase victim cooperation and the offender's willingness to plead guilty to lesser charges by a threatened felony charge of child endangerment.

In addition, three scenarios prototypically were involved when the interests of the mother might not coincide with that of her children: (1) an abused mother is alleged to have abused her children; (2) both mother and children are abused by the same male perpetrator; and (3) children are exposed to domestic violence but are not abused themselves. For each scenario, respondents answered these questions: Would your office report the

mother to the child protection agency? Would your office prosecute the mother in the first scenario for the abuse of her children? Would your office report or prosecute the mother in scenarios 2 and 3 for failure to protect her children from abuse or exposure to domestic violence? Table 12.1 shows prosecutors' responses to these questions.

We know that a large number of women who are victims of domestic violence have minor children in the household. Currently, we are expecting women to report all acts of abuse; however, the results of such reporting may expose her to loss of custody of the children (nearly automatic in some jurisdictions when a report of child endangerment is being investigated) and even in extreme cases may subject her to threats of prosecution for child abuse or child endangerment either because of her own activity or because of her inability to resolve her own battering. We can expect that, as this dilemma becomes more widely publicized, many women will simply refuse to seek needed assistance despite long-term risk to the safety and well-being of themselves and their children. It is not surprising that litigation on this point has already begun. Already, a class action was filed in federal court against the Child Services Administration and the New York City Police Department, claiming that both had a practice of taking children from victims of domestic violence and putting them in foster care, regardless of whether the child was in danger (Lemon, 2000).

ARE THERE ALTERNATE MODELS EMPOWERING VICTIMS THAT PROSECUTORS CAN FOLLOW?

We believe that it is incumbent on proponents of extreme measures, such as prosecutorial no-drop policies or coercion of victims to achieve convictions, to determine if less disruptive measures would accomplish the same goals. First, the reasons for case attrition are either benign, due to the victim having accomplished her needs before the conclusion of the case, or they could be addressed through far less restrictive practices. For example, victim cooperation with prosecution may depend far more on factors that the criminal justice system can implement on its own without trying to coerce the victim. For many years, police have had vastly improved incident report forms that require detailed information on domestic assaults. Photographs of bruises and interviews with many parties can make the officer an effective witness to a prosecution without involving the victim. Similarly, the presence of videotaped testimony may make later victim testimony unnecessary. At the prosecutor's office, the frequency and quality of meeting with victims and victim advocates within the prosecutor's offices (or similar advocates) are critical to sustaining a victim's desire to prosecute a case (Weisz, 1999). Any of these options are well within the control of the police and prosecutor, who can then influence the victim to continue prosecution—if such actions are in her own best interests. Otherwise, we believe that victims should be allowed to participate in the key decision of whether to prosecute a batterer.

It may be that these less intrusive measures may accomplish the bulk of the intent of no-drop policies. After all, the basic reason for such policies has been the understanding that most cases are dropped at victim request, yet it is functionally difficult to determine if the victim does so of her own

volition or as a result of intimidation or discouragement by rigid practices in the prosecutor's office.

Second, prosecutors can make additional efforts to address victim's needs more satisfactorily and to provide greater support. Fears of intimidation may be partially addressed by making the victim's reasons for discontinuance more visible, and therefore, more appropriate for resolution. Simply forcing defendants to appear in court at arraignment accomplishes both some level of "offender intimidation," providing an opportunity for the prosecutor to determine if there are issues of victim intimidation, and also to insist that the defendant abide by certain restrictions, such as no contact with the victim and no further battery as a condition of release. When such restrictions are imposed, a violation can be used to justify incarceration before trial and to signal which cases require aggressive action by the system. When properly administered, certain pretrial diversions— a succession of battering and attendance at treatment programs—may accomplish the same result as actual conviction, with few costs to the system or to the victim. Ignoring the efficacy of such processing in favor of no-drop policies would appear to unnecessarily dissipate scarce resources.

Third, a long-term training program to sensitize court personnel, funding of a well-staffed advocacy program as described later, and active efforts to train victims on the judicial process and their rights may all serve the purpose of reducing case attrition without imposing a "no-drop policy." It has been noted that prosecutors, being trained as aggressive lawyers, typically lack the innate ability to handle social problems or even to be comfortable addressing victims' feelings. This makes it difficult for them to speak to victims in a nurturing, rather than an overbearing, manner (Mills, 1997).

Relatively modest changes in the prosecution of cases, such as inviting women to file complaints in informal and confidential settings at locations other than the prosecutor's office (emergency rooms, female-run facilities, etc.), could start the process of committing the victim to prosecution. The theory is that an "affective" approach that attempts to involve the victim in the decision to prosecute would demonstrate that the system does not prejudge her as being either hopeless or helpless, but instead demonstrates a willingness to nurture and empower her (Mills, 1997).

There is persuasive evidence that increased contact of prosecutors with victims can dramatically enhance the prospects of guilty verdicts, regardless of whether coercive policies toward victims are in place.

In a recent study, Belknap et al. (1999) analyzed 2,670 case dispositions in a Midwestern court and reported that 44% resulted in a guilty verdict, 51% were dismissed, and 5% resulted in a not-guilty verdict. Not surprisingly, prosecutors blamed the victims for the high dismissal rate. They said it was due to the victims' failure to appear. Belknap noted that, in reality, this was not the case, because in many instances the victim was not even told of relevant court dates; in other cases, there appeared to be precious little positive feedback from the prosecutor to encourage victim cooperation.

Belknap et al. (1999) reported that

the best predictors of court outcome is how many times the prosecutor met with the victim. The more often the prosecutor met with the victim, the greater the likelihood that the defendant was found guilty, was fined more, and received a greater number of days sentenced to both probation and incarceration. (p. 9)

She also observed that victims were at times more afraid of the courts and the law than they were of the danger posed by the offender. As a result, her recommendation of making the court system more user-friendly for victims and with more informal contacts

with prosecutors could reduce the concerns of the woman, making her more likely to voluntarily testify and enhance the probability of convictions without coercion.

Fourth, a relatively modest change in court procedures could accomplish much of the perceived reasons for a no-drop policy. Specifically, it could become the policy that although cases without actual injury may be freely dropped at the request of the victim, in cases in which an injury did occur, the victim could be told to cooperate with the prosecution unless she appears in open court and explains on the record why she wants the charges to be dropped. Along with her testimony, the criminal history of the offender would greatly assist the court in determining the likelihood of intimidation compared with the victim's genuine belief that the case does not warrant prosecution. Along with the offender's criminal history, this would help identify cases of victim intimidation and expose the reasons for the victim's decisions to the prosecutor and the judge. It also addresses the fact that in many cases alleged victim noncooperation is more a function of the failure of the prosecutor and court to communicate effectively with the victim.

It has been asserted that, in many cases, victims in fact wanted to go to court to "teach their abuser a lesson" but few wanted to have them convicted of a crime. Having a mandated appearance before dropping a case would make certain that cases were not being dropped because of miscommunications between the prosecutor, the court, and the victim and would give an opportunity for the victim to be heard in court (Belknap et al., 2001). A sympathetic judge would then be able to explain if, in his or her opinion, continued prosecution could further the victim's interests without coercion.

Fifth, in large jurisdictions, specialized domestic violence units may provide more informed and efficient prosecution of cases. In most jurisdictions, younger less experienced prosecutors handle a variety of misdemeanor cases on an assembly-line basis. A group of dedicated prosecutors with specialized training may allow for improved efficiency in operations that would enhance conviction rates. Even in smaller jurisdictions, having a designated prosecutor handle all such cases could accomplish similar results. In either case, "vertical prosecution,"—having one prosecutor handle a given case from intake to final disposition—greatly increases the likelihood of involvement of the prosecutor and victim cooperation.

Sixth, no-drop policies may be needed, even if solely targeted to repeat batterers or chronic offenders such as those who have either previously attacked the same victim or who have a chronic criminal history. Our growing knowledge base shows that "serial batterers" account for many, if not most, incidents and account for the vast bulk of serious injuries. Therefore, the test of a more limited policy may provide most of the societal benefits advanced in support of general no-drop policies while targeting seriously limited resources toward those that clearly deserve such attention.

In contrast, those offenders who have the greatest likelihood to respond to more rehabilitative approaches would then have the resources needed to access these less coercive services. Of equal significance, this is in accordance with victim preferences. The vast majority of domestic violence victims, unlike victims of nondomestic assault, want a degree of criminal justice intervention, but only if it is rehabilitative in its orientation rather than punitive.

This would address our primary concern that no-drop policies fail to recognize that neither victims nor batterers are a monolithic group. Victims have broad ranges of motives for their preferences of criminal justice involvement. All offenders will not respond the same to intervention, nor do they reflect the same degree of potential danger.

CAN COMPREHENSIVE PROSECUTORIAL PROGRAMS HAVE AN IMPACT ON DOMESTIC VIOLENCE? A CASE STUDY

A recent study (Buzawa et al., 1999) in Quincy District Court of the impact on victims and offenders of a comprehensive program on the control of domestic violence in QDC, a court cited as a model in the Violence Against Women Act. The role of the prosecutors and the effects of their practices on offenders and victims may be worth analysis as a case study. In Massachusetts, the district attorney decides the charges that are ultimately placed against a defendant, often, but not always, based on police recommendation. It is aggressive prosecution, but not the no-drop policies used in some jurisdictions. Overall, during the course of the study, 26% of the cases were not prosecuted, 25% of cases were continued without a finding (usually to give the offender time to attend counseling), and the remainder was prosecuted through conviction.

In this environment, there were a striking number of charges brought against offenders. The researchers found that in the 353 study cases, the total number of criminal charges issued by the prosecutor was 505 compared with 501 issued by police officers—virtually the same. In addition, the average number of prosecutorial charges was 1.43 compared with 1.53 by the police.

Although the QDC is a full arrest jurisdiction in action as well as policy, these data suggest that neither prosecutors nor the police "overcharge" or even use all of the charges that are justified in the incident. For example, if an offender was charged with assault and battery (the prototypical charge used in 42% of the cases by the police and

47% of cases by prosecutors), we would expect to find additional charges involving the specific conduct (i.e., breaking and entering, destruction of property, stalking, trespassing, disorderly conduct, etc.). The analysis did not find multiple charging behavior by either the police or the prosecutors. Additionally, we would expect in the actions of a proactive police and court that there would be somewhat fewer charges made by the prosecutor. This is because some police charges may lack sufficient legal evidence for the case to go forward.

Analysis did not stop at the raw number of charges filed by the police and prosecutors because some research has suggested that prosecutor charges in domestic violence cases have been routinely downgraded to less serious offenses such as generic disorderly conduct or disturbing the peace (Cahn, 1992; Lerman, 1981; Pleck, 1987; Schmidt & Steury, 1989); this study found that only 0.4% of cases was for disorderly conduct.

There are two notable areas in which prosecutors were found more likely to charge than the police: First, the charge of violation of a restraining order was the most common charge on the part of both parties. This charge was leveled in 16.6% (88) cases by the police and in 19.6% (99) by the prosecutor. This is important because it suggests that prosecutors may be better able to elicit information regarding restraining order violations than the police or that they were quick to file charges for those violating restraining orders subsequent to arrest.

When only charges involving actual acts of physical violence are aggregated, the prosecutors were more aggressive in charging than were the police, with the exception of attempted murder and aggravated assault. This discrepancy between the prosecutor and the police was most apparent in the area of assault and assault and battery with a dangerous weapon, which in Massachusetts constitutes a significant enhancement of the charges of assault and of assault and battery. In examining the two crimes of assault with a dangerous weapon and assault and battery with a dangerous weapon, the police asserted such charges in 14.1% (74) of the cases overall compared with 23.8% (120) of cases by prosecutors.

These findings suggest that prosecutors were more likely to charge in more objective areas such as restraining order violations, whereas in less objective areas such as attempted murder, for which they may have had legal concerns about proving criminal intent, charges were at times made more objective, being changed to offenses such as assault with a dangerous weapon.

Perhaps the best method for determining whether prosecutors engaged in the process of marginalizing domestic violence offenses was whether they generally reduced charges from major to less serious offenses. Although police filed serious criminal charges in 24.7% (86) cases, this number dropped an insignificant amount to 23.8% (84) for prosecutors.

Victim Preferences

The QDC study found that there were several important measures of the quality of the interaction that took place between the victim and the prosecutor. These included (a) whether the victim wanted the prosecutor to become involved in the incident, (b) whether there were differences in the goals of the victim and those of the prosecutor and how these differences were resolved, (c) whether the victim perceived that the prosecutor helped increase her capabilities to prevent future violence, and (d) her overall satisfaction with the actions of the prosecutor.

Data on victim desire for contact with the district attorney showed great diversity. Although the prosecutor became involved in 91% of the cases in this study, victim's preferences for such contact were more mixed. In response to the question "Did you want to talk to the prosecutor?", a plurality (47.5%) answered affirmatively, a substantial minority did not want such contact, and (21.1%) were ambivalent. The fact that the majority of victims did not want or were ambivalent about contact with the prosecutor suggests that victims perceived a gap between their interests and the interests of the prosecutor. The reasons for this gap are undoubtedly complex but, because victims know that a successful prosecution can be obtained in this jurisdiction through the district attorney's office, a fairly sizable number of victims did not want criminal case processing.

A slight majority of victims did <u>not</u> support aggressive case prosecution. Thirty-seven percent either wanted the charges dropped by the prosecutor or did not even want to go to the prosecutor in the first place, and an additional 14% wanted the charges lowered. On the other hand, 36% of victims were content with the nature of the filed charges, and 10% wanted the prosecutor to increase the severity of the charges. Not surprisingly, approximately 46% of victims directly asked the prosecutor to drop criminal charges against the offender. Despite that request, the vast majority were told that charges would not be dropped. These data were consistent with literature that has repeatedly shown that many victims did not actually want their cases prosecuted. It also shows that despite such preferences, and even formal requests to the prosecutor's office, prosecution in a full enforcement jurisdiction typically continues.

Another important facet of the interaction between the prosecutor and victim is how the prosecutor's actions actually affected her future perceptions and actions. We asked victims in this study a series of questions (anywhere from 3 to 8 months after their initial contact with the prosecutor) about their perceptions of the effects of the prosecutor's

handling of her case. It is not surprising that when asked the specific question about whether the prosecutor "gave you a sense of control over your life," a majority of study victims (57%) answered in the negative. These responses probably reflect the disparity between the stated goals of prosecutors in this jurisdiction (i.e., to treat all domestic violence cases as a crime warranting prosecution) and the far more diverse goals of victims.

A majority of victims (69%) also reported that the prosecutor did not motivate her to take steps to end the abuse, and 60% of the victims reported that they did not feel safer as a result of the actions of the prosecutor. In response to a specific question about whether the prosecutor actually affected the victim's safety, however, 61% believed that their actually safety was either greatly or somewhat increased compared with 30%, who reported no effect on personal safety and 9% who reported a deterioration in personal safety because of the actions of the prosecutor.

These data are significant because they show that, as a group, victims cannot point to any particular benefits in terms of motivating them to end abuse or to feel safer, but the actions the prosecutors took, by processing the charges, were associated with an increase in the sense of personal safety. Nonetheless, it should be noted that in 3 out of every 10 cases, the victim did not report any change in her subsequent safety, and in 9% of the cases, there was a reported decrease in personal safety.

The dilemma is that those victims who reported that contact with the prosecutor did not affect safety or actually decreased it were more likely to have been involved with more dangerous offenders. These men were more likely to have had more extensive criminal histories (16 prior criminal vs. 11 charges), more prior restraining orders taken out against them by the victim and other women (.65 compared with .37), and to have had a greater number of prior periods of probation (1.8 vs. 1.3). Victim reports of the prosecutor not affecting personal safety or decreasing safety may have been well founded in that these women were involved with the more hard-core offenders in our sample who were not deterred by the criminal justice system and who might have been angrier and more prone to retaliation.

Results in a methodologically closely related study in another Massachusetts District Court confirmed that the conclusions of the QDC were not isolated. This latter study reported that the majority of victims preferred that the prosecutor exert control to the offender in ways not involving criminal prosecution. For example, they were almost twice as likely as nonintimate assault victims to report that they wanted the prosecutor to "talk to the offender and then drop the case" and almost 5 times more likely to have wanted the prosecutor to "drop the criminal charges but make the offender go to counseling" as a way to address the incident (Hotaling & Buzawa, 2001).

The Use of Victim Advocacy Services

The QDC has well-developed procedures and funding for victim advocates who are structurally attached to the district attorney's office. Such services were routinely used, and in more than 80% of cases, the victim talked to a victim advocate. This was typically not a perfunctory interaction. Although 20% of the victims talked with an advocate for less than 15 minutes, 36% spent 15 to 45 minutes, and a plurality (42%) spent 45 minutes or more with an advocate. When the reasons for the time disparity were discussed, victims reported that in many cases, especially for those involving restraining orders or outside counsel, more time was unnecessary.

Satisfaction with the time spent with a victim advocate is a significant measure of the efficacy of such services. In this case, 81% were either very or somewhat satisfied with time spent. The remaining 19%, who were somewhat or very dissatisfied or ambivalent, present an interesting contrast.

Although the reasons for the expressed dissatisfaction are unclear, in some cases it may be due to victim perceptions that the victim advocate either did not provide the services desired or did not spend enough time with the victim for her to detail her wishes. In still other cases, it could be a reflection of the victim advocate's structural position as part of the district attorney's office and his or her orientation to try to proceed with the prosecution of cases. More than three quarters of victims (77.1%) said they would want to talk to the victim advocate again if a similar incident reoccurred.

The Victim's Level of Satisfaction With the Prosecutor's Office

Despite the victim's general reticence regarding charging, the majority was of respondents were satisfied with the actions of the prosecutor. Fully 65% said they were either "very" or "somewhat" satisfied compared with 33.5% who were dissatisfied to some degree. Another 2% of the sample did not express an opinion on this issue.

Overall levels of satisfaction appeared related to whether the prosecutor affected the victim's safety. For example, among those who felt the prosecutor had increased their personal safety, fully 83% reported high levels of global satisfaction. On the other hand, global satisfaction did not appear related to specific survey items asking whether the prosecutor motivated the victim to end the abuse or whether victims felt safer as a result of prosecutorial contact. The reason for this disparity is not well understood. Perhaps victims as a group expected only a limited role from the prosecutor. It may be that many victims did not really believe the prosecutor was responsible for increasing their level of control or even to have felt safer, but decided their level of satisfaction on the basis of whether they were actually made safer by the overall actions of the prosecutor and, by extension, the rest of the criminal justice system.

Levels of satisfaction with the prosecutor were significantly higher for victims who felt that the prosecutor had increased their safety. Fully 83% of those reporting increased safety were satisfied compared with much lower levels of satisfaction among those who perceived the prosecutor as not making them safer. In general, levels of victim satisfaction with the prosecutor did not vary significantly by offender's criminal history. Although the data are in the direction of suggesting that satisfaction is inversely related to the extensiveness of offender criminal history, the differences are not strong enough to support such a finding.

In contrast, in the second study of a district court (Orange District Court) in another Massachusetts jurisdiction, Buzawa and Hotaling (2001) reported that the victims' level of satisfaction with the prosecutor's office was not very high and was, in fact, lower than with the police, victim's advocates, and the court. The most common reason cited for their dissatisfaction with the prosecutor is instructive: The victims believed that the actions of the prosecutor would ultimately be harmful to the victim. Fifty percent of the domestic assault victims felt the prosecutor acted either too harshly or that the prosecutor's actions would eventually be harmful to them. None of the nondomestic assault victims in this study cited these reasons for any dissatisfaction with the prosecutor, suggesting this phenomenon was directly related to the aggressive handling of domestic violence cases undertaken in this jurisdiction.

In short, the QDC and Orange District Court studies suggest that tensions between victims and the prosecutor offices are not transitory or likely to disappear simply because many, if not most, prosecutors are obviously committed to ending domestic violence through increased prosecution. In fact, to the extent institutions assume decision-making power as opposed to trying to gain victim cooperation, or if necessary, defer to victim preferences in some situations, there may be negative consequences. It is likely that victim cooperation and, indirectly, practical use of the system, will decrease for a substantial group of domestic violence victims. The line between well-intentioned assistance and perceptions of attacking victim autonomy may be one of the criminal justice system's most difficult remaining dilemmas.

NOTE

1. Ideally, such an enterprise combines the inherent powers and capabilities of the respective agencies—both within and apart from the criminal justice system. This is the conclusion that Jolin and Moore (1997) reached from their review of studies examining a coordinated community response system to battering. An important end product may be that such "partnerships" lower batterer recidivism.

CHAPTER 13

Judicial Innovations: Diversions From the Criminal Justice System

THE LACK OF A COORDINATED RESPONSE FROM THE JUDICIARY

Although virtually every state has passed domestic violence statutes, until recently, the judicial response to sexual and family violence has neither been as comprehensive nor as advanced as the police. Why? The police, however grudgingly, are fully expected to follow the laws as written. Although prosecutors have the power to exercise discretion, their discretion has begun to be limited by active oversight or even by the initiation of no-drop policies discussed in the previous chapter.

In contrast, judges have the express responsibility to adjudicate criminal responsibility and the conduct of offenders. Although many, if not most, are willing to experiment with innovative approaches, others are largely unsympathetic with the goals and methods espoused in domestic violence legislation and often are disturbed by potential impingement of a defendant's rights. Due to their unique position, they can effectively refuse to enforce statutes, and the ability of most victims to contest judicial decisions in misdemeanor cases is in practice virtually nonexistent.

Research in the study of what works in the judiciary is less advanced (or at least less disseminated) than in the case of the police or even prosecutors. Although many policy analyses have been published by victim rights advocates, feminist attorneys, and law reviews that strongly advocate further change, issues of judicial operational performance have not been widely circulated. Nonetheless, the national consensus needed to force systemic change has begun to coalesce, imparting a current degree of uncertainty exceeding that of the police.

As a result, judicial management of domestic violence cases has only recently gained saliency as a public issue. Initial attention was the result of occasional newspaper series exploring the extent to which the system does not work or sporadic outcries to an especially outrageous unguarded public comment by a trial court judge who, at a minimum, was unaware of the political necessity to refrain from critiquing abuse victims. Such attitudes are not atypical. Although unspoken, they are endemic and systematized. The degree to which these attitudes still prevail is unclear. Clearly, there are still many judges who hold victims largely responsible for their victimization and do not see such cases appropriate for judicial intervention (Hemmens, Strom, & Schlegel, 1998).

Similarly, because most commentaries on the judicial response have been published in law journals or advocacy publications and are based on nonquantitative measures, there has not been a research catalyst for change equivalent to the Minneapolis Domestic Violence Experiment (MDVE). Therefore, operational change that has occurred is more a product of the impact of professional groups such as the National Council of Juvenile and Family Court Judges, the American Bar Association, the State Justice Institute, and the National Judicial College the orientation and training of individual administrators and the push of federal funding from the Violence Against Women Act (see Valente, Hart, Zeya, & Malefyt, 2001).

As a result of such factors, the current performance of judges is even more inconsistent than that of the police. Davis Adams, director of EMERGE, the country's oldest treatment program for batterers (located in Massachusetts) with intimate experience with the system in that state, best summed up his conclusions as follows: "In Massachusetts, everyone has the rhetoric down. But when you're dealing with individual cases, that's when the consistency really breaks down" (Polochanin, 1994).

A report published by the *Boston Globe* ("Records Show," 1994) used the Massachusetts database on the history and disposal of restraining orders, a good indicator of the commitment of judges to these crimes, showed startling variations in enforcement between different counties. In some counties, including Suffolk County (Boston), more than 60% of such claims of violation were dismissed. In other jurisdictions, as few as 18% of cases were dismissed. Similarly, sentencing of the offenders to jail time for restraining order violation ranged from 0% to 26%, with even the high estimates well below expectations when the considering that applicable domestic

violence statute clearly favored stiff punishment for violating restraining orders.

The reasons for the discrepancy appear to reflect the operations and attitudes of courts. Adams faults many judges in whom he now sees a backlash because they are "sick and tired of hearings about battered women" ("Records Show," , 1994). This was partially confirmed by detailed analysis of individual court statistics demonstrating that some judges would rarely dismiss cases, whereas others might dismiss up to 75% under certain circumstances. Regardless of the reasons, it appears that there is a virtual patchwork approach toward handling domestic cases, sometimes even within the same jurisdiction.

CASE DISPOSITION BY THE JUDICIARY

Historically, cases that are not filtered out of the system by action or inaction of the police or by victims or prosecutors often received summary dispositions by the judiciary. Although it would be easy to overgeneralize, judges, at least in the past, shared the consensus of prosecutors that most domestic violence cases could not readily be helped by the full prosecution of an offender (Dobash & Dobash, 1979; Field & Field, 1973). Given the organizational context of extreme time pressures and limited resources, it is not surprising that in the past it was repeatedly noted that judges minimized domestic violence cases and disproportionately dismissed them (Parnas, 1970, 1973).

Similarly, until the full effect of the ongoing recent reforms, the sentencing of convicted domestic violence offenders has been quite lenient, with few offenders sentenced to serve any time in jail (Sherman, 1993). One study was made in Ohio of all misdemeanor domestic violence assault charges in the state during 1980. This research was conducted after Ohio passed a new domestic violence statute designed to sensitize the criminal justice system to the problems of battered women. Although termed misdemeanors, many of these cases involved injuries and potentially serious conduct that in another context would have been termed felonies (Quarm & Schwartz, 1983).

The sentences imposed graphically illustrate how the crimes were trivialized. Of 1,408 cases, 1,142 (81%) were dismissed. Of the 1,142 dismissed cases, 1,062 (93%) were dismissed because the victim requested this action (for the vast variety of reasons described in this chapter) or failed to appear. Of the remaining 256 cases, 166 guilty verdicts or pleas were received. Despite being in a jurisdiction otherwise noted for harsh sentencing, only 60 miscreants (36%) spent any time in jail, with one third (20) spending between 1 and 15 days (including time spent in jail awaiting trial), one third (20) between 16 and 30 days, and only one third (20 out of the original 48 cases) more than 20 days. Similarly, only 12% of the miscreants were fined more than $100. Simple probation, instead of imprisonment or fines, was the sentence in almost two thirds of the cases (Quarm & Schwartz, 1983).

The same results were reported in several other studies even when, in the rare occasion, domestic violence cases were treated as felonies. Another study, also conducted in Ohio, reported that even in the rare circumstance that a domestic violence defendant was convicted and received a prison sentence, sentence terms were shorter then they were for other types of offenders (Erez & Tontodonato, 1990). Similarly, in one study conducted in Alaska, the overall result of court actions (after taking into account "voluntary dismissals") was that domestic violence offenders were less likely to be convicted, and if convicted, they were less likely to be sentenced to jail (Miethe, 1987).

Why did such results occur, even in the face of rather blunt statutory directives to enhance the response to domestic violence? There are few empirical studies that have surveyed judicial attitudes to explain behavior. We can, however, surmise that several key factors are involved. First, trial criminal court judges are attorneys, primarily recruited directly from the ranks of prosecutors or indirectly after a prosecutor has become a successful defense attorney. For the reasons we described earlier, prosecutors have long had a troubled history in responding to these offenses. Becoming a defense attorney would be unlikely to change their attitudes toward aggressive enforcement.

Second, judges are in a unique position to impose their own will on a case. Since this crime has never received the mandatory minimum sentences meted out in certain drug and other offenses, they can, if they choose, ignore statutory directions. Because of "separation of powers," such decisions cannot be overturned by the legislature. Moreover, as judges they do not have to justify sentencing and other case dispositions to victims, prosecutors, or defense attorneys. As the vast majority of domestic violence cases are treated by the system as misdemeanors, the operating reality is that there is no appeal from their decisions.

The study of so-called "gender bias" in the courts has for the last few years received significant research attention, especially from feminist writers and their political allies. As a result of claims of gender bias, the National Organization for Women (NOW) Legal Defense and Education Fund worked with the National Association of Women Judges to study systemic gender bias in the courts (Schafran, 1990). By 1989, 30 states had such gender bias task forces. Interestingly, it has long been assumed that gender bias is not simply, or even at this time, primarily a case of intentional ill will against women. Instead, it is more likely to be differential treatment in situations in which gender should not be considered as a result of stereotypical beliefs about the gender's temperament, expectations, and proper roles (California Gender Bias Task Force, 1996).

Such attitudes were found to exist by the judges and by their staff. For example, the California 1996 task force reported that 53% of male court personnel thought that women exaggerated domestic violence complaints. Not surprisingly only about one quarter of female court personnel shared these beliefs. Similarly, whereas 40% of the male court personnel believed that domestic violence cases should be diverted or that counseling should be used rather than prosecution, only 21% of female court staff agreed with this (Hemmens et al., 1998).

Hemmens and colleagues (1998) summarized the findings of the state reports and found that gender bias was most prevalent in domestic violence cases. Although a significant part of their findings related to the actions of prosecutors and defense attorneys, many reports commented on inappropriate attitudes and actions by the judiciary. For example, Utah in 1990 reported that cases of domestic violence were minimized compared with nondomestic assaults (Utah Gender Bias Task Force, 1990). The Maryland report stated that "51% of male attorneys and 68% of the female attorneys believed that judges sometimes failed to view domestic violence as a crime" (Hemmens et al., 1998).

Hemmens and colleagues (1998) quoted several particularly egregious examples cited in the state sponsored gender bias studies. For example,

> A state trial court judge commented, "I have difficulty finding where this defendant's (the husband) done anything wrong, other than slapping her (his wife). Maybe that was 'justified' " (Utah, 1990, p. 44). The Massachusetts study revealed that

some victims report improper or irrelevant questions during court proceedings. Over three-fourths of the responding attorneys said judges sometimes allow questions as to what the victim did to provoke the battering. Comments made by judges included "Why don't you get a divorce" and "Why are you bothering the court with this problem?" (Massachusetts, 1989, p. 90). (Hemmens et al., 1998, p. 24)

Third, even the more enlightened judges who have sought to provide an adequate answer to such crimes have faced real issues. They are aware that the evidence of which party was at fault can be quite tangled in many cases, creating relatively weak cases when presented at trial. Even when guilt is clear, many have long acted on the assumption that their goal was primarily to "rehabilitate" the domestic violence offender, not primarily to punish him. This has been seen by many as being responsive to victims who want rehabilitation, not punitive results. Not surprisingly, it was recently noted that in most courts the likelihood and duration of jail sentences has simply not been increased as a result of recent reforms, although this did not prove true in an in-depth study of case dispositions in New York City (Peterson, 2001).

We recognize that judicial decisions toward leniency, when prompted by evidentiary challenges or respect for genuine victim preferences, is, on balance, positive. We have certainly met many judges whose commitment to the resolution of domestic violence cases cannot be questioned, nor can their actions in these difficult cases be second-guessed. We are, however, less sanguine that the result of judicial action in many, if not most, courtrooms truly reflects victim preferences and not preexisting judicial attitudes to rapidly dispose of this part of a judge's overwhelming caseload. Unfortunately, the effect of judicial attitudes and practices that negate the importance of this crime, like those of prosecutors before them, cascades throughout the criminal justice system.

Frankly, the judiciary has always retained the potential to lead the criminal justice system by example or direction. They are the ultimate authority, with the power to ratify or negate the actions of the police and prosecutors, as well as to define the parameters and seriousness of a particular crime. They may use such power to compel effective action or, as in the past, strongly imply that domestic violence is not a "real" crime.

The cost of judicial action that is not conducted properly is high. In many cases, victims have essentially been deprived of legal protection, and offenders may have perceived that the whole matter was "no big deal." Additionally, police with policies that emphasized the role of arrest or that even made arrest mandatory undermined such cases, resulting in their being routinely dismissed or in the sentencing trivializing the inherent serious nature of an assault.

The fact is that few systemic efforts have been made to coordinate the actions of the judiciary. To date, although individual judiciary actions are being examined, no one has really attempted to force consistency in actions among the thousands of judges nationwide. In this manner, the response of the judiciary, compared with those of the police or prosecutors, is even more problematic. Many judges lead their communities in the fight against domestic violence. Others, sometimes even in the same jurisdiction, treat such cases lightly or even resent their role in flooding the court docket with misdemeanor cases that are often dismissed.

The federal Violence Against Women Act (1994) reauthorized in 2000, attempted to address this inconsistency by establishing standards, providing technical assistance, and funding improvements to those courts not yet increasing efforts toward a proactive response. Although not being at all coercive toward the courts, it provided guidance by highlighting achievements of innovative efforts by designating model courts such as the Quincy District Court. Databases and evaluations also began to develop in an effort to confirm the relative performance of particular courts. Also, by establishing new federal crimes and enforcement responsibilities, there is increased pressure for courts to take these crimes more seriously.

In the absence of any judicial uniformity, the following is a discussion of several major changes now being evaluated and adopted, specifically the move to systematically divert appropriate cases at an early stage out of the criminal system through mediation and court-mandated counseling, the development of specialized courts, and an integrated approach to handling domestic violence cases is explored in Chapter 15.

COURT-SPONSORED DIVERSIONS

Many members of the judiciary have recognized that one of the primary reasons the criminal justice system has been ineffective has been the relative inflexibility of treatment modalities and an inability to focus limited resources by diverting offenders with little history of violence. Two models of diversion from the system have been developed: (a) court sponsored mediation and (b) batterer counseling by court mandate as a condition for pretrial diversion or as a part of sentencing subsequent to a guilty plea or trial verdict.

Although not strictly part of the "criminal justice" response to domestic violence, in reality, mediation and mandated batterer treatment have both been widely adopted and advocated by many courts as alternatives to continued case prosecution. Hence, it is appropriate to examine these options as part of the criminal justice process. Such efforts are popular, at least in principle, with the public. In one community survey, respondents far preferred court-sponsored mediation to conviction for abuse followed by jail or even probation (Stalans, 1996; Stalans & Lurigio, 1995). Similarly, a 1992 public poll favored "counseling," not arrest (Klein et al., 1997). Only if the female victim was punched or "hit hard" did the percent favoring arrest increase to between 50% and 90%, depending on the degree of injury inflicted (Klein et al., 1997). Clearly, both mediation and counseling have a legitimate, although bounded, scope of support by the public, as well as by many, if not most, agency administrators.

In contrast to public support, the extent to which victims favor these approaches is not certain. Hotaling and Buzawa (2001) reported in this study that only 13% of victims preferred mediation as an alternative to court prosecution, and less than a third preferred "informal meetings" with a court official to work out a judicially enforced solution. This was often not for punitive reasons, however, because more than two thirds of victims believed psychological counseling for offenders, such as batterer treatment, offered the greatest potential for preventing reoffending, whereas fewer believe traditional criminal justice sanctions would be effective.

COURT-SPONSORED MEDIATION PROGRAMS

In contrast to informal efforts by police to settle a domestic assault at the scene, formal mediation uses the services of a skilled intermediary. Parties are shown how to resolve serious differences without resorting to violent or otherwise inappropriate behavior. Based on an assumption of cooperation among discordant parties, mediation is largely a "self-help" process by which the impartial mediator facilitates conflict resolution. The mediator does not have the authority to mandate any particular settlement but instead typically seeks to develop a process for solving disputes nonviolently. Marital conflict mediation has experienced phenomenal growth as a means of having a client-controlled, less expensive system of settling disputes (including divorces) among spouses (Hilton, 1993). In fact, it has been observed that courts now use mediation as the "first avenue" of trying to effect an interpersonal dispute (Umbreit, 1995). This is true despite the fact that best estimates are that between 50% and 80% of all marriages referred by the courts to mediators involve family violence (Maxwell, 1999; Newmark, Harrell, & Salem, 1995).

Mediation efforts to contain domestic violence have several precedents. Crisis intervention centers nationwide have been set up to diffuse many kinds of interpersonal disputes, including domestic violence. These efforts, although a vital component of society's response to domestic violence, are not covered in this book. A detailed, if somewhat dated, study of such programs is contained in "Domestic Violence Mediation Demands Careful Screening" (Ray, 1982).

The mediation programs of more direct relevance to this book have been the use of pretrial mediation sponsored by prosecutors' offices and structured mediation in divorce cases in which the threat of criminal prosecution is evident. These programs may be run by prosecutorial or judicial staff or may be contracted out using the services of local crisis management agencies.

Court-sponsored divorce-related mediation is widely used in cases of domestic violence. Virtually all studies of divorce mediation suggest that domestic violence is prevalent in divorce mediations, with estimates of the co-occurance at 50% to 80% of all mediated divorce cases (Kurz, 1996; Maxwell, 1999; Pearson, 1997). Despite this, where such court-sponsored programs exist, mediation generally resolves 50% to 70% of referrals without further judicial input. Although typically divorce mediators have the responsibility of advising parties that they can "opt out" and pursue criminal conduct if domestic violence has occurred, Pearson (1997) and Thoennes et al (1995) each noted that less than 5% of such cases were excluded from mediation due to domestic violence.

Types of Mediation Programs

Formal mediation programs are extraordinarily varied. They start with an initial referral of the case either by a prosecutor, victim advocate, or the attorney for one of the parties. Some programs use a structured framework seeking to teach long-term dispute resolution in a nonviolent context or to negotiate key aspects of legal separation through divorce-related mediation. Some have even included initial direct sessions with a mediator and a surrogate or advocate for the "adversary."

A typical mediation session involving intimates is designed to use a neutral trained facilitator or mediator to provide both parties with a safe and structured forum in which they can express their needs and aspirations in a relationship and hear those of the other party. Stated succinctly, "the mediator is an advocate of a fair process" (Moore, 1997). This is true whether the parties' shared goal is to "reform" the relationship or to end it with a minimum of rancor and collateral damage to the parties or their children.

The mediator will typically spend the majority of his or her efforts trying to facilitate negotiations by making each side understand the reasonable requests of the other party and appeal to both parties desires to achieve a "fair result." The process of mediation is thus designed to be "self-empowering" to each of the participants, giving both a degree of "buy in," hence making them responsible for the decisions that are reached. To the extent achieved, the result may be far more readily accepted then those "mandated" by a court or other "supreme decision maker."

Mediating relationships with domestic violence components would need to add additional essential components. Clearly, it cannot be the subject of the "mandatory" mediation divorce statutes with which some states are experimenting. Also, during the course of the mediation, both parties would be taught that past violence could not be tolerated and that constructive techniques for expressing anger must be developed. Similarly, the victim should be given guidance about her legal rights and available support systems for victims of battering. This practice has been widely adopted; at this time virtually all modern divorce-related mediation services have protocols on how to handle cases of domestic violence (Thoennes et al., 1995).

In other programs, individual counseling of both the accused offender and the victim precedes joint sessions between the spouses. This lessens the immediate trauma of the incident, allows a careful evaluation of the parties' commitment to mediation, begins teaching each party his or her rights and responsibilities, and may provide requisite psychological counseling. To memorialize the process and reinforce the commitment to change, a formal signed mediation agreement is usually prepared that sets forth mutually agreed on goals.

Some mediation programs therefore accept only couples in which the assailant has conditionally admitted that he or she did assault the victim. This type of mediation begins to resemble a conditional sentencing and is an adaptation of the typically nonjudgmental tenet of mediation. Ultimately, the result is a "contract" or "agreement" that sets forth the conflict resolution strategies and behavioral modifications to which each party agrees. Typically, such an agreement would include "nonabuse" covenants as well as commitments to attend substance abuse or anger control therapy when needed (Hilton, 1993).

Enforcement of mediation agreements to ensure future nonviolence is then handled by careful case monitoring, often under the auspices of a court's probation department (if part of a sentencing arrangement) or, more informally, by cognizant prosecutorial staff if a criminal case has been suspended pending the outcome of the mediation. Mediation programs are best coupled with a firm prosecutorial commitment that if monitoring or victims' reports disclose violation of the mediation agreement, a suspended prosecution would be reinstated for both the original act of violence and any new offenses. Lerman (1982) provided a good analysis of the components of such a program. In her article, she also detailed the many problems and limitations attendant to this type of diversion.

Does Mediation Reduce Violence?

Although there have been few empirical studies, some findings have suggested that in appropriate cases, alternate programs such as mediation provide approximately equal reductions in the rate of recidivism compared with traditional sentencing. Early studies found the District of Columbia's mediation service to be effective in reducing future violence and mediation was considered fair by both parties (Davis, Tichane, & Grayson, 1980).

Of course, many authors believe it is inappropriate to compare recidivism rates with a criminal justice system known in the past to avoid domestic assault cases. These authors— who are often quite hostile to most court-sponsored diversion programs, including mediation—assert that such comparisons are irrelevant. They believe the real comparison should be to the ideal outcome attainable in a nonsexist legal system (Stallone, 1984). Despite the merit of this critique—we should, after all, aim for the best response possible— comparisons between real-world alternatives do remain the best indicators of useful social policy. This being the case, it is essential to consider carefully the comparative advantages and limitations of mediation.

Advantages of Mediation

Mediation has several significant advantages. The theory behind the use of mediation as a diversionary program is that the abuser, and even at times the abused party, usually denies the criminality of spouse abuse. Mediation finesses the need for such a determination (or, put another way, improperly refuses to make such a finding). The process and techniques for settling conflicts without violence are taught to both offender and victim. Some have favored this as a method of circumventing an impersonal court system that discriminates against the needs of women. It further serves as a method of educating both parties about their legal rights and responsibilities. Of even more significance, it addresses the apparent desires of many victims who have repeatedly indicated in most surveys that, as a group, they do not want continued prosecution through conviction.

Even more significant, past chapters in this book have demonstrated amply that many, if not most, victims prefer alternatives to the "command and control" orientation of the criminal justice system. Many such victims, as shown in Chapter 12, are presently dissatisfied with the decisions or at least the processes of the criminal justice system handling of their case. We predict that such discomfort will only increase as prosecutors place more aggressive attention on claims of "child endangerment" and when there will not be a pretext that the victims' interests are of paramount importance. In mediation cases, the parties, facilitated by the mediator, tailor make decisions that may be best for them, and, as they perceive, for their children.

Despite intensive time commitments for counselors and mediators, most cases do not require much of the far scarcer and costlier prosecution and judicial resources. Consequently, mediation may be considered expedient to an overburdened system facing gridlock in trial courts. Perhaps in comparison to traditional prosecution, studies have shown that participants of effective programs view the process as being fair and generally rate it favorably, at least in comparison with the vagaries of the traditional, overworked, and somewhat cynical court system (B. E. Smith, 1983). If the mediators are prepared for the possibility of domestic violence and are correspondingly careful to equalize power relationships and maintain mechanisms to intervene actively if it appears that violence is likely to recur, some authors have stated that mediation may prove beneficial even in the context of domestic violence (Johnston & Campbell, 1993; Yellot, 1990).

Limits of Mediation

Mediation shares some of the basic tenets, and hence limitations, of the "conciliatory" style of policing. Specifically, mediators are not as a profession inclined to fix blame on either party's behavior in a relationship. As a result, mediation fails to define explicitly either a "victim" or an "aggressor" and does not make value judgments regarding their actions. Mediation as a strategy allows a batterer to avoid the criminal justice process. Therefore, some offenders may be better able to continue denying the criminality of their actions. In fact, it is possible that by implying that neither party is solely responsible, an assailant may be encouraged to view his conduct as not being expressly wrong but merely the result of a problematic relationship in which his actions are at least is partially attributable to "provocations" by the victim.

The basic concern with mediation is that, if inappropriately used, the result may be continued victim subjugation, with

clear criminal acts treated as a by-product of a "dysfunctional" relationship between "involved parties." At worst, mediators might even inadvertently facilitate domestic abuse by ignoring the criminal nature of an assault and assuming that there is mutual responsibility for the physical aggression of one party, by explicitly assigning a higher value to facilitating agreement than addressing violent behavior, and by trivializing past and potential future assaults in the mediation "contracts" or "agreements" (Hilton, 1991, 1993; Ellis, 1993). By analyzing transcripts of mediations, Cobb (1992) described how mediators ignored past violence in their effort to reach a "therapeutic" mediation. From this, she concluded (without presenting any empirical data) that mediation likely increased the risk of further injury to the abused party (Cobb, 1992). Sometimes this ignorance may not be intentional because, as we noted earlier, virtually all mediation services have established protocols on handling domestic violence mediation. Despite such policies, it has been observed that the mediator never uncovers many instances of violence because of an inability to draw out the information or because of reluctance to ask probing questions in private interviews (Pearson, 1997). Other times, mediation is a "single shot" or a time-limited activity, and the mediator cannot recognize an unfolding pattern of abuse, particularly if the victim is affected by posttraumatic stress (Maxwell, 1999). An ineffective mediation may have unfortunate results even beyond missing an opportunity to effectively intervene by prosecuting a crime (Pirro, 1982). Mediation, even if ineffective at stopping violence, increases the likelihood of the family staying together, at least during the period of the mediation. It is well known that intimacy and frequency of contact increases potential for conflicts. If the mediation is unsuccessful at stopping a prior assailant from committing repeat acts of violence, there is a real probability that it may create more harm for a victim than if the case had not been diverted from the criminal justice system.

Those who critique mediation believe that cases of repeat assault should be treated as a crime rather then subject to mediation as part of a "conflict situation." If not, the opportunity for identifying, sanctioning, and deterring future violent behavior might be lost.

Somewhat dated research by B. E. Smith (1983) suggests that violence even after mediation is no idle concern, reporting that 36% of victims reported more violence after mediation and that 41% had increased fears of revenge. Of course, this study did not answer what percentage of these women would have had such a poor result without mediation because they were already a population at risk. Nor by the nature of the study (one program) could it reflect the potential for conflict management of all the various forms of mediation. Ellis (1993) noted the lack of any empirical evidence to support conclusions of a harmful effect. His review of mediation efforts, in fact, noted a small number of studies and did not find such a negative pattern. Not surprisingly, most mediators also vehemently deny allegations that they were simply "mediating violence."

For this reason, we need to synthesize these findings. There is a role for mediation, but perhaps it might best be reserved for less serious cases of threats of or actual assault. An example is cases in which, if there was an assault, there was no weapon involved, no injury, and no likelihood of serious injury. Other examples are cases in which mediation is preferred by both parties; in which there is no prior history of violence, or in which the specific violence appears to be more in the context of "mutual conflict" than of one disempowered party (typically the woman) being continually victimized by an intimate partner.

In stating this, we recognize that this limitation may create intake or selection problems for such programs, given the lack of agreement over the definition of severe abuse. Using this criterion to disqualify a couple might, for example, include even one incident that involves major injury or weapon use. The key would be that participation by a couple with a long-recorded history of prior incidents should be severely restricted. This would certainly be consistent with the increased trend in many statutes to recategorize a repeat misdemeanor domestic assault as a felony, subjecting the assailant to the potential for far more severe sentencing.

Mediation in this context should also carefully preserve the record of the violence that may have precipitated the mediation, perhaps in the form of mutually signed agreements in which violent episodes are described so that in case of a subsequent assault, the prosecutor will be able to invoke laws for habitual offenders or at least know the type of offender with which he or she is presented.

Requirements placed on the conduct of both parties also limit the appropriate use of mediation. Obviously, because a mediation program requires the participation of both parties to be effective, it is not appropriate for separated parties or in cases in which either party does not seek reconciliation (Greenstein, 1982). Similarly, it should not be used, even if both parties are willing, if one party is unable to adequately represent his or her interests. Should the proposed mediator believe that inappropriate temperament, past traumatic shock, or strongly ingrained belief in a master–subordinate relationship is present, an adversarial process with a victim advocate would be far superior (Lerman, 1984). These concerns have contributed to legislation in many states, which explicitly exempt domestic violence victims from required mediation in divorce cases (Hart, 1992).

In some jurisdictions, the use of divorce-related mediation in the presence of an active domestic violence restraining order has been hotly contested. Some mediation agencies such as the Court Mediation Service of Maine flatly refuse to take any such cases, because they believe mediation between parties with obviously unequal bargaining power is inappropriate (Pearson, 1997). Similarly, even the American Bar Association's Family Law Section Task Force, the Academy of Family Mediators, and the Association of Family and Conciliation Courts have called for formal restrictions on mediation in the presence of violence. In most instances, however, mediation remains available, although not mandated, even if past instances of domestic abuse have occurred.

Mediation programs also require a continued commitment of state and local funding. Too often, mediation and other "demonstration projects," announced with great fanfare by federal and state funding agencies, are started, proven initially effective, and continued for a time. In subsequent periods of budgetary austerity, however, the push for efficiency in terms that are easily quantifiable becomes overwhelming. Mediation programs are uniquely vulnerable to such disillusion because they are highly dependent on the qualifications and time commitments of the mediators. Degradation of results may easily occur if quantifiable measures of efficiency, such as cases per mediator, become the litmus test of efficacy. Unfortunately, accountability of mediation is low because of the necessary secrecy of most mediation efforts. Therefore, systemic decay caused by insufficient funding or a decline in organizational commitment may not immediately be realized.

Finally, implicit in mediation is the assumption that the parties should be able to compromise disparate interests to maintain a previously dysfunctional relationship. Those arguing that precedence should be given to violence abatement have directly challenged the implied primary goal of family unit maintenance. From that perspective, mediation is an attempt to address family maintenance concerns without changing the underlying

neglect of women's legitimate interests in self-protection (Stallone, 1984). Introducing the potentially conflicting goal of family maintenance may diminish the importance of ending violence.

There also may be a more subtle effect. Many battered women advocates fear that in the zeal to reach a mutually satisfactory accommodation, victims may be "pressured" into abstaining from aggressive or "provocative behavior," thus achieving the abuser's goal of dominating a relationship without the necessity of even resorting to violence. For example, we assume a mediator would not react well to claims of such "provocative behavior" as failing to adequately perform household chores; however, the woman might be told not to protest if the man does not do any household chores or stays out all night, leaving his wife to care for minor children. We know that it is precisely these types of conflicts that often precipitate many acts of intimate violence. Should the mediator tell the woman that she must be willing to agree with her partner to avoid a beating? In this context, what must be addressed is the inability of the man to resolve inevitable familial conflicts without resorting to violence rather than a "conflict" to be mediated.

Without overstating the point, it is critical that mediation should not be allowed if there is evidence of serious, repetitive violence. Otherwise, the guise of keeping a family together will further restrict a woman's autonomy, as well as the ability of the criminal court to further intervene. Similarly, a feminist critique of divorce-court-sponsored mediation has developed, arguing that the common practice of "mandatory" mediation in divorce cases, regardless of domestic violence, deprives women of their right to be recognized as victims of a crime and might even decrease their safety while the case is being "mediated" compared with aggressive prosecution of domestic violence (Gagnon, 1992; Hart, 1990).

Has Mediation Limited or Aggravated Domestic Violence?

The previous discussion clearly demonstrates that mediation in the context of domestic violence has public support, is widely used, and is far less expensive to the system than traditional criminal justice processing. What is less clear is whether empirical research has demonstrated the actual impact of mediation on participants. Although such limitations to court-sponsored mediations to date are real, empirical research has not found that divorce-court-related mediations, the most typical form, have increased the disempowerment of women or increased the likelihood of violence during or following participation in the mediation process. One study following a series of cases reported a steady and relatively sharp decrease in abuse during the year following termination of the mediation (Ellis & Stuckless, 1996).

A second comprehensive study used a variety of data techniques to explore how domestic violence issues impacted divorce-related mediation (Pearson, 1997). Pearson reported that through training of mediators, the presence of criminal court alternatives, and other safeguards, the chance of negative impacts on victims did not appear significant. As a result, satisfaction with the entire mediation process was not negatively correlated with a past history of domestic violence (Ellis, 1993; Ellis & Stuckless1996; Pearson, 1997, quoting Davis et al., 1995; Newmark et al., 1995).

BATTERER INTERVENTION PROGRAMS

The Role of Batterer Intervention Programs in a Divergent Offender Group

Although counseling and mediation share the distinction of being programs to divert offenders from the criminal justice system, they present some real distinctions with counseling programs, having one key advantage over mediation for more serious cases of abuse. The focus of counseling is firmly on inappropriate actions of the offender and the necessity of modifying this behavior. As a result, it may more predictably lead the offender to realize that he has acted inappropriately and needs to change his behavior in contrast with the conflict-resolution model implied by mediation.

Many judges now realize that traditional sentencing fines or incarceration have only had a limited and indirect effect on batterers, in which violence is typically unpredictable and irrational. Instead, a growing realization has been that sentencing, to be effective, must contain elements of batterer treatment. The way prosecution and courts have handled this, although by no means uniform, has been through pretrial diversion of offenders into treatment programs, or, after conviction, a split sentence that includes treatment component.

There is increasing evidence to suggest that criminal justice interventions are more likely, or perhaps *only* likely, to be effective when combined with a treatment component (Andrews & Bonta, 1994; Bonta, 1997; Dutton, 1998; Gendreau, Cullen, & Bonta, 1994). Furthermore, as discussed earlier in this book, we now recognize that offenders are a diverse group with a wide range of attitudes, personality characteristics, and behaviors. First and foremost, recent research has clearly disclosed that for many of the most severe batterers, the act of domestic assault is merely one manifestation of a pattern of violent behavior reflected by numerous arrests and convictions for violence against family members, relatives, intimates, acquaintances, and strangers. For this group, requiring batterer treatment with its focus on intimate partner violence may be of limited effect, given the overall problem of violent tendencies. To date, virtually all programs have ignored such distinctions and in fact only address batterer violence in the context of intimate relationships.

In addition, some batterers simply wrongly perceive that society tolerates (or has tolerated) domestic violence as part of an overall patriarchal society (see Chapter 4). The mere fact of criminal justice intervention in itself, regardless of type of independent rehabilitation efforts, might signify to this group that domestic violence is no longer acceptable. For many of these offenders, a continuing relationship with the victim or minor dependent children increases the importance to them of stopping unacceptable conduct even without formal therapeutic intervention. For others, rehabilitation, with or without incarceration, is more effective. For them, violence may be attributable to deeply rooted personality characteristics and closely related to substance abuse or dysfunctional expressions of emotions. For these offenders, it is necessary to address a much broader range of issues than typically encompassed in batterer treatment programs. Incapacitation as well as supplemental or alternative rehabilitation interventions may be the only methods that can prevent recidivism. It is unlikely that any intervention (short of lengthy incarceration) without effective rehabilitation will be effective (Dutton, 1988; see also Saunders, 1993).

In fact, without effective treatment, even if repeat violence by known offenders is prevented, unexpected consequences may result. For example, it is possible that offenders will adopt alternative and potentially equally harmful yet less legally liable behaviors, such as sexual assault, verbal aggression, threats, and stalking. Alternatively, they may simply alter targets to other family members or a different partner. The point is that merely increasing the fear of arrest and ultimate incarceration is unlikely to stop all forms of violence on the part of batterers without targeted interventions.

Characteristics of Batterer Intervention Programs

Batterer intervention programs generally operate on the implicit assumption that batterers change behavior after altering their attitudes, perceptions, and interpersonal skills. Whether such a program can be effective under a court order has not been fully documented. After all, treatment programs rely on a series of assumptions, some of which have not yet been empirically proven. It is assumed that character traits or inappropriate learned behavior patterns favoring violence lead to recurrent violent explosions. Most programs also assume that these patterns are consistent among batterers, or at least that batters will respond to a standardized intervention. From this, it is assumed that batterers can change their behavior but only after altering such attitudes, perceptions, and interpersonal skills through intervention of skilled counselors.

It is also assumed that the offender wants to be rehabilitated. If not, rehabilitation as a process may be difficult, and compliance may simply evolve into an offender's learning how to say what the treatment program administrator or therapist wants to hear, not real attitudinal change. Paradoxically, some offenders appear to have had their conduct reinforced by being exposed to other batterers whose retrograde misogynist comments might be routinely made and not effectively challenged (Harrell, 1991).

Proper intervention begins with an understanding that classification of batterers and the availability of appropriate programs for different types of offenders are critical. For example, it has been argued that those batterers found to be generally antisocial and suffering from serious psychopathology should not be included in standardized batterer treatment programs because they are unlikely to respond positively. When included in such programs, their victims may be in increased danger; they are led to believe that the offender is "improving" and they therefore remain with him during the treatment period (Gondolf, 1988). Instead, this type of offender may require long-term, extensive court supervision, coupled with more individually based treatment.

In a later study, however, Gondolf and White (2000) reported that 60% of "repeat reassaulters," which constituted 20% of program participants, showed no serious personality dysfunction or psychopathology. They argued that therefore batterer counseling might be appropriate for many of these seemingly high-risk offenders.

In Chapter 3 of this volume, "Risk Markers for Offenders and Victims," we demonstrated the covariance between domestic violence and a variety of factors such as poverty, substance abuse, personality disorders, and employment. Although the need for an individualized response to batterer psychopathology remains uncertain, few would disagree with the premise that additional treatment must be targeted for those whose battering coincides with severe substance abuse. Simply treating someone with anger control therapy is unlikely to succeed when the critical trigger is the loss of inhibition caused by severe alcoholic binges.

This may be significant because apart from batterer programs housed within correctional facilities, program access to counseling as a diversion from the criminal justice system must be restricted to those most likely to benefit from it. Courts have historically been reluctant to categorize batterers or otherwise recognize different types to try to determine the likelihood of success. Some programs use formal contracts to match offender commitments to change their behavior and attend counseling sessions with an agreement from the prosecution regarding his future actions. Within limits, such agreements may be tailor-made to the offender's individual behaviors or needs (Chalk & King, 1998). For example, given the strong correlation between substance abuse and domestic violence, they may contain intermediate goals such as cessation of substance abuse or prevention of any further contact with the victim until counseling has been completed. Naturally, the long-term goal of all such programs is to rehabilitate the offender, ending his propensity for violence. Therefore, effective programs should reflect the diversity among batterers (National Research Council 1998; Saunders, 1993). The prosecutor's office might handle case screening with assistance from domestic violence specialists or in an integrated treatment model coordinated through probation.

Similarly, even the timing of treatment programs has a significant impact on their success. Counseling ideally would begin almost immediately after a violent episode, when the offender feels most remorseful, most frightened of the criminal justice system, and most receptive to demands for change. There is a sound therapeutic basis for such early intervention. It is well known that the period immediately after the battering incident may see the defendant most amenable to behavioral change. Avoiding long court proceedings typically lasting more than 6 months from incident to conviction (and then longer for sentencing) may actually increase the impact of counseling and its ultimate chance of success. Consequently, most intervention programs now hold the offender accountable by forcing him to acknowledge criminal conduct, even if in the context of a "no contest" plea to a charge of assault before addressing the violent behavior.

Programs for clinical assistance to domestic violence batterers have been in existence for more than 25 years. One trend has been the direct involvement of the criminal justice system in increasing the flow of client referrals from judicial proceedings. By the mid-1980s, it was estimated that one third of offenders being seen by counselors came from court referrals (Goolkasian, 1986).

The increasing relative importance of court referrals has changed the direction of many programs. Mental health practitioners initially had maintained that the profound personality changes needed to eliminate deeply ingrained violent tendencies would be most likely when the client chose counseling, voluntarily identifying behavior as problematic. Although this may indeed be true, many batterers are not sufficiently determined to take or at least complete independent corrective action. This is especially true of batterers who, as a class, have often been described as denying the essential deviance of their acts and therefore do not seek treatment voluntarily. Instead, they appear to need prodding with the threat of court sanctions to enroll in—and complete—counseling programs.

Court involvement may be accomplished through the initial diversion of the suspect before trial or as part of the court's oversight (through probation) of his sentence. Diversion to counseling before trial also has been informally handled by prosecutors, formally through administrative procedures (as in the federally funded demonstration projects noted earlier), or even by statute, allowed in many of the domestic violence statutes.

In addition, court-mandated counseling is rapidly growing as a part of sentencing or as a condition of a plea bargain. In fact, Rebovich's (1996) study of large prosecutor's offices found that fully 50% relied on post charge diversion options suspending case processing while the offender is treated. Eighty percent of prosecutors using such programs believed that they were effective. It was interesting that 63% of the programs were pretrial diversions despite the fact that 66% of the offices described how they had instituted no-drop policies. Pretrial diversion was thereby often incorporated into no-drop policies, with fully 93% of the prosecutors reporting that successful completion resulted in all charges being dropped compared with only 7% demanding conviction, albeit on lesser charges (Rebovich, 1996).

Program Characteristics and Conditions for Participation

Suspension of prosecution is a critical element to diversionary use of counseling. In such instances, the criminal case is not heard or the sentence is suspended if the offender agrees to and attends required counseling sessions. If a counseling program is indeed deemed successful for a particular offender, then, after an established time—typically 6 months to 1 year—the original suspended prosecution is dropped and records of the original offense are destroyed or "filed."

Alternatively, if the offender leaves counseling or recidivates, the prosecutor is (at least theoretically) committed to prosecuting both the original and any subsequent offenses. The counseling itself would typically be handled by community-based mental health professionals rather than by probation officers; however, subsequent case tracking to monitor for new offenses, violation of terms of probation, or other court orders would be handled by probation officers.

The fact is that the act of battering indicates the existence of a potential for continued violence, even when batterer intervention programs are instituted. As such, it may be critical to distinguish risks for future violent by offenders based on a host of factors and risk markers such as prior criminal history and age at first offense (Buzawa et al., 1999), heavy substance use and psychopathology (Gondolf, 1997), victim input (Buzawa, et al., 1999; Hotaling & Buzawa, 2001; Weisz, 1999), and even batterers' self-assessments. Despite efforts to develop a valid predictive instrument that would best assess when treatment programs could be a safe substitute for incarceration, no such categorization is available, nor is one likely to appear in the future, given the vast array of factors involved (e.g., situational variables such as access to the victim, further substance abuse, offender compliance) that may prove to be intervening variables (Gondolf, 1997).

Counseling used for pretrial diversion should be considered different from counseling imposed as a form of sentence. In the former case, prosecutors must be cognizant of the responsibility to protect defendants' constitutional rights; this includes making certain defendants know that charges will be reinstated if they quit the counseling program.

In summary, batterer treatment programs cannot be viewed in isolation from a strong criminal justice presence enforced by the prosecution and courts. In an National Institute of Justice–sponsored analysis of batterer intervention programs, Healey, Smith, and O'Sullivan (1998) listed, among other things, the following relationships between such programs and the criminal justice system that they thought would increase the likelihood of program success:

- Expedited disposition of domestic violence cases by the system, so that if the offender does not remain in treatment, the alternative is stark and credible
- Specialized domestic violence courts with centralized dockets, again to reinforce the credibility of the system
- Rapid collection of relevant offender data to ensure similarity for diversion and that the type of program used is best matched to the offender
- Coordination of batterer intervention with substance abuse treatment with the periodic monitoring by probation officers of the offender's substance abuse status

- Attention to the needs and risks to children
- Resources devoted to minority victim safety, including victim advocates and others who can quickly intervene if a batterer treatment program is failing

Advantages of Batterer Intervention Programs

There are several distinct advantages of court-sponsored treatment interventions, especially as a diversion from the criminal justice system or as part of a split sentence. They finesse the greatest weakness of the criminal justice system its inability to prevent victims or prosecutors from dismissing charges. By selective use of counseling as a diversion, the finite resources available in the system may also be more effectively focused on recidivist batterers or cases in which the potential for serious continued violence appears greatest based on past or current attitudes and behaviors.

Pretrial diversion to counseling is also appropriate in the many instances in which the judicial sentence would undoubtedly be probation, perhaps coupled with counseling. In these cases, the ideal is to accomplish behavioral change quickly without incurring the heavy transactional costs to the judicial system or the necessity of labeling the offender as a convicted miscreant risking secondary deviance or costing the victim and her family. Finally, because it is considered less "punitive" then an adjudicated sentence and conviction for a domestic violence offense, the actual therapy can start literally months before treatment is imposed as a condition of sentence. As already noted, early intervention tends to be far more effective at facilitating long-term behavioral change.

Limitations of Batterer Intervention Programs for Diversion or Sentencing

Batterer intervention programs have certain costs and severe administrative limitations.

Treatment, other than on a group basis, is time intensive and expensive to an otherwise overloaded system. Meanwhile, research suggests that the most effective programs may require long commitments to therapy because differences in recidivism have been observed between shorter, less intensive therapies and a 9-month program incorporating mental health and substance abuse treatments for the offender and even assistance to the victims of the original abuse (Gondolf, 1999). Moreover, the costs of batterer intervention programs are greatly increased by the high percentage of offenders who do not complete treatment. A national survey of batterer treatment programs conducted in the 1980s reported program attrition rates to average 40% (Pirog-Good & Stets, 1986).

Furthermore, the cost of counseling is but one component of this continued case monitoring, and case tracking by probation officers is both necessary and expensive. When an offender loses contact with the probation officer or the prosecutor's office, it is relatively easy for him to push the limits of a treatment program, gaining little real benefit. For this reason, costs of counseling indigent offenders far exceed those for voluntary dismissals in which the prosecutor merely agrees to a negotiated plea followed by minimally supervised probation.

Many advocates do not necessarily understand this conflict over scarce resources. It certainly can be argued that more funds are needed and should be provided for shelters and services for battered women rather than counseling for offenders (Stanko, 1989). We recognize this position is morally difficult to refute. After all, the needs of victims of crimes should intuitively take precedence over those of an offender. The unfortunate reality is that shelters can realistically provide only a brief respite from abuse for some women, "harden targets," and sometimes help the victim make major life changes. If,

however, an offender is not rehabilitated, violence is likely to recur with either the same or another victim. For this reason, allocation of resources to offender counseling, if successful, may prove far more cost-effective than shelters or, at the least a good complement to them.

It has also been suggested that counseling could be more effective if it is part of a split sentence and coupled with incarceration to reinforce the importance of changing behaviors. Although incarcerating abusers may deter others by labeling this behavior as clearly criminal, surrounding abusers with other violent men in a prison environment may increase violent tendencies on their release. Indeed, some researchers have suggested that it may even teach them how to become "nonviolent terrorists" who are better able to commit abuse effectively and legally (Gondolf, 1992), perhaps by stalking or through other forms of harassment. Alternatively batterers form their own "support groups," reinforcing each other's behaviors.

There is anecdotal information that incarceration may indeed have these unanticipated effects. For example, we have been told that in recent years the Quincy (Massachusetts) Probation Department has had cases in which batterers continued to violate restraining orders and harassed their victims from jail by using friends, relatives, or other proxies. In fact, two incarcerated abusers have been indicted in Massachusetts for hiring fellow inmates who were to be released to murder their spouses (Klein, 1994a).

Impact of Batterer Intervention Programs

Despite the fact that many states now mandate treatment for men convicted of domestic assault or as a condition of deterred sentencing, it is currently difficult to give an overall assessment of their efficacy. A meta-analysis of seven studies examining the impact of batterer intervention reported no profound effect for treatment, with a recidivism rate of 32% for the treated offenders and 34% for the control group. Further analysis of research relying on police and court data for rates of reoffending found only a modest effect—14% for treated offenders compared with 22% for the control group (Levesque, 1998). A National Institute of Justice analysis perhaps best summarized current concerns:

> While numerous evaluations of batterer interventions have been conducted, domestic violence researchers concur that findings from the majority of these studies are inconclusive because of methodological problems, such as small samples, lack of random assignment or control groups, high attrition rates, short or unrepresentative program curriculums, short follow-up periods, or unreliable or inadequate sources of follow-up data (e.g. only arrest data, only self-reported data, or only data from the original victim). Among evaluations considered methodologically sound, the majority have found modest but statistically significant reductions in recidivism among men participating in batterer interventions. (Healey et al., 1998, p. 8)

One easily measured criterion is the short-term goal of program completion. It does appear that court-mandated programs have higher rates of completion than those serving voluntary participants. Rates for program completion may also be different because of the documented ability of offenders to deny the irrational and criminal nature of their conduct. Without a judicial order, batterers may enter a program during the "honeymoon" or "remorseful stage" of a typical domestic violence cycle. When this mood changes, the voluntary offender may quickly drop out without some form of court or administrative sanction.

Furthermore, there is evidence suggesting that batterers who are voluntary participants to treatment are more likely to reoffend than those who are court referred. Gondolf (1997) conducted a 15-month follow-up of 840 batterers in four cities and reported that 44% of voluntary participants reoffended compared with 29% reoffending by court-ordered participants. It is at possible that this differential offender response may be due to the threat of further criminal justice involvement by offenders already in the court system rather than the treatment itself.

Hamberger and Hastings (1993) summarized existing studies on the demographic profile of hard-core offenders. What is perhaps most disheartening, although not altogether unexpected, is that this profile mirrors that of the hard-core offender that the MDVE replication studies suggested were not particularly affected by other interventions such as arrest.

Although completion rates are themselves important, the longer term and far more significant goal is to prevent offenders from reoffending. All programs have criteria by which they determine program success; however, there is an increasing and positive tendency to use competency-based criteria rather than program completion. If a batterer attends half of a 26-week course or attends irregularly, he may not technically meet program completion requirements even if he did achieve the program goals of attitudinal changes. Contrast this with an offender who attended all sessions but who did not participate nor make any attitudinal changes, such as accepting responsibility for his actions. The latter would have technically "completed" the program, but success in changing attitudes is, at best, problematic (Bennett & Williams, 2001); it is hardly a resounding success if an offender continues to engage in violence despite having completed the counseling program.

Therefore, the definition of when a program ends for an individual—for example, at a set number of sessions or when psychological testing shows a likelihood of long-term personality or response change—affects success rates. Deschner (1984), Hamberger and Hastings (1986), and Hawkins and Beauvais (1985) all reported that the mental health of the abuser at the end of the program appears to be important to long-range prospects for success. Similarly, future studies of the effect of such rehabilitative programs should assess offenders to determine if individual characteristics of the offender—such as age, race, ethnic origin, prior histories of crime, and substance-abuse profile—significantly bear on rates of program success.

Although the two concepts are not the same, in addition to only being a measure of short-term success, program completion may provide a reasonably good indicator of future recidivism. Studies that have assessed the frequency of recurring violence as a measurement of program effectiveness have tended to show far different rates of recidivism for those who complete the program versus those who quit. Among program completers, reported rates of recidivism have varied considerably across different studies.

Hamberger and Hastings (1993) reviewed of 28 studies of the effect of treatment programs on batterers. They noted that dependent on whether success is defined as the complete cessation of violence versus reduction in frequency or severity of violence, rates of recidivism ranged from 4% to 16% to as high as 47%. It is also noteworthy that several studies have not attributed much of an overall effect of treatment on subsequent rates of violence (Taylor, Davis, & Maxwell, 2001).

Of course, it is possible that the variability in reported recidivism may be an artifact of several factors, including the studies' small sample sizes, the varying sampling techniques, the different measures of recidivism (including the time period being measured), and the fact that the people responsible for program implementation wrote much of the evaluative research, clearly presenting potential conflicts

of interest. For example, Dutton (1987) freely acknowledged that the subjects in his 1986 study were batterers whose participation and treatment were determined in part by their willingness to participate in the treatment program. The extremely low recidivism rate reported in his study may therefore be partially attributable to the self-selection of a group that was likely to be positively affected. Recidivism data in other studies originated in a national survey of violence abatement programs (Pirog-Good & Stets, 1986) or estimates of recurrence obtained from victims, batterers, and police reports. Thus, variability in reported recidivism rates might reflect not only probable success or failure rates of various programs but also the variance in treatment selection criteria and the sources of recidivism data.

Several smaller scale studies that compared recidivism of these two groups, however, have shown differences. Dutton (1986) and Hamberger and Hastings (1986) found significantly lower rates of recidivism among program completers compared with studies of Gondolf (1984), Halpern (1984), and Hawkins and Beauvais (1985), in which no truly significant differences were found between those who completed and those who dropped out of treatment programs.

It appears that until fairly recently much research in this area has reported the impact of treatment in isolation. This, of course, is merely an abstract of reality. Far more important is that mandated batterer programs may synergistically affect other aspects of the criminal justice system. For example, court-mandated counseling may well have an indirect role in mediating the success of arrest. Dutton and Strachan (1987) found an apparent contradiction in the literature in recidivism after arrest. They reported that studies showing that arrest reduced recidivism used short-term measurements of success, often 6 months, as in Sherman and Berk's (1984a)

MDVE. In their own study, however, they found that recidivism increased considerably, to almost 40%, within 30 months after the arrest, when no further criminal justice action or batterer treatment followed the initial arrest. This was compared with an overall recidivism rate of 4% in the group that received counseling after arrest. In fact, they found that 84% of the wives of arrested and treated men reported no further acts of severe violence directed toward them during the entire 30-month follow-up period in the group in which the offenders were subjected to treatment programs. Consequently, a great long-term decrease in recidivism might occur when arrest was paired with subsequent treatment (Dutton, 1986).

Therefore, Dutton's research tentatively suggested that although arrest had only a short-term deterrent effect, arrest plus an effective treatment program may have a long-term impact. Similarly, Ford and Regoli's (1993) research in Indianapolis found that court-mandated counseling as a condition of either diversion or probation reduced the chance of violence during the 6 months following case settlement (but before completion of counseling). It was no more effective than any other case outcome, however.

Types of Batterer Intervention Programs

We should also resist considering the category of treatment programs as a monolithic entity. Such programs can and do vary enormously in structure and even in their purpose. This obviously may affect the rates of program success. For example, the sophistication and size of a program and the type of counseling (group vs. individual sessions) intuitively would seem to have the potential to produce different rates of program success.

Gondolf (1984) has already reported that the number and duration of sessions are determinative factors in the odds of successful batterer treatment.

Currently, the preferred approach to batterer intervention has been to focus on matching offenders with an appropriate program (Healey et al., 1998). As Saunders (1993) noted, treatment programs are likely to be more effective if they are designed to accommodate different types of batterers. For example, a treatment program that did not effectively deal with alcohol abuse might not fully address the unique problems of an alcoholic who is abusive when drunk.

Although each treatment program is perforce unique, it is conceivable that programs may have differential rates of success depending on the qualifications or treatment pursued, style of the program (group or individual), and its length and duration. The dilemma is that current typologies based on personality types are not of great value because of both the comprehensive assessments needed and the lack of appropriate programs once these assessments are actually made (Healey et al., 1998). Furthermore, one study examining the utility of batterer typologies reported that many batterers were classified differently and that professionals had great difficulty selecting the appropriate subtype (Langhinrichsen-Rohling, Huss, & Ramsey, 2000).

Because of numerous methodological issues—including high attrition rates, lack of statistical evaluations, lack of control groups, and nonrandom assignment to treatment groups—few definitive conclusions can be made. Perhaps we are now in the long, slow process of moving from the relatively sterile question of whether treatment works to a more productive exploration of the efficacy of many possible interventions with particular types of offenders.

CHAPTER 14

The Role of Restraining and Protective Orders

THE INCREASING ROLE OF THE CIVIL COURTS

Civil courts also have a role to play in responding to domestic assault. Although such courts primarily litigate suits between private parties, they long have had the power to issue injunctive decrees. Until specific domestic violence statutes were passed, however, injunctive decrees or orders for protection in the context of domestic assault were infrequent. In fact, before the 1970s, women typically had to begin divorce proceedings even to be eligible for protective orders (Chaudhuri & Daly, 1992).

Other avenues of civil law were until recently also quite problematic for victims of such crimes. On its face, this was surprising because we have long known that the criminal justice system and attendant courts see relatively few cases of domestic violence committed in the middle and professional social classes. Although such violence occurs, it is not typically reported to the police or prosecutors or, until recently, even recognized by doctors and others who might otherwise be expected to demand intervention (American Medical Association Council of Scientific Affairs, 1992). For this comparatively small group of victims, assistance might be received from civil lawsuits for damages as well as from protective orders. In most such cases the defendant has assets and a job from which wages may be garnished to support a judgment. The theoretical basis for an award is easy to establish because civil courts, since the English common law, allow private recovery for claims of the intentional infliction of personal injury. Currently, private suits as well as motions for a protective order might easily include recompense for the costs of new shelter, moving expenses, medical care, and child support.

Not surprisingly, some attorneys have also specialized (or at least have agreed to take) civil cases for assault and battery or intentional infliction of emotional distress against victims. In several well-publicized incidents in Massachusetts, defendants, including the head judge of a major city in the state, were found responsible to their victims for civil damages. Not surprisingly, virtually all such cases were settled out of court under sealed court orders, but apparently for relatively high monetary amounts (English, 1992). Naturally, because of court backlogs and the need for the defendant to possess discrete seizable assets, such private lawsuits remain only a marginal resource to stop battering, at least for the foreseeable future.

Instead, the primary weapon of civil courts has been the gradual, inconsistent growth in issuance of civil protective orders. Because they were in theory always readily available, why has such a potent resource for victims not assumed a primary role in the control of domestic violence? As we will explain, the reality is that because of the influence of court attitudes and legal precedents, the latent strengths of such a proceeding have to date often been outweighed by their limitations.

The power to issue this type of injunctive order historically was considered ancillary, or secondary, to the court's substantive power to decide matters of law and try issues of fact. Because the issuance of such orders was not the court's primary purpose, together with the concerns just described, judges historically used injunctive orders sparingly. They were primarily initiated at the request of a prosecutor or by claimants in civil court to limit otherwise uncontrollable threats. Restraining order use was also limited because judges and prosecutors, as lawyers, tend to be process oriented. They remain acutely aware of the limited authority to issue prior restraints on conduct without notice, and also aware of the danger of infringing on a respondent's constitutional rights. As a result, courts routinely required high standards of proof, often to the degree of "beyond a reasonable doubt" that the respondent posed a threat to the complainant. One of the recent significant innovations in judicial responses to domestic violence has therefore been the adoption of statutes and policies encouraging judges to grant injunctive orders to immediately stop abuse.

There is virtually no disagreement that domestic violence victims need protective orders. In one recent study, 68% of women seeking a restraining order had been victimized by prior violence (Carlson, Harris, & Holden, 1999). Another study reported that more than 50% of women applying for restraining orders had been injured during the incident that led to the issuance of the order (Harrell & Smith, 1996).

Research in two Colorado counties reported that women filing for temporary restraining orders experienced an average of 13 violent acts in the year before filing. Similar findings were reported in Dane County, Wisconsin, where approximately one third of women filing for ex parte orders were assaulted at least 10 times in the 3 months before filing (M. Johnson & Elliott, 1997).

Beginning with Pennsylvania in 1976, all 50 states and the District of Columbia had enacted laws providing victims of domestic violence direct access to courts via protective orders by the early 1990s (Keilitz, 1994). Before that statute, women typically had to initiate divorce proceedings to be eligible for a protective order in a divorce or family court (Chaudhuri & Daly, 1992). Such orders may be permanent or preliminary in nature. Orders of shorter duration are called temporary restraining orders (TROs). They are also frequently ex parte orders, meaning that the party being restrained need not be represented for relief before a hearing for a permanent injunction. Civil restraining orders were in fact developed expressly as a technique for advocates of battered women to circumvent the reluctance of police, prosecutors, and criminal courts to properly handle domestic violence cases (Klein, 1996; Schechter, 1982).

The Process of Protective Orders

Protective orders differ from a criminal prosecution in that they are heard in general purpose or family courts and rely on the civil powers of the court to judge disputes or a specialized family court's authority to resolve marital and familial matters. Courts typically attempt representation of both parties at a hearing prior to issuance of any permanent or even preliminary injunctions. If the matter is urgent, however, such as the threat of immediate violence, courts may authorize ex parte orders to remain in effect for a short time without the alleged offender being present (hence, "ex parte").

In criminal cases, judges always had the power to issue "no-contact" orders in the context of an ongoing criminal case, making a civil order of protection moot. Although criminal orders are important to victims and typically are sought by victim advocates in the context of ongoing prosecutions, these are not discussed here. Rather, they might be more properly viewed as part of the case-processing strategy rather than an independent vehicle for victim protection.

In addition, although not directly related to their customary mission, several jurisdictions have given criminal courts the power to issue permanent and preliminary injunctions and temporary restraining orders apart from an ongoing criminal case. For example, as early as 1977, New York State gave both criminal and county courts concurrent jurisdiction over domestic violence with equal powers to issue temporary restraining orders and permanent injunctions. This has the potential to dramatically enhance criminal courts' ability to divert appropriate cases from the criminal justice system without relying on another court to assume jurisdiction.

Because the issuance of a restraining order is not a criminal case, civil rules of procedure apply. The proceedings are explicitly designed to prevent future unlawful conduct rather than punish past criminal behavior (Finn, 1989). Hence, the evidentiary standard is preponderance of the evidence rather than beyond a reasonable doubt.

Although, as described earlier, protective orders are customarily issued by civil courts, they are directly relevant to the criminal justice system. Violation in the context of domestic violence is now punishable not

only by a contempt of court finding, it also constitutes an independent ground for justifying, or in many states mandating, a warrantless arrest. In Massachusetts, a fairly typical state, violation of a civil order is a misdemeanor punishable by incarceration for up to 30 months in the County House of Corrections. In other states, violation remains punishable by contempt of court, the traditional mechanism for enforcement. This might be slow and cumbersome, but it does allow for severe punishment.

Several types of domestic violence–related protective orders have become common. In addition to general civil protection orders or TROs, which have been specifically adopted for domestic violence cases in all states and the District of Columbia, most states have enacted protection orders ancillary to a divorce or other marital proceeding. Although specific statutes vary, divorce-related orders require evidence of likelihood of improper conduct before issuing an order, typically for past physical abuse to the plaintiff-divorcee or the children. The broad scope of marital orders parallels that of the generalized protective order statutes. In addition, because these are coupled with interim custody and support orders, their immediate impact may be considerable.

Advantages of Relying on Protective Orders

For a variety of reasons, civil protective orders have the potential to assume a central role in society's response to domestic violence. First, the courts have far wider discretion to fashion injunctive relief, unlike strict sentencing restraints that are typically imposed on many judiciary proceedings. Most states confronting the issue have expressly provided judges the authority to grant any relief that is available and warranted by their state constitution. For example, courts often issue the following protective orders in domestic violence cases:

- Orders prohibiting further contact with the victim either in person, by telephone, or through the mail
- Orders for the offender to enter counseling
- Orders limiting visitation rights to minor children
- Orders to vacate a domicile
- Orders to allow the victim the exclusive use of certain personal property, such as a car, even if title is in the name of the restrained party
- Orders to prevent stalking

This list should not be viewed as exhaustive in that this is a court's equity power to fashion suitable relief. To accomplish this, a court may restrain any type of improper conduct and will not be limited to granting any particular remedy. Instead, it is meant to be tailor-made for the specific situation.

Second, protective orders give the judicial system an opportunity for prospective intervention to prevent likely abuse. This avoids the necessity of requiring proof of past criminal conduct beyond a reasonable doubt. This is particularly useful for cases in which threats, intimidation, or prior misdemeanor activity suggest that the potential for serious abuse is quite high yet the violence has not yet occurred. Hence, protective orders may be the best and, at times, the only timely remedy to prevent abuse from escalating by intervening before commission of an actual assault. This, plus the existence of flexible terms, has the potential for far better intervention strategies than the blunt instrument of criminal law.

Third, because violation of an order is now a criminal offense in all states, the existence of the order itself provides a potent mechanism for police to stop abuse—that is, the right to arrest and subsequently convict for violation of its terms. When made aware of a no-contact order, a well-trained officer can easily prove a prima facie case of its violation (usually just making contact) compared with the more difficult task of determining probable cause of commission of substantive crimes. As discussed in Chapter 7, federal and state initiatives now mandate that police departments keep records of such orders so that an officer can retrieve the information from a dispatcher or by computer at the same time the suspect is checked for warrants. Despite this, in our own research we have repeatedly found that many officers simply had no idea whether an order existed. Nonetheless, the use of protective orders makes it more likely that police will act decisively by giving officers an independent method for verifying recidivism and providing evidence that a victim is willing to pursue legal redress.

Fourth, when the police respond to a protective order, they may be more inclined to take action to forestall their own legal liability. Otherwise, the victim's counsel might later present such an order to establish that an officer failed to "carry out required duties." Although cut back by recent court cases, in the eyes of the officer, breach of this duty might make the officer and the police department potentially liable if an injury occurs and the order is not enforced. Even if legal liability does not occur, the officer's actions will be "second guessed," decreasing his or her odds of promotion.

Fifth, obtaining a protective order from a court may have the effect of empowering the victim. Specifically, an order will usually give her unfettered control over her home and other essential assets. Knowledge that the local police can enforce such an order should make the victim more secure and most offenders less likely to resume abuse. Such empowerment may be dramatic in that the victim, if assisted by a knowledgeable advocate, has the potential for far more control of the proceedings than in a prosecution. After obtaining a protective order, she can overcome indifference or even hostility among prosecution and court personnel. She can also retain more control by using or withholding the injunction, or paradoxically, choosing whether or not to alert police of a violation. Although it may appear to be illogical to obtain and then not actually use an injunction in a state that has adopted mandatory arrest and prosecution policies, this may be the only method for the victim to prevent the system from inexorably gaining total control over both the victim and offender.

Sixth, in many dimensions, civil protective orders incur far fewer victim costs than criminal prosecution. Specifically, the mere issuance of a protective order does not jeopardize the job of an offender as might arrest, conviction, or even possible incarceration. Although this might not seem important to an outsider, incarceration often interferes with alimony or child-care payments. Hearings themselves are far less likely to require a significant time commitment from the victim. Fear of offender retaliation should also significantly lessen in that harm from violating a protective order is prospective in nature. The victim might constantly remind the offender of what could happen if he violates the order rather than angrily remembering a punishment that has already been inflicted.

Seventh, divorce-related injunctive orders have an additional unique role. Counselors familiar with obtaining injunctive orders typically represent women in such cases. Family court or domestic relations judges and court personnel are also frequently knowledgeable about the scope of, and protection against, domestic violence. Even in no-fault divorce states, the family court judges make property allocations in the absence of the parties' agreement and decide contested custody cases. Under such circumstances, obtaining a protective order may deter future contact and thereby modify the offender's previously uncontrollable behavior.

Eighth, relief can be far timelier than in criminal cases. Because civil protective orders are meant to deter future abuse rather than sanction past criminal activities, there are far fewer delays from the time relief is sought until it is granted. In a civil court, a preliminary hearing can usually be scheduled within 1 to 2 days after the complaint is filed. In contrast, criminal hearings often are delayed excessively due to failure to serve the defendant, an overwhelmingly crowded court docket, or continuances—often at the behest of the defendant whose attorney uses delaying tactics. Even in progressive courts committed to handling domestic violence cases aggressively, the average period of delay between case intakes to disposition can stretch 6 to 8 months (Buzawa et al., 1999).

Ninth, protective orders can be useful if criminal case prosecution would be problematic. Examples include situations where the evidence of actual assault is unclear, if the victim would be a poor or reluctant witness, or when, because of alcoholism or drug abuse, she might be unable to get a conviction (Finn & Colson, 1990). Frankly, although we believe the needs of the criminal justice system should take a distant second place to those of the victim, the reality is that overloaded dockets may cause less serious or more problematic cases to be dropped unless aggressively pushed by a victim or her advocate. In these cases, protective orders may be the most realistic protection for victims, however imperfect.

Limitations of Protective Orders

Despite statutory provisions to use protective orders in domestic violence cases, a number of factors have limited their use. First, at least in the past, the primary obstacle was that the actual issuance of an order relied on judicial discretion, and enforcement was problematic at best. For reasons discussed earlier, many judges remained reluctant to issue decrees. Although the legislative intent may be to grant such orders freely when needed, courts have always considered pre-judgment injunctive relief to be a significant restriction on personal liberty and, at the least, ancillary to their primary mission of adjudicating contested facts (Quinn, 1985; Waits, 1985). They were never issued as a matter of course, and judges, in fact, required past commission of serious domestic violence before issuing an order when not expressly required by statute. Such reticence is natu-rally increased when an ex parte order of the type common in a TRO is considered and a respondent's constitutionally protected liberty and property rights are curtailed without effective due process (e.g., initially he may not even be told about the order).

In fact, the primary legal critique in the past of ex parte orders has been that they deprived defendants of constitutional rights. For example, although the reference may be somewhat dated, the motivation is clear in the following passage in which, in 1985, the administrative judge of the New York City Family Court circulated the following memorandum to all family court judges in New York City (Golden, 1987):

> The propriety of issuing such an order with-out . . . notice to petitioners raises I believe due process questions because this practice denies petitioners timely notice of respon-dent's allegations and an opportunity to prepare an adequate defense. . . . Although this issue is certainly within the discretion of each judge, I urge that you discuss the above . . . [to] be aware of the conse-quences of their issuing . . . orders of protection. (p. 324)

Constitutional arguments were at first based on a series of U.S. Supreme Court cases wherein ex parte prejudgment orders were subject to due process restrictions. Without exploring these in depth, the U.S. Supreme Court has long mandated that ex parte actions balance private rights being abridged with the governmental reasons for action, the intrinsic fairness of the existing proceedings, and the probable value of providing additional safeguards (*Mathews v. Eldridge,* 1976, citing *Fuentes v. Shevin,* 1972; *Mitchell v. W. T. Grant,* 1974).

A 1994 report suggests that such difficul-ties persisted. The authors did find that most petitioners (96%) who appeared at the hearing were granted some protective orders. Despite statutory encouragement of granting broad orders, however, petitioners found their requests for relief were significantly cut back (Gondolf, McWilliams, Hart, & Stuehling, 1994).

The importance of this is that when the courts significantly cut back requested relief; effective protection to the victim may be dramatically curtailed. For example, a no-contact order is nearly universally requested, because its violation is far easier to prove, and contact typically precedes active harassment or violence. The report found that almost 50% of victims requesting such actions were refused, however. Similarly, depending on location, requested financial support was denied for 40% to 88% of the requesters. This might be crucial for many economically dependent women. Even requests for weapons confiscation were denied in 88% of the cases despite obvious correlations to future violence. The authors noted that this could lead many advocates for battered women to conclude that the purpose of the law enabling issuance of protective orders was not being fulfilled (Gondolf et al., 1994).

In short, although the application of these laws may be upheld when taken to an appel-late or supreme court, this has little immedi-ate relevance for many victims. They may confront a hostile judge who knows that a denial of a preliminary injunction or a TRO is, in reality, unlikely to be appealed. Under such circumstances, judges have ignored the availability of TROs—at least in the past—and in one state even actively lobbied to have the law repealed (Lerman, 1984). Similarly, less than ringing endorsement of such orders by senior judges demonstrates that victims and their advocates may continue to encounter difficulty in having these orders routinely issued.

Despite the judicial resolution of any constitutional restraints on protective orders, recent studies have confirmed that many judges do not issue or dramatically curtail restraining orders (Solender, 1998). Such judicial restrictions are often the result of overly zealous interpretations of procedural requirements made especially difficult for inexperienced advocates (Zorza & Klemperer, 1999). Because of this, at least one commentator has termed the issuance of protective orders as "useless" (Barnett, 2000, p. 358).

A further difficulty is that, as a practical matter, the process of obtaining an injunctive order must both be initiated and pursued by the victim. Despite often being handicapped by a posttraumatic stress reaction and the necessity to take legal actions against a spouse, she may also face seemingly arcane procedural requirements and indifference— or sometimes even hostility of court personnel or the judiciary (Goolkasian, 1986; Waits, 1985). Similarly, victims often hesitate to file restraining orders because of fear of retaliation by the victim, fear of disbelief, and even fear of unfamiliar and unfriendly courtroom rituals (Ptacek, 1999).

As we noted earlier, to be truly effective and enforced, police departments must have obtained copies or at least have a readily available reliable source of the terms of the order. Although the victim might receive a copy, it may not be readily available, and the police might legitimately worry that they are exceeding terms of the order or it might have expired, thereby exposing them to charges of false arrest. For this reason, best practices should require court clerks to actually notify police departments. In fact, such computerized systems often exist, but may not be coordinated or kept current because they suffer from budgetary pressures and overall neglect.

Significant information gaps still exist as a result of these systemic failures. Although the 1994 Violence Against Women Act (VAWA) and its 2000 reauthorization have begun to assess and improve such systems, truly effective databases are relatively rare even as of this date. Fourth, there is still no uniformity of statutes or policies in granting protective orders, the availability of such protective orders for any particular case may be greatly limited by statute or, even more frequently, by arcane and often unpublished court administrative rules. Such restrictions are constantly in flux as statutes and administrative policies are revised. A list of some representative restrictions is useful, however:

- Lifestyle factors of the victim and offender often curtail the ability of granting an order. Several states do not allow orders to be issued to former spouses, and some do not allow orders to be issued to people who have never been formally married, even if they are intimates.
- Administrative limitations have been placed on the type of past conduct that may be used to justify imposition of a restraint. Some states have required proof of actual physical abuse and refuse to grant protective orders in cases of threats or intimidation.
- Limitations have been administratively placed on ex parte TROs—arguably the most important form of protective order given the strong potential for immediate violence. These continue to reflect the judiciary's ambivalence toward using what they see as an extraordinary remedy.
- Numerous procedural limitations exist in many states, including filing fees (which may be waived) or an inability of a victim to obtain an emergency order at nighttime or on weekends—precisely the time when

she is most at risk. (Finn, 1989; Finn & Colson, 1998)

Fifth, there is a real danger of such orders being inappropriately used to undermine domestic violence enforcement by claiming that society "has done all we can do" to help its victims, and therefore advocates should be satisfied. In reality, even when they are granted, there are real intrinsic limits to the efficacy of injunctive orders. Research has demonstrated that hard-core recidivists are not deterred by prospects of the social stigma associated with an arrest or even incarceration (Buzawa et al., 1999). Such offenders are unlikely to stop merely because of another piece of paper. The only effective method of stopping them is for a district attorney to determine that a felony prosecution is warranted, followed by conviction and incarceration, often for an extended period. Although protective orders stop many potential offenders, the use of protective orders for "hard-core" offenders may prove an illusory remedy, allowing many people to think they have solved the problem without, in fact, having handled the worst offenders.

In addition to these limitations, which apply to all protective orders, there are additional reasons why divorce-specific protective orders have not been used more often. By their nature, marital orders are limited to cases involving formal marriage, not alternative lifestyles. Even in the former case, many state courts require an aggrieved spouse to initiate divorce proceedings to retain jurisdiction. In addition, the entire no-fault divorce movement and the pressure of high caseloads encourage court personnel and the judiciary to try to limit clearly adversarial actions.

Despite lack of any empirical evidence, some of the judiciary (along with many divorce attorneys representing men in divorce cases) have expressed concern that women in a divorce might be motivated to allege domestic violence falsely in an attempt to influence custody or property allocation. Because of such fears, orders are not often immediately granted or are granted ex parte for only a short period. Although this might be legally justifiable, this does set significant roadblocks to their use.

Actual Use of Protective Orders

Originally, use of protective orders was quite restrictive. One of the authors of this book participated in developing and analyzing a research program conducted by the Massachusetts Committee on Criminal Justice and funded by the U.S. Bureau of Justice Statistics. This program examined domestic violence practices in eight randomly selected police agencies in the state from October 1986 to December 1986. Despite well-developed laws offering general civil- and divorce-related injunctions and official policy to use such orders, police rarely reported having encountered victims protected by injunctive decrees. In fact, out of the 86 domestic violence cases that the officers reported, only 15 protective orders were found to be in effect (Holmes & Bibel, 1988).

Even when an officer reported that a victim was protected by a TRO and a warrantless arrest could be made if terms were violated, arrests were made in only 3 of the 15 cases, or 20% of the potential offenders. This was compared with 11 arrests in the 171 incidents or 7% in which a TRO had not been issued. In its final report, the Massachusetts Committee on Criminal Justice (Holmes & Bibel, 1988) stated that because the arrest rate in which a court order was in effect was higher than without such an order, this demonstrated the efficacy of protective orders. Nonetheless, because TROs were present in less than 10% of the cases and because even in their presence a rather anemic 20% arrest rate occurred, the report's enthusiasm appeared to be premature. Of attorneys surveyed, 53% reported that judges rarely or never imposed sanctions against violators; however, 40% of judges stated that they often used sanctions (Gender Bias Commission of the Supreme Court, 1989, cited in Klein, 1994a).

Evidence suggests that this was not atypical during this period. In 1987, in all of New York State, only 25,000 protective orders were issued, compared with 2,000 orders issued in 1990 in a model court (The Quincy District Court of Massachusetts [QDC]), a jurisdiction of only 250,000 people. Meanwhile, in all of Massachusetts in 1993, more than 50,000 TROs were granted, a number that has been increasing at the rate of 10,000 per year (Klein, 1994a). The incidence of protective orders sought and granted appears to be as related to current events—such as spectacular instances of celebrity murders or stalking—as it is to the steady need for such orders. Ptacek (1999) suggested that media attention played a critical role in forcing the judiciary to be more responsive to domestic violence victims:

> More than anything else, it seems, judges fear public humiliation in the news media. They don't fear feminists or other advocacy groups: indeed, refusing to bend to the pressure of such groups is a mark of judicial pride, perhaps, especially in a state where judges are appointed rather than elected. One judge who trains other judges on domestic violence said that when she encounters antipathy for battered women or resistance to issuing restraining orders in her trainings, she responds with the question: "Why do you want your name on the front page of the *Boston Globe*?" (Ptacek, 1999, p. 61)

Despite this, a recent study confirms that restraining orders are still not enforced. Kane (1999) reported the effects of breaking the terms of restraining orders in two Boston police precincts. His report was unequivocal: The violation of a restraining order by itself did not automatically lead to an arrest despite its being required under Massachusetts's law (Kane, 1999).

When Will Women Use Restraining Orders?

There has also been research on the conditions under which battered women will be able to use the court system effectively to obtain restraining orders. Women who are economically dependent on their abusers obviously are at greater financial risk then those that are financially independent. Not surprisingly, economic dependence has been found to have a great impact on the victim's perseverance in obtaining a permanent restraining order (Muscat & Iwamoto, 1993). Similarly, the extent and frequency of abuse may so terrify women that the most severely impacted victims may paradoxically be the most likely to fail to obtain a permanent order.

There is also a predictable interaction between the demands of court procedures and the crisis attendant to being a victim of battering. It has long been known that to use the courts effectively, as with most criminal justice agencies, it is best to present an appearance of a calm demeanor, remembering exactly what has occurred and the expectations that the person has of the agency. In contrast, battered women as a corollary of abuse, often develop symptoms of posttraumatic stress disorder (PTSD). They may act forgetful, confused, and indecisive—conditions that directly contribute to being marginalized by many court personnel (McGregor & Hopkins, 1991). Similarly the unwillingness of many victims to discuss the details of abuse in front of an audience may, along with the time-consuming steps needed to obtain a restraining order, account for attrition by many victims (Fiedler, Briar, & Pierce, 1984; cf. Ptacek, 1995, who reported that embarrassment for many victims was combined with overall fear of appearing in front of unknown and intimidating judges and other court personnel).

Are Protective Orders Effective?

A number of studies have reported on the actual efficacy of the TRO process in preventing abuse. In an early study conducted before the enhanced enforcement typical of modern statutes, Grau, Fagan, and Wexler (1985) suggested that TROs, when used in isolation and without the full commitment by the prosecutors, courts, and police, were ineffective. The researchers interviewed 270 recipients of TROs and found that the orders were generally ineffective in reducing either the rate or the severity of abuse by serious abusers. Indeed, 60% of the victims studied were abused again regardless of the presence or absence of restraining orders.

A second comprehensive study by the Urban Institute also demonstrated that restraining orders do not always deter battering. In a comprehensive study (Harrell, Smith, & Nemark, 1993) of the impact of 779 protective orders issued in 1991, researchers interviewed both victims and batterers in Denver and Boulder, Colorado. Not surprisingly, the interviews disclosed that TROs were sought by 56% of those that had previously been injured, not those merely worried about future attacks. These typically were not trivial injuries, with approximately 40% of those injured needing medical care. The order did appear to have an impact among most offenders. Although most offenders tried to "work things out" or "talk their way out of the order," only 4% contested its terms. More important, according to both victims and batterers, 85% of the offenders subsequently did obey all conditions of the protective order (Harrell et al., 1993). The impact was not uniform for all provisions of the order. Instead, compliance was best at its core—the cessation of violence. In contrast,

offenders as a group largely ignored provisions requiring economic support.

In short, although abuse may have largely ceased, it is clear that the mere issuance of a protective order does little to stimulate the respondent to support his family. In common with most divorce or separation statistics, 88% of victims with permanent orders and 81% of those with TROs stated that they had not received any money for support despite protective orders to the contrary. In addition, a clear majority of men refused to honor child support provisions (Harrell et al., 1993).

Further, respondents contacted 75% of the victims with permanent no-contact orders. This noncompliance was statistically similar to the 80% of victims who were contacted when they were without any permanent orders. Finally, collateral effects were observed. Although physical abuse might stop, other behaviors that we might generically call stalking began: 52% of victims reported unwanted phone calls, 21% said they were actually tracked or stalked, and 21% stated that the respondent entered her residence in violation of the order (Harrell et al., 1993). Since the time of these studies, all states have implemented anti-stalking statutes that allow restraining orders for stalking behavior against intimates or former intimates. Their impact appears similarly discouraging, however. When women obtained restraining orders for the specific purpose of stopping an offender from stalking, the vast majority reported that the orders were violated (Tjaden & Thoennes, 1998).

Such behavior occurred across the board with few readily apparent victim-relationship characteristics predictive of success or failure. Although women with children were more likely to be assaulted, severity of past incidents and the relative duration of abuse were not closely related. Fully 93% of the batterers believed that the police or the courts would intervene if they did not comply—a clear requirement for deterrence. The real correlates appeared to be the man's behavior toward the issuance of the court order. When permanent orders were resisted in court by the abuser or when he attempted in court to obtain child custody or to remain in the house, recurrent abuse was far more likely (Harrell et al., 1993).

Although the Urban Institute study lent some credence to the potential for TROs, it was less sanguine about the actual prospects for obtaining a permanent injunction. Only 60% of those who had obtained a TRO sought a permanent order (Harrell et al., 1993). It is unclear why the remainder did not. Some presumably achieved all that they required through the TRO. Other victims, however, might have been discouraged by difficulties in court (restrictive court hours, limited court locations, high fees, and other judicial impediments to action) or feared retaliation.

The latter is a real concern because despite actual cessation of abuse, the study reported that most female victims (68%) would be hesitant to return to court if their partner violated the restraining order. This was largely in response to her fear of revenge by the offender. In addition, 58% said it "wouldn't help," and 57% said it "would worsen the problem." Also, the TRO might not be served to the respondent, a necessary precondition to issuance of a permanent order (Harrell et al., 1993).

A more recent study by Mears et al. (2001) reported that positive effects of restraining orders were not apparent despite the fact that seeking and obtaining a protective order represented active victim efforts to seek outside support in preventing revictimization. The researchers reported that there was virtually no additional protection from revictimization due to the issuance of a protective order if protection was measured as the number of days from original to second victimization. Instead, they found that there was no statistically significant difference between those receiving a protective order, those simply arrested, and those who had a protective order coupled with arrest for violation of a protective order. If anything, they found that women from low-income communities who obtained protective orders were at increased risk for revictimization (Mears et al., 2001).

In contrast, a study sponsored by the National Center for State Courts appeared to cast the outcome of protective orders in a much more favorable light, reporting that victims of domestic violence who were interviewed 1 and 6 months after obtaining a protective order, generally perceived that well-being was positively impacted by issuance of protection orders. Furthermore, this impact increased over time. Incidents of reabuse were low, and 95% said they would obtain a protective order again (Keilitz, Hannford, & Efkeman, 1997). Similarly, several recent studies of victim attitudes toward restraining orders said they felt more "empowered" by the restraining order process, but only if they were able to document the abuse via having a restraining order issued, thereby sending the message that the abuse was wrong (Fischer & Rose, 1995; Ptacek, 1999).

Perhaps the distinction between these studies is the how effectiveness outcomes were measured. If we examine "effectiveness" on the basis of preventing further acts of violence, little positive impact is shown by these studies; however, this does not mean that when reabuse occurs that police will ignore the subsequent event. In fact, the police and official reaction to the protective order might affect future abuse. In any event, other studies now clearly show that women feel "empowered" or "protected" by such orders, and the lifting of fear is itself valuable.

THE COMPLEX
PROBLEM OF REABUSE

A number of studies have documented the extent of the problem of reabuse even in the face of protective orders. This warrants further study as to when and why such reabuse occurs. One study found that more than 15% of all restraining order defendants were arrested for violating the orders within 6 months of their issuance (Isaac, 1994). Still other offenders presumably violate protective orders, but these are not reported because of victim fears of retaliation or loss of control in a jurisdiction with mandatory arrest or no-drop prosecution policies.

Grau et al.'s (1985) initial research suggested that aggregating offenders might mask two markedly different offender subpopulations. Although it is reasonably clear that hard-core offenders are not deterred, a different result occurs when analyzing the behavioral impact of those that were apparently less addicted to an abusive lifestyle. For those with less serious prior histories of family violence or in which the abuser was less violent, future acts of domestic violence did decline significantly.

A second study conducted in a model court tends to reinforce Grau's analysis. A comprehensive study in the QDC reported that in 1990, almost 50% of 663 male restraining order defendants reabused the same victim within 2 years; 34% were arrested for violations of restraining orders and 95% became subjects of new orders reflecting new incidents. Such substantial reoffending behavior appeared heavily correlated to age and prior criminal history with younger men and those with prior criminal history most likely to reoffend (Klein, 1996).

In all of Massachusetts in 1992, more than 6,000 individuals were arrested for violating restraining orders. Of these offenders, almost 1,000 were placed on probation. In short, these studies graphically demonstrate that

although our operating assumption is that court restraining orders should dramatically affect the cycle of abuse, unfortunately, to date, there is little empirical evidence that such an impact occurs for all types of batterers. A number of other studies have found that revictimization is a serious problem, ranging from between 23% to 50% of women who have sought protective orders (see especially Carlson et al., 1999; Chaudhuri & Daly, 1992, Harrell & Smith, 1996; & Klein, 1996). In addition, the 1997 Keilitz study, although generally finding that protective orders were effective (72% were not battered within 1 month and 65% were not battered at the follow-up), also reported that prior criminal history of the offender in a protective order was strongly correlated with both future violence in general and the severity of the subsequent violence (Keilitz et al., 1997).

Our discussion of the deterrent effect of restraining orders assumes that prosecutors and courts will actively enforce protective orders once issued; however, recently published accounts of excessive rates of dismissals of such cases suggest that such an assumption must be tested further. If it is found that the prosecutorial and judicial organizations fail to enforce such orders within a relatively short period, batterers, victims, and the community at large will know this is reality. Under such circumstances, deterrence will inevitably become less effective, and protective orders may begin to atrophy into a useless, even cynical vehicle to quell public demands for action.

There is not yet a consensus as to which factors predict when restraining orders will be violated and reabuse occur; however, several tentative hypotheses have been advanced. For example, Harrell and Smith (1996) observed that victimization was higher among those having dependant, minor children. Carlson et al. (1999) observed that revictimization occurred more frequently in lower socioeconomic and minority groups. Both of these conclusions may be due to simple predictable aspects of family life. If minor children are in the households, a batterer may take extraordinary risks to ensure continued visitation. Financial issues, especially court-ordered support, will exacerbate the offender's feelings of being wronged (e.g., being forced to pay support without visitation rights).

In addition, a consistent body of research appears to be developing that relates violation of protective orders to prior criminal history. Harrell and Smith (1996) found that prior offenders were likely to reoffend. Similarly, in his review of the QDC Klein (1996) reported this relationship. Buzawa et al.'s 1999 research, also in the QDC, reinforced the findings of the earlier Klein research. They found that offenders who had restraining orders had the most violent and abusive criminal histories and the highest rates of substance abuse, as well as the highest rate of reoffending. Although that study was, by definition, one that examined cases of reabuse, it clearly reinforced the perception that restraining orders might be effective for the overall population, but for the subpopulation of offenders with an extensive criminal history, it had little or no positive impact (Buzawa et al., 1999).

Research suggesting that protective orders are ineffective based on reoffending may be misleading. Women tend to take out restraining orders disproportionately when offenders have criminal histories of violent behavior (Waul, 2000). Keilitz et al. (1997) reported that 80% of those seeking protective orders had an offender who had prior criminal histories; Klein (1996) found that 65% had prior criminal arrest histories. Waul (2000) reported that women whose partners had a prior criminal record with at least one domestic violence offense were significantly more likely to obtain a protective order than women whose partners did not have prior domestic violence charges.

Similarly, Buzawa et al. (1999) reported that victims seeking restraining orders sought them against offenders who averaged twice the criminal history of the offenders whose victims did not seek restraining orders. A simple comparison of reoffending rates for those who did and did not seek restraining orders would not provide a valid comparison, at least at an aggregate level. Instead, this could simply represent an artifact of the differential population seeking restraining orders compared with those victims who did not. We hope that future research will clarify the role of past criminal history by isolating this crucial variable to measure its seemingly overwhelming significance. In any event, at this stage, it appears premature to conclude that restraining orders "do not work."

The fact is that it is extraordinarily difficult to determine generally the efficacy of restraining orders. We know that a substantial number of domestic violence victims who seek restraining orders will be subject to reabuse. We also know that there are some factors, such as the presence of minor children, lower levels of income, and, perhaps most important, past criminal history, that appear to predict the likelihood of reabuse and hence, in the broadest sense, make a restraining order "ineffective." We believe it premature to marginalize the role of restraining orders, especially because, as noted earlier, most victims believe that the issuance of protective orders does have merit. We are also aware that most research, at least until the QDC study, did not control for past criminal history in determining whether restraining orders were effective at preventing reabuse. Hence, any conclusion of the "failure" or intrinsic limits of protective orders is, to our minds, premature.

CHAPTER 15

Innovations in Judicial Processing and Disposition

THE ROLE OF SPECIALIZED DOMESTIC VIOLENCE COURTS

Specialized courts have been started with the primary purpose of handling domestic violence. From the earliest effort in Philadelphia through innovations in Los Angeles and Chicago, there are now more than 200 domestic violence courts, and the number is growing steadily (Karan, Keilitz, & Denard, 1999; Winick, 2000).

There are three primary reasons for such courts. First, when there is no specialized court, domestic violence cases can result in a series of uncoordinated, overlapping, and even contradictory cases. For example, just two acts of violence may cause concurrent actions in one civil court for issuance of a restraining order, a second civil courtroom for violation of an existing restraining order, criminal courts for prosecution of each separate offense (the original assault and each additional action are, after all, separate offenses), a court to hear issues of custody for minors, and finally, a court case for property and other disputes in connection with divorce proceedings.

Each of these courts typically has highly structured and often arcane intake procedures and operating rules. Hearings are held in different courts, usually in different buildings, and often result in differing, even conflicting decisions. Differences in procedural requirements, case knowledge, and even the temperaments of individual judges may confuse even the most motivated attorney—and be absolutely baffling to their clients.

Costs and emotional trauma for the victim, the family, and even the offender are greatly increased, and the certainty of outcome is clouded. The numbers of such appearances and their emotional costs for victims and their children can be staggering. One commentator noted a particularly egregious case involving a Kentucky couple that occurred during 1995–1996. Instances of the husband, Robert Graves, beating his wife, Karen, were the subject of 16 hearings in front of 10 judges in civil and criminal courts. In addition, three family law cases, including one for divorce, were heard by three judges and involved eight hearings. Richard, as the batterer, was enrolled in three court-ordered anger control and substance abuse programs, and advocates from at least four agencies tried to help Karen and her children. As the author noted, there was no evidence that any of the agencies or courts communicated with each other, despite Karen's recorded pleas that they do so. Ultimately, after 2 years of this, Robert killed Karen with a shotgun and then committed suicide. After this, the courts issued a report (D. Epstein, 1999). Fortunately, most cases do not have such tragic outcomes resulting from the abject failure of the judicial system to communicate internally. Nonetheless, the impact of the lack of coordination between courts and agencies is truly staggering, imposing court costs on the victim, her family, and as we discuss later, even the batterer and the courts.

Second, as discussed in Chapter 11, there has been an explosion of criminal cases plaguing our courts. Nationwide, the necessity of dealing with drug-related and street-crime offenses throughout the 1990s and now acts of terrorism in 2001 and 2002 has relegated misdemeanor domestic violence to low priority, resulting in pressures for case dismissal or inordinate delays. Contributing to this is the fact that domestic violence cases have become the fastest growing part of the domestic relations caseload. In recent years, new policy mandates, given to the police and prosecutors alike, have flooded the courts with new domestic violence cases (Ostrom & Kauder, 1998). Therefore, issues of court processing time have become of even greater concern in virtually all courts (D. Epstein, 1999). Even in a model general-purpose court, the average processing time for domestic violence cases was 6 months. This time lapse is highly significant because the majority of women who are revictimized are at greatest risk within the first month following the earlier incident (Buzawa et al., 1999).

Third, victim advocates have long maintained that court personnel still have a strong antivictim bias. Judges and their staff fail to understand the psychological, social, and economic reasons that some victims stay with batterers, may not follow procedural guidelines, and may not fully cooperate with efforts to prosecute a case through to conviction. This has resulted in concern that the court processing of domestic assault cases results in more lenient case processing. Educating and providing experience to court personnel in handling domestic violence is essential. In reality, however, a general-purpose court cannot be thoroughly familiar with every type of offense it handles. The institution of specialized domestic violence courts would effectively limit such problems by allowing a system to concentrate educational and training resources on a small cadre of committed personnel and allow increased scrutiny of serious domestic violence cases.

For these reasons, the more than 200 domestic violence courts in the country have removed domestic assault cases from general courts, which handle a myriad of civil and criminal cases, or from general purpose criminal courts. The typical method is to establish a family court or a court that exclusively specializes in handling domestic violence.

By definition, a specialized domestic violence court is an integrated system that handles both civil protective orders (and their violations) and criminal domestic violence cases. It provides for integrated adjudication of all aspects of the victim–offender relationship. It is not, as some might believe, a court that typically tries to increase the jail sentences of offenders. In most cases, these courts did not attempt to increase the severity of sanctions but rather to implement a rehabilitating approach toward sentencing (Crowell & Burgess, 1996; Peterson, 2001). Typically, however, formal arrangements are present to integrate the court with counseling, treatment, substance abuse programs and resources for victims and their children. Specialized court personnel are trained in coordinating case management, linking the current case to any related pending cases or those that are subsequently filed (Winick, 2000).

These courts have been found to expedite the handling of requests for protective orders and their enforcement. Personnel in such courts tend to be more sympathetic and typically better trained than those who handle a variety of criminal (and even civil) pleadings and actions. Such specialized courts have also become agents for change, both within their own jurisdictions and as a result of affiliation with national groups. For example, in 1994 the National Council of Juvenile and Family Court Judges, published the *Model State Code on Domestic and Family Violence* through the Family Violence Project.

This effort produced a suggested code that treated domestic violence as requiring early intervention, mandatory arrest for violation of protective orders and certain domestic-related crimes, and specified conditions of arrest; it also set forth the expected standards for prosecution and victim assistance by prosecutors. Perhaps because of the background of its membership, it also focused on the problems of child protection and custody in domestic violence cases, an area often ignored in other codes.

How Do These Special Courts Operate?

In 1991, in what may have been the first of its type in the nation, a specific Philadelphia courtroom was dedicated to serving the 5,000 people each year who sought emergency restraining orders after normal business hours (e.g., from 5:00 p.m. to 8:30 a.m.). Victim advocates were quoted as saying this single innovation reduced the time spent getting an order from 3 hours to 30 minutes ("Special Court," 1991).

Of even greater importance, these cases were, for the first time, being heard by specially trained masters, not police commissioners who concurrently heard bail hearings and criminal arraignments and issue bench warrants. Victim support services were provided by volunteers from Women Against Abuse (a local advocacy and shelter group),

who on a regular basis staffed the courtroom from 5:00 p.m. to 2:00 a.m., helped victims fill out lengthy forms and securing legal assistance for indigents ("Special Court," 1991). Such an environment intrinsically appears more likely to encourage victims to pursue requests for assistance. Although not as effective as the foregoing, another method of having such courts assist domestic violence victims during off hours would be to statutorily authorize clerks and clerk magistrates working night hours to issue restraining orders without the necessity of obtaining a judicial signature.

In another case, Milwaukee adopted an innovative approach for dealing with victims who had previously preferring that their cases not go forward. The city established a special domestic violence court in September, 1994. Included in the operations of the court was a procedure for highly structured, 90-day scheduling that decreased disposition time and ensured rapid case processing. Officials believed this would make victims less likely to change their minds about cooperating (or to be pressured by offenders to do so). In addition, victims would be less likely to be in danger from batterers if they could reduce the processing time for cases, especially because the court was committed to severe sanctions. Finally, city officials believed that conviction rates would improve.

In the past, in all New York counties, a victim could have her case heard simultaneous in family court, criminal court, and the supreme court. These courts each have their own judges, attorneys, and related agencies. Authorities in Kings County, New York (Brooklyn), tried another approach, implementing a specialized felony domestic violence court in June 1996. Officials intended to create an integrated response between criminal justice and social service agencies through a model court responsible for all aspects of domestic violence.

In response to the success of this court, as well as similar courts throughout the country, the state courts of New York initiated an experiment in 4 of the 62 counties of the state (the Bronx, Westchester, Monroe, and Rensselear Counties) in January 2001. Judge Jonathan Lippman, the state's chief administrative judge, initiated this reform. He developed a special-purpose domestic violence court using trial judges from the existing state supreme court (trial level). Families referred to such courts were assigned to these judges and were offered social services, such as victim counseling, in addition to traditional legal assistance.

An additional factor influencing this State Court initiative was that the New York courts had previously had highly successful experiences with special purpose drug courts for non-violent drug offenders. These courts were able to divert many offenders from developing a long record for serious felonies. There was also a realization that because of factors unique to New York's fractured court systems, domestic violence cases were seen by a multiplicity of courts, including the state supreme courts, surrogate of family courts, and other tribunals.

Judge Lippman said the expectation was that the number of total cases would dramatically decline when the system moved from its pilot phase to the inclusion of all state courts. At the time this pilot effort was initiated, there were 80,000 domestic violence cases, 20,000 contested divorces, and about 200,000 family court cases involving custody or "family offenses," including any type of assault, sexual abuse, abuse or neglect of children, threatening, and stalking. Judge Lippman estimated that combining cases could reduce the total number of separate court cases by about 50,000 per year. In addition, although unstated, was the expectation that, over the long term, the effectiveness of these courts would further reduce caseloads (Mansnerus, 2001).

Central to the establishment of all such courts was developing a core of knowledgeable court personnel empowered to provide a comprehensive, coordinated response to all aspects of family violence usually at a unified intake center. Knowledgeable clerks at that center assist personnel from various agencies and private advocates. Case assignment is then made to one judge, who becomes responsible for all aspects of the case. This is considered a necessary to dramatically minimize time needed to familiarize the court with relevant facts and reduce inconsistent rulings. Similarly, case-processing time is usually dramatically curtailed because the courts are not subject to the demands of other, higher profile cases.

Dade County's Domestic Violence Court Experiment took the approach of focusing on implementing dual treatment for both battering and substance abuse (Goldkamp, 1996). Unlike other domestic violence courts, their focus was primarily on the treatment of violent behavior and substance abuse rather than on the integration of civil and criminal cases or on providing additional social services.

What Are the Operational Needs and Advantages of Specialized Courts?

There are few intrinsic drawbacks to the institution of such specialized courts if provided with fair but committed judges and sufficient resources.

Judicial Requirements

The first factor in the success of a domestic violence court is that the public must be assured that judges are committed to ending abuse. They also must not be perceived as biased either toward victims or batterers. If not, the legitimacy of their subsequent orders would suffer. We suspect that this is not a major concern, because research has begun to report that these courts as a whole favor rehabilitation, not retribution, in their approach to sentencing (Crowell & Burgess, 1996; Peterson, 2001), but procedural safeguards and strict impartiality of judges must be maintained.

In addition to necessary perceptions of fairness, it must be recognized that an effective judge in a domestic violence court must understand the dynamics of domestic violence at a level far beyond that of simply knowing legal issues. Success or failure is not dependent on conviction of the offender given that the parties and characteristics of the offense are usually well known. Instead, it depends on the development of therapeutic jurisprudence in which the judge must not only dispense "justice" but also develop and supervise a sentencing structure that will rehabilitate an offender. This is complicated by the fact that offenders and victims usually have ongoing relationships, often intimate, and that the victim may not be at all committed to case prosecution, as discussed at length several earlier chapters. Furthermore, she may act in ways adverse to her long-term interests. Likewise, issues regarding child welfare and fragile economic and community support networks mean a range of options that might ideally be available are not practicable. Although a judge typically would dispense justice through sentencing, therapeutic justice entails the additional task of addressing the long-term needs of the victim and her family as well as the offender.

Resource Issues

The primary disincentive to establishing specialized courts is that additional resources are at least initially required to ensure the success of these courts. This has been demonstrated by the experiences of the Milwaukee Domestic Violence Court (R. C. Davis et al., 1998). If sufficient resources are not allocated, however, such courts would inevitably begin to develop procedures that would informally "limit" demand. The primary cost factor from the standpoint of many court administrators who must operate on highly constrained budgets is the high level of support resources that must be allocated to a domestic violence judge, which are far beyond those of most judicial officers. These are necessary to coordinate the complicated legal, financial, and treatment aspects of such cases. From that we must concede that if traditional measures of "cost per case" or "cases handled per judge" are used alone, special purpose courts are not as "efficient" as general-purpose courts. After all, the latter have the luxury of being able to balance their caseload between sporadic "crisis driven" work and the more prosaic and predictable motion and trial practice that constitutes the bulk of their workload. However, by not having multiple cases in the system and the increased probability of programs effective in preventing reoffending, the "savings" of domestic violence courts are significant.

To understand the comparative advantages of a domestic violence court in terms of total resources consumed, we must explore what limits are placed on a typical system using general-purpose courts. As demonstrated earlier in this chapter, one of the primary limitations involves overlapping jurisdiction in which the actions of a batterer may at times require the attention of several courts. This problem can be compounded by the fact that multiple civil and criminal cases may be present in different jurisdictions within a state or even in different states. Currently, databases are not sufficiently integrated to enable each case to be treated as an underlying systemic problem. As a result, victims and their advocates often do not have proof of prior orders, and batterers in one situation can escape attention as a multiple offender. Creating a specialized court, the mandate of which is to coordinate all civil and criminal actions related to a particular couple, inevitably reduces the likelihood of overlapping, inconsistent, and inadequate judicial reaction to chronic battering, thereby reducing the total resources needed to address the problem.

Although perhaps counterintuitive, the ability of well-funded specialized courts to rapidly process cases also becomes a major cost benefit to the system. We know the question is usually presented from the viewpoint of those who argue that given the inherent budgetary pressures in courts today, why should victims of this crime get extra resources to allow fast case disposition?

The answer to this legitimate question requires knowledge of the dynamics of domestic violence. An extensive body of research has documented strong tendencies for domestic violence to escalate over time. Research has also shown that repeat acts of violence occur quickly, usually within a month of the previous incident (Buzawa et al., 1999). Even if court personnel did not primarily care about the victim's welfare, rapid case processing tends to prevent multiple offenses, including felonies, from clogging their system.

Similarly, the training of court personnel and judges to handle such cases may prevent the phenomena of massive numbers of cases being dropped by victims without resolution of underlying issues. Although perhaps of most direct benefit to the victim, this also prevents the offender from engaging (and being held liable) for additional criminal offenses and helps prevent often-concurrent child abuse and other related problems. For these reasons, the initial investment in such specialized courts will not only better serve victims, offenders, and their families, but may actually save the criminal justice system money in the long term.

INTEGRATED DOMESTIC VIOLENCE CASE MANAGEMENT

Regardless of whether specialized courts are set up, recent efforts have suggested that the use of integrated case management for domestic violence cases may prove beneficial. Although initial reforms focused first on police followed by the prosecutors as discrete entities with their own individual outputs and measures of efficacy, the recognition of a dysfunctional criminal justice system has realigned current thinking to focus on systemic reform using enhanced coordination among agencies (Hart, 1995).

A number of initiatives, typically funded by federal or state government, were begun in the early 1990s to influence the actual behavior of responding agencies and the courts. These model interagency efforts were built on the developing knowledge of "best practices," which tended to emphasize coordinated intervention of all agencies.

Although many programs may be administered under the auspices of prosecutor's offices, they rely on the active involvement and sponsorship of the judiciary. An "integrated" response must be interorganizational, with dedicated teams comprising the prosecutor, the police, and probation officers (often court personnel). These teams must be willing to work with and receive input from nongovernmental service providers, including battered women's advocates and the leaders of shelters and batterer treatment programs. The key element for deeming a program to be truly integrated is an administrative commitment from all agencies to successfully deflect competing demands for scarce resources, to avoid acting unilaterally, and to inculcate in subordinates a real passion for addressing the problems presented by serious repeat offenders and the needs of their victims.

Once again, resource issues are important, not so much for the initiation of a "task force" as for the effort needed to "reach out" to others to whom the cause is but one of many conflicting time demands. Hence it is essential to provide specialized domestic violence training to sensitize staff to victim needs and to develop materials providing victims information on available assistance, the availability of temporary restraining orders, and the role of each agency in providing assistance.

Interagency responses are even more essential when officials are dealing with the problem of stalking. As stated earlier, it may be impractical because the activity in question may simply be a precursor to violence. One study found that police departments do not typically ask domestic violence victims about stalking when responding to an assault. Most police departments do not request officers to question victims about earlier experiences with the offender (Buzawa et al., 1999). This makes it difficult for prosecutors to recognize that an additional charge for stalking can and should be presented at the time of arraignment for the assault charge. In such circumstances, a vital component of success is well-developed coordination between police officers who can recognize and document a pattern of stalking and prosecutors who are willing to process such cases aggressively despite the lack of immediate injury. Otherwise, stalking legislation will be of limited efficacy.

There are numerous methods by which interagency coordination has been developed. Perhaps the most formal are those that are led by and based primarily on integrating all criminal justice agency actions. Although there are many models as to what constitutes an integrated system, one insightful report (Karan et al., 1999, p. 78) suggested that the following elements were essential:

- Interagency collaboration
- Comprehensive victim advocacy
- Effective prearrest procedures
- Effective postarrest procedures
- Multiagency intake
- Integrated case processing
- Effective prosecution and defense
- Effective treatment programs
- Monitoring and judicial review
- Integrated data collection and distribution

The focus of this list indicates the numerous ties by which one agency can complement the effective actions of one agency and how information about chronic offenders can be shared. Some early examples of officially sponsored integrated systems may help to illustrate both the shared and distinct features of each system.

Quincy District Court

As described in earlier chapters, the Quincy District Court (QDC) has been a national model for the systematic treatment of abusers, from initial intake through closely supervised probation and active collaboration with several recognized treatment programs.

The approach the QDC has taken begins with police policies mandating aggressive intervention. Consistent with applicable Massachusetts's statutes, the QDC does not rigidly follow a mandatory case processing approach (e.g., it does not absolutely mandating either arrest or prosecution through conviction, although arrest is the customary initial reaction). In this regard, it is different from some "models" such as those of Santa Barbara or Seattle where state statute or administrative decree requires that all cases be brought to the police department to be processed to conviction.

Although Massachusetts' statutes only mandate arrest on violation of restraining orders, police departments in the QDC have uniformly developed policies that emphasize proactive arrests. Unlike many jurisdictions, these policies are rigorously enforced. For example, past research has shown that in the city of Quincy, police arrest 75% of abusers when called to respond to domestic abuse incidents (Klein, 1994b).

Following arrest, the district attorney's office successfully prosecutes approximately 70% of those charged with domestic violence offenses. Additional instances of abuse or violation of a restraining order are also dealt with according to policies emphasizing judicial supervision of offenders. Judges in the QDC sentence most offenders to probation, organizationally contained within the court system (Klein, 1994a).

The QDC's probation department developed an integrated protocol for the supervision of this caseload that includes batterers' group treatment, abstinence from alcohol and drugs, and strict adherence to extant civil orders and intensive supervision (Klein, 1994a). Community-based supervision (probation) is the usual punishment for domestic violence offenses in Quincy. Those who end up incarcerated do so for violation of that court-ordered community supervision (Klein, 1994a).

In keeping with an integrated treatment model, the court supervision of treatment programs for offenders is extensive. The QDC uses two programs for the treatment of male batterers, EMERGE (one of the first such programs in the country) and Common Purpose. The duration of both programs is approximately 1 year with weekly meetings. Moreover, staff members periodically check with victims to confirm continued no-abuse.

San Francisco, California

In 1980, the San Francisco District Attorney's Office received one of the first national demonstration grants to improve the response of law enforcement agencies to domestic violence. Within 1 year, they had one of the first comprehensive law enforcement policies for domestic violence in California, the district attorney had established a specialized unit for vertical prosecution of felony domestic violence cases, and more than 1,500 victims had received legal advocacy and counseling.

The key in San Francisco's model was the vertical prosecution method used for all felony cases. A single trained prosecutor handled the case from start to finish, interfacing with the

police, the court, and probation personnel, thereby coordinating the actions of all other agencies. In addition, the Criminal Justice Advocacy Unit provided victim advocacy services for felony domestic violence assaults. Due to the success of this unit in handling felony domestic violence cases, the unit also developed an advocacy unit for misdemeanor charges.

Pima County, Arizona

Pima County (Tucson) has a mandatory arrest policy, bringing most offenders to the jurisdiction's courts. The courts then reinforce such actions through administrative decrees ordering mandatory filing even if the victim is reluctant or hostile. This is coupled with an enforced no-drop policy, regardless of the victim's statements or recantations, if the prosecutor determines this is warranted. Training on the causes and social control of domestic violence as well as the appropriate response is systematically provided to law enforcement and prosecution. Complementing these are comprehensive written policies regarding filing and charging offenders, preliminary hearing requirements, and written standards for pleas and sentencing. Detailed conditions for allowing release of offenders are also provided, including near automatic no-contact orders enforceable by revocation of the release.

King County, Washington

In King County (Seattle), domestic violence charges are filed whenever there has been a domestic violence call leading to arrest. Police forward an incident report to prosecutors within 10 days of the domestic violence call. In the case of a report but no arrest, the victim is contacted to inform her of her legal options.

This jurisdiction has also established a victim support project within the prosecutor's office. The Victim Assistance Unit of the King County Prosecutor's Office provides direct advocacy services to victims of misdemeanors. Its primary goals are to provide victim support, solicit victim cooperation, and enhance case survival rates. The unit is mandated to contact the victim and interview her as soon as possible after the assault. Victims are then mailed follow-up information packets on court procedures and the protections made available to domestic violence victims. The program also includes special volunteers to accompany many victims to court.

As in San Francisco, the Special Assault Unit of the prosecutor's office, with its own victim coordinator, handles the most serious felony cases. The unit also employs vertical prosecution methods (using the same personnel for all phases of the case from intake to sentencing) in cooperation with the Victim Assistance Unit.

COMMUNITY INTERVENTION PROJECTS

Alternate, or at times supplementary, approaches to criminal justice agency–led coordination have also been tried. Shepard (1999) described how Community Intervention Projects (CIPs) have acted to coalesce nongovernmental groups into effective advocacy organizations that in turn provide assistance to agencies in reforming, improving, and coordinating institutional responses. The earliest adopter of that model was Duluth, Minnesota, discussed in the following section.

Duluth, Minnesota

The first such system was the Duluth Domestic Abuse Intervention Project (DAIP; Shepard, 1999) in which a number of non-governmental agencies assisted in the development of an innovative response by the criminal justice agencies. Because of the emphasis of this volume, our focus is on the impact on the criminal justice system,

although a variety of improvements in the provision of housing and medical and other services to victims have been pioneered in this jurisdiction.

Duluth was, in fact, the first jurisdiction in the nation to adopt mandatory arrest policies. It has since coupled mandating arrest with an intervention strategy emphasizing a coordinated response from all elements of the criminal justice system. A "flexible" no-drop prosecution policy was adopted in which victims were subpoenaed into court and strongly told that the office would not drop charges merely because the victim and offender reconciled. In effect, the victim became the witness for the state. Each element—the police, prosecutors, judges, and probation officers— was given written guidelines for case processing.

The effect was to increase the level of awareness of key personnel, establish a preferred method of handling such cases, and ultimately to limit discretion of agencies to ignore such guidelines (either through departmental sanctions or via exposure to lawsuits). In addition, and perhaps of equal importance, an independent monitoring entity, the Domestic Abuse Intervention Project, was established as financially independent from the criminal justice system. It functioned as a referral and monitoring agency for batterers who have been mandated by court to attend education groups.

Innovative approaches to the treatment of batterers were also developed. Batterers were typically assigned to counseling or treatment programs. These well-developed programs featured audio-visual material to supplement classic treatment materials. Based on the success of the Duluth model, similar programs coordinating the activities of agencies and nongovernmental bodies were instituted in numerous other states including Minnesota, Colorado, California, Wisconsin, and Washington (Tift, 1993).

INTEGRATED COORDINATING COUNCILS

A third model involves setting up integrated coordinating councils to provide more effective communication, goal setting, and case collaboration (Shepard, 1999). Although the critical work (and determinants of success) for such courts are best measured at the local or community level, impetus for successful implementation has often started with statewide coordinating councils. These were established fairly early, often in the 1970s, and by the mid-1990s had become a regular feature in most states. In fact, the National Council of Juvenile and Family Court Judges reported in 1995 that of the 43 state domestic violence coalitions surveyed, 23 had already organized coordinating councils or task forces (Shepard, 1999). This effort has greatly increased since then because of the influx of federal funding that started with the 1994 passage of the Violence Against Women Act that both encouraged and funded such efforts.

These statewide organizations, often using funds from VAWA, in turn helped to develop local umbrella coalitions that often had large numbers of agencies participating in problem resolution. Problems were then addressed by "subcommittees" that would focus on traditional criminal justice activities (law enforcement and the courts) while other subcommittees worked on service provision for battered women, medical recognition and treatment needs, community education, and addressing specific needs of ethnic and immigrant communities.

Does the Struggle Against Stalking Demand a Coordinated Response ?

Although it is beyond the scope of this book—and frankly would be quite presumptuous—to try to develop a universal "ideal" response to acts of domestic violence, the problem of stalking may show how a coordinated response is needed to make an impact on many such crimes.

We have found that passage of anti-stalking laws by themselves, no matter how detailed, are an insufficient response to stalking. The sheer number of cases appears to be growing, and the headlines demonstrate with depressing regularity that society has been unable to cope with the problem and prevent high numbers of murder-suicides. As discussed in Chapter 3, many stalkers operate under a delusional framework that justifies obsessive actions, apart from all indications that such conduct is neither appreciated by the victim nor encouraged by society. In fact, in the context of domestic violence, stalking is the area engendering the most social approbation: The victim has clearly terminated the abusive relationship, but the abuser refuses to give up. Mere passage of anti-stalking statutes, as with those involving domestic violence in general, has not deterred hard-core offenders. Under these circumstances, it is critical that stalking be placed within an overall context of a cohesive systemic response.

To date, no research has studied the efficacy of the new anti-stalking initiatives nor empirically demonstrated the impact of coordinated agency intervention techniques. As in cases of domestic violence, past reforms outlawing stalking have not necessarily led to a decrease for the more serious repeat offenders. In this case, it is necessary but insufficient to have the police, prosecutors, and the judiciary act in common purpose to stop harassment. The foregoing must be coupled with education for victims with effective treatment or extended incarceration of the stalker. Experience suggests that both elements will prove difficult.

In addition, as we discussed in Chapter 3, there is a causal relationship between witnessing of domestic violence or experiencing child abuse in childhood and later manifestations of stalking or similar crimes. Although we suggest some methods to deal with stalkers in a coordinated sense, the fact is that long-term counseling of children from abusive families may be far more effective for society than later efforts to prevent psychologically damaged adults from acting out largely preprogrammed tendencies to stalk.

A Coordinated Approach to Stalking

As noted earlier, domestic violence stalkers are likely to constitute among the most persistent and potentially dangerous offenders. The response to such a group must be given careful consideration and be coordinated in both criminal justice and social welfare agencies.

As with all domestic violence–related crimes, police need to be on the front line. They will need both additional training from caseworkers and prosecutors and access to modern technology to cope effectively with the myriad forms of stalking. Training should entail the following:

- Knowledge of the characteristics of stalking and tendency of stalkers to escalate
- Existence of new statutory powers in preventing stalking
- The desirability of having the offender brought under court jurisdiction via filing criminal complaints
- Explaining self-help to victims, including "target hardening" (reducing their risk of victimization), residence security, and actions to take in a crisis
- The importance of periodic follow-up by uniformed patrol officers to monitor stalking
- Developing a realistic appraisal of the potential danger of a particular stalker, using, if needed, specialized officers or assistance of court-mandated counselors or forensic psychologists

Assessing future behavior and risk based on threats or repetitive, obnoxious behavior is qualitatively different from investigating a typical domestic violence crime, apprehending an offender, or other common police tasks. Despite this, it is a crucial skill with unique features. We suggest that each department use the training materials that are by now widely available and train officers on appropriate responses.

These would include having the officer develop an accurate risk assessment, ask the victim appropriate questions, and help her identify and document any escalating patterns of stalking, threats that are actually made, existence of protective orders, offender's past criminal history, or past instances of domestic violence involving the offender. In addition to their general responsibility to protect victims, it may be in the police department's interests to forestall claims of negligence by aggressively carrying out their duties.

In addition to training, when responding to a stalking, police should (as with all domestic violence–related offenses) have in place an effective information system readily accessible to all patrol officers containing data on the existence of protective orders, complaints for stalking, domestic violence–related convictions, and addresses and phone numbers of both offenders and victims.

We do not normally advocate specialized domestic violence units, believing instead that every officer should be familiar with common patterns of domestic violence, but stalking may present a unique circumstance. One particularly effective program (the Los Angeles Threat Management Unit) is run as a separate unit. Forensic psychologists provide support to assess the potential for violence. Although this might prove difficult to duplicate and is especially relevant in Los Angeles because of the concentration of celebrities, the volume and serious nature of requests for help in stalking may justify a specialized unit in many other cities. Prosecutors and judicial personnel, including judges, should also participate both by receiving training on the importance of early intervention to prevent an assault and by telling officers what evidence is necessary to bring charges and later to sustain a conviction.

In short, agencies must consider stalking a serious crime requiring interagency coordination before a tragedy occurs. Judges in turn will be challenged to understand and apply the full range of potential sentences for stalkers, including possibly demanding psychological (threat assessment) evaluations before release, releases made conditional on wearing electronic bracelets, imposing especially rigorous probation oversight, and adopting similar measures.

Because of their position, the judiciary and other criminal justice personnel share a unique responsibility to be public advocates and to make the public, victims, and potential offenders aware that the problem of stalking is serious, illegal, and will not be tolerated. Therefore, in addition to providing guidance to the police and rigorously trying key cases, they should consider whether it also their responsibility to increase community recognition of the problem by developing and distributing victim-oriented guides at no cost. An example of this is the pamphlet "What to Do If You Are Being Stalked," developed and distributed by the National Victim Center. As part of seminars to the community, these guides could be distributed to the police, domestic violence shelters, and hotlines for even wider distribution.

Finally, as in all cases, prosecutors and the judiciary should also be encouraged to make their operations more user-friendly, adding victim support where financially possible. In addition, although it might not be legally required in a particular jurisdiction, someone in the judicial system—that is, the probation department—should be assigned to tell victims when

a stalker is being conditionally released lest she is dangerously unprepared.

DO INTEGRATED PROGRAMS WORK?

The implementation of integrated criminal justice systems raises several theoretical concerns, primarily related to resource allocation and potential conflicts in roles and missions. As to resource concerns, the issues are reasonably straightforward. First, there is a need for adequate space and personnel for coordinating a forum, to ensure victim privacy for interviews, and to reduce lengthy delays during the intake process (D. Epstein, 1999). Today many prosecutors and courts already struggle to find adequate space in which to talk to victims privately, away from the offender, his attorney, and the general public. Second, current data systems, despite the influx of VAWA and state funds, still often cannot be adequately linked to provide needed, and often critical, information for case processing.

Third, not only is there a need for resources to provide extensive judicial training, there often is "burn-out" of line personnel, especially prosecutors, victim advocates, and even judges. Although the issue has not been resolved for the providers of services to victims in the judicial area, some courts now provide for the rotation of judges, solving the problem of burnout but probably also further increasing the costs and time required for judicial training (D. Epstein, 1999).

Fourth, there may not be sufficient funding provided for the additional services required for batterers, victims, and their children. If a therapeutic approach is attempted without the resources to follow through, there potentially may be a greater adverse impact than if traditional, more punitive approaches were followed by "traditional" courts. For example, many victims believe that once a batterer enters treatment, they are "safe" and are more likely to remain with him. If personnel needed to ensure quality treatment and monitor offender compliance are not available, victims might actually be in increased danger.

There is a second major theoretical concern with community wide initiatives: the potential conflict inherent in organizations with different roles and missions. In a system led by criminal justice agencies, conflicts are predictable. Clearly, police, prosecutors, judges, and probation officers all have, to some extent, different agendas and measures of success. For example, if police are required to devote substantially more resources to domestic violence, they might appropriately ask for similar resources to be allocated by other agencies. Prosecutors may believe that a full enforcement program in which all offenders are brought forward through arrest brings forward cases that are inappropriate for prosecution, thereby diluting even more an already limited resource. Even if committed to domestic violence prevention, judges may believe the scales are being tilted too far to weak cases with insufficient evidence leaving offenders without adequate due process.

The potential for conflicts in goals increases exponentially when non-governmental bodies are given decision-making roles. These conflicts can be with established agencies or with each other. For example, it is common for battered women advocates to argue for a full-enforcement mandatory arrest policy. As we addressed in Chapter 8, this may not be the best policy. In any event, it will cause severe resource strains on the entire criminal justice system. Similarly, it is not at all uncommon for conflicts to arise among groups seeking funding for victim support services (such as shelters, medical treatment, child care) and groups seeking additional funding for expensive and more individualized batterer intervention

programs that are more likely to yield success. In addition to simple conflicts over resources, there may be serious philosophical differences between those ideologically committed to treat every act of domestic violence as a proper matter for retribution from the criminal justice system compared with those that believe most offenders should be "diverted" from the system and "rehabilitated" without stigma.

To some extent, coordinated community programs have been able to "paper over" these fundamental issues. This has occurred because in recent years, especially since 1994, VAWA and COP (Community Oriented Policing) Office funds have allowed all agencies to receive some degree of additional funding simply through their participation. Although somewhat cynical, we believe that federal and state directed funding is likely to diminish significantly because of the impact of other social and world problems that require even greater funding (e.g., terrorism). When this happens, the conflicts in the roles and missions will be exacerbated because of an inability to fund all these programs at their current levels.

What Is the Real Impact of Integrated Model Programs

Assuming that the funding is provided and missions are agreed on, there are still issues as to the overall effect of even well-planned, comprehensive intervention programs. Unfortunately, effective valuation of a coordinated approach to domestic violence is still somewhat premature, although the need for rigorous study to determine what works, for whom, under what conditions, and at what cost is clearly recognized (Chalk & King, 1998). The devil is in the details.

As described throughout this volume, virtually all research to date appears (somewhat artificially) to evaluate the impact of discrete actions by particular agencies. The National Institute of Justice started the trend, of course, when it funded and then aggressively promoted the results of the Minneapolis Domestic Violence Experiment and the subsequent six "replication" studies. Reasons for this were simple: The designs were "experimental" and hence considered of greater "scientific" value than other methodologies. In addition, the economics-based approaches of "deterrence" fit a more expedient and punitive-oriented ideology that was prevalent at the time.

Possibly as a result of this factor for an excessive time, evaluative research as to the effect of communitywide reforms on the overall crime of domestic violence has been tentative at best. Far more studies review the impact of a particular type of policing practice without understanding that the impact truly depends on the political and social milieu in which it takes place and the interdependence of that agency with the actions of other criminal justice and even private groups. This perhaps has been the bane of research in this field. We may review many well-designed studies that report the result of quasi-experimental research but have yet to see many cases of in-depth, community-based analysis that can conclusively demonstrate which parts of a system function effectively, let alone with maximum efficiency.

Indeed, often the conclusions reached seemed, at least to us, to have implicitly rejected rival hypotheses without testing them, which a rigorous systemic analysis would have explored. For example, without specifying any particular work, we have seen many agency-sponsored evaluations in which "full enforcement" of a mandatory arrest policy was lauded because "statistics" showed that fewer acts of domestic violence were committed in the city. We have never seen any such report state that a possible reason for the drop in reported crimes was not the positive effect of the police but rather that when the jurisdiction

follows full-enforcement policies in many minority or immigrant communities, the percentage of victims requesting assistance could have simply dropped. These communities were, after all, already more prone to view police with suspicion. Then when victims became aware that arrest was mandatory and might have its own serious consequences, some simply would not call the police, preferring to tolerate the violence rather than expose a family member to arrest and prosecution.

Similarly, in the long run, increased arrests might largely become irrelevant in any particular community if prosecutors simply dismiss such cases. Even when prosecutors are committed, judges may treat these cases lightly for the reasons described in Chapter 12. To complete the loop, even when judges freely issue protective orders, their ultimate efficacy is often greatly compromised when police fail to arrest or prosecutors refuse to prosecute restraining order violations. Even how such programs are publicized—with an orientation toward the funding agency, practitioners, or fellow academicians rather than to potential batterers and their victims—may enter into the equation of a program's real success. No wonder a plethora of "rigorous" quasi-experimental studies of the impact of particular reform have led to inconsistent, often flatly contradictory results

The widely variant studies demonstrate the inability of researchers to clearly identify the one agency and their specific actions that could prevent reoffending. To gain a more comprehensive understanding, many researchers now realize that the study of a single action, such as arrest, by one agency, such as police, will be insufficient. As a result, there has been greater recognition of the need to study the combined effects of community-based interventions (Buzawa & Buzawa, 1996; Shepard, 1999; Steketee, Levey, & Keilitz, 2000; Tolman & Weisz, 1995).

Unfortunately, such studies intrinsically are far more difficult than the discrete work typically funded by government agencies. To be useful, they require intimate knowledge of the organizational and financial commitments made in a location and the social and economic milieu of the jurisdictions studied. Many are now beginning to recognized that previous study models focusing on an individual outcome may not be effective for future evaluation studies.

> The merging emphasis on integrated, multi-faceted, community-based approaches to treatment and prevention services, in particular, presents a new dilemma in evaluating family violence interventions: comprehensive interventions are particularly difficult, if not impossible, to implement as well as study using experimental or quasi-experimental designs. (Chalk & King, 1998, p. 59)

The need for evaluating a community's comprehensive response to domestic violence has begun to generate results, even if they have been inconclusive to date. Comprehensive community intervention projects have been studied for the longest period. As one of the first programs, Duluth was the site for some of the earliest studies.

The Duluth model became nationally known for its effectiveness at bringing about the institutional changes needed to facilitate a coordinated intervention. They were successful at working with the Duluth Police Department in the early 1980s to implement a mandatory arrest policy and a batterer treatment program. Shepard and Pence (1999) reported on institutional measures of success finding that batterers were arrested more often, prosecuted successfully, and ordered into counseling at greater rates after program initiation. Similarly, Gamache et al., (1988) studied three parallel programs and reported the same increase in the statistics customarily relevant to criminal justice agencies. Similarly, as described in detail in Chapter 12, Buzawa

et al. (1999) found in the QDC project that virtually all measures of criminal justice functioning—arrest, prosecution, conviction, and attendance at batterer treatment programs as well as high levels of victim satisfaction—were positive indicators of a well-functioning system.

Unfortunately, the end point of evaluation cannot be the successful processing of cases, that is, the number of arrests, convictions, or similar measures. Instead, we must look at batterer- and victim-centered indicia of success. This approach has not yet provided consistent or clear results.

Shepard (1992, 1999) examined the performance of a CIP and its relationship to reoffending over a 5-year period. Unfortunately, although the system might have an effect on batterers, she did not find that any particularly aggressive treatment modality had a profound affect on batterer recidivism.

> No combination of the interventions studied (i.e. jail time, civil or criminal court intervention, completion of the men's program, number of sessions attended) determined whether a man was identified as a recidivist. Men who had been abusive for a shorter duration before the program, court ordered to have a chemical dependency, abused as children, and previously convicted for non-assault crimes were more likely to be recidivists. This study suggests that batterer characteristics were more important than the types of intervention provided in determining recidivism. However, the impact of coordination itself was not examined because all of the men in the sample lived in a community that had a coordinated community response. (Shepard, 1999, p. 5)

In short, batterer characteristics, not treatment, appeared to determine the likelihood of recidivism.

Similarly, Buzawa et al. (1999) reported that although agency measures of effectiveness were positive, the actual impact on recidivism was really not that dramatic.

A coordinated domestic violence response was largely achieved. Victims and offenders dealt with agencies in this jurisdiction with shared goals and apparent resources to carry these out . . . despite this aggressive enforcement, recidivism rates remained quite high. (Buzawa et al., 1999, p. 164)

Similarly, several other studies that measured offender behavior have reported inconsistent results. For example, R. C. Davis and Taylor (1997) found no significant differences in the number or severity of new offenses as reported by victims. In contrast, Murphy, Musser, and Maton (1998) examined the impact of a Community Intervention Project in Baltimore, Maryland, on 235 cases in 1994. They reported that the number of court sanctions was associated with lower rates of reoffending. Recidivism was measured as new charges for battering, violation of a restraining order, or other domestic violence offenses, however.

In contrast to the somewhat ambiguous results of comprehensive programs on batterer violence, most studies have reported increased levels of victim satisfaction as a result of maintaining integrated programs. In the QDC, research found that as a group, most victims were highly satisfied with the actions of the system and each of the component organizations. The majority of victims (84%) ultimately did find their experience positive, did report their safety increased generally, and would call for intervention of criminal justice services in any future, similar incident. According to victim interviews conducted 1 year after the study incident, however, the majority of new assaults were not reported to the police—49% according to victim interviews, compared with 22% in official data (Buzawa et al., 1999).

Similarly, R. C. Davis and Taylor (1995) explored how comprehensive programs might lead to victims being more likely to call the police thus engaging the community

agencies most likely to ultimately help victims end abuse. In another case examining a pilot program in Westchester County, New York, it was reported that victim behavior changed in terms of their commitment to the system. Instead of widespread case attrition, victims followed through on 82% of the charges in the domestic violence prosecution unit. Of those charges, more than 94% of the defendants were convicted (Pirro, 1982). Nonetheless, the same study suggests that such programs need constant attention to continue to affect these crimes. It noted that other programs had reported impressive reductions of voluntary dismissals and an increase in domestic violence offenders' being ultimately held accountable. These attributes disappeared when organizational and personnel changes were made (Pirro, 1982). Clearly, even to sustain the relatively modest goal of victim commitment to the integrated process, agencies must not treat this as merely another public relations cause with short-term goals but instead as a long-term effort with the payoff measured by incremental victories.

Finally, in an evaluation that measured changes both on victim's attitudes and offender behavior, Orchowsky (1999) studied the Alexandria (Virginia) Domestic Violence Intervention Program, a CIP response to domestic violence. A series of victim interviews were conducted both in Alexandria (106) and, as a control without a CIP, in Virginia Beach (64). Victims in Alexandria reported victim satisfaction with services received as well as a decrease in nonphysical revictimization, although there was little impact on physical victimization—the most serious issue. These results, although based on a relatively small study, confirm the effect of such programs on victims but the lack of any dramatic effect on violence itself.

The overall lack of a dramatic reduction in future acts of violence perhaps should not be surprising. In Chapter 1, we discussed a recent study of domestic violence (Dugan et al., 2001), which found that 48 of the 50 largest jurisdictions reported only a modest and sometimes even contradictory impact on the relationship between money spent in handling domestic violence and future rates of domestic homicides.

Perhaps the cause of the inconsistent results that we have often reported in this book is not the failure of researchers to study the proper unit of analysis, nor a natural tendency to over generalize findings. Instead, violence reduction by the most serious potential offenders may be too much to expect of any system, whether or not that system is well coordinated. Indeed, we have theorized that attention to the problem and the development of comprehensive treatment programs and victim support services may work for a majority of violent families for whom the problems are primarily situational in nature or, somewhat less definitively, are related to substance abuse. Unfortunately, relatively few actors repeatedly commit most serious acts of domestic violence. We now know that these offenders tend to have extensive prior criminal histories and are typically violent toward a host of people involving intimates, other family members, "friends," and strangers. It is true and unfortunate that even the most professional and highly coordinated programs designed to respond to domestic violence cannot be expected to have an impact on these miscreants directly through rehabilitation or helping reduce family stress. For these individuals, the only reasonable "assistance" a system can provide is the concurrent development of "fast-track" and severe prosecution, followed by lengthy incarceration.

References

Abraham, M. (2000). Isolation as a form of marital violence: The South Asian immigrant experience. *Journal of Social Distress and the Homeless, 9,* 221–236.

Adams, D. (1994). *Boston Globe.*

Adamson, J. L., & Thompson, R. A., (1998). Coping with interparental verbal conflict by children exposed to spouse abuse and children from nonviolent homes. *Journal of Family Violence, 13,* 213–232.

Albrecht, S. F. (2001). Stalking, stalkers, and domestic violence. Relentless fear and obsessive intimacy. In J. A. Davis (Ed.), Stalking crimes and victim protection: Prevention, intervention, threat assessment, and case management (pp. 69–80). Boca Raton, FL: CRC Press.

American Medical Association Council of Scientific Affairs. (1992). Violence against women: Relevance for medical practitioners. *Journal of the American Medical Association, 267,* 3184–3189.

American Psychiatric Association. (1987). *Diagnostic and statistical manual of mental disorders* (3rd ed., rev.). Washington, DC: Author.

Andrews, B., & Brewin, C. R. (1990). Attributions of blame for marital violence: A study of antecedents and consequences. *Journal of Marriage and the Family, 52,* 757–767.

Andrews, D.A., & Bonta, J. (1994). *The psychology of criminal conduct.* Cincinnati, OH: Anderson.

Bachman, R. (1992). *Death and violence on the reservation: Homicide, family violence and suicide in American Indian populations.* Westport, CT: Auburn House.

Bachman, R., & Coker, A. L. (1995). Police involvement in domestic violence: The interactive effects of victim injury, offender's history of violence, and race. *Violence and Victims, 10,* 91–106.

Bachman, R., & Saltzman, L. E. (1995). *Violence against women: Estimates from the redesigned survey* (BJS Publication No. 154-348). Washington, DC: Bureau of Justice Statistics, U.S. Department of Justice.

Balos, B., & Trotsky, I. (1988). Enforcement of the domestic abuse act in Minnesota: A preliminary study. *Law and Inequality, 6,* 83–125.

Bannon, J. (1974). *Social conflict assaults. Detroit, MI.* Unpublished report for the Detroit Police Department and the Police Foundation.

Barancik, J. I., Chattergee, B. F., Greene, Y. C., Michenzi, E. M., & Fife, D. (1983). Northeastern Ohio Trauma Study. I. Magnitude of the problem. *American Journal of Public Health, 73,* 746–751.

Bard, M. (1967). Training police as specialists in family crisis intervention: A community psychology action program. *Community Mental Health Journal, 3,* 315–317.

Bard, M. (1970). *Training police in family crisis intervention.* Washington, DC: Government Printing Office.

Bard, M. (1973). The role of law enforcement in the helping system. In J. R. Snibbe & H. M. Snibbe (Eds.), *The urban policeman in transition: A psychological and sociological review* (pp. 407–420). Springfield, IL: Charles C Thomas.

Bard, M., & Zacker, J. (1974). Assaultiveness and alcohol use in family disputes. *Criminology, 12,* 281–292.

Bardach, E. (1977). *The implementation game: What happens after a bill becomes a law.* Cambridge, MA: MIT Press.

Barnett, O. W. (2000, October). Why battered women do not leave, Part 1: External inhibiting actors within society. *Trauma, Violence & Abuse, 1,* 343–372.

Barnett, O. W., Fagan, R. W., & Booker, J. M. (1991). Hostility and stress as mediators of aggression in violent men. *Journal of Family Violence, 6,* 219–241.

Barnett, O. W., & Fagan, R. W. (1993). Alcohol use in male spouse abusers and their female partners. *Journal of Family Violence, 8,* 1–25.

Barnett, O. W., & Hamberger, L. K. (1992). The assessment of martially violent men on the California Psychological Inventory. *Violence and Victims, 7,* 15–28.

Barnett, O. W., Lee, C. Y., & Thelen, R. E. (1997). Differences in forms, outcomes, and attributions of self-defense and control in interpartner aggression. *Violence Against Women, 3,* 462–481.

Barnett, O. W., Martinez, T. F., & Keyson, M. (1996). The relationship between violence, social support, and self-blame in battered women. *Journal of Interpersonal Violence, 11,* 221–233.

Barnett, O. W., Miller-Perrin, C. L., & Perrin, R. L. (1997). *Family violence across the life span.* Thousand Oaks, CA: Sage.

Bassett, S. (1980). *Battered rich.* Port Washington, NY: Ashley Books.

Batterer is walking time bomb. (1993, November 14). *Boston Globe,* p. 1.

Bayley, D. H. (1986). The tactical choices of police patrol officers. *Journal of Criminal Justice, 14,* 329–348.

Belknap, J. (1995). Law enforcement officers' attitudes about the appropriate response to woman battering. *International Review of Victimology, 4,* 47–62.

Belknap, J., Fleury, R. E., Melton, H. C., Sullivan, C., & Leisenring, A. (2001). To go or not to go? Preliminary findings on battered women's decisions regarding court cases. In H. Eigenberg (Ed.), *Woman battering in the United States: Till death do us part* (pp. 319–326). Prospect Heights, IL: Waveland.

Belknap, J., Graham, D. L. R., Allen, P. G., Hartman, J., Lippen, V., & Sutherland, J. (1999, October/November). Predicting court outcomes in intimate partner violence cases: Preliminary findings. *Domestic Violence Report, 5,* 1–2, 9–10.

Bell, C. C., & Mattis, J. (2000). The importance of cultural competence in ministering to African American victims of domestic violence. *Violence Against Women, 6,* 515–532.

Bell, D. (1984). The police responses to domestic violence: A replication study. *Police Studies, 7,* 136–143.

Bennett, L. W., Tolman, R. M., Rogalski, C. J., & Srinivasaraghavan, J. (1994). Domestic abuse by male alcohol and drug addicts. *Violence and Victims, 9,* 359–368.

Bennett, L. W., & Williams, O. J. (2001). Intervention programs for men who batter. In C. Renzetti, J. Edleson, & R. K. Bergen (Eds.), *Sourcebook on violence against women* (pp. 261–278). Newbury Park, CA: Sage.

Bent-Goodley, T. (2001). Eradicating domestic violence in the African American community: A literature review and action agenda. *Trauma, Violence & Abuse: A Review Journal, 2,* 316–330.

Berk, R., & Newton, P. (1985). Does arrest deter wife battery? An effort to replicate the findings of the Minneapolis spouse abuse experiment. *American Sociological Review, 50,* 253–262.

Berk, R. A., Fenstermaker, S., & Newton, P. J. (1990). *An Empirical Analysis of police responses to incidents of wife battery.* In G. T. Hotaling, D. Finkelhor, J. T. Kirkpatrick, & M. A. Straus (Eds.), *Coping with Family Violence* (pp. 158–168). Newbury Park, CA: Sage.

Berk, R. A., & Sherman, L. (1988). Police responses to family violence incidences: An analysis of an experimental design with incomplete randomization. *Journal of the American Statistical Association, 83,* 70–76.

Berk, S. F., & Loseke, D. R. (1980–1981). "Handling" family violence: Situational determinants of police arrests in domestic disturbances. *Law and Society Review, 15,* 317–346.

Berk, S. F., Campbell, A., Klap, R., & Western, B. (1992). Beyesian analysis of the Colorado Springs spouse abuse experiment. *Criminal Law and Criminology, 83,* 170–200.

Best, J. (1999). *Random violence: How we talk about new crimes and new victims.* Berkeley: University of California Press.

Bethel, C. A., & Singer, L. R. (1981–1982). Mediation: A new remedy for causes of domestic violence. *Vermont Law Review, 6,2; 7,1.*

Binder, A., & Meeker, J. (1988). Experiments as reforms. *Journal of Criminal Justice, 16,* 347–358.

Binney, V., Harkell, G., & Nixon, J. (1981). *Leaving violent men: A study of refuges and housing of battered women.* London: Woman's Aid Federation and Department of Environment.

Bittner, E. (1967). The police on skid row: A study of peace keeping. *American Sociological Review, 32,* 699–715.

Bittner, E. (1970). *The functions of the police in modern society.* Washington, DC: National Institute of Mental Health.

Bittner, E. (1974). Florence Nightingale in pursuit of Willie Sutton: A theory of the police. In H. Jacob (Ed.), *The potential for reform of criminal justice.* Beverly Hills, CA: Sage.

Bittner, E. (1990). *Aspects of police work.* Boston: Northeastern University Press.

Black, A., & Reiss, A. (1967). Studies in law enforcement in major metropolitan areas (Field Survey 3, 2 vols). Washington, DC: U.S. Government Printing Office.

Black, D. (1976). *The behavior of law.* New York: Academic Press.

Black, D. (1980). *The manners and customs of the police.* New York: Academic Press.

Blumstein, A., Cohen, J., & Nagin, D. (Eds.). (1978). *Deterrence and incapacitation: Estimating the effects of criminal sanctions on crime rates.* Washington, DC: National Academy of Sciences.

Boffey, P. M. (1983, April 5). Domestic violence: Study favors arrest. *New York Times,* p. L1.

Bograd, M. (1988). Feminist perspectives on wife abuse: An introduction. In K. Yllö & M. Bograd (Eds.), *Feminist perspectives on wife abuse* (pp. 11–27). Newbury Park, CA: Sage.

Boon, J. C. W., & Sheridan, L. (2001). Stalker typologies: A law enforcement perspective. *Journal of Threat Assessment, 1,* 75–97.

Bowker, L. H. (1982). Police services to battered women. *Criminal Justice and Behavior, 9,* 476–494.

Bowker, L. (1983). *Beating wife beating.* Toronto: Lexington Books.

Bowman, C. G. (1992) Commentary—The arrest experiments: A feminist critique. *The Journal of Law and Criminology, 83,* 201–208.

Boyer, P. (1978). *Urban masses and moral order in America, 1820–1920.* Cambridge, MA: Harvard University Press.

Boyle, C. (1980, Spring). Violence against wives—the criminal law in retreat? *Northern Ireland Quarterly, 31,* 565–586.

Bradford, J. M., & Bourget, D. (1986). Sexually aggressive men. *Psychiatric Journal of the University of Ottawa, 12,* 169–173.

Bradley v. State 1 Miss. (1 Walker) 156 (1824).

Braga, A. A., Weisburd, D. L., Waring, E. J., Mazerolle, L. G., Spelman, W., & Gajewski, F. (1999). Problem-oriented policing in violent crime places: A randomized controlled experiment. *Criminology, 37*(3), 541–580.

Breedlove, R., Sandker, D. M., Kennish, J. W., & Sawtell, R. K. (1977). Domestic violence and the police: Kansas City. In M. Wilt & J. Bannon (Eds.), *Domestic violence and the police: Studies in Detroit and Kansas City*. Washington, DC: Police Foundation.

Breslau, N., Davis, G.C., Andreski, P., & Peterson, E. (1991). Traumatic events and posttraumatic stress disorder in an urban population of young adults. *Archives of General Psychiatry, 48*, 216–222.

Brookoff, D. (1997). Drugs, alcohol and domestic violence in Memphis. National Institute of Justice Research Preview. Washington, DC: U.S. Department of Justice.

Brown, S. (1984). Police responses to wife beating: Neglect of a crime of violence. *Journal of Criminal Justice, 12*, 277–288.

Browne, A., Salomon, A., & Bassuk, S. (1999). The impact of recent partner violence on poor women's capacity to maintain work. *Violence Against Women, 5*, 393–426.

Bruno v. Codd, 396 N.Y.S. 2nd 974, NY, Sup Ct (1977). Reversed in part 407 N.Y.S. 2nd 105 (1978).

Buchanan, D., & Perry, P. (1985). Attitudes of police recruits toward domestic disturbances: An evaluation of family crisis intervention training. *Journal of Criminal Justice, 13*, 561–572.

Bui, H. N., & Morash, M. (1999). Domestic violence in the Vietnamese immigrant Community: An exploratory study. *Violence Against Women, 5*, 769–795.

Burgess, A. W., Baker, T., Greening, D., Hartman, C., Burgess, A. G., Douglas, J., & Halloran, R. (1997). Stalking behaviors within domestic violence. *Journal of Family Violence, 12*, 389–403.

Burris, C. A., & Jaffe, P. (1983). Wife abuse as a crime: The impact of police laying charges. *Canadian Journal of Criminology, 25*, 309–318.

Burt, M. R., Newmark, L. C., Jacobs, L. K., & Harrell, A. V. (1998, July). *1998 Report: Evaluation of the STOP Formula Grants Under the Violence Against Women Act of 1994*. Washington, DC: Urban Institute.

Buzawa, E. (1978). *Traditional responses to domestic disturbances*. Paper presented at the Michigan Sociological Association, Detroit, MI.

Buzawa, E. (1982). Police officer response to domestic violence legislation in Michigan. *Journal of Police Science and Administration, 10*, 415–424.

Buzawa, E., & Austin, T. (1993). Determining police response to domestic violence victims. *American Behavioral Scientist, 36*, 610–623.

Buzawa, E., Austin, T., & Buzawa, C. (1995). Responding to crimes of violence against women: Gender differences vs. organizational imperatives. *Crime & Delinquency, 41*, 443–466.

Buzawa, E., & Buzawa, C. (1985). Legislative trends in the criminal justice response to domestic violence. In A. Lincoln & M. Straus (Eds.), *Crime and the family*. New York: Charles C Thomas.

Buzawa, E., & Buzawa, C. (Eds.). (1990). *Domestic violence: The criminal justice response*. Westwood, CT: Auburn House.

Buzawa, E. S., & Buzawa, C. G. (1996). *Domestic violence: The criminal justice response* (2nd ed.). Thousand Oaks, CA: Sage.

Buzawa, E., & Hotaling, G. (2000, September). *The police response to domestic violence calls for assistance in three Massachusetts towns: Final report*. Washington, DC: National Institute of Justice.

Buzawa, E., & Hotaling, G. (2001, June), *An examination of assaults within the jurisdiction of Orange district court: Final Report*. Washington, DC: National Institute of Justice.

Buzawa, E., Hotaling, G., Klein, A., & Byrne, J. (1999, July). *Response to domestic violence in a pro-active court setting: Final Report.* Washington, DC: National Institute of Justice.

Byrne, C. A., Arias, I., & Lyons, C. M. (1993). *Attributions for partner behavior in violent and nonviolent couples.* Paper presented at the annual meeting of the Southeastern Psychological Association, Atlanta, GA.

Byrne, C., Kilpatrick, D., Howley, S., & Beatty, D. (1999). Female victims of partner versus nonpartner violence: Experiences with the criminal justice system. *Criminal Justice and Behavior, 26,* 275–292.

CA A 363 (1991).

CA A 226 (1993).

CA S 178 (1993).

Caesar, P. L., & Hamberger, L. K. (Eds.). (1989). *Treating men who batter.* New York: Springer.

Cahn, N. (1992). Prosecuting domestic violence crimes. In E. Buzawa & C. Buzawa (Eds.), *Domestic violence: The changing criminal justice response* (pp. 95–112). Westwood, CT: Auburn House.

Cahn, N., & Lerman, L. (1991). Prosecuting woman abuse. In M. Steinman (Ed.), *Woman battering: Policy responses* (pp. 95–112). Cincinnati, OH: Anderson Publishing and Academy of Criminal Justice Sciences.

California Gender Bias Task Force. (1996). *Achieving equal justice for women and men in the courts. The draft report of the Judicial Advisory Committee on Gender Bias in the Courts.* San Francisco: Access and Fairness Advisory Committee, Administrative Office of the Courts.

Campbell, J. C., Kub, J. E., Belknap, R. A., & Templin, T. N. (1997). Predictors of depression in battered women. *Violence Against Women, 3,* 271–293.

Campbell, J. C., & Soeken, K. L. (1999). Women's responses to battering over time. *Journal of Interpersonal Violence, 14,* 21–40.

Cannavale, F., & Falcon, W. (1986). *Improving witness cooperation.* Washington, DC: Government Printing Office.

Canton v. Harris 109 S Ct 1197. (1989).

Carlson, B. E. (1984). Children's observations of interpersonal violence. In A. Roberts (Ed.), *Battered women and their families: Intervention strategies and treatment programs.* New York: Springer.

Carlson, B. E. (1991). Outcomes of physical abuse and observations of marital violence among adolescents in placement. *Journal of Interpersonal Violence, 6,* 526–534.

Carlson, B. E. (2000). Children exposed to intimate partner violence: Research findings and implications for intervention. *Trauma, Violence and Abuse: A Review Journal, 1,* 321–342.

Carlson, M. J., Harris, S. D., & Holden, G. W. (1999). Protective orders and domestic violence: Risk factors for re-abuse. *Journal of Family Violence, 14,* 205–226.

Carmody, D. C., & Williams, K. R. (1987). Wife assault and perceptions of sanctions. *Violence and Victims, 2,* 25–39.

Chalk, R., & King, P. A. (1998). *Violence in families: Assessing prevention and treatment programs.* Washington, DC: National Academy Press.

Chaney, C. K., & Saltzstein, G. H. (1998). Democratic control and bureaucratic responsiveness: The police and domestic violence. *American Journal of Political Science, 42,* 745–768.

Chaudhuri, M., & Daly, K. (1992). Do restraining orders help? Battered women's experience with male violence and legal process. In E. Buzawa & C. Buzawa (Eds.), *Domestic violence: The changing criminal justice response* (pp. 227–254). Westwood, CT: Auburn House.

Coates, C. J., & Leong, D. J. (1980). *Conflict and communication for women and men in battering relationships.* Denver Anti-Crime Council. Washington, DC: Department of Justice, LEAA.

Coates, C. J., Leong, D. J., & Lindsey, M. (1997, July). *Personality differences among batterers voluntarily seeking treatment and those ordered to treatment by the court.* Paper presented at the Third National Family Violence Research Conference, Durham, NH.

Cobb, S. (1992, May). *The domestication of violence in mediation: The social construction of disciplinary power in law.* Paper presented at the Law and Society Conference, Philadelphia, PA.

Cohen, L. E., & Felson, M. (1979). Social change and crime rate trends: A routine activities approach. *American Sociological Review, 44,* 588–608.

Cohen, M., Miller, T., & Wiersema, B. (1995). *Crime in the United States: Victim costs and consequences: Final report.* Washington, DC: U.S. Department of Justice.

Cohn, E., & Sherman, L. (1987). *Police policy on domestic violence 1986: A national survey* (Report 5). Washington, DC: Crime Control Institute.

Coker, D. (2000). Shifting power for battered women: Law, material resources, and poor women of color. *U.C. Davis Law Review, 33,* 1009–1055.

Coker, D. (2001). Feminism and the criminal law: Crime control and feminist law reform in domestic violence law: A critical review. *Buffalo Criminal Law Review, 4,* 801–848.

Cole, G. (1984). The decision to prosecute. In G. Cole (Ed.), *Criminal justice: Law and politics* (5th ed.). Monterey, CA: Brooks/Cole.

Coleman, D. H., & Straus, M. A. (1986). Marital power, conflict, and violence in a nationally representative sample of American couples. *Violence and Victims, 1,* 141–157.

Coleman, F. (1997). Stalking behavior and the cycle of domestic violence. *Journal of Interpersonal Violence, 12,* 420–432.

Coleman, F., & Straus, M. (1983). Alcohol abuse and family violence. In E. Gottheil, K. A. Druley, T. E. Skoloda, & H. M. Waxman (Eds.), *Alcohol, drug abuse, and aggression* (pp. 104–124). Springfield, IL. Charles C Thomas.

Congressional Record. (1980). 126 Cong. Rec. 24, 120.

Connecticut State Police. (2000). 1999 data. Middletown, CT: Crime Analysis Unit.

Corvo, K. N. (1992). Attachment and violence in the families of origina of domestically violent men. *Dissertation Abstracts International, 54,* 1950A.

Coulter, M. L., Kuehnle, K., Byers, R., & Alfonso, M. (1999). Police-reporting behavior and victim-police interactions as described by women in a domestic violence shelter. *Journal of Interpersonal Violence, 14,* 1290–1299.

Crank, J. P. (1998). *Understanding police culture.* Cincinnati, OH: Anderson.

Cretney, A., & Davis, G. (1997). Prosecuting domestic assault: Victims failing courts or courts failing victims? *The Howard Journal, 36,* 146–157.

Crowell, N. A., & Burgess, A. W. (1996). *Understanding violence against women.* Washington, DC: National Academy Press.

Cupach, W. R., & Spitzberg, B. H. (1998). Obsessive relational intrusion: Incidence, perceived severity and coping. *Violence and Victims, 15,* 357–372.

Cupach, W. R., & Spitzberg, B. H. (2000). Obsessive relational intrusion: Incidence, perceived severity, and coping. *Violence and Victims, 15,* 357–372.

Dabbs, J. M., Frady, R. L., Carr, T. S., & Beach, N. F. (1987). Saliva, testosterone and criminal violence in young adult prison inmates. *Psychosomatic Medicine, 49,* 174–182.

Dabbs, J. M., Jurkovic, G. J., & Frady, R. L. (1991). Salivary testosterone and cortisol among late adolescent male offenders. *Journal of Abnormal Child Psychology, 19,* 469–478.

Dabbs, J. M., Ruback, R. B., Frady, R. L., & Hopper, C. H. (1988). Saliva testosterone and criminal violence against women. *Personality and Individual Differences, 9,* 269–275.

Davidson, T. (1977). Wifebeating: A recurring phenomenon throughout history. In M. Roy (Ed.), *Battered women* (pp. 187–206). London: Routledge.

Davis, L. V., & Srinivasan, M. (1995). Listening to the voices of battered women: What helps them escape violence. *Affilia, 10,* 49–69.

Davis, P. (1983). Restoring the semblance of order: Police strategies in the domestic disturbance. *Symbolic Interaction, 6,* 261–278.

Davis, R., Tichane, M., & Grayson, D. (1980). *Mediation and arbitration as alternatives to criminal prosecution in felony arrest cases: An evaluation of the Brooklyn Dispute Resolution Center.* New York: Vera Institute of Justice.

Davis, R. C., & Erez, E. (1998). *Immigrant populations as victims: Toward a multicultural criminal justice system.* Research in brief. Washington, DC: National Institute of Justice.

Davis, R. C., & Smith, B. (1995). Domestic violence reforms: Empty promises of fulfilled expectations. *Crime and Delinquency, 41,* 541–552.

Davis, R. C., Smith, B. E., & Nickles, L. (1998). Prosecuting domestic violence cases with reluctant victims: Assessing two novel approaches in Milwaukee. In *Legal interventions in family violence: Research findings and policy implications* (pp. 71–72). Washington, DC: National Institute of Justice and the American Bar Association.

Davis, R. C., & Taylor, B. G. (1997). A proactive response to family violence: The results of a randomized experiment. *Criminology, 35,* 307–333.

Davis, R. C., Taylor, B. G., & Titus, R. M. (1997). Victims as agents: Implications for victim services and crime prevention. In R. C. Davis, A. J. Lurigio, & W. G. Skogan (Eds.) *Victims of crime* (2nd ed.). Thousand Oaks, CA: Sage.

Dawson, M., & Dinovitzer, R. (2001). Victim cooperation and the prosecution of domestic violence in a specialized court. *Justice Quarterly, 18,* 595–622.

DeKeseredy, W. S. (2000). Current controversies on defining nonlethal violence against women in intimate heterosexual relationships: Empirical implications. *Violence Against Women, 6,* 728–746.

DeKeseredy, W. S., & MacLeod, L. (1997). *Women abuse: A sociological story.* Toronto, Canada: Harcourt Brace.

DeKeseredy, W. S., Saunders, D. G., Schwartz, M. D., & Alvi, S. (1997). The meanings and motives for women's use of violence in Canadian college dating relationships: Results from a national survey. *Sociological Spectrum, 17,* 199–222.

Deschner, J. (1984). *The hitting habit: Anger control for battering couples.* New York: Free Press.

DeShaney v. Winnebago County Dept of Social Services 109 S. CT 998 (1989).

Dietz, P., Matthews, D. B., Van Duyne, C., Martell, D. A., Parry, C., Stewart, M., Warren, J., & Crowder, J. D. (1991). Threatening and otherwise inappropriate letters to Hollywood celebrities. *Journal of Forensic Sciences, 36,* 185–209.

Dobash, R. E., & Dobash, R. (1979). *Violence against wives: A case against the patriarchy.* New York: Free Press.

Dobash, R. E., & Dobash, R. P. (1992). *Violence against wives: A case against the patriarch.* New York: Free Press.

Dobash, R. E., & Dobash, R. P. (2000). Evaluating criminal justice interventions for domestic violence. *Crime and Delinquency, 40,* 252–270.

Doctors falter on spotting abuse. (1992, June 22). *Boston Globe,* p. 18.

Doggett, M. E. (1992). *Marriage, wife-beating and the law in Victorian England.* London: Weidenfeld and Nicholson.

Dolon, R., Hendricks, J., & Meagher, M. (1986). Police practices and attitudes toward domestic violence. *Journal of Police Science and Administration, 14*(3), 187–192.

Dugan, L., Nagin, D., & Rosenfeld, R. (2001). *Exposure reduction or backlash? The effects of domestic violence resources on intimate partner homicide: Final report.* Washington, DC: U.S. Department of Justice.

Dunford, F. W. (1990). System-initiated warrants for suspects of domestic assault: A pilot study. *Justice Quarterly, 7,* 631–653.

Dunford, F. W., Huizinga, D., & Elliott, D. (1989). *The Omaha domestic violence police experiment: Final report to the National Institute of Justice and the City of Omaha.* Boulder, CO: Institute of Behavioral Science.

Dunford, F. W., Huizinga D., & Elliot D. S. (1990). The role of arrest in domestic assault: The Omaha Police Experiment. *Criminology, 28,*183–206.

Dunham, K., & Senn, C. Y. (2000). Minimizing negative experiences: Women's disclosure of partner abuse. *Journal of Interpersonal Violence. 15*(3), 251–261.

Dutton, D. (1986). Wife assaulters' explanations for assault: The neutralization of self-punishment. *Canadian Journal of Behavioral Science, 18,* 381–390.

Dutton, D. (1987, July). *The prediction of recidivism in a population of wife assaulters.* Paper presented at the Third International Family Violence Conference, Durham, NH.

Dutton, D. (1988). *The domestic assault of women: Psychological and criminal justice perspectives.* Boston: Allyn & Bacon.

Dutton, D. (1995). *The domestic assault of women: Psychological and criminal justice perspectives.* Boston: Allyn & Bacon.

Dutton, D. (1998). *The abusive personality: Violence and control in intimate relationships.* New York: Guilford.

Dutton, D., Hart, D. S., Kennedy, L., & Williams, K. (1990). Arrest and the reduction of repeat wife assault. In E. Buzawa & C. Buzawa (Eds.), *Domestic violence: The criminal justice response* (pp. 118–128). Westwood, CT: Auburn House.

Dutton, D., & Strachan, C. (1987, July). *The prediction of recidivism in a population of wife assaulters.* Paper presented at the Third National Conference for Family Violence Researchers, Durham, NH.

Dutton-Douglas, M. A. (1992). Treating battered women in the aftermath stage. *Psychotherapy in Private Practice, 10,* 93–98.

Edleson, J. L. (1993). Advocacy services for battered women. *Violence Update, 4,* 1–10.

Edleson, J. L. (1996). Controversy and change in batterers' programs. In J. Edleson & Z. Eisikovits (Eds.), *Future interventions with battered women and their families,* pp. 154–169. Thousand Oaks, CA: Sage.

Edleson, J. L. (1999). Children's witnessing of adult domestic violence. *Journal of Interpersonal Violence, 14,* 839–870.

Edleson, J. L., & Brygger, M. P. (1986). Gender differences in reporting of battering incidents. *Family Relations, 35,* 377–382.

Edwards, S. M. (1989). *Policing domestic violence: Women, law and the state.* London: Sage.

Eigenberg, H. (Ed.). (2001). *Women battering in the United States: Till death do us part.* Prospect Heights, IL: Waveland.

Eigenberg, H. M. (2001). *Woman battering in the United States: Till death do us part.* Prospect Heights, IL: Waveland.

Eigenberg, H. M., Scarborough, K. E., & Kappeler, V. E. (1996). Contributory factors affecting arrest in domestic and non-domestic assaults. In H. Eigenberg (Ed.), *Women battering in the United States: Till death do us part* (pp. 269–326). Prospect Heights, IL: Waveland.

Elias, R. (1993). *Victims still: The political manipulation of crime victims.* Newbury Park, CA: Sage.

Ellenberger, H. (1955). Psychological relationships between the criminal and his victim. *Archives of Criminal Psychodynamics 2*, 257–290.

Elliot, D. S. (1989). Criminal justice procedures in family violence crimes. In M. Tonry & N. Morris (Eds.), *Family violence* (pp. 427–480). Chicago: University of Chicago Press.

Ellis, D. (1993). Family courts, marital conflict mediation and wife assault. In N. Z. Hilton (Ed.), *Legal responses to wife assault: Current trends and evaluation* (pp. 165–187). Newbury Park, CA: Sage.

Ellis D., & Stuckless, N. (1996). *Mediating and negotiating marital conflicts*. Thousand Oaks, CA: Sage.

Ellis, J. W. (1984). Prosecutorial discretion to charge in cases of spousal assault: A dialogue. *Journal of Criminal Law and Criminology, 75*, 56–102.

Emerson, C. D. (1979). Family violence: A study by the Los Angeles County Sheriff's Department. *Police Chief, 46*, 48–50.

Emerson, R. M., Ferris, K. O., & Gardner, C. B. (1998). On being stalked. *Social Problems, 45*, 289–314.

English, B. (1992, June 22). Billing abusers for the damage. *Boston Globe*, p. 15.

Eppler, A. (1986). Battered women and the equal protection clause: Will the Constitution help them when the police won't? *Yale Law Journal, 95*, 788–809.

Epstein, D. (1999). Effective intervention in domestic violence cases: Rethinking the roles of prosecutors, judges, and the court system. *Yale Journal of Law and Feminism, 11*, 3–50.

Epstein, S. (1987). The problem of dual arrest in family violence cases. In *The law enforcement response to family violence*. New York: Victim Services Agency.

Erez, E., & Belknap, J. (1998). In their own words: Battered women's assessment of the criminal processing system's response. *Violence and Victims, 13*, 251–268.

Erez, E., & Tontodonato, P. (1990). The effect of victim participation in sentencing on sentence outcomes. *Criminology, 28*, 451–474.

Fagan, J. A. (1988). Contributions of family violence research to criminal justice policy on wife assault: Paradigms of science and social control. *Violence and Victims, 3*, 159–186.

Fagan, J. A. (1996). The criminalization of domestic violence: Promises and limits. *NIJ Research Report*. Washington, DC: National Institute of Justice.

Fagan, J. A., & Browne, A. (1994). Violence between spouses and intimates: Physical aggression between women and men in intimate relationships. In A. J. Reiss & J. A. Roth (Eds.), *Understanding and preventing violence* (Vol. 3, pp. 115–191). Washington, DC: National Research Council, National Academy of Sciences.

Fagan, J. A., Stewart, D. K., & Hansen, K. V. (1983). Violent men or violent husbands? Background factors and situational correlates. In D. Finkelhor, R. J. Gelles, G. T. Hotaling, & M. A. Straus (Eds.), *The dark side of families* (pp. 49–68). Beverly Hills, CA: Sage.

Fantuzzo, J. W., DePaola, L. M., Lamberg, L., Martino, T., Anderson, G., & Sutton, S. (1991). Effects of interparental violence on the psychological adjustment and competencies of young children. *Journal of Consulting and Clinical Psychology, 59*, 258–265.

Fantuzzo, J. W., & Mohr, W. (1999). Prevalence and effects of child exposure to domestic violence. *The Future of Children, 9*(3), 21–32.

Faragher, T. (1985). The police response to violence against women in the home. In J. Pahl (Ed.), *Private violence and public policy* (pp. 16–48). London: Routledge and Kegan Paul.

Farrell, G. (1995). Preventing repeat victimization. In M. Tonry and D. P. Farrington (Eds.), *Building a safer society: Strategic approaches to crime prevention*. (Crime and Justice, vol. 19, pp. 469–534). Chicago, IL: University of Chicago Press.

Farrell, G., & Pease, K. (1993). *Once bitten, twice bitten: Repeat victimization and its implications for crime prevention* (Crime Prevention Unit Paper No. 46). London: Home Office.

Farrell, G., Phillips, C., & Pease, K. (1995). Like taking candy: Why does repeat victimisation occur? *British Journal of Criminology, 35*:3: 384–399.

Farrington, K. M. (1980). Stress and family violence. In M. A. Straus & G. T. Hotaling (Eds.), *Social causes of husband-wife violence* (pp. 94–114). Minneapolis: University of Minnesota Press.

Fattah, E. A.(Ed.). (1986). *From crime policy to victim policy.* New York: Macmillan.

Fattah, E. A. (1991). *Understanding criminal victimization.* Englewood Cliffs, NJ: Prentice Hall.

Faulk, R. (1977). Men who assault their wives. In M. Roy (Ed.), *Battered women: A psychosociological study of domestic violence* (pp. 180–183). New York: Van Nostrand.

Feder, L. (1996). The importance of offender's presence in the arrest decision when police respond to domestic violence calls. *Journal of Criminal Justice, 12,* 279–305.

Feder, L. (1997). Domestic violence and police response in a pro-arrest jurisdiction. *Women & Criminal Justice, 8*(4), 79–98.

Feder, L. (1998). Police handling of domestic violence calls: Is there a case for discrimination? *Crime & Delinquency, 44,* 139–153.

Federal Bureau of Investigation. (1992). *Crime in the U.S.: 1991.* Washington, DC: U.S. Government Printing Office.

Feld, L. S., & Straus, M. (1989). Escalation and desistance of wife assault in marriage. *Criminology, 27,* 141–161.

Felson, R. B. (1996). *Violent disputes and calling the cops: The role of chivalry and social relationships.* Paper presented at the annual meetings of the American Sociological Association.

Felson, R. B., & Ackerman, J. (2001). Arrests for domestic and other assaults. *Criminology, 39,* 655–676.

Felson, R. B., Messner, S. F., & Hoskin, A. (1999). The victim-offender relationship and calling the police in assaults. *Criminology, 37,* 931–947.

Ferraro, K. (1989a). The legal response to women battering in the United States. In J. Hanmer, J. Radford, & E. Stanko (Eds.), *Women, policing, and male violence* (pp. 155–184). London: Routledge & Kegan Paul.

Ferraro, K. (1989b). Policing women battering. *Social Problems, 36,* 61–74.

Ferraro, K., & Pope, L. (1993). Irreconcilable differences: Battered women, police, and the law. In N. Z. Hilton (Ed.), *Legal responses to wife assault: Current trends and evaluation* (pp. 96–126). Newbury Park, CA: Sage.

Fiedler, D., Briar, K. H., & Pierce, M. (1984). Services for battered women. *Journal of Sociology and Social Welfare, 11,* 540–557.

Field, M., & Field, H. (1973). Marital violence and the criminal process: Neither justice nor peace. *Social Service Review, 47,* 221–240.

Finchman, F. D., & Beach, S. R. H. (1999). Conflict in marriage: Implications for working with couples. *Annual Review of Psychology 50,* 47–77.

Finesmith, B. K. (1983, Winter). Police response to battered women: A critique and proposals for reform. *Seton Hall Law Review,* 74–109.

Finkelhor, D., Hotaling, G. T., & Yllö, K. (1988). *Stopping family violence: Research priorities for the coming decade.* Newbury Park, CA: Sage.

Finn, P. (1989). Statutory authority in the use and enforcement of civil protection orders against domestic abuse. *Family Law Quarterly, 24,* 43–73.

Finn, P. (1991). Civil protection orders: A flawed opportunity for intervention. In M. Steinman (Ed.), *Woman battering: Policy responses* (pp. 155–190). Cincinnati, OH: Anderson.

Finn, P., & Colson, S. (1990). *Civil protection orders: Legislation, current court practice, and enforcement.* Washington, DC: National Institute of Justice.

Finn, P., & Colson, S. (1998). Civil protection orders. In *Legal interventions in family violence: Research findings and policy implications* (pp. 43–47). Washington, DC: National Institute of Justice.

Firestone, D. (1995, April 5). Giuliani and council clash on domestic violence effort. *New York Times*, p. 83.

Fischer, K., & Rose, M. (1995). When "enough is enough": Battered women's decision making around court orders of protection. *Crime and Delinquency, 41*, 414–429.

Fisher, B., Cullen, F., & Turner, M. (2002). Being pursued: Stalking victimization in a nation study of college women. *Criminology & Public Policy, 1*, 257–308.

Fitzpatrick, D., & Halliday, C. (1992). *Not the way to love: Violence against young women in dating relationships.* Amherst, Canada: Cumberland County Transition House Association.

Fletcher, A. (1995). *Gender, sex and subordination in England 1500–1800.* New Haven, CT: Yale University Press.

Florida (1990). *Report of the Florida Supreme Court Gender Bias Study Commission.*

Foa, E. B., & Riggs, D. (1994). Posttraumatic stress disorder and rape. In R. S. Pynoos et al. (Eds), *Posttraumatic stress disorder: A clinical review* (pp. 1333–1363). Lutherville, MD: Sidran.

Follette, V. M., Polusny, M. A., Bechtle, A. E. & Naugle, A. E. (1996). Cumulative trauma: The impact of child sexual abuse, adult sexual assault, and spouse abuse. *Journal of Traumatic Stress, 9*, 25–35.

Follingstad, D. R., Brennan, A. F., Hause, E. S., Polek, D. S. & Rutledge, L. L. (1991). Factors moderating physical and psychological symptoms of battered women. *Journal of Family Violence, 6*, 81–95.

Ford, D. A. (1983). Wife battery and criminal justice: A study of victim decision-making. *Family Relations, 32*, 463–475.

Ford, D. A. (1984, August). *Prosecution as a victim power resource for managing conjugal violence.* Version of the paper presented at the annual meeting of the Society for the Study of Social Problems, San Antonio, TX.

Ford, D. A. (1987, July). *The impact of police officers' attitudes toward victims on the disinclination to arrest wife batterers.* Paper presented at the Third International Conference for Family Violence Researchers, Durham, NH.

Ford, D. A. (1988, November). *Preventing wife battery through criminal justice.* Paper presented at the annual meeting of the American Society of Criminology, Chicago.

Ford, D. A. (1990). The preventative impacts of policies for prosecuting wife batterers. In E. Buzawa & C. Buzawa (Eds.), *Domestic violence: The criminal justice response.* Westwood, CT: Auburn House.

Ford, D. A. (1991). Prosecution as a victim power resource: A note on empowering women in violent conjugal relationships. *Law and Society Review, 1*, 313–334.

Ford, D. A. (1992). *Training project on family violence for Indiana law enforcement officers: Final report.* Washington, DC: Department of Justice.

Ford, D. A. (1993). *The Indianapolis domestic violence prosecution experiment. Final report submitted to the National Institute of Justice.* Washington, DC: U.S. Department of Justice.

Ford, D. A., & Burke, M. J. (1987, July). *Victim initiated criminal complaints for wife battery: An assessment of motives.* Paper presented at the Third National Conference for Family Violence Researchers, Durham, NH.

Ford, D., & Regoli, M. J. (1992). The preventive impact of policies for prosecuting wife batterers. In E. S. Buzawa & C. G. Buzawa (Eds.), *Domestic violence: The changing criminal justice response* (pp. 181–207). Westport, CT: Greenwood.

Ford, D., & Regoli, M. J. (1993). The criminal prosecution of wife assaulters: Process problems, and effects. In N. Zoe Hilton (Ed.), *Legal responses to wife assault: Current trends and evaluation.* Newbury Park, CA: Sage.

Ford, D. A., Reichard, D. Goldsmith, S., & Regoli, M. J. (1996). Future directions for criminal justice policy on domestic violence. In E. Buzawa & C. Buzawa (Eds.), *Do arrests and restraining orders work?* Thousand Oaks, CA: Sage.

Forrell, C. (1990–1991). Stopping the violence: Mandatory arrest and police tort liability for failing to assist battered women. *Berkeley Women's Law Journal, 6,* 215–263.

Franklin, D. L. (2000). *What's love got to do with it? Understanding and healing the rift between Black men and women.* New York: Simon & Schuster.

Freeman, M. (1980). Violence against women: Does the legal system provide solutions or itself constitute the problem? *British Journal of Law and Society, 7,* 216–241.

Frey, S., & Morton, M. (1986). *New world, new roles: A documentary history of women in pre-industrial America.* New York: Greenwood.

Fridell, L. A., & Pate, A. M. (2001). Death on patrol: Killings of American law enforcement officers. In R. Dunham & G. Alpert (Eds.), *Critical issues in policing: Contemporary readings* (pp. 636–680). Prospect Heights, IL: Waveland.

Frieze, I. H., & Browne, A. (1989). Violence in marriage. In L. Ohlin & M. Tonry (Eds.), *Family violence.* Chicago: University of Chicago Press.

Frye, V., Wilt, S., & Schomberg, D. (2000). *Female homicide in New York City, 1990–1997.* Retrieved from www.ci.nyc.ny.us/html/doh/pdf/ip/female97.pdf

Fuentes v. Shevin, 407 U. S. 67 (1972).

Fyfe, J.J., Klinger, D. A., & Flavin, J. M. (l997). Differential police treatment of male-on-female spousal violence. *Criminology, 35,* 455–473.

Gagnon, A. (1992). Ending mandatory divorce mediation for battered women. *Harvard Women's Law Journal, 15,* 272–294.

Gaines, L., Kappeler, V., & Vaughn, J. (1999). *Policing in America* (3rd ed.). Cincinnati, OH: Anderson.

Gamache, D. J., Edleson, J. L., & Schock, M. D. (1988). Coordinated police, judicial and social service response to woman battering: A multi baseline evaluation across three communities. In G. R. Hotaling, D. Finkelhor, J. T. Kirkpatrick, & M. A. Straus (Eds.), *Coping with family violence: Research and policy perspectives* (pp. 193–209). Newbury Park, CA: Sage

Gana, J. A., Stewart, D. K., & Hansen, K. V. (1983). Violent men or violent husbands? Background factors and situational correlates. In D. Finkelhor, R. J. Gelles, G. T. Hotaling, & M. A. Straus (Eds.), The dark side of families: Current family violence research (pp. 49–68). Thousand Oaks, CA: Sage.

Garland, D. (2001). *The culture of control: Crime and social order in contemporary society.* Chicago: University of Chicago Press.

Garner, J. (1990). *Alternative police responses to spouse assault: The design of seven field experiments.* Unpublished manuscript.

Garner, J., & Clemmer, E. (1986). Danger to police in domestic disturbances: A new look. In *National Institute of Justice: Research in Brief.* Washington, DC: Department of Justice.

Garner, J., & Maxwell, C. (2000). What are the lessons of the police arrest studies? In S. Ward & D. Finkelhor (Eds.), *Program Evaluation and Family Violence Research* (pp. 83–114). New York: Haworth.

Gartin, P. (1991). *The individual effects of arrest in domestic violence cases: A reanalysis of the Minneapolis Domestic Violence Experiment: Final Report.* Washington, DC: National Institute of Justice.

Gartner, R., & MacMillan, R. (1995). The effect of victim offender relationship on reporting crimes of violence against women. *Canadian Journal of Criminology, 37,* 393–430.

Geberth, V. (1992, October). Stalkers. *Law and Order*, 138–143.

Gelles, R. J. (1972). *The violent home: A study of physical aggression between husbands and wives*. Beverly Hills, CA: Sage.

Gelles, R. J. (1983). An exchange/social control theory. In D. Finkelhor, R. J. Gelles, G. T. Hotaling, & M. A. Straus (Eds.), *The dark side of families: Current family violence research* (pp. 151–165). Beverly Hills, CA: Sage.

Gelles, R. J. (1993a). Constraints against family violence: How well do they work? *American Behavioral Scientist, 36*, 575–586.

Gelles, R. (1993b). Through a sociological lens: Social structure and family violence. In Gelles, R. & Loseke, D. (Eds.), *Current controversies on family violence* (pp. 31–47). Newbury Park, CA: Sage.

Gelles, R. J. (2000). Estimating the incidence and prevalence of violence against women: National data systems and sources. *Violence Against Women, 6*, 784–804.

Gelles, R., & Loseke, L. (1993). *Current controversies on family violence*. Newbury Park, CA: Sage.

Gelles, R. G., & Straus, M. A. (1978). Determinants of violence in the family: Towards a theoretical integration. In W. R. Burr, R. Hill, F. I. Nye, and I. L. Reiss (Eds). *Contemporary theories about the family* (Vol. 1, Ch. 21). New York: Free Press.

Gelles, R., & Straus, M. (1985). Violence in the American family. In A. J. Lincoln & M. A. Straus (Eds.), *Crime in the family* (pp. 88–110). Springfield, IL: Charles C Thomas.

Gelles, R., & Straus, M. (1988). *Intimate violence*. New York: Simon & Schuster.

Gibbs, J. (1985). Deterrence theory and research. *Nebraska Symposium on Motivation, 33*, 87–130.

Giles-Sims, J. (1983). *Wife battering: A systems theory approach*. New York: Guilford.

Golden, J. F. (1987). Mutual orders of protection in New York State family offense proceedings: A denial of "liberty" without due process of law. *Columbia Human Rights Law Review, 18*, 309–331.

Goldkamp, J. (1996). *The role of drug and alcohol abuse in domestic violence and its treatment: Dade County's domestic violence court experiment, Final Report*. Philadelphia: Crime and Justice Institute.

Goldstein, H. (1990). *Problem-oriented policing*. New York: McGraw-Hill.

Gondolf, E. W. (1984). *Men who batter: An integrated approach stopping wife abuse*. Homes Beach, FL: Learning.

Gondolf, E. W. (1988). Who are those guys Toward a behavioral typology of batterers. *Violence and Victims, 3*, 187–203.

Gondolf, E. W. (1992). Discussion of violence in psychiatric evaluations. *Journal of Interpersonal Violence, 7*, 334–349.

Gondolf, E. W. (1997). Patterns of reassault in batterer programs. *Violence and Victims, 12*, 373–387.

Gondolf, E. W. (1998). *Assessing woman battering in mental health services*. Thousand Oaks, CA: Sage.

Gondolf, E. W. (1999). Characteristics of court-mandated batterers in four cities: Diversity and dichotomies. *Violence Against Women, 5*, 1277–1293.

Gondolf, E. W., Fisher, E., & McFerron, J. R. (1988). Racial differences among shelter residents: A comparison of Anglo, Black and Hispanic battered. *Journal of Family Violence, 3*, 39–51.

Gondolf, E. W., Fisher, E. R., & McFerron, R. (1991). Racial differences among shelter residents: A comparison of Anglo, Black, and Hispanic battered women. In R. Hampton (Ed.), *Black family violence: Current research and theory* (pp. 103–113). Newbury Park, CA: Sage.

Gondolf, E. W., McWilliams, J., Hart, B., & Stuehling, J. (1994). Court response to petitions for civil protection orders. *Journal of Interpersonal Violence, 9,4*.

Gondolf, E. W., & White, R. J. (2000). "Consumer" recommendations for batterers programs. *Violence Against Women, 6,* 198–217.

Goodman, L. A., Koss, M. P., Fitzgerald, L. F., & Puryear-Keita, G. (1993). Male violence against women: Current research and future directions. *American Psychologist, 48,* 1054–1058.

Goolkasian, G. A. (1986). The judicial system and domestic violence: An expanding role. *Response, 9,* 2–7.

Gordon, M. (2000). Definitional issues in violence against women: Surveillance and research from a violence research perspective. *Violence Against Women, 6,* 747–826.

Gormley, W. T. (1989). *Taming the bureaucracy: Muscles, prayers and other strategies.* Princeton, NJ: Princetown University Press.

Governor's Commission on Violence Against Women. (2000). *Annual Report, 1998-1999.* Phoenix, AZ: Author.

Grau, J., Fagan, J., & Wexler, S. (1985). Restraining orders for battered women: Issues of access and efficacy. In C. Schweber & C. Feinman (Eds.), *Criminal justice politics and women: The aftermath of legally mandated change* (pp. 13–28). New York: Haworth.

Green, H. W. (1984). *Turning fear to hope.* Nashville, TN: Thomas Nelson.

Greenfeld, L. A., Rand, M. R., Craven, D., Flaus, P. A., Perkins, C. A., Ringel, C., Warchol G., Matson, C., & Fox, J. (1998). Violence by intimates: Analysis of data on crimes by current or former spouses, boyfriends and girlfriends (NCJ-167237). Washington, DC: U.S. Department of Justice, Bureau of Justice Statistics.

Greenstein, H. (1982). *Role of mediation in domestic violence cases.* Chicago: American Bar Association, Special Committee on Resolution of Minor Disputes.

Gruber, J. (1987). *Controlling bureaucracies.* Berkeley: University of California Press.

Gundle, R. (1986). Civil liability for police failure to arrest: *Nearing v. Weaver. Women's Rights Law Reporter, 3/4.*

Halpern, R. (1984). *Battered women's alternatives: The men's program component.* Paper presented to the American Psychological Association, Toronto, Canada.

Hamberger, K. L., & Hastings, J. H. (1986). *Characteristics of male spouse abusers: Is psychopathology part of the picture?* Paper presented at the American Society of Criminology, Atlanta, GA.

Hamberger, L. K., & Hastings, J. E. (1989). Counseling male spouse abusers: Characteristics of male treatment completers and dropouts. *Violence and Victims, 4,* 275–286.

Hamberger, L., & Hastings, J. (1993). Court mandated treatment of men who assault their partner. In N. Z. Hilton (Ed.), *Legal responses to wife assault: Current trends and evaluation* (pp. 182–229). Newbury Park, CA: Sage.

Hamberger, L. K., Lohr, J. M., Bunge, D., & Tolin, D. F. (1997). An empirical classification of motivation for domestic violence. *Violence Against Women, 3,* 401–423.

Hamby, S. L., Poindexter, V. C., & Gray-Little, B. (1996). Four measures of partner violence: Construct similarity and classification differences. *Journal of Marriage and the Family, 58,* 127–139.

Hamilton, B., & Coates, J. (1993). Perceived helpfulness and use of professional services by abused women. *Journal of Family Violence, 8,* 313–324.

Hammond, N. (1977). *Domestic assault: A report on family violence in Michigan.* Lansing: State of Michigan.

Hampton, R. L. (1987). Family violence and homicides in the Black community: Are they linked? In R. L. Hampton (Ed.), *Violence in the Black family: Correlates and consequences* (pp. 135–186). Lexington, MA: Lexington Books.

Hampton, R., Carrillo, R., & Kim, J. (1998). Violence in communities of color. In R. Carrillo & J. Tello (Eds.), *Family violence and men of color: Healing the wounded male spirit* (pp. 1–30). New York: Springer.

Hanmer, J., Radford, J., & Stanko, E. (1989a). Improving policing for women: The way forward. In J. Hanmer, J. Radford, & E. Stanko (Eds.), *Women, policing and male violence: International perspectives* (pp. 185–201). London: Routledge & Kegan Paul.

Hanmer, J., Radford, J., & Stanko, E. (1989b). Policing men's violence: An introduction. In J. Hanmer, J. Radford, & E. Stanko (Eds.), *Women, policing and male violence: International perspectives* (pp. 1–12). London: Routledge & Kegan Paul.

Hanmer, J., Radford, J., & Stanko, E. (Eds.). (1989c). *Women, policing and male violence: International perspectives.* London: Routledge & Kegan Paul.

Hanmer, J., & Saunders, S. (1984). *Well founded fear: A community study of violence to women.* London: Hutchinson.

Hanson, R. K., Cadsky, O., Harris, A., & Lalonde, C. (1997). Correlates of battering among 997 men: Family history, adjustment, and attitudinal differences. *Violence and Victims, 12,* 191–208.

Hare, R. D. (1993). *Without conscience: The disturbing world of the psychopaths among us.* New York: Pocket Books.

Harrell, A. (1991). *Evaluation of court ordered treatment for domestic violence offenders* [final report]. Washington, DC: Urban Institute.

Harrell, A., & Smith, B. (1996). Effects of restraining orders on domestic violence victims. In E. Buzawa & C. Buzawa (Eds.), *Do arrests and restraining orders work?* (pp. 214–242). Thousand Oaks, CA: Sage.

Harrell, A., Smith, B., & Newmark, L. (1993, May). *Court processing and the effects of restraining orders for domestic violence victims.* Washington, DC: Urban Institute.

Harris v. McRae, 448 U.S. 297 (1980).

Harris, R. N. (1973). *The police academy: An inside view.* New York: John Wiley.

Hart, B. (1986). Lesbian battering: An examination. In K. Lobel (Ed.), *Naming the violence: Speaking out about lesbian battering* (pp.173–189). Seattle, WA: Seal.

Hart, B. (1988). Safety for women: Monitoring batterers' programs. Harrisburg, PA: Pennsylvania Coalition Against Domestic Violence.

Hart, B. (1990). Gentle jeopardy: The further endangerment of battered women and children in custody mediation. *Mediation Quarterly, 7,* 317–330.

Hart, B. (1992). *State codes on domestic violence: Analysis, commentary and recommendations.* Reno, NV: National Council of Juvenile and Family Court Judges.

Hart, B. (1993). Battered women and the criminal justice system. *American Behavioral Scientist, 36,* 624–638.

Hart, B. (1995). *Coordinated community approaches to domestic violence.* Paper presented at the Strategic Planning Workshop on Violence Against Women, National Institute of Justice, Washington, DC.

Hartman, H. H. (1999, June–July). Aggressive prosecution requires money, not more mandates. *Domestic Violence Report.* Kingston, NJ: Civic Research Institute.

Hartog, H. (1976). The public law of a county court: Judicial government in eighteenth century Massachusetts. *American Journal of Legal History, 20,* 282–329.

Hasting, J. E., & Hamberger, L. K. (1988). Personality characteristics of spouse abusers: A controlled comparison. *Violence and Victims, 3,* 31–48.

Hatty, S. (1989). Policing male violence in Australia. In J. Hanmer, J. Radford, & E. Stanko (Eds.), *Women, policing and male violence: International perspectives* (pp. 70–89). London: Routledge & Kegan Paul.

Hawkins, R., & Beauvais, C. (1985). *Evaluation of group therapy with abusive men: The police record.* Paper presented at the American Psychological Association, Los Angeles.

Healey, K., Smith, C., & O'Sullivan, C. (1998, February). *Batterer intervention: Program approaches and criminal justice strategies.* Washington, DC: National Institute of Justice.

Hemmens, C., Strom, K., & Schlegel, E. (1998). Gender bias in the courts: A review of the literature. *Sociological Imagination, 35,* 22–42.

HI H 2712 (1992).

Hilton, N. Z. (1991). Mediating wife assault: Battered women and the new family. *Canadian Journal of Family Law, 9,* 29–53.

Hilton, N. Z. (Ed.). (1993). *Legal responses to wife assault: Current trends and evaluation.* Newbury Park, CA: Sage.

Hirschel, J. D., & Buzawa, E. S. (In press). Understanding the context of dual arrest with directions for future research. *Violence Against Women.*

Hirschel, J. D., Dean, C., & Lumb, R. (1994). The relative contribution of domestic violence to assault and injury of police officers. *Justice Quarterly, 11,* 99–117.

Hirschel, J. D., & Hutchison I. W. (1992). Female spouse abuse and the police response: The Charlotte, North Carolina, experiment. *Journal of Criminal Law and Criminology, 83,* 73–119.

Hirschel, J. D. & Hutchison I.W. (1996). Realities and implications of the Charlotte Spousal Abuse Experiment. In Eve S. Buzawa and Carl G. Buzawa, eds. *Do Arrests and Restraining Orders Work?* Thousand Oaks, CA: Sage, pp. 54-82.

Hirschel, J. D., & Hutchison, I. W. (2001, January). The relative effects of offense, offender, and victim variables on the decision to prosecute domestic violence cases. *Violence Against Women, 7,* 46–61.

Hirschel, J. D., Hutchison, I. W., & Dean, C. W. (1992). The failure of arrest to deter spouse abuse. *Journal of Research in Crime and Delinquency, 29,* 7–33.

Hirschel, J. D., Hutchison, I. W., Dean, C. W., Kelley, J. J., & Pesackis, C. E. (1991). *Charlotte Spouse Assault Replication Project: Final Report.* Washington, DC: US Department of Justice.

Hirschel, J. D., Hutchison, I. W., Dean C. W., & Mills, A. (1992). Review essay on the law enforcement response to spouse abuse: Past, present, and future. *Justice Quarterly, 9,* 247–283.

Hoff, L. A. (1990). *Battered women as survivors.* New York: Routledge.

Holmes, W. M. (1993). Police arrests for domestic violence. *American Journal of Police, 12,* 101–125.

Holmes, W. M., & Bibel, D. (1988). *Police response to domestic violence: Final report.* Washington, DC: Bureau of Justice Statistics.

Holtzworth-Munroe, A., & Anglin, K. (1991). The competency of responses given by martially violent versus nonviolent men to problematic marital situations. *Violence and Victims, 6,* 257–269.

Holtzworth-Munroe, A., & Hutchinson, G. (1993). Attributing negative intent to wife behavior: The attributions of martially violent versus non violent men. *Journal of Abnormal Psychology, 102,* 206–211.

Holtzworth-Munroe, A., Meehan, J. C., Herron, K., Rehman, U., & Stuart, G. L. (2000). Testing the Holtzworth-Munroe and Stuart (1994) batterer typology. *Journal of Counseling and Clinical Psychology, 68,* 1000–1019.

Holtzworth-Munroe, A., Smutzler, N., & Sandin, E. (1997). A brief review of the research on husband violence. Part II: The psychological effects of husband violence on battered women and their children. *Aggression and Violent Behavior, 2,* 179–213.

Holtzworth-Munroe, A., & Stuart, G. (1994). Typology of male batterers: Three subtypes and the differences among them. *Psychological Bulletin, 116,* 476–497.

Homant, J. R., & Kennedy, D. B. (1984). Content analysis of statements about policewomen's handling of domestic violence. *American Journal of Police, 3,* 265–283.

Homant, J. R., & Kennedy, D. B. (1985). Police perceptions of spouse abuse: A comparison of male and female officers. *Journal of Criminal Justice, 13,* 29–47.

Hotaling, G. T., & Buzawa, E. (June, 2001). *An Analysis of Assaults in Rural Communities: Final Report.* Federal Grant #MA0095–400, US Department of Justice, Office of Community Oriented Policing Services.

Hotaling, G. T., & Straus, M. A., with Lincoln, A. (1989). Intrafamily violence and crime and violence outside the family. In L. Ohlin & M. Tonry (Eds.), *Family violence* (pp. 315–376). Chicago: University of Chicago Press.

Hotaling, G. T., & Sugarman, D. B. (1986). An analysis of risk makers in husband to wife violence: The current state of knowledge. *Violence and Victims, 1,* 101–124.

Hotaling, G. T., & Sugarman, D. B. (1990). The primary prevention of wife assault. In R. T. Ammerman & M. Herson (Eds.), *Treatment of family violence: A source book.* New York: John Wiley.

Howell, M. J., & Pugliesi, K. L. (1988). Husbands who harm: Predicting spousal violence by men. *Journal of Family Violence, 3,* 15–27.

Hughes, H. M. (1988). Psychology and behavior correlates of family violence in child witnesses and victims. *American Journal of Orthopsychiatry, 58,* 77-90.

Hughes, H. M., Parkinson, D., & Vargo, M. (1989). Witnessing spouse abuse and experiencing physical abuse: A "double whammy"? *Journal of Family Violence, 4,* 197–209.

Humphreys, I. C., & Humphreys, W. O. (1985). Mandatory arrest: A means of primary and secondary prevention. *Victimology, 10,* 267–280.

Hutchison, I. W., & Hirschel, J. D. (1998). Abused women: Help seeking strategies and police utilization. *Violence against Women; 4,* 436–456.

Hutchison, I. W., Hirschel, D., & Pesackis, C. E. (1994). Family violence and police utlization. *Violence and Victims, 9*(4), 299–313.

International Association of Chiefs of Police. (1993). *Training key #16,handling disturbance calls.* Gaithersburg, MD: International Association of Chiefs of Police.

Ireland, T., & Widom, C. S. (1994). Childhood victimization and risk for alcohol and drug arrests. *International Journal of the Addictions, 29,* 235–274.

Isaac, N. (1994). Men who batter, profile from a restraining order database. *Archives of Family Medicine, 3,* 50–54.

Jacobsen, N. J. (1994). Rejoinder to Lipchik and Geffner. *Family Therapy News, 25.*

Jacobson, N. S., & Gottman, J. M. (1998). *When men batter women: New insights into ending abusive relationships.* New York: Simon & Schuster.

Jacoby, J. (1980). *The American prosecutor: A search for identity.* Lexington, MA: Lexington Books.

Jaffe, P., Hastings, E., Reitzel, D., & Austin, G. (1993). The impact of police laying charges. In N. Z. Hilton (Ed.), *Legal responses to wife assault: Current trends and evaluation* (pp. 62–95). Newbury Park, CA: Sage.

Jaffe, P., Wilson, S., & Wolfe, D. (1986). Promoting changes in attitudes and understanding of conflict resolution among child witnesses of family violence. *Canadian Journal of Behavioral Science Review, 18,* 356–366.

Jaffe, P., Wolfe, D., Telford, A., & Austin, G. (1986). The impact of police charges in incidents of wife abuse. *Journal of Family Violence, 1,* 37–49.

Jasinski, J. L. (1996). *Structural inequalities, family and cultural factors, and spousal violence among Anglo and Hispanic Americans.* Unpublished doctoral dissertation, University of New Hampshire, Durham.

Johnson, H. (2000). The role of alcohol in male partners' assault on wives. *Journal of drug issues, 30,* 725–741.

Johnson, H. (2001). Contrasting views of the role of alcohol in cases of wife assault. *Journal of Interpersonal Violence, 16,* 54–72.

Johnson, I. M. (1990). A loglinear analaysis of abused wives' decisions to call the police in domestic-violence disputes. *Journal of Criminal Justice, 18,* 147–159.

Johnson, M. (1995). Patriarchal terrorism and common couple violence: Two forms of violence against women. *Journal of Marriage and the Family, 57,* 283–294.

Johnson, M. (2000). Paper presented at the Workshop on Gender Symmetry. Arlington, VA: National Institute of Justice.

Johnson, M., & Elliott, B. (1997). Domestic violence among family practice patients in midsized and rural communities. *Journal of Family Practice, 44,* 391–400.

Johnston, J. R., & Campbell, L. E. G. (1993). A clinical typology of interparental violence in disputed custody divorces. *American Journal of Orthopsychiatry, 63,* 190–199.

Jolin, A., & Moore, C. A. (1997). Evaluating a domestic violence program in a community policing environment: Research implementation issues. *Crime and Delinquency, 43,* 279–297.

Jones, A., & Schechter, S. (1992). *When love goes wrong.* New York: HarperCollins.

Jones, D. A., & Belknap, J. (1999). Police responses to battering in a progressive pro-arrest jurisdiction. *Justice Quarterly, 15,* 249–273.

Joseph, J. (1997). Women battering: A comparative analysis of Black and White women. In G. K. Kantor & J. L. Jasinski (Eds.), *Out of darkness: Contemporary perspectives on family violence* (pp. 161–1690). Thousand Oaks, CA: Sage.

Kahn, A. S. (1984). The power war: Male response to power loss underequality. *Psychology of Women Quarterly, 6,* 234–247.

Kalmuss, D. (1984). The intergenerational transmission of marital aggression. *Journal of Marriage and the Family, 46,* 11–19.

Kamphuis, J. H., & Emmelkamp, P. M. (2001). Traumatic distress among support-seeking female victims of stalking. *American Journal of Psychiatry, 158,* 795–798.

Kane, R. (1999). Patterns of arrest in domestic violence encounters: Identifying a police decision-making model. *Journal of Criminal Justice, 27,* 65–80.

Kantor, G. K., & Asdigian, N. (1997). When women are under the influence: Does drinking or drug use by women provoke beatings by men? In M. Galanter (Ed.), *Recent developments in alcoholism. Volume 13: Alcoholism and violence* (pp. 315–336). New York: Plenum.

Kantor, G. K., & Jasinski, J. L. (1998). *Dynamics and risks factors in partner violence.* In J. L. Jasinski & L. M. Williams (Eds.), *Partner violence. A comprehensive review of 20 years of research* (pp.1–43). Thousand Oaks, CA: Sage.

Kantor, G. K., & Straus, M. (1987). The "drunken bum" theory of wife beating. *Social Problems, 34,* 213–230.

Kantor, G. K., & Straus, M. A. (1989). Substance abuse as a precipitant of wife abuse victimization. *American Journal of Alcohol Abuse, 15,* 173–189.

Kappeler, V. (1997). *Critical issues in police civil liability* (2nd ed.). Prospect Heights, IL: Waveland.

Kappeler, V., Blumberg, M., & Potter, G. (2000). *The mythology of crime and criminal justice* (3rd ed.). Prospect Heights, IL: Waveland.

Karan, A., Keilitz, S., & Denard, S. (1999). Domestic violence courts: What are they and how should we manage them? *Juvenile & Family Court Journal, 71,* 75–86.

Kaufman Kantor, G. K. (1996). Alcohol and spousal abuse: Ethnic differences. In M. Galanter (Ed.), *Recent developments in alcoholism.* New York: Plenum.

Kaufman Kantor, G. K., & Jasinski, J. (Eds.). (1997). *Out of darkness: Contemporary research perspectives on family violence.* Newbury Park, CA: Sage.

Kaufman Kantor, G. K., & Straus, M. A. (1990). Response of victims and the police to assaults on wives. In M. A. Straus & R. J. Gelles (Eds.), *Physical violence in*

American families: Risk factors and adaptations to violence in 8,145 families (pp. 473–486). New Brunswick, NJ: Transaction.

Kaukinen, C. (2002). The help-seeking decisions of violent crime victims: An examination of the direct and conditional effects of gender and the victim-offender relationship. *Journal of Interpersonal Violence, 17,432–456.*

Keilitz, S. (1994). Civil protection orders: A viable justice system tool for deterring domestic violence. *Violence and Victims, 9,* 79–84.

Keilitz, S. (2000, October). *Specialization of domestic violence case management in the courts: A national survey.* NIJ Research Conference on Violence Against Women and Family Violence, Washington, DC.

Keilitz, S. L., Hannaford, P. L., & Efkeman, H. S. (1997). *Civil protection orders: The benefits and limitations for victims of domestic violence: Executive summary.* Washington, DC: Department of Justice.

Kelling, G. L., & Cole, C. M. (1997). *Fixing broken windows: Restoring order and reducing crime in our communities.* New York: Kessler.

Kemp, A., Rawlings, E. I., & Green, B. L. (1991). Post-traumatic stress disorder (PTSD) in battered women: A shelter sample. *Journal of Traumatic Stress, 4,* 137–148.

Kemp, A., Green, B. L., Hovanitz, C., & Rawlings, E. I. (1995). Incidence and correlates of post-traumatic stress disorder in battered women. *Journal of Interpersonal Violence, 10,* 43–55.

Kemp, C. H., Silverman, F. N., Steele, B. F., Droegenmuller, W., & Silver, H. (1962). The battered child syndrome. *Journal of the American Medical Association, 181,* 17–24.

Kessler, R. C., Sonnega, A., Bromet, E., Hughes, M., & Nelson, C. B. (1995). Posttraumatic stress disorder in the National Comorbidity Survey. *Archives of General Psychiatry, 52,* 1048–1060.

Kilpatrick, D. G., Acierno, R., Renick, H., Saunders, B. E., & Best, C. L. (1997). A 2-year longitudinal analysis of the relationship between violent assault and substance use in women. *Journal of Counseling and Clinical Psychology, 65,* 834–847.

Kinports, K., & Fischer, K. (1993). Orders of protection in domestic violence cases: An empirical assessment of the impact of the reform statutes. *Texas Journal of Women and Law, 2,* 163–276.

Klein, A. (1994a). *Recidivism in a population of court-restrained batterers after two years.* Unpublished doctoral dissertation, Northeastern University, Boston.

Klein, A. (1994b). *Spousal/Partner assault: A protocol for the sentencing and supervision of offenders.* Boston: Production Specialties.

Klein, A. (1996). Re-abuse in a population of court-restrained male batterers: Why restraining orders don't work. In E. S. Buzawa & C. G. Buzawa (Eds.), *Do arrests and restraining orders work?* (pp. 192–213). Thousand Oaks, CA: Sage.

Klein, E., Campbell, J., Soler, E., & Ghez, M. (1997). *Ending domestic violence: Changing Public perceptions/halting the epidemic.* Thousand Oaks, CA: Sage.

Klinger, D. (1995). Policing spousal assault. *Journal of Research in Crime and Delinquency, 32,* 308–324.

Koehler, L. K. (1980). *Women of the republic: Intellect and ideology in revolutionary America.* Chapel Hill: University of North Carolina Press.

Kosky, R. (1983). Childhood suicidal behavior. *Journal of Child Psychology and Psychiatry and Allied Disciplines, 24,* 457–468.

Koss, M. P., Goodman, L. A., Browne, A., Fitzgerald, L. F., Kita, G. P., & Russo, N. F. (1994). *Male violence against women at home, at work, and in the community.* Washington, DC: American Psychological Association.

Kulwicki, A. D., & Miller, J. (1999). Domestic violence in the Arab American population: Transforming environmental conditions through community education. *Issues in Mental Health Nursing, 20,* 199–215.

Kurz, D. (1992). Battering and the criminal justice system: A feminist view. In E. Buzawa & C. Buzawa (Eds.), *Domestic violence: The changing criminal justice response* (pp. 21-40). Westwood, CT: Auburn House.

Kurz, D. (1996). Separation, divorce, and woman abuse. *Violence Against Women, 2*, 63–81.

Labaton, S. (1989, December 29). New tactics in the war on drugs tilt scales of justice off balance. *New York Times.*

Langan, P., & Innes, C. (1986). *Preventing domestic violence against women.* Washington, DC: Bureau of Justice Statistics, Department of Justice.

Langhinrichsen-Rohling, J., Huss, M. T., & Ramsey, S. (2000). The clinical utility of batterer typologies. *Journal of Family Violence, 15*, 37–53.

Langhinrichsen-Rohling, J., Palarea, R., Cohen, J., & Rohling, M. (2000). Breaking up is hard to do: Unwanted pursuit behaviors following the dissolution of a romantic relationship. *Violence and Victims, 15*, 73–90.

Langhinrichsen-Rohling, J., Smutzler, N., & Vivian, D. (1994). Positivity in marriage: The role of discord and physical aggression against wives. *Journal of Marriage and the Family, 56*, 69–79.

Langley, R., & Levy, R. (1977). *Wife beating: The silent crisis.* New York: Dutton.

Langley, R., & Levy, R. (1978). Wife abuse and the police response. *FBI Law Enforcement Bulletin, 47*, 4-9.

Laub, J. H. (1997). Patterns of criminal victimization in the United States. In R. C. Davis, A. J. Lurigio, & W. G. Skogan (Eds.), *Victims of crime* (2nd ed., pp. 9–26). Thousand Oaks, CA: Sage.

Laub, J. H., & Sampson, R. J. (2001). Understanding desistance from crime. In M.Tonry (Ed.), *Crime & Justice: A Review of Research.* Chicago: University of Chicago Press.

Lawrenz, F., Lembo, R., & Schade, S. (1988). Time series analysis of the effect of a domestic violence directive on the number of arrests per day. *Journal of Criminal Justice, 16*, 493–498.

Lemon, N. (2000, October/November). Review of New York Symposium on Domestic Violence. *Domestic Violence Report*, pp. 5–6.

Lempert, R. (1987, June 21). Spouse abuse: Ann Arbor rushed into arrest ordinance without studying side effects. *Ann Arbor News.*

Lempert, R. (1989). Humility is a virtue: On the publicization of policy relevant research. *Law and Society Review, 23*, 145–161.

Lentz, S. (1999). Revisiting the rule of thumb: An overview of the history of wife abuse. In L. Feder (Ed.), *Women and domestic violence: An interdisciplinary approach* (pp. 9–27). Binghampton, NY: Haworth.

Leonard, K. E. (1993). Drinking patterns and intoxication in marital violence: Review, critique, and future directions for research. In *Alcohol and interpersonal violence: Fostering multidisciplinary perspectives* (NIH Research Monograph No. 24, pp. 253–280). Rockville, MD: U.S. Department of Health and Human Services.

Leonard, K. E., & Blane, H. T. (1992). Alcohol and marital aggression in a national sample of young men. *Journal of Interpersonal Violence, 7*, 19–30.

Lerman, L. (1981). *Prosecution of spouse abuse innovations in criminal justice response.* Washington, DC: Center for Women Policy Studies.

Lerman, L. (1982). Expansion of arrest power: A key to effective intervention. *Vermont Law Review, 7*, 59–70.

Lerman, L. (1984). Mediation of wife abuse cases: The adverse impact of informal dispute resolution of women. *Harvard Women's Law Journal, 7*, 65–67.

Lerman, L. G. (1992). The decontextualization of domestic violence. *Journal of Criminal Law and Criminology, 83*(1), 217–240.

Levesque, J. R. (1998). Emotional maltreatment in adolescents' everyday lives: Further sociolegal and social service provisions. *Behavioral Sciences and the Law, 16,* 237–263.

Levinson, D. (1989). *Family violence in cross-cultural perspective.* Newbury Park, CA: Sage.

Lie, G. Y., Schilit, R., Bush, J., Montagne, M., & Reyes, L. (1991). Lesbians in currently aggressive relationships: How frequently do they report aggressive past relationships. *Violence and Victims, 62,* 121–135.

Liebman, D. A., & Schwartz, J. A. (1973). Police programs in domestic crisis intervention: A review. In J. R. Snibbe & H. M. Snibbe (Eds.), *The urban policeman in transition* (pp. 421–472). Springfield, IL: Charles C Thomas.

Lipton, D., Martinson, R., & Wilks, J. (1975). *The effectiveness of correctional treatment.* New York: Praeger.

Lloyd, S. (1997). The effects of violence on women's employment. *Law & Policy, 19,*159–167.

Lloyd, S., Farrell, G., & Pease, K. (1994). *Preventing repeated domestic violence: A demonstration project in Merseyside* (Crime Prevention Unit Paper, No. 49). London: Home Office.

Lloyd, S., & Taluc, N. (1999). The effects of male violence on female employment. *Violence Against Women, 5,* 370–392.

Loulan, J. (1987). *Lesbian passion.* San Francisco: Spinsters/Aunt Lute.

Loving, N. (1980). *Responding to spouse abuse and wife beating: A guide for police.* Washington, DC: Police Executive Research Forum.

Loving, N., & Quirk, M. (1982). Spouse abuse: The need for new law enforcement responses. *FBI Law Enforcement Bulletin, 51*(12), 10–16.

Lyon, E. (1997). Poverty, welfare and battered women: What does the research tell us? Welfare and Domestic Violence Technical Assistance Initiative. Harrisburg, PA: National Resource Center on Domestic Violence.

Lyon, E., & Goth Mace, P. (1991). Family violence and the courts: Implementing a comprehensive new law. In D. D. Knudsen & J. L. Miller (Eds.), *Abused and battered: Social and legal responses to family violence* (pp. 167–180). New York: Aldine de Gruyter.

Maguire, E. R., Kuhns, J. B. Uchida, C. D., & Cox, S. M. (1997, August). Patterns of community policing in non-urban America. *Journal of Research in Crime and Delinquency, 34,* 368–394.

Mahoney, P., & Williams, L. (1998). Sexual assault in marriage: Prevalence, consequences, and treatment of wife rape. In J. Jasinski & W. Williams (Eds.), *Partner violence: A comprehensive review of 20 years of research.* Thousand Oaks, CA: Sage.

Maiuro, R. D., Cahn, T. S., & Vitaliano, P. P. (1986). Assertiveness deficits and hostility in domestically violent men. *Violence and Victims, 1,* 279–289.

Maiuro, R. D., Cahn, T. S., Vitaliano, P. P., Wagner, B. C., & Zegree, J. B. (1988). Anger, hostility, and depression in domestically violent versus generally assaultive men and nonviolent control subjects. *Journal of Consulting and Clinical Psychology, 56,* 17–23.

Makepeace, J. (1997). Courtship violence as process: A developmental theory. In A. P. Cardarelli (Eds.), *Violence between intimate partners: Patterns, causes, and effects* (pp. 29-47). Boston: Allyn-Bacon.

Malefyt, M., Little, K., & Walker, A. (1998). *Promising practices: Improving the criminal justice system's response to violence against women.* Washington, DC: National Institute of Justice.

Manning, P. (1978). The police: Mandate, strategies and appearances. In P. Manning & J. Von Mannen (Eds.), *Policing: A view from the street.* Santa Monica, CA: Goodyear.

Manning, P. (1988). *Symbolic interaction: Signifying calls and police response.* Cambridge, MA: MIT Press.

Manning, P. (1993a). The preventive conceit: The black box in market context. *American Behavioral Scientist, 36,* 639–650.

Manning, P. (1993b). The preventive conceit: The black box in market context. In E. Buzawa & C. Buzawa (Eds.), The impact of arrest on domestic assault [Special issue]. *American Behavioral Scientist, 36,* 639–650.

Manning, P. (1996). The preventive conceit: The black box in market context. In E. S. Buzawa & C. G. Buzawa (Eds.). *Do arrests and restraining orders work?* (pp. 83–97). Thousand Oaks, CA: Sage.

Manning, P. (1997). *Police work: The social organization of policing.* Prospect Heights, IL: Waveland.

Manning, P. (2000). Community-based policing. In G. P. Alpert and A. R. Piquero (Eds.), *Community policing: Contemporary readings* (2nd Ed., pp. 23–34). Prospect Heights, IL: Waveland.

Manning, P., & Van Maanen, J. (Eds.). (1978). *Policing: A view from the street.* Santa Monica, CA: Goodyear.

Mansnerus, L. (2001, January). Family strife is subject of new courts. *New York Times.*

Mapes, C. (1917). Sexual assault. *The urologic and cutaneous review, 21,* 430.

Margolin, G. (1998). Effects of witnessing violence on children. In P. K. Trickett & C. J. Schellenbach (Eds.), *Violence against children in the family and the community* (pp. 57–101). Washington, DC: American Psychological Association.

Margolin, G., John, R., & Gleberman, L. (1988). Affective responses to conflictual discussions in violent and nonviolent couples. *Journal of Consulting and Clinical Psychology, 56,* 24–33.

Martin, D. (1976). *Battered wives.* San Francisco: Glide.

Martin, D. (1978). Battered women: Society's problem. In J. R. Chapman & M. Gates (Eds.), *The victimization of women* (pp. 111–141). Beverly Hills, CA: Sage.

Martin, D. (1979). What keeps a woman captive in a violent relationship?: The social context of battering. In D. M. Moore (Ed.), *Battered women* (pp. 33–57). Beverly Hills, CA: Sage.

Martin, M. (1997): Double your trouble: Dual arrest in family violence. *Journal of Family Violence, 12,* 139–157.

Martin, S. E. (1993). Female officers on the move? A status report on women in policing. In R. G. Dunham & G. P. Alpert, *Critical issues in policing* (2nd ed., pp. 327–347). Prospect Height, IL: Waveland.

Massachusetts Supreme Judicial Court (1996). *Annual Report of the Massachusetts Court System.* Fiscal Years 1981–1996. Boston: Supreme Judicial Court.

Mastrofski, S. D. (1999). *Policing for people.* Washington, D.C. Police Foundation.

Mastrofski, S. D., Snipes, J. B., & Supina, A. E. (1996). Compliance on demand: The public's respone to specific requests. *Journal of Research in Crime and Delinquency, 33,* 269–305.

Mastrofski, S. D., & Uchida, C. (1993). Transforming the police. *Journal of Research on Crime and Delinquency, 30,* 330–358.

Mastrofski, S. D., Worden, R. E., & Snipes, J. B. (1995). Law enforcement in a time of community policing. *Criminology, 33*(4), 539–563.

Mathews v. Eldridge, 424 U.S. 319 (1976).

Matoesian, G. M. (1993). *Reproducing rape: Domination through talk in the courtroom.* Cambridge, MA: Blackwell.

Maxfield, M. (1987). Household composition, routine activity, and victimization: A comparative analysis: *Journal of Quantitative Criminology, 3,* 301–320.

Maxwell, C., & Bricker, R. (1999, March 11). *The nature of police and citizens interactions within the context of intimate and domestic conflict and violence.*

Paper presented the Annual Meeting of the Academy of Criminal Justice Sciences, Orlando, FL.

Maxwell, C., Garner, J., & Fagan, J. (2001). *The effects of arrest on intimate partner violence: New evidence from the spouse assault replication program. Research in Brief.* Washington, DC: National Institute of Justice.

Maxwell, J. P. (1999). Mandatory mediation of custody in the face of domestic violence: Suggestions for courts and mediators. *Family & Conciliation Courts Review, 37,* 335–356.

McGregor , H., & Hopkins, A. (1991). *Working for change: The movement against domestic violence.* Sydney, Australia: Allen & Unwin.

McLeod, M. (1984). Women against men: An examination of domestic violence based on an analysis of official data and national victimization data. *Justice Quarterly, 1,* 171–192.

Mears, D. P., Carlson, M. J., Holden, G., & Harris, S. D. (2001). Reducing domestic violence revictimization: The effects of individual and contextual factors and type of legal intervention. *Journal of Interpersonal Violence, 16,* 1260–1283.

Mederer, H. J., & Gelles, R. J. (1989). Compassion or control: Intervention in cases of wife abuse. *Journal of Interpersonal Violence, 4,* 25–43.

Mednick, S. A., Gabrielli, W. F., & Hutchison, B. (1987). Genetic factors in the etiology of criminal behavior. In S. A. Mednick, T. E. Moffitt & S. S. Stack (Eds.), *The causes of crime* (pp. 74–91). Cambridge, UK: Cambridge University Press.

Meloy, J. R. (1996). Stalking (obsessional following): A review of some preliminary studies. *Aggression and Violent Behavior, 1,* 147–162.

Meloy, J. R. (1997). The clinical risk management of stalking: "Someone is watching over me . . .". *American Journal of Psychotherapy, 51,* 174–184.

Meloy, J. R. (1998). The psychology of stalking. In J. R. Meloy (Ed.), *The psychology of stalking* (pp. 2–24). San Diego, CA: Academic Press.

Meloy, J. R., Cowett, P. Y. , Parker, S., Hofland, B., & Friedland, A. (1997). Do restraining orders restrain? Finally some data. *Proceeding of the American Academy of Forensic Sciences, 3,* 173.

Meloy, J. R., Davis. B., & Lovette, J. (2001). Risk factors for violence among stalkers. *Journal of Threat Assessment, 1,* 3–16.

Meloy, J. R., & Gothard, S. (1995). Demographic and clinical comparison of obsessional followers and offenders with mental disorders. *American Journal of Psychiatry, 152,* 258–263.

Meloy, J. R., Rivers, L., Siegel, L., Gothard, S., Naimark, D., & Nicolini, J. R. (2000). A replication study of obsessional followers and offenders with mental disorders. *Journal of Forensic Sciences, 45,* 147-152.

Mendelsohn, B. (1956, July). The victimology. *Etudes Internationale de PsychoSociologie Criminelle,* 23–26.

Miccio, K. (2000). Notes from the underground: Battered women, the wtate and conceptions of accountability. *Harvard Women's Law Journal, 23,* 133–166.

MI H 4308 (1994).

Miethe, T. D. (1987). Stereotypical conceptions and criminal processing: The case of the victim offender relationship. *Justice Quarterly, 4,* 571–593.

Mignon, S. I., & Holmes, W. M. (1995). Police response to mandatory arrest laws. *Crime and Delinquency, 41,* 430–443.

Miller v. California, 413 U.S. 15 (1973).

Miller, B., Nochajski, T., Leonard, K., Blane, H., Gondoli, D., & Bowers, P. (1990). Spousal violence and alcohol/drug problems among parolees and their spouses. *Women in Criminal Justice, 1,* 55–71.

Miller, N. (1997). *domestic violence legislation affecting police and prosecutor responsibilities in the United States: Inferences from a 50-state review of state statutory codes.* Alexandria, VA: Institute for Law and Justice.

Miller, N. (2000). *A legislative primer on state domestic violence-related legislation: A law enforcement and prosecution perspective.* Alexandria, VA: Institute for Law and Justice.

Miller, S. (1999). *Gender and community policing: Walking the Talk.* Boston: Northeastern University Press.

Miller, S. (2001). The paradox of women arrested for domestic violence: Criminal justice professionals and service providers respond. *Violence Against Women, 7,* 1339–1376.

Miller, S. L., & Wellford, C. F. (1997). Patterns and correlates of interpersonal violence. In A. P. Cardarelli (Ed.), *Violence between intimate partners: Patterns, causes and effects* (pp. 90–100). Boston: Allyn & Bacon.

Miller, T. R., Cohen, M. A., & Wiersema, B. (1996). *Victims costs and consequences: A new look.* Washington, DC: National Institute of Justice.

Mills, L. G. (1997). Intuition and insight: A new job description for the battered woman's prosecutor and other more modest proposals. *UCLA Women's Law Journal, 7,* 183–199.

Mills, L. G. (1998). Mandatory arrest and prosecution policies for domestic violence: A critical literature review and the case for more research to test victim empowerment approaches. *Criminal Justice and Behavior, 25,* 306–318.

Mills, L. G. (1999). Killing her softly: Intimate abuse and the violence of state interventions. *Harvard Law Review, 113,* 551–613.

Mitchell v. W.T. Grant (1974).

Moe, T. M. (1987). An assessment of the positive theory of "Congressional Dominance." *Legislative Studies Quarterly, 2,* 475–520.

Mofitt, T. E., & Caspi, A. (July, 1999). *Findings about partner violence from the Dunedin Multidisciplinary Health and Development Study: Research in Brief.* Washington, DC: National Institute of Justice.

Moffit, T., Robins, R., & Caspi, A. (2001). A couples analysis of partner abuse with implications for abuse prevention policy. *Criminology & Public Policy, 1,* 5–36.

Moore, A. M. (1997). *Intimate violence: Does socioeconomic status matter?* In A. P. Cardarelli (Ed.), *Violence between intimate partners: Patterns, causes and effects* (pp. 90–100). Boston: Allyn & Bacon.

Morash, M., Bui, M., & Santiago, A. (2000). Gender specific ideology of domestic violence in Mexican origin families. *International Review of Victimology, 1,* 67–91.

Morris, A. (1987). *Women, crime, and criminal justice.* Cambridge, MA: Blackwell.

Morrison, J. A. (2000). Protective factors associated with children's emotional responses to chronic community violence exposure. *Trauma, Violence, & Abuse: A Review Journal, 1,* 299–320.

Morse, B. J. (1995). Beyond the conflict tactics scale: Assessing gender differences in partner violence. *Violence and Victims, 10,* 251–272.

Mullen, P. E., Pathe, M., & Purcell, R. (2000). *Stalkers and their victims.* Cambridge, UK: Cambridge University Press.

Murphy, C., Musser, P., & Maton, K. (1998). Coordinated community intervention for domestic abusers: Intervention system involvement and criminal recidivism. *Journal of Family Violence, 13,* 263–284.

Muscar, B. T., & Iwamoto, K. K. (1993). *Abused women in the restraining order process: A study of their likelihood of completion.* Unpublished mansucript, American Sociological Association.

Mustaine, E., & Tewksbury, R. (1999). A routine activity theory explanation for women's stalking victimizations. *Violence Against Women, 5,* 43–62.

Myers, M. A., & Hagan, J. (1979). Private and public trouble: Prosecutors and the allocation of court resources. *Social Problems, 26,* 439–451.

Nagin, D. (1998). Criminal deterrence research at the outset of the twenty first century. In M. Tonry (Ed.), *Crime and justice: An annual review of research* (Vol. 23, pp. 1–42). Chicago: University of Chicago Press.

National Clearinghouse on Domestic Violence. (1980). *Battered women: A national concern.* Rockville, MD: Author.

National Crime Victimization Survey. (1994). Washington, DC: U.S. Government Printing Office.

National Criminal Justice Association (1993). *Project to develop a model anti-stalking code for states. Final summary report for the National Institute of Justice.* Washington, DC: Government Printing Office.

National District Attorneys Association. (1980). *Prosecutor's responsibility in spouse abuse cases.* Alexandria, VA: National District Attorneys Association, National Criminal Justice Reference Service.

National Research Council. (1998). *Understanding violence against women.* Washington, DC: Author.

National Victim Center. (1993, February). What to do if you are being stalked. In *Helpful guide for victims of stalking.* New York: Author.

Newmark, L., Harrell, A., & Salem, P. (1995). Domestic violence and empowerment in custody and visitation in custody and visitation cases. *Family and Conciliation Courts Review, 33,* 30–62.

O'Brien, M., John, R. S., Margolin, G., & Erel, O. (1994). Reliability and diagnostic efficacy of parents' reports regarding children's exposure to marital aggression. *Violence and Victims, 9,* 45–62.

O'Donovan, D. (1988). Femiphobia: Unseen enemy of intellectual freedom. *Men's Studies Review, 5,* 5–8.

Office for Victims of Crime. (1999). *Breaking the cycle of violence: Recommendations to improve the criminal justice response to child victims and witnesses.* Washington, DC: Office of Justice Programs.

Office of the Attorney General, State of California. (1999). Report on Arrest for Domestic Violence in California, 1998. Sacramento, CA.

O'Leary, K. D. (1993). Through a psychological lens: Personality traits, personality disorders and levels of violence. In R. Gelles & D. Loseke (Eds.), *Current controversies on family violence* (pp. 7–31). Newbury Park, CA: Sage.

Oliver, W. (1999). *The violent social world of Black men.* San Francisco: Jossey Bass.

O'Neil, J. M. (1981). Patterns of gender role conflict and strain: The fear of femininity in men's lives. *The Personal Guidance Journal, 60,* 203–210.

O'Neil, J. M., & Nadeau, R. A. (1999). Men's gender role conflict, defense mechanisms, and self-proective defensive strategies: Explaining men's violence against women from a gender role socialization perspective. In M. Harway & J. M. O'Neil (Eds.), *What causes men's violence against women* (pp. 86–116). Thousand Oaks, CA: Sage.

Oppenheim v. Kridel, 140 N.E. 227,228 (N.Y. 1923).

Oppenlander, N. (1982). Coping or copping out: Police service delivery in domestic disputes. *Criminology, 20,* 449–465.

Orchowsky, S. J. (1999). *Evaluation of a Coordinated Community Response to Domestic Violence: The Alexandria Domestic Violence Intervention Project: Final Report.* Washington, D.C.: National Institute of Justice.

Osofsky, J. (1999). The impact of violence on children. *Domestic Violence and Children, 9,* 33–49.

Ostrom, B. J., & Kauder, N. B. (Eds.). *Examining the work of state courts, 1997: A national perspective from the court statistics project.* Williamsburg, VA: National Center for State Courts.

Pagelow, M. D. (1981). *Woman battering: Victims and their experiences.* Beverly Hills, CA: Sage.

Pagelow, D. M. (1984). *Family violence.* New York: Praeger.

Pahl, J. (1985). *Private violence and public policy: The needs of battered women and the response of the public services.* London: Routledge & Kegan Paul.

Painter, K., & Farrington, D. P. (1998). Marital violence in Great Britain and its relationship to marital and non-marital rape. *International Review of Victimology, 5,* 257–276.

Palarea, R. E., Zona, M. A., Lane, J. C., & Langhinrichsen-Rohling, J. (1999). The dangerous nature of intimate relationship stalking: Threats, violence and associated risk factors. *Behavioral Sciences and the Law, 17,* 269–283.

Paris Adult Theatres v. Slaton, 413 U.S. 49 (1973).

Parnas, R. I. (1967). The police response to the domestic disturbance. *Wisconsin Law Review, 2,* 914–960.

Parnas, R. I. (1970). Judicial response to intra-family violence. *Minnesota Law Review, 54,* 585–644.

Parnas, R. I. (1973). Prosecutorial and judicial handling of family violence. *Criminal Law Bulletin, 9,* 733–769.

Parnas, R. I. (1993). Criminal justice responses to domestic violence. In L. Ohlin & F. Remington (Eds.), *Discretion in criminal justice: The tension between individualization and uniformity* (pp. 175–210). Albany, NY: SUNY Press.

Pate, A., & Hamilton, E. (1992). Formal and informal deterrents to domestic violence: The Dade County Spouse Assault Experiment. *American Sociological Review, 57,* 691–697.

Pate, A., Hamilton, E., & Annan, S. (1991). *Metro-Dade Spouse Assault Replication Project: Draft Final Report.* Washington, DC: Police Foundation.

Pearce, J., & Snortum, J. (1983). Police effectiveness in handling disturbance calls: An evaluation of crisis intervention training. *Criminal Justice and Behavior, 10,* 71–92.

Pearson, J. (1997). Mediating when domestic violence is a factor: Policies and practices in court-based divorce mediation programs. *Mediation Quarterly, 14,* 319–335.

Pease, K., & Laycock, G. (1996). *Revictimization: Reducing the heat on hot victims. research in action.* Washington, DC: National Institute of Justice.

Pepinsky, H. E. (1976). Police patrolman's offense-reporting behavior. *Journal of Research in Crime and Delinquency, 13,* 33–47.

Peterson, R. R. (2001). Comparing the processing of domestic violence cases to non-domestic violence cases in New York City Criminal Courts: Final Report. New York: New York City Criminal Justice Agency.

Pierce, G., & Deutsch, S. (1990). Do police actions and responses to domestic violence calls make a difference? A quasi experimental analysis. *Journal of Quantitative Criminology, 17–42.*

Pierce, G. L., & Spaar, S. (1992). Identifying households at risk of domestic violence. In E. S. Buzawa and C. G. Buzawa (Eds.). *Domestic violence: The changing criminal justice response* (pp. 59–78). Westport, CT: Greenwood.

Pierce, G., Spaar, S., & Briggs, B. (1988, November). *Character of calls for police work.* NIJ Report. Washington, DC: Department of Justice.

Pirog-Good, M. A., & Stets, J. (1986). Program for abusers: Who drops out and what can be done. *Response, 9,* 17–19.

Pirro, J. (1982). Domestic violence: The criminal court response. *New York State Bar Journal, 54,* 352–357.

Pirro, J. (1997, October). *Commission on domestic violence fatalities: Report to the governor*. Albany, NY: Commission on Domestic Fatalities.

Pleck, E. (1979). Wife beating in nineteenth-century America. *Victimology, 4,* 60–74.

Pleck, E. (1987). *Domestic tyranny*. Oxford, UK: Oxford University Press.

Pleck, E. (1989). Criminal approaches to family violence 1640–1980. In L. Ohlin & M. Tonry (Eds.), *Crime and justice: A review of research* (Vol. 11, pp. 19–58). Chicago: University of Chicago Press.

Polochanin, D. (1994, July 30). Programs to treat men who batter fall short of need. *The Boston Globe*.

Pressman, B. M. (1984). *Family violence: Origins and treatment*.

Prince, J. E., & Arias, I. (1994). The role of perceived control and the desirability of control among abusive and nonabusive husbands. *American Journal of Family Therapy, 22,* 126–134.

Ptacek, J. (1995). Disorder in the courts: Judicial demeanor and women's experience seeking restraining orders. (Doctoral dissertation, Brandeis University, 1995). *Dissertation Abstracts International, 56,* 1137.

Ptacek, J. (1999). *Battered women in the courtroom: The power of judicial responses*. Boston: Northeastern University Press.

Punch, M. (1985). *Conduct unbecoming*. London: Macmillan.

Quarm, D., & Schwartz, M. (1983). Legal reform and the criminal court: The case of domestic violence. *Northern Kentucky Law Review, 10,* 199–225.

Quarm, D., & Schwartz, M. (1985). Domestic violence in criminal court: An examination of new legislation in Ohio. In C. Schweber and & C. Feinman (Eds.), *Criminal justice politics and women: The aftermath of legally mandated change* (pp. 29–46). New York: Haworth.

Quinn, D. (1985). Ex parte protection orders: Is due process locked out? *Temple Law Quarterly, 58,* 843–872.

Radford, J. (1987). Legalizing woman abuse. In J. Hanmer & M. Maynard (Eds.), *Women, violence and social control* (pp. 135–151). London: Macmillan.

Radford, J. (1989). Women and policing: Contradictions old and new. In J. Hanmer, J. Radford, & B. Stanko (Eds.), *Women, policing and male violence* (pp. 13–45). London: Routledge & Kegan Paul.

Raj, A., & Silverman, J. (2002): Violence against immigrant women: The roles of culture, context, and legal immigrant status on intimate partner violence. *Violence Against Women, 8,* 367–398.

Ray, L. (Ed.). (1982). Domestic violence mediation demands careful screening. In *Alternative means of family dispute resolution* (pp. 417–427). Washington, DC: American Bar Association.

Reaves, B., & Hart, T. (2000). *Law enforcement management and administrative statistics, 1999: Data for individual state and local agencies with 100 or more officers*. Washington, DC: Bureau of Justice Statistics, U.S. Department of Justice.

Rebovich, D. (1996). Prosecution response to domestic violence. Results of a survey of large jurisdictions. In E. Buzawa & C. Buzawa (Eds.), *Do arrests and restraining orders work?* Thousand Oaks, CA: Sage.

Records show uneven domestic violence effort. (1994, September 25). *Boston Globe*, pp. 1, 28–29.

Reed, D., Fischer, S., Kantor, G., & Karales, K. (1983). *All they can do . . . Police response to battered women's complaints*. Chicago: Chicago Law Enforcement Study Group.

Reiss, A. J. (1971). *The police and the public*. New Haven, CT: Yale University Press.

Reiss, A. J. (1986). Official and survey crime statistics. In E. A. Fattah (Ed.), *Crime policy to victim policy* (pp. 53–79). New York: St. Martin's.

Reiss, A. J., Jr., & Roth, G. A. (Eds).(1993). *Understanding and preventing violence.* National Research Council. Washington, DC: National Academy.

Rennison, C. M. (2001, June) *Criminal victimization 2000: Changes 1999–2000 with trends 1993–2000.* Washington, DC: U.S. Department of Justice.

Rennison, C. M., & Welchans, S. (2000). *Intimate partner violence* (Publication No. NCJ178247). Washington, DC: Bureau of Justice Statistics.

Renzetti, C. (1997). Violence and abuse among same sex couples. In A. Cardarelli (Ed.), *Violence between intimate partners: Patterns, causes and effects* (pp. 70–89). Needham Heights, MA: Allyn and Bacon.

Renzetti, C. (1999). The challenge to feminism posed by women's use of violence in intimate relationships. In S. Lamb (Ed.). *New versions of victims: Feminists struggle with the concept* (pp. 42–56). New York: New York University Press.

Rhode Island Domestic Violence and Reporting Unit. (2000). 1999 data. Wakefield, RI: Rhode Island Supreme Court.

Riggs, D. S., Kilpatrick, D. G., & Resnick, H. S. (1992). Long-term psychological distress associated with marital rape and aggravated assault: A comparison to other crime victims. *Journal of Family Violence, 7,* 283–296.

Riggs, D. S., & O'Leary, K. D. (1989). The development of a model of courtship aggression. In M. A. Pirog-Good & J. Stets (Eds.), *Violence in dating relationships: Emerging social issues* (pp. 53–71). New York: Praeger.

Riggs, D. S., & O'Leary, K. D. (1992). *Violence between dating partners: Background and situational correlates of courtship aggression.* Unpublished manuscript.

Ringquist, E. (1995). Political control and policy impact in EPA's Office of Water Quality. I *American Journal of Political Science, 39,* 336–363.

Roberts, A. R. (1987). Psychosocial characteristics of batterers: A study of 234 men charged with domestic violence offenses. *Journal of Family Violence, 2,* 81–93.

Roberts, A. R. (1988). Substance abuse among men who batter their mates. *Journal of Substance Abuse Treatment, 5,* 83–87.

Robinson, A. (2000). The effect of a domestic violence policy change on police officers' schemata. *Criminal Justice and Behavior, 27,* 600–624.

Robinson, A., & Chandek M. (2000a). Philosophy into practice? Community policing units and domestic violence victim participation. *Policing: An International Journal of police strategies and Management, 23,* 280–302.

Robinson, A. L., & Chandek, M. S. (2000b). Differential police response to black battered women. *Women & Criminal Justice, 12(2/3),* 29–61.

Rosenbaum, A., & Hoge, S. L. (1989). Head injury and marital aggression. *American Journal of Psychiatry, 146,* 1048–1051.

Rosenbaum, A., & Lurigio, A. J. (1994). An inside look at community policing reform: Definitions, organizational changes and evaluation findings. *Crime & Delinquency, 40,* 299–314.

Rosenbaum, D. P., & Lurigio, A. J. (1998). An inside look at community policing reform: Definitions, organizational changes, and evaluation findings. In G. P. Alpert and A. R. Piquero (Eds.), *Community policing: Contemporary readings* (2nd Ed., pp. 201–214). Prospect Heights, IL: Waveland.

Rosenbaum, A., & O'Leary, K. D. (1981). Marital violence: Characteristics of abusive couples. *Journal of Consulting and Clinical Psychology, 49,* 63–76.

Rosenfeld, B. D. (1992). Court ordered treatment of spouse abuse. *Clinical Psychological Review, 12,* 205–226.

Rossman, B. B. (1998). Descartes's Error and posttraumatic stress disorder: Cognition and emotion in children who are exposed to parental violence. In G. W. Holden, R. Geffner, & E. N. Jouriles (Eds.), *Children exposed to marital violence* (pp. 223–256). Washington, DC: American Psychological Association.

Rossman, B. B. R. (2001). Long-term effects of exposure to adult domestic violence. In S. A. Graham-Bermann & J. L. Edelson (Eds.), *Domestic violence in the lives of children: The future of research, intervention and social policy* (pp. 35–66). Washington, DC: American Psychological Association.

Rothman, D. J. (1980). *Conscience and convenience: The asylum and its alternatives in progressive America.* Boston: Little, Brown.

Rouse, L. P. (1984). Models, self-esteem, and locus of control of factors contributing to spouse abuse. *Victimology: An International Journal, 9,* 130–141.

Roy, M. (Ed.). (1977). *Battered women: A psychosociological study of domestic violence.* New York: Van Nostrand Reinhold.

Salamon, L., & Wamsley, G. (1975). The federal bureaucracy: Responsive to whom?. In E. Rieselbach (Ed.), *People v. Government.* Bloomington: Indiana University Press.

Salmon, M. (1986). *Women and the law of property in early America.* Chapel Hill: University of North Carolina Press.

Saltzman, L., Fanslow, J., McMahon, P., & Shelley, G. (1999). *Intimate partner violence surveillance: Uniform definitions and recommended data elements.* Atlanta, GA: Centers for Disease Control and Prevention.

Sampson, R. J., & Wilson, W. J. (1995). Toward a theory of race, crime, and urban inequality. In J. Hagan & R. D. Peterson (Eds.), *Crime and inequality* (pp. 37–54). Stanford, CA: Stanford University Press.

Sanders, A. (1988). Personal violence and public order: The prosecution of "domestic" violence in England and Wales. *International Journal of the Sociology of Law, 16,* 359–382.

Saunders, D. (1993). Husbands who assault: Multiple profiles requiring multiple responses. In N. Z. Hilton (Ed.), *Legal responses to wife assault* (pp. 9–36). Newbury Park, CA: Sage.

Saunders, D. G. (1995). The tendency to arrest victims of domestic violence. *Journal of Interpersonal Violence, 10,* 147–158.

Saunders, D. G., & Size, P. B. (1986). Attitudes about woman abuse among police officers, victims and victim advocates. *Journal of Interpersonal Violence, 1,* 24–42.

SC S 1287 (1994).

Schafran, L. H. (1990). Overwhelming evidence: Reports on gender bias in the courts. *Trial, 26,* 28–35.

Schechter, S. (1982). *Women and male violence: The visions and struggle of the battered women's movement.* Boston: South End.

Schechter, S., & Gary, L. T. (1988). A framework for understanding and empowering battered women. In M. A. Straus (Ed.), *Abuse and victimization across the life span* (pp. 240–253). Baltimore: Johns Hopkins University Press.

Schmidt, J., & Steury, E. H. (1989). Prosecutorial discretion in filing charges in domestic violence cases. *Criminology, 27,* 487–510.

Schulman, M. (1979). *A survey of spousal violence against women in Kentucky* (Study No. 792701 for the Kentucky Commission on Women). Washington, DC: Department of Justice.

Schwartz, M. D. (1991). Series wife battering victimizations in the National Crime Survey. *International Journal of Sociology of the Family, 19,* 117–136.

Schwartz, M. D., & DeKeseredy, W. S. (1997). *Sexual assault on the college campus: The role of male peer support.* Thousand Oaks, CA: Sage.

Scott, K., Schafer, J., & Greenfield, T. (1999). The role of alcohol in physical assault perpetration and victimization. *Journal of Studies on Alcohol, 60,* 528–536.

Scott v. Hart, No. C-76-2395 (N.D. Cal. 1976). SD H 1286 (1992).

Sellers, C. S. (1999). Self-control and intimate violence: An examination of the scope and specification of the general theory of crime. *Criminology, 37,* 375–404.

Shepard, M. (1992). Predicting batterer recidivism five years after invervention. *Journal of Family Violence, 7,* 167–178.

Shepard, M. (1999). *Evaluating coordinated community responses to domestic violence.* Paper by the National Resource Center on Domestic Violence or the Pennsylvania Coalition Against Domestic Violence.

Shepard, M., & Pence, E. (1988). The effect of battering on the employment status of women. *Affilia, 3,* 55–61.

Shepard, M., & Pence, E. (1999). Coordinated community responses to domestic violence: Lessons from Duluth and beyond. Thousand Oaks, CA: Sage.

Sheptycki, J. W. E. (1991). Using the state to change society: The example of domestic violence. *Journal of Human Justice, 3,* 47–66.

Sheptycki, J. W. E. (1993). *Innovations in policing domestic violence.* Newcastle upon Tyne: Athenaeum.

Sheridan, L., Davies, G. M., &Boon, J. C. (2001). The course and nature of stalking: A victim perspective. *Howard Journal of Criminal Justice, 40,* 215–234.

Sherman, L. W. (1990). Police crackdowns: Initial and residual deterrence. In A. J. Reiss (Ed.), *Modern policing* (Vol. 12, pp. 159–230). Chicago: University of Chicago Press.

Sherman, L. (1992). The influence of criminology on criminal law: Evaluating for misdemeanor domestic violence. *Journal of Criminal Law and Criminology, 85,* 901–945.

Sherman, L. (1993). *Policing domestic violence: Experiments and dilemmas.* New York: Free Press.

Sherman, L. W. & Berk, R. A. (1984a). *The Minneapolis Domestic Violence Experiment.* Washington, DC: Police Foundation.

Sherman, L. W., & Berk, R. A. (1984b). The specific deterrent effects of arrest for domestic assault. *American Sociological Review, 49,* 261–272.

Sherman, L. W., & Cohn, E. G. (1989). The impact of research on legal policy: The Minneapolis Domestic Violence Experiment. *Law and Society Review, 23,* 117–144.

Sherman, L. W., & Cohn, E. G. (1989). The impact of research on legal policy: The Minneapolis Domestic Violence Experiment. *Law and Society Review, 23,* 117–144.

Sherman, L. W., Schmidt, J. D., Rogan, D. P., Smith, D. A., Gartin, P. R., Cohn, E. G., Collins, D. J., & Bacich, A. R. (1992a). The variable effects of arrest on criminal careers: The Milwaukee Domestic Violence Experiment. *Journal of Criminal Law and Criminology, 83,* 137–169.

Sherman, L. W., Smith, D. A., Schmidt, J. D., & Rogan, D. P. (1992b). Crime, punishment and stake in conformity: Legal and informal control of domestic violence. *American Sociological Review, 57,* 680–690.

Short, L. (2000). Survivors' identification of protective factors and early warning signs for intimate partner violence. *Violence Against Women, 6,* 272–281.

Shotland, R. L., & Straw, M. K. (1976). Bystander response to an assault: When a man attacks a woman. *Journal of Personality and Social Psychology, 34,* 1990–1999.

Sigler, R. T. (1989). *Domestic violence in context.* Lexington, MA: Lexington Books.

Silvern, L., Karyl, J., Waelde, L., Hodges, W. F., Starek, J., Heidt, E., & Min, K. (1995). Retrospective reports of parental partner abuse: Relationships to depression, trauma symptoms and self-esteem among college students. *Journal of Family Violence, 10,* 177–202.

Simon, T., & Mercy, J. (2001, June). *Injuries from Violent Crime: 1992–1998.* Washington, DC: Bureau of Justice Statistics, U.S. Department of Justice.

Simon, T., & Perkins, C. (2001). *Injuries from violent crime, 1992–1998: Special Report.* U.S. Department of Justice, Bureau of Justice Statistics.

Simons, R. L., Wu, C. I., & Conger, R. D. (1995). A test of various perspectives on the intergenerational transmission of domestic violence. *Criminology, 33,* 141–170.

Skogan, W. (1981). *Issues in the measurement of victimization.* Washington, DC: Government Printing Office.

Skogan, W. (1990). *Disorder and decline: Crime and the spiral of decay in American neighborhoods.* New York: Free Press.

Skogan, W. G., & Harnett, S. M. (1997). *Community policing, Chicago style.* New York: Oxford University Press.

Skolnick, J. H. (1975). *Justice without trial.* New York: John Wiley. (Original work published 1966)

Skolnick, J. H., & Bayley, D. H. (1988). Theme and variation in community policing. In M. Tonry & N. Morris (Eds.), *Crime and justice: A review of research, 10.* Chicago: University of Chicago Press.

Smart, C. (1986). Feminism and law: Some problems of analysis and strategy. *Journal of the Sociology of Law, 14,* 109–123.

Smith, A. (2000). It's my decision, isn't it? A research note on battered women's perceptions of mandatory intervention laws. *Violence Against Women, 6*(12), 1384–1402.

Smith, B. E. (1983). *Non-stranger violence. The criminal court's response.* Washington, DC: Department of Justice, NIJ.

Smith, B. E., Davis, R., Nickles, L., & Davies, H. J. (2001). *Evaluation of efforts to implement no-drop policies: Two central values in conflict: Final report.* Washington, DC: National Institute of Justice.

Smith, D. A. (1986). The neighborhood context of police behavior. In A. J. Reise, Jr., & M. Tonry (Eds.), *Communities and Crime,* Vol. 8 of *Crime and Justice A Review of Research.*

Smith, D. A. (1987). Police response to interpersonal violence: Defining the parameters of legal control. *Social Forces, 65,* 767–82.

Smith, D. A., & Klein, J. (1984). Police control of interpersonal disputes. *Social Problems, 31,* 468–481.

Snell, J. E., Rosenwald, P. J., & Robey, A. (1964). The wife beater's wife: A study of family interaction. *Archives of General Psychiatry, 11,* 107–113.

Solender, E. K. (1998). Report on miscommunication problems between the family courts and domestic violence victims. *Women's Rights Law Reporter, 19,* 155–160.

Sonkin, D., Martin, D., & Walker, L. E. (1985). *Group treatment for men who batter women.* New York: Singer.

Spaccarelli, S., Coatworth, J. D., & Bowden, B. S. (1995). Exposure to serious family violence among incarcerated boys: Its association with violent offending and potential mediating variables. *Violence and Victims, 10,* 163–182.

Special court is aiding home violence victims. (1991, December 26). *New York Times,* p. 17.

Spitzberg, B. H., & Cupach, W. R. (2002). The inappropriateness of relational intrusion. In R. Goodwin & D. Cramer (Eds.), *Inappropriate relationships* (pp. 191–219). Mahwah, NJ: Erlbaum.

Stagg, V., Wills, G. D., & Howell, M. (1989). Psychopathology in early childhood witnesses of family violence. *Topics in Early Childhood Special Education, 9,* 73–87.

Stalans, L. J. (1996). Family harmony or individual protection? *American Behavioral Scientist, 39,* 433–448.

Stalans, L. J., & Finn, M. A. (1995). How novice and experienced officers interpret wife assaults: Normative and efficiency frames. *Law and Society Review 29,* 287–321.

Stalans, L. J., & Lurigio, A. J. (1995). Lay and professionals' beliefs about crime and criminal sentencing. *Criminal Justice and Behavior, 17,* 333–349.

Stallone, D. R. (1984). Decriminalization of violence in the home: Mediation in wife battering cases. *Law and Inequality, 2,* 493–505.

Stanford, R., & Mowry, L. (1990). Domestic disturbance to danger rate. *Journal of Police Science and Administration, 17,* 244–249.

Stanko, E. A. (1982). Would you believe this woman? In N. H. Rafter & E. A. Stanko (Eds.), *Judge, lawyer, victim, thief: Women, gender roles and criminal justice.* Boston: Northeastern University Press.

Stanko, E. A. (1985). *Intimate intrusions: Women's experience of male violence.* New York: Routledge.

Stanko, E. A. (1989). Missing the mark? Police battering. In J. Hanmer, J. Radford, & B. Stanko (Eds.), *Women, policing and male violence* (pp. 46–49). London: Routledge & Kegan Paul.

Star, B. (1978). Comparing battered and nonbattered women. *Victimology, 3,* 32–44.

Stark, E. (1984). *The battering syndrome: Social knowledge, social therapy, and the abuse of women.* Unpublished doctoral dissertation, State University of New York—Binghamton.

Stark, E. (1992). Framing and reframing battered women. In E. Buzawa & C. Buzawa (Eds.), *Domestic violence: The changing criminal justice response* (pp. 271–292). Westwood, CT: Auburn House.

Stark, E. (1993). Mandatory arrest of batterers: A reply to the critics. *American Behavioral Scientist, 36,* 651–680.

Stark, E., & Flitcraft, A. (1988). Violence among intimates: An epidemiological review. In V. B. Van Hasselt, R. L. Morrison, A. S. Bellack, & M. Hersen (Eds.), *Handbook of family violence* (pp. 293–317). New York: Plenum.

Stark, E., & Flitcraft, A. (1996). *Women at risk: Domestic violence and women's health.* Thousand Oaks: CA: Sage.

Steele, B. F. (1976). Violence within the family. In R. F. Helfer & C. H. Kempe (Eds.), *Child abuse and neglect: The family and the community.* Cambridge, MA: Ballinger.

Steinmetz, S. K. (1980). Violence prone families. *Annals of the New York Academy of Sciences, 347,* 351–265.

Steinmetz, S. K., & Straus, M. A. (1974). *Violence in the family.* New York: Harper & Row.

Steketee, M. W., Levey, L. S., & Keilitz, S. L. (2000). *Implementing an integrated domestic violence court: Systemic change in the District of Columbia.* State Justice Institute.

Stets, J. E. (1991). Psychological aggression in dating relationships: The role of interpersonal control. *Journal of Family Violence, 6,* 97–114.

Stets, J. E., & Straus, M. A. (1990). Gender differences in reporting marital violence and its medical and psychological consequences. In M. A. Straus & R. J. Gelles (Eds.), *Physical violence in American families: Risk factors and adaptations to violence in 8,145 families* (pp. 151–166). New Brunswick, NJ: Transaction.

Stith, S. M., & Farley, S. C. (1993). A predictive model of male spousal violence. *Journal of Family Violence, 8,* 183–201.

Straus, M. A. (1973). A general systems theory approach to a theory of violence between family members. *Social Science Information, 12,* 105–125.

Straus, M. A. (1977). A sociological perspective on the prevention and treatment of wife-beating. In *Battered women* . In M. Roy (Ed.), pp. 196–239. New York: Van Nostrand Reinhold.

Straus, M. A. (1977–1978). Wife beating: How common and why? *Victimology: An International Journal, 2,* 443–458.

Straus, M. A. (1980). Wife beating: How common and why. In M. A. Straus & G. T. Hotaling (Eds.), *Social causes of husband wife violence*. Minneapolis: University of Minnesota Press.

Straus, M. A. (1983). Ordinary violence, child abuse, and wife beating: What do they have in common? In D. Finkelhor, R. J. Geeles, G. T. Hotaling, & M. A. Straus (Eds.), *The dark sie of families* (pp. 213–234). Beverly Hills, CA: Sage.

Straus, M. A. (1986). Medical care costs of intrafamily assault and homicide. *Bulletin of the New York Academy of Medicine, 6,* 556–561.

Straus, M. A. (1989). *Manual for the Conflict Tactics Scales*. Durham: University of New Hampshire, Family Violence Research Laboratory.

Straus, M. A. (1990). The National Family Violence Surveys. In M.A. Straus and R. J. Gelles (Eds). *Physical violence in American families: Risk factors and adaptations to violence in 8,145 families* (pp. 3–16). Brunswick: Transaction.

Straus, M. A. (1996). Identifying offenders in criminal justice research on domestic assault. In E. S. Buzawa & C. G. Buzawa (Eds.). *Do arrests and restraining orders work?* (pp. 14–29). Thousand Oaks, CA: Sage.

Straus, M. A. (1997). Physical assaults by women partners: A major social problem. In M. R. Walsh (Eds.), *Women, men, and gender: Ongoing debates* (pp. 210–221). New Haven, CT: Yale University Press.

Straus, M. A. (November 20, 2000). Comments made at the National Institute of Justice, Workshop on Gender Symmetry, Washington, D.C.

Straus, M. A. (1999). *The controversy over domestic violence by women: A methodological, theoretical, and sociology of science analysis*. In X. Arriaga & S. Oskamp (Eds.), *Violence in intimate relationships* (pp. 17–44). Thousand Oaks, CA: Sage.

Straus, M. A., & Gelles, R. (1986). Social change and change in family violence from 1971 to 1985 as revealed by two national surveys. *Journal of Marriage and the Family, 48,* 465–479.

Straus, M. A., & Gelles, R. J. (1990). How violent are American families: Estimates from the National Family Violence Resurvey and other studies. In M. Straus & R. Gelles (Eds.), *Physical violence in American families: Risk factors and adaptations in 8,145 families* (pp. 95–112). New Brunswick, NJ: Transaction.

Straus, M. A., Gelles, R. J., & Steinmetz, S. K. (1980). *Behind closed doors: Violence in the American family*. Garden City, NY: Anchor.

Straus, M. A., & Hotaling, G. T. (Eds.). (1980). *Social causes of husband wife violence*. Minneapolis: University of Minnesota Press.

Straus, M. A., & Ramirez, I. L. (1999, November). *Criminal history and assault of dating partners: The role of gender, age of onset, and type of crime*. Paper presented at the American Society of Criminology annual meeting, Toronto.

Straus, M. A., & Smith, C. (1990). Violence in Hispanic families in the United States: Incidence rates and structural interpretations. In M. Straus & R. Gelles (Eds.), *Physical violence in American families: Risk factors and adaptations in 8,145 families* (pp. 95–112). New Brunswick, NJ: Transaction.

Studies find domestic violence roots in childhood abuse, economic stress. (1992, June 5). *Boston Globe*.

Sugarman, P. B., & Hotaling, G. T. (1989). Violent men in intimate relationships: An analysis of risk markers. *Journal of Applied Social Psychology, 19,* 1034–1048.

Sullivan, C. M., & Bybee, D. I. (1999). Reducing violence using community based advocacy for women with abusive partners. *Journal of Consulting & Clinical Psychology, 67,* 48–59.

Sullivan, C. M., & Keefe, M.(1998). *Evaluations of advocacy efforts to end intimate male violence against women*. St. Paul: Minnesota Center Against Violence & Abuse.

Sullivan, C. M., Tan, C., Basta, J., Rumptz, M., & Davidson, W. S. II (1992). An advocacy intervention program for women with abusive partners: Initial evaluation. *American Journal of Community Psychology, 20,* 309–332.

Swan, S. C., & Snow, D. L. (2002). A typology of women's use of violence in intimate relationships. *Violence Against Women, 8,* 286–319.

Szinovacz, M. E. (1983). Using couple data as a methodological tool: The case of marital violence. *Journal of Marriage and the Family, 45,* 633–644.

Taylor, B. G., Davis, R. C., & Maxwell, C. D. (2001). The effects of a group batterer treatment program: A randomized experiment in Brooklyn. *Justice Quarterly, 18,* 171–201.

Teran, L. J. (1999). Barriers to protection at home and abroad: Mexican victims of domestic violence and the violence against women act. *Boston University International Law Journal, 17,* 1–70.

Thistlewaite, A., Woolredge, J., & Gibbs, D. (1998). Severity of dispositions and domestic violence recidivism. *Crime and Delinquency, 44,* 388–398.

Thoennes, N., Salem, P., & Pearson, J. (1995). Mediation and domestic violence: Current policies and practices (special issue). *Family and Conciliation Courts Review, 33,* 6–29.

Tift, L. (1993). *Battering of women.* Boulder, CO: Westview.

Tjaden, P., & Thoennes, N. (1998). *Prevalence, incidence and consequences of violence against women: Findings from the National Violence Against Women Survey.* Washington, DC: National Institute of Justice.

Tjaden, P., & Thoennes, N. (2000). *Extent, nature, and consequences of intimate partner violence: Findings from the National Violence Against Women Survey.* Washington, DC: U.S. Department of Justice.

Tolman, R. (1992). Psychological abuse of women. In R. Ammerman & M. Hersen (Eds.), *Assessment of family violence: A clinical and legal sourcebook.* New York: John Wiley.

Tolman, R. M., & Bennett, L. (1990). A review of quantitative research on men who batter. *Journal of Interpersonal Violence, 5,* 87–118.

Tolman, R. M.. & Edleson. J. L. (1995). Interventions for men who batter: A review of research. In S. M. Stith & M. A. Straus (Eds.), *Understanding partner violence: Prevalence, causes, consequences, and solutions* (pp. 211–255). Minneapolis, MN: National Council on Family Relations.

Tolman, R., & Weisz (1995). Coordinated community intervention for domestic violence: The effects of arrest and prosecution on recidivism of woman abuse perpetrators. *Crime & Delinquency, 41,* 481–495.

Tracey Thurman et al. v. City of Torrington, Connecticut, 595 F. Supp. 1521 (D. Connecticut 1984).

Tsai, B. (2000). Note: The trend toward specialized Domestic Violence Courts: Improvements on an effective innovation. *Fordham Law Review, 68,* 1285–1320.

Uchida, C., Brooks, L., & Koper, C. (1987). Danger to police during domestic encounters: Assaults on Baltimore county police, 1984–1986. *Criminal Justice Policy Review, 2,* 357–371.

Umbreit, M. S. (1995). Mediating interpersonal conflicts. A pathway to peace. West Concord, MN: CPI.

Ursel, J. (1995). *Winnipeg family violence court evaluation.* Working Document WD1995-2e. Department of Justice, Ottawa, Canada.

U.S. Attorney General's Task Force on Family Violence. (1984). *Final report.* Washington, DC: U.S. Government Printing Office.

U.S. Commission of Civil Rights. (1978). *Battered women: Issues of public policy.* Washington, DC: Government Printing Office.

U.S. Commission on Civil Rights. (1982). *Under the rule of thumb: Battered women and the administration of justice.* Washington, DC: National Institute of Justice.

U.S. Department of Justice, Office of Justice Programs (1991, May). Stalking and Domestic Violence: Report to Congress. Rockville, Maryland: National Criminal Justice Reference Service.

U.S. Department of Justice, Office of Justice Programs, Bureau of Justice Statistics. (1994, November). *Violence between intimates.* Washington, DC: Government Printing Office.

U.S. Department of Justice (1998). *Stalking and domestic violence: The third annual report to Congress under the Violence Against Women Act.* Washington, DC: U.S. Department of Justice, Violence Against Women Grants Office.

U.S. Department of Justice. (1999). *The Clinton administration's law enforcement strategy: Combating crime with community policing and community prosecution.* Washington, DC: Author.

U.S. Department of Justice (May, 2001). *Stalking and domestic violence: Report to congress.* NCJ 186157. Rockville, MD: National Criminal Justice Reference Service.

Utah Gender Bias Task Force. (1990). *Utah Task Force on Gender and Justice: Report to the Utah Judicial Council.* Salt Lake City, UT: Administrative Office of the Courts.

Valente, R. L., Hart, B. J., Zeya, S., & Malefyt, M. (2001). The Violence Against Women Act of 1994: The federal commitment to ending domestic violence, sexual assault, stalking, and gender-based crimes of violence. In C. Renzetti, J. Edleson, & R. K. Bergen (Eds.), *Sourcebook on violence against women* (pp. 279–302). Newbury Park, CA: Sage.

Van Maanen, J. (1973). Observations on the making of policemen. *Human Organization, 32,* 407–417.

Van Maanen, J. (1974). Working the street: A developmental view of police behavior. In H. Jacob (Ed.), *The potential for reform of criminal justice* (pp. 83–130). Beverly Hills, CA: Sage.

Van Maanen, J. (1975). Police socialization: A longitudinal examination of job attitudes in an urban police department. *Administrative Science Quarterly, 20,* 207–228.

Van Maanen, J. (1978). Observations on the making of policemen. In P. Manning & J. Van Maanen (Eds.), *Policing: A view from the street* (pp. 123–146). Santa Monica, CA: Goodyear.

Vera Institute of Justicex (1977). *Felony arrests: Their prosecution and disposition in New York City's courts.* New York: Author.

Victim Services Agency. (1988). *The law enforcement response to family violence: A state by state guide to family violence legislation.* New York: Author.

Von Hentig, H. (1941, March–April). Remarks on the interaction of perpetrator and victim. *Journal of Criminal Law, Criminology, and Police Science, 31,* 303–309.

50. Von Hentig, H. (1948). *The criminal and his victim.* New Haven, CT: Yale University Press.

Von Hirsch, A. (1985). *Past or future crimes: Deservedness and dangerousness in the sentencing of criminals.* New Brunswick, NJ: Rutgers University Press.

Waaland, P., & Keeley, S. (1985). Police decision making in wife abuse: The impact of legal and extralegal factors. *Law and Human Behavior, 9,* 355–366.

Waits, K. (1985). The criminal justice system's response to battering: Understanding the problem, forging the solutions. *Washington Law Review, 60,* 267–329.

Wallace, H. (1996). *Family violence: Legal, medical, and social perspectives.* Boston: Allyn & Bacon. Walker, L. (1979). *Battered women.* New York: Harper & Row.

Walker, L. (1979). *The battered woman.* New York: Harper & Row.

Walker, L. (1990). Psychological assessment of sexually abused children for legal evaluation and expert witness testimony. *Professional Psychology: Research and Practice, 21,* 344–353.

Walker, S. (1991). *Police accountability: The role of citizen oversight.* Belmont, CA: Wadsworth.

Walker, S. (2000). *Sense and Nonsense about Crime and Drugs: A Policy Guide. Fifth Edition.* Belmont, CA: Wadsworth.

Walker, S., Spohn, C., & DeLeone, M. (1996). *The color of justice: Race, ethnicity, and crime in America.* Belmont, CA: Wadsworth.

Walters, G. D. (1992). A meta-analysis of the genecrime relationship. *Criminology, 39,* 595–613.Wan, A.M. (2000). Battered women in the restraining order process: Observations on a court advocacy program. *Violence Against Women,* 6:6, 606-632.

Warnken, W. J., Rosenbaum, A., Fletcher, K. E., Hoge, S. K., & Adelman, S. A. (1994). Head-injured males: A population at risk for relationship aggression. *Violence and Victims, 9,* 153–166.Waul, M. (2000). Civil protection orders: An opportunity for intervention with domestic violence victims. *Georgetown Public Policy Review, 6,* 51–68.

Waul, M. R. (2000, Fall). Civil protection orders: An opportunity for intervention with domestic violence victims. *The Georgetown Public Policy Review, 6,* 51–70.

Weaver, T. L., & Clum, G. A. (1995). Psychological distress associated with interpersonal violence: A meta-analysis. *Clinical Psychology Review, 15,* 115–140.

Weisz, A. N. (1999). Legal advocacy for domestic violence survivors: The power of an informative relationship. *Families in Society: The Journal of Contemporary Human Services, 80,* 138–147.

West, C. (1998): Lifting the "political gag order": Breaking the silence around partner violence in ethnic minority families. In J. L. Jasinski & L. M. Williams (Eds.), *Partner violence. A comprehensive review of 20 years of research* (pp. 184–209). Thousand Oaks, CA: Sage.

West, T. C. (1999). *Wounds of the spirit: Black women, violence, and resistance ethics.* New York: New York Univesrity Press.

Westley, W. (1970). *Violence and the police: A sociological study of law, custom and morality.* Cambridge, MA: MIT Press.

Wetzel, L., & Ross, M. A. (1983). Psychological and social ramifications of battering: Observations leading to a counseling methodology for victims of domestic violence. *Personnel and Guidance Journal, 61,* 423–428.

Whetstone, T. (2001). Measuring the impact of a domestic violence coordinated response team. *Policing: An International Journal of Police Strategies & Management, 24,* 371–398.

Whitcomb, D. (2002, March). Prosecutors, kids, and domestic violence cases. *National Institute of Justice Journal,* pp. 3–9.

Widom, C. S. (1989). The cycle of violence. *Science, 244,* 160–166.

Widom, C. S. (1992). *Cycle of violence: Research in brief.* Washington, DC: U.S. Department of Justice.

Widom, C. S., & Maxfield, M. G. (2001). *An update on the "cycle of violence"* (Research in Brief). Washington, DC: National Institute of Justice.

Williams, K. (1976). The effects of victim characteristics on violent crimes. In W. F. McDonald (Ed.), *Criminal justice and the victim* (pp. 177–213). Beverly Hills, CA: Sage.

Williams, K. R., & Hawkins, R. (1989). The meaning of arrest for wife assault. *Criminology, 27,* 163–181.

Williams, O. J. (1999). Working in groups with African American males who batter. In R. Carrillo & J. Tello (Eds.), *Family violence and men of color: Healing the wounded male spirit* (pp. 74–94). New York: Springer.

Wills, D. (1997). Domestic violence: The case for aggressive prosecution. *UCLA Women's Law Journal, 7,* 173–199.

Willson, P., McFarlane, J., Malecha, A., Watson, K., Lemmey, D., Schultz, P., Gist, J., & Fredland, N. (2000). Severity of violence against women by intimate partners and associated use of alcohol and/or illicit drugs by the perpetrator. *Journal of Interpersonal Violence, 15,* 996–1008.

Wilson, J. Q. (1968). *Varieties of police behavior.* Cambridge, MA: Harvard University Press.

Wilson, J. Q. (1989). *Bureaucracy: What government agencies do and why they do it.* New York: Basic Books.

Wilson, J. Q., & Hernstein, R. (1985). *Crime and human nature.* New York: Simon and Schuster.

Wilson, J. Q., & Kelling, G. (1982). Broken windows: The police and neighborhood safety. *Atlantic Monthly, 249,* 29–38.

Wilt, M., & Bannon, J. (1977). *Domestic violence and the police: Studies in Detroit and Kansas City.* Washington, DC: Police Foundation.

Winick, B. J. (2000). Applying the law therapeutically in domestic violence cases. *University of Missouri at Kansas City Law Review, 69,* 33.

Winkel, F. H. (1999). Repeat victimization and trauma susceptibility: Prospective and longitudinal analyses. In J. J. M. van Dijk, R. G. H. van Kaan, & J. Wemmers (Eds.), *Caring for crime victims: Selected proceedings of the 9th International Symposium on Victimology.* Monsey, New York: Criminal Justice Press.

Wolfe, D. A., Jaffe, P., Wilson, S. K., & Zak, I. (1985). Children of battered women: The relation of child behavior to family violence and maternal stress. *Journal of Consulting and Clinical Psychology, 53,* 657–665.

Wolfgang, M. (1958). *Patterns of criminal homicide.* Philadelphia: University of Pennsylvania Press.

Wolfgang, M., & Ferracuti, F. (1967). *The subculture of violence.* London: Tavistock.

Wolfgang, M., & Ferracuti, F. (1982). *The subculture of violence* (2nd ed.). London: Tavistock.

Wood, B. D., & Waterman, R. W. (1991). The dynamics of political control of bureaucracy. *American Political Science Review, 85,* 801–828.

Wood, B. D., & Waterman, R. W. (1994). *Bureaucratic dynamics.* Boulder, CO: Westview.

Woods, L. (1978). Litigation on behalf of battered women. *Woman's Rights Legal Reporter, 7*(2), 35.

Woods, S. J. (1999). Normative beliefs regarding the maintenance of intimate relationships among abused and nonabused women. *Journal of Interpersonal Violence, 14,* 479–491.

Worden, A. P. (1993) The attitudes of women and men in policing: Testing conventional and contemporary wisdom. *Criminology, 31,* 203–237.

Worden, A. P. (2001). *Models of community coordination in partner violence cases: A multi-site comparative analysis: Final report.* Washington, DC: U.S. Department of Justice.

Worden, R. E., & Pollitz, A. A. (1984). Police arrests in domestic disturbances: A further look. *Law and Society Review, 18,* 105–119.

Worden, R. E., & Shepard, R. (1996). Demeanor, crime and police behavior: A reexamination of the Police Services Study data. *Criminology, 34,* 83–205.

Wright, J. A., Burgess, A. G, Burgess, A. W., Laszlo, A. T., McCrary, G., & Douglas, J. (1996). A typology of interpersonal stalking. *Journal of Interpersonal Violence, 11,* 487–502.

Wuest, J., & Merritt-Gray, M. (1999). Not going back: Sustaining the separation in the process of leaving abusive relationships. *Violence Against Women, 5,* 110–133.

Yegidis, B. L., & Renzy, R. B. (1994). Battered women's experience with a preferred arrest policy. *Affilia, 9,* 60–70.

Yellot, A. (1990). Mediation and domestic violence: A call for collaboration. *Mediation Quarterly, 8, 39–50.*

Yllö, K. (1984). The status of women, marital equality, and violence against wives: A contextual analysis. *Journal of Family Issues, 5,* 307–320.

Yllö, K. (1988). Political and methodological debates in wife abuse research. In K. Yllo & M. Bograd (Eds.), *Feminist perspectives on wife abuse* (pp. 28-50). Newbury Park, CA: Sage.

Yllö, K. (1993). Through a feminist lens: Gender, power, and violence. In R. Gelles & D. Loseke (Eds.), *Current controversies on family violence* (pp. 46-62). Newbury Park, CA: Sage.

Yllö, K., Gary, L., Newberger, E. H., Pandolfino, J., & Schechter, S. (1992, October). *Pregnant women abuse and adverse birth outcomes.* Paper presented at the annual meeting of Society for Applied Sociology, Cleveland, OH.

Yllö, K., & Straus, M. A. (1990). Patriarchy and violence against wives: The impact of structural and normative factors. In M. A. Straus & R. J. Gelles (Eds.), *Physical violence in American families: Risk factors and adaptations to violence in 8,145 families* (pp. 473–486). New Brunswick, NJ: Transaction.

Zalman, M. (1991, November). *A review of state statutes concerning the police role in domestic violence.* Paper presented at the American Society of Criminology Annual Meeting, San Francisco.

Zimring, F., & Hawkins, G. (1973). *Deterrence.* Chicago: University of Chicago Press.

Zlotnick, C. K., Kohn, R., Peterson, J., & Pearlstein, T. (1998). Partner physical victimization in a national sample of American families. *Journal of Interpersonal Violence, 13,* 156–166.

Zona, M., Sharma, K., & Lane, J. (1993). Comparative study of erotomanic and obsessional subjects in a forensic sample. *Journal of Forensic Sciences, 38,* 894–903.

Zoomer, O. J. (1989). Policing women beating in the Netherlands. In J. Hanmer, J. Radford, & B. Stanko (Eds.), *Women, policing and male violence* (pp. 125–154). London: Routledge & Kegan Paul.

Zorza, J. (1994). Woman battering: High costs and the state of the law (Special issue). *Clearinghouse Review, 28,* 383–395.

Zorza, J., & Klemperer, J. (1999, April/May). The Internet-based domestic court preparation project: Using the Internet to overcome barriers to justice. *Domestic Violence Report, 4,* 49–50, 59–60.

Zorza, J., & Woods, L. (1994). *Analysis and policy implications of the new police domestic violence studies.* New York: National Center on Women and Family Law.

Index

About the Authors

Eve S. Buzawa is Professor and the Chairperson of the Department of Criminal Justice at University of Massachusetts–Lowell. She received her bachelor of arts degree from the University of Rochester and her master's and doctoral degrees from the School of Criminal Justice, Michigan State University. Buzawa has been conducting research in the areas of the criminal justice response to family violence and policing for more than 25 years. She is the author of several books and numerous journal articles. In addition, she has been the recipient of numerous federal, state, and local research grants. She is past President of the Society of Police and Criminal Psychology, past President of the Northeast Association of Criminal Justice Sciences, and past Board Member for the Academy of Criminal Justice Sciences. She is past President of the Society of Police and Criminal Psychology, past President of the Northeast Association of Criminal Justice Sciences, and past Board Member for the Academy of Criminal Justice Sciences.

Carl G. Buzawa is Vice-President at Textron Systems Corporation. He received his Bachelor of Arts degree from the University of Rochester in Political Science and History, a master's of science degree from the University of Michigan in Political Science, and a law degree from Harvard Law School. He has an extensive publication history in the area of family violence. He also has helped lead his company's efforts in addressing domestic violence in the workplace.